"A meticulously researched history of one of the US Army's greatest regiments. *Birth of a Regiment* incorporates many sources not previously available to historians studying the 504th Parachute Infantry Regiment and adds impressive new insights to previous accounts of the early years of the 'Devils in Baggy Pants.'"

—General David Petraeus, US Army (Ret.), former commander of the 504th Parachute Infantry Regiment (1995–1997), as well as of the 101st Airborne Division, the Surge in Iraq, US Central Command, and Coalition and US Forces in Afghanistan

"The 504th PIR was a singularly competent Airborne combat force. From North Africa to the concentration camps, its reputation was second to none. Slogging through the Italian mountains to performing seemingly impossible tasks in Holland to repelling repeated armored attacks in the Bulge, its extraordinary leadership from Col Tucker to the most junior enlisted, provided the 82nd Airborne the tip of its bayonet. The extraordinary work performed by Frank van Lunteren is worthy of their accomplishments. To understand the 'Why' of the regiment's greatness, the author places you inside the unit where the singular ethos of the regiment is born, nurtured and matured into an extraordinary tool for good. General's Ridgway and Gavin recognized the exceptional quality of the unit and gave it the toughest jobs with uniformly uncommon results. If you wish to learn how good units are made that transcends time, this book will be an excellent guide."

—Col (Ret) Keith Nightingale, author of *Just Another Day* and *Phoenix Rising*

"This book is long overdue and could not have been written any better. Frank van Lunteren masterfully balances the historical and personal sides of the compelling history of the 504 PIR in World War II. Get to know dozens of 504 veterans personally. Extensive interviews are included, along with letters, photos, and memoirs. This book added new insights and eyewitness accounts I had not seen before. You are not just reading about the birth of a regiment, but also about the birth of the American Paratrooper and the legendary accomplishments of many who served."

—Phil Rosenkrantz, Author of *Letters from Uncle Dave: The 73-year Journey to Find a Missing-In-Action World War II Paratrooper*

BIRTH OF A REGIMENT

The 504th Parachute Infantry Regiment
in Sicily and Salerno

FRANK VAN LUNTEREN

A KNOX PRESS BOOK
An Imprint of Permuted Press

ISBN: 978-1-63758-380-7
ISBN (eBook): 978-1-63758-381-4

Birth of a Regiment:
The 504th Parachute Infantry Regiment in Sicily and Salerno
© 2022 by Frank van Lunteren
All Rights Reserved

Interior maps by Carl Mauro, Jr.

Permuted Press, LLC
New York • Nashville
permutedpress.com

Published in the United States of America
1 2 3 4 5 6 7 8 9 10

Dedicated to all the officers and men who served in the
504th Regimental Combat Team in World War II.
Their sacrifices will *not* be forgotten.

"As the stars that shall be bright when we are dust,
Moving in marches upon the heavenly plain;
As the stars that are starry in the time of our darkness,
To the end, to the end, they remain."
—Laurence Binyon, "For the Fallen" (1914)

"I am in Africa but can't say where."
—Pfc. Edwin E. Decker, B Company in a
letter to his parents, May 18, 1943

"When I jumped I was one of the first to put foot
on enemy territory, quite an adventure."
—Sgt. Robert G. Dew, I Company in a letter
to his parents, August 6, 1943

"We were advised that we would not receive any
anti-aircraft fire along the Sicilian coast."
—2nd Lt. Delor M. Perow, C Company 307th
Airborne Engineers Battalion

"Stories of what their isolated units accomplished
are almost unbelievable."
—John Thompson on the 504th PIR, *Chicago Tribune*, July 27, 1943

"Altavilla and 424 were part of their warrior
saga written in their blood and sweat."
—Seymour Korman, *Chicago Tribune*, September 19, 1943

Contents

Acknowledgments xiii

Introduction xvii

Chapter 1: The Airborne Pioneers.. 1
Fort Benning, Georgia
June 1940–April 1942

Chapter 2: The Original Cadre 11
Georgia, Alabama, Louisiana, North Carolina
May–June 1942

Chapter 3: Losing Half a Cadre 20
Fort Benning, Georgia
June–September 1942

Chapter 4: Captain Beall's Challenge...35
Fort Bragg, North Carolina
October–November 1942

Chapter 5: Change in Command...49
Fort Bragg, North Carolina
December 1942–February 1943

Chapter 6: Preparation for Overseas Deployment.............................59
Fort Bragg, North Carolina
March 1943

Chapter 7: Across the Atlantic 74
Camp Edwards, New York City, Casablanca
April–May 1943

Chapter 8: EGB447 86
Oujda, Algeria
May–June 15, 1943

Chapter 9: Training in Tunisia 106
Kairouan, Tunisia
June 16–30, 1943

Chapter 10: 'X Battalion' 114
Kairouan, Tunisia
July 1–9, 1943

Chapter 11: Kouns and the Machine Gunners 127
Sicily
July 9–11, 1943

Chapter 12: Saga of HQ and G Companies 152
Sicily
July 9–11, 1943

Chapter 13: Saga of H Company 176
Sicily
July 9–11, 1943

Chapter 14: Saga of I Company 189
Sicily
July 9–13, 1943

Chapter 15: Baptism of Fire... 206
Sicily
July 11–July 12, 1943

Chapter 16: Friendly Fire 228
Sicily
July 11–July 12, 1943

Chapter 17: "The Most Anguishing Experience" 239
Sicily
July 11–July 12, 1943

Chapter 18: Unfolding the Fiasco 260
Sicily
July 12–July 14, 1943

Chapter 19: Charge at Tumminello Pass 274
Sicily
July 17–July 22, 1943

Chapter 20: Garrison Duty 287
Sicily
July 23–August 11, 1943

Chapter 21: EGB448 296
Oujda, Algeria
Kairouan, Tunisia
August 12–August 24, 1943

Chapter 22: Cancelled Jump on Capua 307
Tunisia and Sicily
August 25–September 12, 1943

Chapter 23: Eight Hours to Countdown 320
Salerno Beachhead
September 13–September 15, 1943

Chapter 24: Regaining Lost Ground 335
Salerno Beachhead
September 16–September 17, 1943

Chapter 25: On the Wrong Hill... 350
Salerno Beachhead
September 17, 1943

Chapter 26: Recapture of Hill 424.. 363
Salerno Beachhead
September 17, 1943

Chapter 27: Strike and Hold... 377
Salerno Beachhead
September 18–September 30, 1943

Chapter 28: Prisoners of War.. 393
Oflag 64 and Stalag II-B
July 1943–May 1945

Postscript.. 405
Appendix A: List of officer transfers June 1942–April 1943 409
Appendix B: Order of Battle in the United States 412
Appendix C: Order of Battle for Operation Husky –
            July 9/10, 1943.. 415
Appendix D: Order of Battle on Sicily – July 22, 1943 421
Appendix E: Order of Battle for Operation Avalanche –
            September 9, 1943.. 423
Appendix F: List of Distinguished Service Cross Recipients............ 425
List of Contributing Veterans... 427
Published Works.. 429
About the Author... 433
Endnotes.. 435
Index.. 461

ACKNOWLEDGMENTS

I n July 2014, my first book, *The Battle of the Bridges: The 504th Para-chute Infantry Regiment in Operation Market Garden*, was published. It was the first of five volumes that cover the World War II (WWII) service record of an entire parachute infantry regiment (PIR). Never before has such a detailed history about a regiment been written. This book is the first part of the series. Back in August 2007, when I Company veteran Francis X. Keefe asked me to write down the saga of the 504th, I could have never realized what a colossal task I would undertake. I am glad he pushed me over the years to complete it.

It has been my aim to devote as equally as possible the amount of data on each of the campaigns. You will read about the different replacement groups; from which pools were they created? When were they sent overseas? What it is like to arrive at a frontline position and be placed in an outpost? How did these paratroopers respond to their first battle? The story of this book ends in Naples and continues in the earlier published book, *Spearhead of the Fifth Army*.

I got to know Cooper Beverley-Meise in June 2014, and we have corresponded ever since. Her uncle, Garland Cooper, was killed at Den Heuvel farm (see *The Battle of the Bridges*) and Cooper helped me obtain several newspaper clippings that I tracked down online. She also encouraged me along the writing process and helped me search for information on several troopers. Together, we organized a large 504th PIR WWII Veterans and Family Reunion in Fort Bragg.

Mike Bigalke shared various reports linked to the early regimental campaigns and the 3rd Battalion cadre photo. Italian historian

Federico Peyrani, the unit historian of Schwere Panzer-Abteilung 504, answered several questions by email.

I traced the last surviving officer from the activation cadre, Brigadier General (Ret.) Henry "Hank" J. Muller, Jr., in January 2017. Muller was the original personnel officer, and despite his high age of 99 years, he had a remarkably clear memory of those early days in May, June, and July 1942. He would eventually rise during WWII to be 11th Airborne Division Intelligence officer and planner of the famed Los Baños Raid. Muller died on January 31, 2022 at age 104.

Many people contributed material and valuable information in the form of recollections, diaries, letters, photographs, and other documents. First of all, I would like to thank Kim, Shannon, and Steve Mandle, children of the late William D. Mandle, for allowing me to use numerous photographs from their late father's collection. Walt Ranta made several rosters and photos of his late father Arne Ranta available. Allen Schoppe and Dennis Kennedy donated unique rosters, correspondence, and photographs from their collections. Peggy Shelly kindly assisted in obtaining copies of questionnaires from the United States Army Military History Institute. Tammy Horton of the Maxwell Air Force Base Archives provided the escape and evasion reports of several paratroopers.

Marcia Ray generously shared a wealth of information on B Company veterans, including her late father, Edwin Decker. Rosie McNaughton supplied letters and photos of her late father Henry Paquet, killed near Altavilla. Pete Puhalla did the same for his uncle Frank A. Puhalla, killed on Hill 424. Travis Smith shared the privately printed memoir of his father, Captain Elbert Frank Smith. Linda Brown retyped the wartime letters of her father, Sergeant Gordon Gould.

In April 2016, I located the son of James O. Eldridge of C and G Companies, Jimmy Eldridge, who sadly never got to know his father. He kindly shared numerous letters and photographs that gave me insight in his father's wartime service. Help was also received from Ken Thieme—grandson of cadre officer Robert Erickson—who supplied not only information about his grandfather but also the 2nd Battalion cadre photo. Doug Adams answered numerous questions about the wartime service of his late father, Colonel (Ret.) Emory Adams, Jr. The late Linda Caplin did the same for her father, Major William R. Beall, who was killed in the Sorrento Peninsula. I first met Priscilla Elledge in Fort Bragg in February 2017, and she copied various documents and letters of her late father James Goethe for me.

In spring 2018, I traced down John and Kim Kouns, son and granddaughter of the late Colonel Charles W. Kouns. They supplied not only his Sicily story but also scans of post-war correspondence with author Clay Blair. Laurie Utterback kindly shared the wartime letters and memoirs of former Lieutenant Thomas E. Utterback, her grandfather. Carl Mauro designed the outstanding maps based on my unskilled sketches; it enables production of small action maps.

Corresponding with the families of paratroopers was one of the most enjoyable aspects of my research. I especially enjoyed these exchanges, as I often could provide families with company photos or other information they wanted to know while I learned much from them about family members who had been in the 504th. If you, too, have a relative or friend who was in the 504th PIR in World War II, I would love to hear from you. Please don't hesitate to contact me at macfrank82@hotmail.com.

So many people contributed to helping this book come to pass that it is impossible for me to mention them all, but I deeply thank those who contributed whose names may not appear here. Gayle Wurst, my agent, attended the earlier mentioned reunion in Fort Bragg and once again supported me to get this book in print. Roger Williams and Kate Monahan of Post Hill Press realized the historical value of this story and made this book come to reality.

My final word of thanks must go to the 504th Parachute Infantry Regiment for making me an Honorary Member in appreciation of my ongoing research on the unit in World War II. With this fourth book, I can once more pay tribute to "my regiment." By the time of publication, eighty years have passed since the activation of the finest airborne unit. Strike and hold!

Frank van Lunteren
Arnhem, The Netherlands
February 24, 2022

INTRODUCTION

I f one takes a critical look at the historiography of the 82nd Airborne Division in World War II, many books are dealing with the 505th Parachute Infantry Regiment (PIR). Even in division histories and studies of the Sicilian campaign, the accomplishments of the 505th are always broadly measured. The 504th PIR, however, seems to be forgotten. True, many authors mention the actions (briefly) of some lieutenants—often only three of them—but other actions of the 3rd Battalion are overlooked. To explain this incomplete view is simple; all authors drew either on Major William R. Beall's account of the campaign or publications from Major General James Gavin, who also depended heavily on Beall's report. Even the composer of the 82nd Airborne Division's official wartime account of the battles of Sicily and Italy used Beall's report verbatim.

Many veterans of the 504th Regimental Combat Team were reluctant to talk about the Sicily jump or the war in general. They were much more modest, as was their regimental commander, than Gavin's 505th PIR. Gavin's troops demonstrated this attitude already in North Africa prior to Operation Husky, when comedian Bob Hope gave a show for them. He said, "Well, I'm certainly happy to be here today with the famous 82nd Division!" To his surprise, the troopers shouted vehemently, "No, no! 505!...505!...505!"[1]

The former regimental commander of the 504th PIR—Major General Reuben H. Tucker III—had long since passed away when Gavin had his memoir *On to Berlin* published in 1978, Gerard Devlin's *Paratrooper!* in 1979, Allen Langdon's *Ready* (about the 505th PIR), bestselling author Clay Blair's *Ridgway's Paratroopers* in 1986, and

William Breuer's classic *Geronimo!* in 1989. The story of Gavin's stand on Biazzo Ridge on July 11, 1943 was immortalized, but the contribution of Tucker's troopers was forgotten.

It seems almost impossible to correct the classic view of the 505th PIR's accomplishments on Sicily. A small number of Gavin's paratroopers not only took all their objectives but also stopped the advance of the Hermann Goering Division toward the American invasion beaches, thus saving basically the entire campaign from disaster. The 504th, in this view, is seen as a regiment that was sent in separately and, apart from the earlier mentioned junior officers, was so scattered that they barely had any influence on the outcome of the battle. I sincerely hope that view will change. Without the actions of Lieutenant Colonel Charles Kouns' 3rd Battalion, it is likely that various elements of the 505th PIR would have been overrun. Also, the dispersed drop of the 504th made it impossible for the Germans to counterattack the way they wanted to.

After the captured paratroopers of the 504th were liberated in 1945, no one took it upon themselves to correct—or update—the reports on the airborne invasion. Thus, the existing historical studies of the American airborne landings on Sicily are largely outdated and unbalanced, as far more veterans of the 505th PIR were consulted than the 504th. Kouns' own story is told here for the first time in his own words. May this book contribute a little in setting straight the accomplishments of the 504th Parachute Infantry Regiment.

CHAPTER 1

THE AIRBORNE PIONEERS

Fort Benning, Georgia

JUNE 1940-APRIL 1942

A t the outbreak of World War II, the world had not yet seen an attack carried out by airborne troops. The war was less than a year old when airborne warfare started with the German attack on the Belgian Fortress of Eben-Emael and a mass drop of their 7th Flieger Division near the Dutch cities of The Hague and Rotterdam on May 10, 1940. Because of these landings, and although the German airborne invasion failed at The Hague, the War Department in Washington decided to experiment with paratroops.

On June 25, 1940, just weeks after the German airborne operations had been conducted, the Commandant of the Infantry School at Fort Benning received orders to form a Test Platoon. The platoon was composed of 1st Lieutenant William T. Ryder, 2nd Lieutenant James A. Bassett, and forty-eight enlisted men who had been selected out of a group of over two hundred volunteers of the 29th Infantry Regiment. With no more than twenty-one parachutes, Warrant Officer Harry Wilson and four riggers started their training in an old iron hangar at Lawson Field, Fort Benning.[2]

Less than two weeks had passed since the first assembly of the Test Platoon when Major William C. Lee visited the group at Lawson Field and told Ryder that he had witnessed demonstrations at the jump towers of New York World's Fair at Hightstown, New Jersey. Lee worked in the Office of the Chief of Infantry and arranged the transfer of the platoon to New Jersey to use the jump towers.[3]

The next day, July 30, every man made five free drops from a 125-foot tower. Next came the 250-foot towers. Ultimately on August 13, the Test Platoon was ready for their first jump into the wild blue yonder. Three days later, the last members made their qualifying parachute drop out of a twin-engine B-18 bomber.

Shortly after, Lee convinced the War Department to purchase two large 250-foot towers from New York World's Fair. They were taken down and reassembled in Fort Benning, Georgia, not far from Lawson Field.[4] The 501st Parachute Battalion was activated on September 6, 1940 under the command of Major William W. Miley at Fort Benning. The Test Platoon was used to cadre the battalion, and Ryder was promoted to captain while Bassett could change the golden second lieutenant bars on his uniforms for silver-colored first lieutenant bars. Months passed by while the 501st Parachute Battalion continued training, and by early 1941, it was considered advanced trained.

At the War Department, plans were drawn to expand the parachute forces with three more battalions before the end of 1941. To supervise the build-up and training of these four battalions, the Provisional Parachute Group Headquarters was activated in in Fort Benning in early March 1941 by the Chief of Infantry. Lee, who had earlier arranged the purchase of two jump towers, was promoted to lieutenant colonel. He was supposed to develop a tactical doctrine for the parachute troops, prepare a study of permanent Tables of Organization and Basic Allowances, and write training manuals.

Lee's first major task, besides choosing his staff, was to provide a cadre for the 502nd Parachute Battalion, which had to be activated on July 1, 1941. As the 501st Parachute Battalion provided the majority of the cadre, it also needed new paratroopers to replace them. But where could Lee find sufficient volunteers?

After conferring with the Office of the Chief of Infantry, Lee was allowed to visit the 8th and 9th Infantry Divisions at Fort Jackson, South Carolina and Fort Benning, Georgia to find the desired quota of men. The 8th Infantry Division provided only a few dozen, while the 9th Infantry Division had a thousand enthusiastic volunteers.

Only about two hundred were needed, and the other men were turned down for the time being. The activation of the 503rd and 504th Parachute Battalions would require more men anyway.[5]

The 504th Parachute Battalion was activated on October 5, 1941 under the command of Major Richard Chase. He had been an original member of the 501st Parachute Battalion and had joined the service in 1937 upon graduating from the Syracuse Commerce University. His Battalion S-3 Officer responsible for planning and operations was Captain Reuben H. Tucker III, who came from the 502nd Parachute Battalion, where he had commanded B Company. "Of all the men who volunteer for the Paratroops," Chase said to journalist Janet Campbell Green, "only two-thirds finish the preliminary training. The reasons for men dropping out vary. The first to be eliminated are those who can't stand up to the physical and mental qualifications."[6]

The training of the individual paratroopers for the four parachute battalions emphasized calisthenics, long marches, a three-mile run daily, scouting and patrolling, map reading, and qualification on all the weapons that were transported by air. The use of a compass was also important as it was expected that paratroopers would need extra help to orient themselves after a drop. Next came the parachute maintenance training, which included packing parachutes and jump training. Jump graduates were awarded silver-plated "jump wings"—a parachute qualification badge designed by Captain William P. Yarborough, a company commander of the 501st Parachute Battalion.

Once assigned to one of the battalions of the Provision Parachute Group, the training was divided into two subsequent phases. First of all, training was on squad, platoon, and company size to blend the individual troopers into a cohesive unit. This phase included exercises both day and night, including more jumps. The troopers also spent considerable time on the rifle range to qualify their marksmanship for a number of weapons. This lasted fourteen weeks. The second phase involved battalion level training on tactical basis and lasted two weeks.[7]

Major General Lesley J. McNair, who commanded the Army Ground Forces, was a great supporter of parachute battalions and argued that this new branch within the U.S. Army could only be used effectively if they would be expanded. He therefore ordered the activation of a number of parachute infantry regiments out of the existing four parachute battalions that would be integrated into them.

In preparation for McNair's plan, a letter was sent on January 9, 1942 to each army corps area. It said, "Qualified men may now be enlisted for parachute troops either directly from civil life or may be procured as volunteers in reception centers. The restriction of procurement of such personnel to volunteers in infantry replacement training centers and men who have had previous military service is removed."[8] To ensure that no volunteers would be prohibited, the letter ended with the following two paragraphs: "Parachute volunteers will be sent from reception centers to infantry replacement training centers for training. While undergoing training, volunteers will be held specifically for parachute unit assignment and will not be made available for assignment to any other unit. Upon completion of thirteen weeks training at infantry replacement centers, all parachute volunteers will be transferred to the Infantry School at Fort Benning, Georgia."[9]

To help the medical officers at the various army reception centers throughout the country, a list of basic requirements had to be made. Captain David E. Thomas, the Group Surgeon of the Provisional Parachute Group Headquarters, wrote an article titled "Selection of the Parachutist," which appeared in *Military Surgeon* magazine and *Military Review*. He wrote:

> A minimum height of 66 inches and weight of 150 lbs. is desired. While it is true that smaller men can make easier landings, a small man does not have the strength required to handle the heavy loads of equipment. A good, little man is very desirable, but most little men are not good enough. Maximum height and weight are 72 inches and 185 lbs. Tall men have trouble getting out of the plane door and exceptionally heavy men may blow out panels of the parachute during the opening shock. Heavy men descend fast, thereby getting hard landings. Tall, thin men, have difficulty tumbling properly.

A vision of 20/40 uncorrected in each eye is required because a man must be able to accurately gauge his height from the ground when landing and must be able to see the equipment to handle it after he lands. Satisfactory color differentiation in the yarn test is also necessary because equipment of various types is dropped by means of colored parachutes. The usual teeth qualifications apply. Men with small bridges are acceptable, but if a plate is worn, the man is not accepted because of the possibility of his losing or breaking the plate.[10]

McNair's plan began to take shape in early April 1942; the Provisional Parachute Group was reformed into the Airborne Command. It meant a promotion for Lee; many of his principal staff officers were also destined to command one of the new parachute infantry regiments. Lieutenant Colonel Theodore L. Dunn, the former Commanding Officer of the Recruiting Detachment of the Provisional Parachute Group Headquarters, was tasked with activating the 504th Parachute Infantry Regiment by General Order Number 2 of the Airborne Command dated April 13, 1942. This activation order was derived from McNair's decision of March 24 and had to be effectuated by May 1.[11]

Dunn was born on February 25, 1904 in Meridian, Mississippi and grew up with heroic stories about the Confederate Army. Dunn graduated from West Point in 1925 and married in 1929 before being sent overseas to the Philippines to serve in the 45th Infantry. The couple settled down in Gumaca, Quezon Province, where Dunn commanded a unit consisting entirely of Philippine soldiers. Three years later, they returned to the States due to a transfer to the Tank School. Dunn was then assigned to the 66th Infantry Regiment and posted in early 1937 to the 114th Infantry Regiment in Panama. That same year, a son was born.

The year 1939 brought a reassignment to the 7th Tank Company at Fort Snelling, Minnesota. A year later, Dunn was again transferred, this time as a major, to a tank battalion in Brownwood, Texas.[12] He found it the right time to try something new when he heard about the paratroops. He volunteered in July 1941 and was assigned in September 1941 to the Provisional Parachute Group Headquarters.

Dunn's task was both difficult and unique; his was the first parachute infantry regiment to be constituted almost entirely of recent jump school graduates. The activation on March 2, 1942 of the first parachute regiment of the U.S. Army, the 503rd Parachute Infantry, had been relatively simple by renumbering the 503rd and 504th Parachute Battalions as the 1st and 2nd Battalions, respectively. A third battalion wasn't activated until June 1942.

The 501st Parachute Battalion was stationed in Panama at the time, and the 502nd Parachute Battalion couldn't contribute either, as they formed the basis of the 502nd Parachute Infantry Regiment activated in March 1942. Thus, the cadre that Dunn had at his disposal to raise the 504th Parachute Infantry was very small: fewer than one hundred officers and men. The majority of them came from the former 503rd and 504th Parachute Battalions. Lieutenant Colonel Chase of the 504th was assigned as Dunn's regimental executive officer.

The recently promoted group of officers included Major Tucker, former S-3 of the 504th Parachute Battalion, was given no specific duty. He does stand on the 1st Battalion cadre photo along with the battalion adjutant, 1st Lieutenant William R. Beall. It is therefore possible that Tucker was involved in the first phase of training the battalion. Why the 1st Battalion Commander, Captain Robert L. Wolverton (West Point 1938), is not on the photo is unknown. On the official list of the cadre officers, no 1st Battalion executive officer is listed. Tucker recalled of the activation: "The 504th Parachute Infantry was born May 1, 1942. At its birth, it weighed in the neighborhood of 86 enlisted men and ten officers. This original cadre came, for the most part, from the 504th Parachute Battalion. (...) Dunn was given command of the regiment and started to build the splendid outfit."[13]

The 2nd Battalion would be initially led by Major John B. Shinberger (West Point 1933) and Captain Robert O. Erickson. Shinberger had commanded the first parachute field artillery battery and C Company of the 501st Parachute Battalion in Panama. Captain Charles H. Chase (West Point 1933) commanded the 3rd Battalion with Captain William Colville, Jr. as his battalion executive officer.

The short Captain Warren R. Williams, Jr. (West Point 1938) served as the Regiment S-3 officer.

Twenty-five-year-old 1st Lieutenant Julian A. Cook from Mount Holly, Vermont was the first regimental adjutant. Cook was born on October 7, 1916. As the youngest of nine children, he chose a military career and graduated from West Point in 1940. He joined the 9th Infantry Division until his best friend, 1st Lieutenant James E. McGinity, decided to join the paratroops in the summer of 1941: "We had been enlisted men together, went to the West Point Prep School and were in the 9th Division at Fort Bragg when he wanted to go into the airborne. He volunteered for it and I was really quite disgusted with the 9th Division so when he went there and said it was good, I went [and] graduated in March of 1942."[14]

Contrary to the first airborne pioneers, the paratroopers who qualified in the spring of 1942 and beyond received a training manual. Their training was becoming less and less experimental compared to the early paratroopers, even though the preparation courses at Lawson Field were very tough. A lot of time was spent on physical training, lectures on map and compass reading, demolitions, codes, infantry tactics, signaling, and unarmed combat. The candidates also learned how to pack their own parachute. Walking in the "frying pan" area was strictly prohibited. Everywhere they went, they had to "double time."

The whole training program was divided into four parts. In the "A" stage, which lasted three weeks, the "men were separated from the boys." The candidates learned to march as a group, ran nine miles every morning before breakfast, learned how to fold and pack their parachutes at the packing sheds, and had calisthenics in the field, starting with side-straddle hops and going the full course to push-ups and other exercises. Push-ups were the regular punishment at Fort Benning when men reacted too slowly or incorrectly in the view of the instructors.

At noontime, the men had chow again, which tasted worse than the food they were served at breakfast. In the afternoon, more running and push-ups followed. Evening chow was again disappointing and remained so even after the paratroopers had joined a parachute infantry regiment, but some men did not complain about the unrecognizable hash.

"A" stage was followed by "B" stage. After having completed the first grueling three weeks, the men now jumped in the afternoons from C-47 mock up fuselages that were four feet above the ground. They also descended from a thirty-five-foot tower in a parachute harness that was suspended from a steel cable. This stage only lasted one week, just like the other two stages that followed. In this stage, a number of men were sent out of the paratroops.

"C" stage became more serious. Now they made free and controlled jumps from one of the three giant 250-foot towers. They started to experience free fall while a wind machine taught them how to control and collapse the canopies of their parachutes.

The last week at Fort Benning was "D" stage, comprising five parachute jumps, including one night jump, out of a C-47 Dakota transport plane at an altitude of 1,500 feet above the ground. They jumped in "sticks" of twelve men. Most candidates had never been in an airplane before, and once near the assigned drop zone, the red light at the right side of the removed cargo door went on. The jumpmaster in the airplane, usually an instructor, yelled, "Is everybody happy!" Following the affirmative reply from the stick, he would give the command, "Stand up and hook up!"

After each man had attached his static line, a line attached to the backpack cover of the main chute, to the anchor line that ran along the top of the fuselage to the door, the instructor would give the order for them to check their own equipment for the last time to make sure that everything was tied up properly.

As soon as the man in the back of the plane was ready, he would yell, "Number Twelve OK" and tap the man in front of him on his shoulder. If he were ready as well, he would call, "Number Eleven OK" and tap the man in front of him. And so on. It just took about forty-five seconds before the man who was closest to the door would say, "Number One OK."

Then the instructor would shout, "Stand in the door." They would shuffle to the door, and the first man stepped in the open door, placing his left foot forward and his hands on the outer edge of the door. Once the green light below the red light appeared, the paratroopers would leap out of the door, the static line pulled the back cover off his main chute, and the prop blasted, inflated the chute, and opened with a terrific shock. Drifting to the ground, they would look around and shout encouragements to each other.

During the training jumps, more emphasis was put on the proper jump procedure than exiting the plane at a fast rate. The sticks were widely spread on the drop zone as a result. Later, while jumping with their regiments, the paratroopers would reverse the priorities: better to jump as quick as possible and land near each other than to jump properly and get dispersed.

After jumping five times, including a night jump, the paratroopers received the desired silver parachute wings pinned on the left pocket of their jackets. It was one of the proudest moments in the life of a paratrooper. They could "blouse" their trousers in their brown leather jump boots and wear the patch of the Airborne Command on their left shoulder until they joined one of the parachute regiments.

Cadre officers on May 1, 1942. Courtesy: John Walsh

Cadre of the 1st Battalion in Fort Benning, May 1, 1942. Major Reuben Tucker standing far left; Lieutenant William Beall far right. Captain Robert Wolverton front row, first on right. Courtesy: Rosie Paquet McNaughton

Cadre of the 2nd Battalion in Fort Benning, May 1, 1942. Major John Shinberger standing far left; Captain Robert Erickson standing far right. Courtesy: Ken Thieme

Cadre of the 3rd Battalion in Fort Benning, May 1, 1942. Captain Charles Chase standing far left; Captain William Colville standing far right. Courtesy: Mike Bigalke

CHAPTER 2

THE ORIGINAL CADRE

Georgia, Alabama, Louisiana, North Carolina

MAY-JUNE 1942

Before new officers and men arrived at the 504th Parachute Infantry Regiment, the cadre had to be prepared for their arrival. On May 1, 1942, the regimental colors were presented to Lieutenant Colonel Theodore L. Dunn, who would be promoted to Colonel in a few weeks' time, and official army photos were taken of the battalion cadres. Each of the three battalions consisted of two officers and eighteen enlisted men at the time of its activation. The remaining four officers and enlisted men would serve in Headquarters and Headquarters Company or Service Company. "The months of May and June were devoted to training the cadre," remembered the Training Officer, Major Reuben Tucker. "An intensive schedule was followed so that the cadre was well prepared to receive the newcomers during the first week of July."[15]

Twenty-five-year-old 1st Lieutenant Henry "Hank" J. Muller, Jr. from Santa Barbara, California became the first regimental personnel officer. Muller was a regular army officer and initially served in B Company of the 1st Infantry Regiment with Captain James "Lou" W. Coutts as his company commander. Coutts had joined the paratroops already in 1941, and Muller decided to follow in his footsteps in early 1942. He was temporarily attached to the 502nd Parachute Battalion upon graduation from Parachute School. Captain Julian A.

Cook told Muller, "That means one of us can't stay." Cook and Muller were respectively the ninth and tenth regular officers who had been assigned to the cadre. "The Army's idea was to spread out the regular officers to avoid what happened after the Civil War," recalled Muller. "They lost so many commanders afterwards, that they didn't want that to happen again. A lot of officers were shifted around much in the early days of the airborne forces. The Army allowed only eight regular officers by a regiment. We didn't have our fillers yet. I think only until I left in July that they got their fillers. I don't remember there was a full complement of junior officers. A contingency was sent by the 1st Battalion to cadre the 3rd Battalion of the 503rd Parachute Infantry Regiment in June."[16]

Front row left to right: Captain Robert Erickson, Major Reuben Tucker, Major Richard Chase, Lieutenant Colonel Theodore Dunn, Major John Shinberger, Captain Charles Chase, and Captain Warren Williams, Jr. Standing behind Erickson is Sergeant Henry Paquet of B Company, who was killed on Hill 424. Courtesy: John Walsh

Captain Charles Wilmarth Kouns, a twenty-eight-year-old native of Salina, Kansas, had married his girlfriend Marion Putnam just two weeks before the activation. He remembered of the cadre: "We met at the Parachute School (Lawson Field, Fort Benning) shortly before Pearl Harbor 1941. Our qualification – five jumps from a plane in flight – was delayed by lack of aircraft. Part of our class was assigned to the 504th Parachute Infantry Regiment as a cadre and nucleus. Teddy Dunn was Commanding Officer, Tucker became the Training Officer. I was assigned Service Company briefly until I was sent to the three months Battalion Commander's Course [of] The Infantry School."[17]

Lieutenant Muller recalled:

> We first billeted in the brick building on the group photo of the cadre. But then we moved to a wooden barracks area near Lawson Field. Our headquarters was set up in single story wooden buildings. I could look out at the window and see Lawson Field. We were right over a cliff, right above the Parachute School. I saw very little of Colonel Dunn in those days. I would see him walk in and out from his office, but I had no direct contact with him. I worked with Captain Julian Cook as I was basically his assistant. The Personnel Officer worked for the S-1.
>
> I remember Major Reuben Tucker as a very gentlemanly commander. He was such a likeable man. But we weren't close at that time as he was a major and I was just a lieutenant. (…) Major John Shinberger was the executive regimental commander [in June 1942]. He was an outgoing officer and often moved around to talk to different people. He asked me one day, "Do you want a leave? I will get you a leave." I answered, "Yes, I would like 10 days." "OK, that is fine." I never thought he would give me that but he did.[18]

It was about mid-July when Muller received a phone call from Lieutenant Colonel Coutts. He recalled:

> Lou Coutts got command of the 507th Parachute Infantry Regiment. He said: "Would you like to come over to be the adjutant?" I answered, "Why? I have

been never been an adjutant." Coutts said, "Well, I have never been a regimental commander." So I decided to join the 507th Parachute Infantry Regiment since there was a chance they would transfer me one day with so many regular officers in the 504th. But Lieutenant Colonel Coutts left one day secretly for England to be the airborne advisor to General Eisenhower for the North Africa invasion. Then Colonel George Millett took charge. He made me a battalion executive officer shortly and sent me to the Officers School in Fort Leavenworth, Kansas.

When I returned to the 507th my old place had been taken. I stood on the ferry crossing the Chattahoochee River when I ran into Lieutenant Colonel [Orin D.] "Hard Rock" Haugen. I knew him from the 502nd Parachute Battalion. He said, "I just got the word to form a regiment – the 511th Parachute Infantry Regiment." I decided to join him and he made me adjutant. When the cadre arrived at Camp Toccoa, Georgia, we had only 30 officers. I was the first day up Mount Currahee. Lieutenant Colonel Haugen said to me, "Hank, I want all the officers up there. We're gonna go for a run." We were still wearing our rain coats and overcoats and ran up that mountain. We hadn't got our fillers yet. A few months I served in the 511th Parachute Infantry Regiment before joining the 11th Airborne Division staff as G-2 officer. I collected the intelligence for the Los Baños Raid.[19]

Detail of the cadre photo on May 1, 1942. Front row: Lieutenant Henry
Muller, Jr., Captains Julian Cook, Charles Kouns, Leslie Freeman, and Robert
Wolverton. Standing between Kouns and Freeman is Sergeant Wallace Ritch,
who was captured on Sicily and is still MIA. Courtesy: John Walsh

All the enlisted cadre members came from the 502nd PIR, and
each company numbered one first sergeant and three staff sergeants,
who would each supervise a platoon until officers arrived to take command.[20] During the first eight weeks of its existence, the regiment was
merely an organization on paper only. A few officers were assigned
every week, like 2nd Lieutenant Charles W. Duncan from Columbia,
South Carolina. Duncan was a regular non-commissioned officer who
had served in the coast artillery from 1932 to 1935 before reenlisting
in the infantry in April 1941. He had previously served in the 503rd
and 504th Parachute Battalions.

In March 1942, 1st Sergeant Duncan served as a cadre member
for I Company of the 502nd PIR before he entered Officer Candidate
School (OCS) at the end of the month. Duncan was commissioned
as second lieutenant in June 1942 and was immediately assigned to
C Company of the 504th PIR. Being one of the first officers in the
company and performing with excellence as a platoon leader, he rose
quickly through the ranks and was given command of B Company
before the regiment went overseas.

The regiment would comprise three battalions, each numbering three rifle companies and a headquarters company. The rifle companies were labeled A, B, and C for the 1st Battalion, D, E, and F for the 2nd Battalion, and G, H, and I for the 3rd Battalion. The three headquarters companies for each battalion were numbered 1, 2, and 3 to indicate to which battalion they belonged to. Second Lieutenant John S. Lekson remembered of the table of organization of the 1st Battalion: "Three rifle companies – A, B and C – formed its fighting backbone. Each rifle company contained three rifle platoons. (...) No weapons platoons were included in the rifle companies. Instead a light machine gun and an automatic rifle were to be dropped with each rifle squad. Orders on the ground would dictate which was to be carried. The battalion was light and it lacked several necessities for sustained ground combat: transportation, and high velocity antitank weapons."[21]

Captain William E. Hornby's Headquarters and Headquarters Company was the overall commanding unit of the regiment. Composed of a Communications Platoon, Reconnaissance Platoon, Regimental Demolition Platoon, Grave Registration Detail, Counter Intelligence Corps (CIC) detachment, and various staff officers and clerks, Headquarters and Headquarters Company could deliver specialists to each of the battalions or rifle companies when needed. For this reason, the Regimental Reconnaissance and Demolition Platoons were divided into three squads. Each could be attached to one of the battalions.

Then there was the 504th Parachute Maintenance Detachment, responsible for the folding and packing of the parachutes, and a Service Company, which was formed out of clerks, cooks, drivers, and other occupancies to support the rifle companies with needed clothing, jump boots, mail, and (food) supplies. First Lieutenant William A. Addison was responsible for the ammunition supply in his function of Munitions Officer. Replacements that were assigned to the regiment during the time it was overseas were almost always put in the "replacement platoon" in Service Company before joining one of the rifle or headquarters companies. Service Company was also responsible for running the base camp of the regiment.

The medical officers and medics served throughout the regiment. The medics were shifted around to get familiar with more than one rifle company. First Regimental Surgeon was twenty-eight-year-old Captain Robert E. Eby, who had earlier been battalion surgeon of the 504th Parachute Battalion and in the regiment from the start. Assistant Regimental Surgeon was twenty-eight-year-old Captain Frederick J. Swift, Jr. The other original surgeons in the regiment were 1st Lieutenants Kenneth I. Sheek and Francis G. Sheehan. In all, there were eight medical officers, a dentist, and sixty enlisted men divided in three battalion medical sections and a small headquarters medical section that handled medical reports, periodic reports, and supplies. A captain and first lieutenant would work as battalion surgeon and assisting surgeon. The Regimental Surgeon and his assistant would often rotate at the battalion sections, carrying out or assisting operations to maintain their level of efficiency.

In combat operations, the regiment would often operate as the 504th Regimental Combat Team. Beside the organic units of the 504th Parachute Infantry Regiment, this included Captain Thomas M. Wight's C Company of the 307th Airborne Engineer Battalion. Wight's unit constructed or repaired barracks, bridges, camp facilities such as showers and stoves, electricity lines, and roads. Airborne engineers also built or repaired bridges, placed or removed mines, and operated assault boats for river crossings. They had a similar table of organization as the rifle companies. Throughout the war, engineers would fight alongside their infantry comrades.

Supporting artillery fire would be provided by Lieutenant Colonel Wilbur M. Griffith's 376th Parachute Infantry Battalion, consisting of four firing batteries equipped with 75mm "pack" howitzers and a headquarters battery. The C Battery of the 80th Airborne Anti-Aircraft Battalion would also be attached several times to the regiment during combat operations. The unit was armed with eight 37mm and later with the British 6-pounder anti-tank guns or 57mm guns, as they were known by the American soldiers. A captain and two lieutenants were in charge of the eighty-men-strong battery, which was divided into a small headquarters component and two platoons numbered 1 and 2.

Whenever the engineers and gunners were attached to the regiment, it was known as the 504th Regimental Combat Team.

Besides all these weapons, spiritual armament was provided by two regimental chaplains: one Catholic, Captain Edwin J. Kozak, and one Protestant, First Lieutenant Delbert A. Kuehl. They were both jump qualified. Kozak was born on August 24, 1911 in Colorado but grew up in Baltimore, Maryland. Upon graduation from high school, he attended St. Hyacinth's Seminary in Granby, Massachusetts. It was there that Kozak entered the priesthood. He was ordained as a priest in the Franciscan Order of Minor Conventuals by Archbishop Michael J. Curley in the Baltimore Cathedral on June 3, 1934. His first parishes were in Fairfield, Connecticut and Detroit before he joined the U.S. Army. Kozak had the honor to be the first American Catholic chaplain to qualify as a paratrooper.[22]

Kuehl was born in January 1917 in Hopkins, Minnesota. He grew up on a farm overlooking the west side of Lake Carlos. The Great Depression caused an abrupt change of the rural life to the city life of Minnetonka a few miles away. As a teenager, Kuehl did not believe in God until he participated in a contest among several Boy Scouts teams. One of the prerequisites was to attend four straight Sunday School meetings. Kuehl decided to put up with it, as it would only be four gatherings. However, as the required Sunday School meetings ended, he found himself enjoying reading the Bible. Finally, he accepted Christ as his savior, a decision that changed his life.

Instead of choosing a career to escape the family poverty, Kuehl decided to enroll at the Northwestern Bible Seminary in 1937. The next step was Bethel University in St. Paul, Minnesota, where he got his associate degree in theology. Back in Alexandria, Minnesota, he also obtained a double degree in history and philosophy.

In early 1942, Kuehl voluntarily joined the U.S. Army as a Protestant chaplain because "I couldn't bear the idea of Hitler and his super race."[23] Commissioned as a lieutenant, Kuehl was sent to Fort Benjamin Harrison in Indiana for chaplains' training. Before his graduation, Kuehl learned about a new army branch: the paratroops. A week later, he was assigned to the 504th Parachute Infantry. He said, "They really put us through the mill. If you made a mistake, it was 50 push-ups.

But I had done construction work in Alaska and worked in the canneries in California to pay my way through college, so I was in pretty good shape."[24]

Five parachute jumps later, Lieutenant Kuehl could proudly wear his wings. No one in the regiment objected to that, but when he appeared on the rifle range to participate in target practice, the gunnery officer raised his eyebrows and asked Kuehl what he was doing there. Despite the discouraging looks and remarks, the chaplain took part in all the tests on the rifle range and came in third out of a group of six hundred men.

His first church service was not so successful, although Kuehl had made customary announcements in the regimental area: "Two men showed up and one of them was drunk. I walked through the camp that night weeping. I prayed and said, 'God, you've got to do something. There are going to be a lot of casualties with these men, and they will need to hear your word.' God answered me, 'If they won't come to you, then you'll have to go to them.'"[25]

This worked; more men started to show up as Kuehl participated in all the physical exercises. It helped create a bond of friendship with many of the troopers.

CHAPTER 3

LOSING HALF A CADRE

Fort Benning, Georgia

JUNE–SEPTEMBER 1942

B ecause new parachute infantry regiments—the 505th, 506th, and 507th—would be activated in the summer of 1942, a cadre had to be drawn from the Airborne Command and the existing parachute regiments. For Colonel Theodore Dunn, it meant the loss of highly valuable officers and non-commissioned officers like Technical Sergeant Woodrow Honea, who became the Warrant Officer of the 507th Parachute Infantry Regiment. Major John B. Shinberger (2nd Battalion) was transferred in early June to the cadre of the American-Canadian First Special Service Force (FSSF) as S-3 officer. He was briefly succeeded by the newly promoted Major Ward S. Ryan (West Point 1938) and then by Captain Robert O. Erickson as acting battalion commander until Major David A. DeArmond (West Point 1935) was placed in command. Erickson was subsequently transferred to the 1st Battalion as both S-2 and S-3.

Dunn's second-in-command, Lieutenant Colonel Richard Chase, left for the newly activated Army Air Force Troop Carrier Command at Stout Field in Indianapolis. Initially, he was accompanied by Major Charles H. Chase, until the latter and Captain Robert L. Wolverton became, respectively, regimental executive officer and battalion commander in the new 506th PIR. First Lieutenants Mark J. Alexander and James E. McGinity both shifted to the cadre of the 505th PIR of

Lieutenant Colonel James M. Gavin, who would become familiar to the 504th later in the war. Captain Arthur A. Maloney was promoted to major and became the executive officer of the new 507th PIR, while 1st Lieutenants Benjamin F. Pearson, Jr. and Gordon K. Smith were elevated to captains under Maloney as S-3 and S-4 officers.

To fill the vacancies left by these departures, Dunn chose officers from the original cadre. Major Reuben H. Tucker III (West Point 1935) became the new regimental executive officer, and Ryan was appointed as 3rd Battalion commander with Captain Leslie G. Freeman as his executive officer. Later in August, Ryan was first reassigned to the Parachute School as executive officer and later to the staff of the 1st Airborne Infantry Brigade as S-3 officer.[26] Ryan's successor, Freeman, had entered the Army in September 1940 and qualified as a paratrooper in March 1942. Although no West Point graduate, his leadership qualities were noticed, and he was made 3rd Battalion commander with the former regimental adjutant, Captain Julian A. Cook (West Point 1940), as battalion executive officer. The 2nd Battalion was trusted to DeArmond with Captain Daniel W. Danielson as his assistant. The recently promoted Major Warren R. Williams, Jr. (West Point 1938) became 1st Battalion commander with Captain George W. Rice as battalion executive officer.

Meanwhile, in July, the War Department had decided to convert the 82nd "All American" Infantry Division of Major General Matthew B. Ridgway, who had succeeded Major General Omar Bradley, to an airborne division. The division had fought in France during World War I, led by Brigadier General William P. Burnham, and consisted of the 325th, 326th, and 328th Infantry Regiments. During those days, the nickname "All American" had been earned as the officers and enlisted men came from all of the forty-eight states in the U.S. Sergeant Alvin C. York of Tennessee had distinguished himself in ferocious battles in the trenches and received the first Medal of Honor in the division. In 1941, Hollywood movie *Sergeant York* was released, and so the wartime legend of the division, in the meantime deactivated, was kept alive.

A few months after the Japanese attack on the naval base at Pearl Harbor in April 1942, the 82nd "All American" Infantry Division had been reactivated at Camp Claiborne, Louisiana. It comprised the 325th, 326th, and 327th Infantry Regiments and several smaller supporting units. Once again, the division was made up of officers and men who came from all over the United States—from California, New York, the rural areas of Montana and Iowa, South Carolina, and Pennsylvania. There were farmers, lawyers, coal miners, cowboys, teachers, high school students, and mountain men. Some had served in the National Guard or the Reserves. Others had no military experience at all when they enlisted.

The division officially became the 82nd Airborne Division on August 15, 1942 and had to transfer a large number of units and men to provide the cadre for a newly activated airborne division, the 101st. The Regimental Surgeon, Captain Robert E. Eby, left the regiment to join this new outfit. The 325th and 326th Glider Infantry Regiments, the 319th and 320th Glider Field Artillery Battalions, and the 307th Airborne Engineer Battalion and the 307th Airborne Medical Battalion were not reassigned.

Dunn's 504th Parachute Infantry Regiment was the first parachute regiment to become an integral part of the 82nd Airborne Division. That same day, another group of recent qualified paratroopers joined the regiment, including twenty-five-year-old 2nd Lieutenant Roy M. Hanna from Castanea Township, Clinton County, Pennsylvania. A graduate from Pennsylvania State University with a B.S. in Food Science, he joined the Pennsylvania National Guard. Because of his college background, Hanna soon climbed up through the non-commissioned officers' ranks until he was a staff sergeant. "The only way you could get out of the 28th Division was to go to OCS, so I went to OCS."[27] Commissioned as second lieutenant, Hanna opted for the paratroops.

The day Hanna received his jump wings, August 15, he found himself assigned to the Machine Gun Platoon of Headquarters Company, 3rd Battalion. "Very little has been written about the short training it had as a Division before entering the war," Hanna recalled of joining, "when this Regiment was a separate unit located at Fort Benning, Georgia. (...) In a comparatively short time, under some great leadership, this division was whipped into shape, trained to be ready for combat, and developed an amazing esprit de corps. Even though I was part of this training I still don't know how it was done."[28]

A tragic loss was suffered in the ranks of C Company when twenty-two-year-old Private Merle R. Williams died in a car accident on August 6. He had just left the Army Base at Fort Benning while on leave. Williams was the first member of the regiment to die during the war, even though it was not battle related. His burial took place ten days later in Inglewood Park Cemetery in his hometown of Inglewood, California. The text "504th Parachute Regt" on his tombstone indicates his strong connection to the regiment.

Captain Charles W. Kouns returned after a three-month absence as a graduate of the Battalion Commanders Course at Fort Benning. He was appointed as Regimental S-3 and was impressed by the progress that had been made. "When I returned, Tucker had training humming," he recalled. Kouns was to supervise "weapons qualification and battle indoctrination." He said:

> One exercise was a night march and simulated meeting engagement. We relied on route markers normal to the training areas but they were not legible in the dark. I struck a match to verify our position and Tucker announced there would be no lights what-so-ever. He asked me if I arranged for "guides." I responded "No" for it would be unrealistic. The penalty for being "lost" was critical because [Major] General Ridgway took a very dim view of subordinates who failed to adhere to their routes and positions as projected in training programs closely monitored by Division.
>
> In this instance, we were lost, but found by the Division and put through the frustrations of "realism" by fouled logistics, surprise losses, etc. to gauge our resiliency to adversity. As such "honing" events phased into combined arms exercises, more effort was devoted to PT for stamina and survival. The whole matrix of pre-combat exertions converted men to soldiers."[29]

Late that month, Ridgway came by with several of his senior staff officers to meet Dunn and the 504th Parachute Infantry Regiment. They were welcomed with the standard military courtesy. Ridgway told Dunn that he wanted to make a parachute jump even though he had never jumped before. Dunn assigned Major Warren R. Williams, Jr. of the 1st Battalion the task of giving the division commander and his staff officers a thirty-minute basic instruction and demonstration on the proper jump training. Williams also supervised some jumps from a raised platform and mock-up planes and a rudimentary briefing of several minutes on how to operate the risers of an opened parachute.

The whole "course" took about two hours. Ridgway became "a little nervous" as the training progressed and he entered the C-47 on the runway to make his first parachute jump.[30] A photo was made on the tarmac of the general and his staff officers in jump suits. Divided into two sticks, an equal number of C-47s took off and approached the DZ in Alabama. Williams acted as jumpmaster of Ridgway's stick. The drop went well, and after landing, Ridgway considered himself "a parachutist of sorts," although he was still not qualified.[31]

Sergeant Ernest W. Parks, one of the original members of D Company, grew up in Forsyth County, North Carolina, where he was born in February 1922. In June 1940, Parks graduated from high school and went with one of his friends to the local army recruitment office. They applied for army service on Hawaii. The local recruiter couldn't promise that they would be sent to Hawaii, so they left disappointed.

A month later, Parks and his friend tried once more at another recruiting office. Again, the recruiter told them that he couldn't offer them a service place in Hawaii. Just as they were heading to the door, the recruiting sergeant changed his mind. He stopped the two possible recruits and told them that he had forgotten a recent request from Hawaii for two young soldiers to start enlistment training. Contrary to what he had said, the sergeant wanted to sign them up for the field artillery. The trick worked; Parks and his friend signed their enlistment papers and received orders to report in Camp Jackson, South Carolina.

It was after about ten days that Parks began to wonder when they would be sent to Hawaii. He approached the drill sergeant and asked him for their departure date. Half drunk, the sergeant remarked with an annoyed loud voice, "What the HELL are you talking about? Who told you you're going to Hawaii?" Parks gave a sheepish reply: "Who? My recruiter did." The drill sergeant looked at him for a few moments and started to laugh. Parks suddenly realized why; he would never go to Hawaii.

Not willing to spend all his army days in the field artillery for which he hadn't volunteered, Parks decided to sign up in early 1942 for the paratroops. He said:

> I had been in training in Fort Benning, Georgia, for only a week or so, when I was ordered to report to a certain officer. I had no idea what lay ahead. The officer presented a letter written to him by my former commanding officer recommending me highly. He told me to learn everything I could during training, for afterwards, I would be offered the jump master position with a promotion to the rank of sergeant.

> The officer was more than a little shocked when I told him I did not want to give an immediate answer. As it turned out, when landing on my fifth jump which qualified me for my wings and status as a paratrooper, I broke a small bone in my foot. This circumstance would have postponed this position for an indefinite period of time. (...)

> In one of my first jumps while qualifying to be a paratrooper, one of the plane's engines conked out. It appeared to be no big deal to land and immediately board another plane for the jump. But, I honestly began to believe the airborne had braver men than myself. I also believed that a living dog is better than a dead lion.[32]

Upon completion of his jump course, Parks was assigned to D Company and promoted "from a lower specialist rating to staff sergeant." The captain appointed Parks as operations sergeant. "I was completely satisfied in every way. The bombing of Pearl Harbor by the Japanese had taken place and would be avenged. Never had I met a group of men who were so loyal and devoted to one another. Our officers, from the second lieutenants to the highest ranking generals, were as one. It seemed like a dream come true."[33]

Another volunteer who had already qualified in the summer of 1941 was Private Lewis P. Fern. Born in New York in 1918, Fern had enlisted on March 12, 1941. He was selected to be Lieutenant Colonel William C. Lee's runner upon his qualification as a paratrooper and served a few weeks in A Company of the 501st Parachute Battalion. Private Fern was promoted to appointed communications sergeant and transferred to the 502nd Parachute Battalion when the 501st was sent to Panama in late 1941. Major James Gavin, the S-3 officer on Lee's staff, arranged his transfer to the Officer Candidate School (OCS) in April 1942, which was also located on the expanding complex of Fort Benning. Three months later, newly minted Lieutenant Fern joined the Mortar Platoon of the 2nd Battalion.

Private Edward P. Haider spent his childhood in St. Paul, Minnesota, where he was born in 1921. Along with four of his high school friends, he walked to the local enlistment office on a warm day in late June of 1942. The old recruiting sergeant asked them which branch they preferred. He said, "Not knowing any better and wanting to show my bravado, I said, 'How about the parachute troops?' I figured this was something new and not many fellas went into that. I figured I would give it a try."[34]

The sergeant handed them enlistment papers, which they needed to fill in and have their fathers sign as they were all under eighteen. Haider managed to convince his father to sign the enlistment papers and returned to the recruiting office the next day. There, he showed up alone; so much for his patriotic friends! But two of them delivered their enlistment papers the next day, and together they were inducted into the army at Fort Snelling, Minnesota.

It took a number of days before Haider and a large group of recruits was sent by train to Camp Wheeler, Georgia to commence their basic infantry training. On the rifle range, Haider was allowed to shoot left-handed, as his firing was accurate. Along with eleven others, he left for Fort Benning to become a paratrooper. He recalled:

> At Benning the training intensified: no more walking, we were double-timing it everywhere. There was half a day self-defense training and packing parachutes. This seemed to take a lot of time, as it should, you didn't want to make a mistake. We had judo lessons for self-defense in the saw dust pits. (...) Many times during this training period I asked myself, "What in the world am I doing in this outfit?" Then I would think about it and strive to do that much better. The training was rough and lasted daylight to dusk – forever moving at double-time speeds.[35]

Haider's endurance during the first weeks paid off. He said,

> ...for that first jump we were all nervous and praying – not knowing what to expect. When the red light above the door went on, the jumpmaster says, "Stand up, hook up." All twenty-two of us stood up and at the jumpmaster's command we checked each other's equipment. Upon the command to stand in the door, we all shuffled forward. The pilot lifts the plane's tail and begins a descent, the light above the door turns green and the jump begins. The jumpmaster taps the first guy on the back of the leg and yells, "Go!" We then all file out, as close as we can get to one another. Sometimes you even got a face-full of silk.

> When you jump, your right leg goes out first, gets caught by the wind and turns your whole body toward the rear of the plane. Frequently you will see your

chute go right over your head as it is blown by the propeller.... We all knew we had to make the required five
jumps to earn our wings – a small metal badge with a
parachute in the middle.[36]

During his fifth jump, Haider's luck ran out, and he broke his legs.
He had to stay for five weeks in the hospital and then got a week's
leave, which he spent traveling to Minnesota to spend three days with
his family. Finally, he got his jump wings, and in October 1942, he was
assigned to 1st Lieutenant George M. Warfield's I Company.

Twenty-three-year-old Private Alfred Burgreen of the 1st Platoon
in I Company recalled that he received his basic infantry training at
Camp Croft, South Carolina. It was there that "the sergeant asked,
'Does anyone want to join the paratroops?' I raised my hand. (...)
My jump training was off platforms and then in a tower three-fourth
up and released. I remember running many miles, including going in a
swamp, dodging machine gun bullets. On my first jump I was so over-
whelmed with curiosity that I had little fear and huge pride. An officer,
Lieutenant [Henry B.] Keep, borrowed the NY Times from me and he
was very friendly."[37]

Herbert C. Lucas grew up in Salem, Oregon, where he was born
on December 11, 1923. Lucas read an article about the paratroops
shortly after the Japanese attack on Pearl Harbor. He recalled:

A month before I joined the Army I read an article
about paratroopers in our local paper. I decided then
and there that I wanted to be a paratrooper. (...)

I went to jump school at Fort Benning in June – July
1942. It was hot and the training was intense and
physically demanding. The first jump was easy compared to the physical demands of the first three
weeks. I was assigned to the 504th from jump school.
I knew nothing of the previous history of the 504th.
At the time I joined, 504 was just a number. The
training was almost as physically demanding as jump

school. I liked all of my fellow troopers and we soon became fast friends. It was in the Frying Pan area that I first met Chaplain Delbert Kuehl. (...) I admired Lieutenant Henry Keep, my first platoon leader in the States. He was very knowledgeable of military tactics and was fair to all the men.[38]

Lucas didn't stay in I Company as he was transferred to the Communications Platoon of Lieutenant Calvin Campbell in Headquarters Company of the 3rd Battalion a few months later. He became a battalion runner for the battalion commander. Private Lucas soon became friends with Privates Bonnie Roberts and William Wheeler and their squad leader, Sergeant Ola Davis.

Private David "Rosie" Rosenkrantz grew up in Los Angeles, where he was born on October 31, 1916. Because of his Jewish background, Rosenkrantz was aware of the threat of Nazi Germany and enlisted on January 29, 1942, just a few weeks after the attack on Pearl Harbor. He applied for the paratroops after his basic infantry training and qualified as a paratrooper. Rosenkrantz soon found himself assigned to H Company.

A number of enlisted men showed obvious leadership potential and were recommended for OCS. Technician 4th Grade Harry F. Welsh from Wilkes-Barre, Pennsylvania was an example. Welsh was promoted three times and bust back in C Company, but early in 1943, Captain Jack Bartley noticed his leadership qualities, encouraging him to enroll in OCS. Welsh joined E Company of the 506th Parachute Infantry Regiment, better known as the *Band of Brothers.*

Luckily, not all the NCOs who attended OCS were assigned to other outfits. Some came back to the outfit but to another company, as it was customary in the U.S. Army to reassign men who had earned a battlefield commission or had graduated from OCS to prevent them from being too friendly with their former comrades. Second Lieutenant Louis A. Hauptfleisch was an exception. He started as a private in F Company, attended OCS, and then was later assigned back to F Company.

First Lieutenant Arthur W. Ferguson of E Company recalled of his first jump:

> I glanced out of the window, and down, and there was the thread-like Chattahoochee River. I didn't look down any more. I concentrated on one thought – I *had* to go out that door. The jump-master yelled over the roar of the plane, "How do you feel men?" The reply in unison, "All right."
>
> Then comes the order, "Stand up and hook up." (Hook up means, hook the static line to a steel cable running the length and near the roof of the plane. This static line pulls the 'chute from your back after you have fallen approximately 100 feet.) Then the command, "Stand in the door." (We had been trained for weeks on how to stand up and hook up and how to stand at the door. I realized now the necessity for the thorough training we had received.) Number one man stood at the door, number two man ready to pivot into the door and out. Number three, four, five, etc., shuffled forward with their left foot forward, holding their balance by holding on to the cable and static line. I was twelfth man, and the door seemed miles and miles and miles away (...)
>
> Deep in my mind I remembered that no officer had ever refused to jump, and I said to myself, "I'm *going* out the door." Suddenly, I was number three man; number two man had pivoted, he's in the door, he's gone – I threw my right foot down, I was in the door, I was gone – into space! I fell for centuries, I forgot to count, then I thought, "something should happen now" – CRASH – a ton of bricks fell on my head – no pain – I was suspended 1000 feet above

the ground – too weak to do anything but hang there – but I was happy.

Everything was quiet (just like it is when snow is falling on a cold winter night). It was beautiful. Silent and still. No experience, no thrill, can never compare with it. I had no sensation of falling whatever. Just suspended.

Then I began to realize I must work hard to make a good landing, so I could walk away. I pulled down hard on my risers, as I had been taught, and let up slowly, to keep from oscillating. Then suddenly the ground rose up and seemed to almost hit me in the face – it was right there before I knew it! I didn't do anything I was taught, but made an old football tumble, which was second nature, and the natural thing for me to do. I stood up, then collapsed to my knees from weakness and joy that I was back on the ground with no injury. Then the perspiration began to flow, and I was drenched in one minute's time. I was joyous – I had overcome all obstacles – and from now on nothing will stand in my way. (...) I fought the hardest battle in my life; I conquered fear, because nothing but will power drove me through that door.[39]

Some of the original cadre members of the 504th Parachute Infantry Regiment left of their own free will. Twenty-four-year-old 2nd Lieutenant Herman C. Hupperich from Baton Rouge, Louisiana commanded the Regimental Demolition Platoon from its inception. Although he "had joined the paratroops in 1941 for adventure" in the 504th Parachute Battalion, Hupperich decided he aspired a career as a pilot and left the regiment in September.[40]

First Lieutenant Erwin B. Bigger was placed in charge of the Regimental Demolition Platoon, which included twenty-two-year-old

Pfc. Darrell G. Harris from San Antonio, Texas. He considered his graduation from the Parachute School

> ...one of the proudest days of our lives. It meant we
> were also entitled to wear the much cherished jump
> boots which only paratroopers were authorized to
> wear in those days. Most troopers had at least two
> pairs – one to wear during duty hours, and one to pol-
> ish and re-polish until a deep, brilliant shine, was built
> up before wearing them into town.
>
> After jump training, my class was divided into two
> groups; one was assigned to communication and the
> other to demolition school. I was assigned to the lat-
> ter where we not only learned to handle explosives but
> also how to operate a steam locomotive, after a fash-
> ion. That is, to say, we didn't become accomplished
> locomotive engineers, but we could build up a head of
> steam, get it rolling, and if we had enough track, bring
> it to a successful halt.[41]

In late September 1942, Colonel Dunn had succeeded along with his cadre to evolve a parachute infantry regiment out of a collection of eager jump-qualified troopers, both pre-war regulars and wartime draftees and volunteers. It was tragic when another fatal casualty was sustained on September 23. Private Gilbert A. Vernier of Headquarters Company, 1st Battalion, died on base of unknown causes. Unfortunately, two more men would die before the 504th Parachute Infantry Regiment was sent overseas.

It was also during this time that an Army Ground Forces inspection took place, which worried Captain Kouns. He had in late August already expressed his concerns to Tucker, the regimental executive officer:

> I had alerted Tucker to impending Battalion tests by
> the Army Ground Forces. I felt we ought to have a

walk-through drill of such a test based on my recent Infantry School problems. Without such practice, I told Tucker we might not measure up so well in troop leadership as we did in marksmanship. Tucker responded with strong emotion: "If we are weak in troop leadership I want to find it out."

A month or so later, our 1st and 2nd Battalions failed their AGF tests. At D-1 Day for the 3rd Battalion test, I was detailed to command the 3rd Battalion for the test, which we passed. Then I returned to training duties. New intensity was devoted to troop leadership (much like sand table situations with actions and orders and critiques).[42]

The regimental newspaper *Propblast* also contributed to bind the members of each company together. As Sergeant George Leoleis of I Company put it, "every platoon thought it was the best."[43] The name *Propblast* was conceived from the original newspaper of the 504th Parachute Battalion with the same name. Lieutenant William R. Dudley and Sergeant Alex R. Fasano had created the first *Propblast*, along with its masthead, for the 504th Parachute Battalion. However, their publication was discontinued when it became part of the 503rd Parachute Infantry. A lively discussion followed in the summer of 1942 when the idea to revive the *Propblast* newsletter was initiated by William E. Chapman, the chief editor.

Finally, it was decided to incorporate *Propblast* with the *Silk and Sweat*, the 1st Battalion's newspaper. The editors of *Propblast* were reinforced by artists Harold L. Dooley, Holley A. Findley, and Mickey Kemble. Lieutenants Reynard Anderson, Shirley Dix, and Harry Cummings acted as editorial advisors. Others were editors representing one of the companies. Dooley became a correspondent after the first issue came out and Findley left. They were replaced by Corporal Howard L. Gregory from B Company (later A Company) and Sergeant Sam D'Crenzo, who invented the cartoon figure Static Line Sammy for *Propblast*. He was a cartographer at 1st Battalion HQ most of the time.

When the second edition came out in October 1942 at Fort Bragg, North Carolina, several changes had taken place among the editors. Lieutenants Anderson and Cummings, too preoccupied with other duties, left the editorial advisor's work to Lieutenant Dix.

The reason that the second *Propblast* came out in Fort Bragg was because the 82nd Airborne Division moved there from Camp Claiborne, Louisiana on October 1. Colonel Dunn's 504th Parachute Infantry had completed its initial five months of training and was now ready to continue training alongside the other units of the division. The original cadre had executed its task properly: it produced a cohesive parachute infantry regiment with its own newspaper. Little did everyone know that one rifle company was not going to stay very long.

CHAPTER 4

CAPTAIN BEALL'S CHALLENGE

Fort Bragg, North Carolina

OCTOBER-NOVEMBER 1942

Afeter arrival in their new home base in Fort Bragg, North Carolina, further training continued. Within a few days, the Regimental Surgeon, Captain Frederick J. Swift, Jr. sustained a fractured ankle on his sixth parachute jump. He was hospitalized and eventually transferred in December on another assignment to the activation cadre of the 513th Parachute Infantry Regiment. With his departure, the most senior surgeons were Captains Roger K. Kalina and Francis G. Sheehan, and for a short time, they were joined by a new Regimental Dentist, Captain William M. Demeritt, Jr.

In late September, the commander of E Company, Captain Philip S. Gage, Jr. (West Point 1936), received the unique opportunity to take an advanced staff course in Fort Leavenworth. He erroneously believed he could subsequently return to his regiment: "When I came back the 82nd had moved on [to Fort Bragg] so I went to the next blossoming new outfit."[44] Gage found himself reassigned to the newly activated 501st Parachute Infantry Regiment.

On October 8, Major General Matthew B. Ridgway got the order to release one of the rifle companies of the 504th PIR to the 503rd, which had received orders to move to Australia. The 503rd PIR also numbered three battalions like the 504th, but its 2nd Battalion (the old 504th Parachute Battalion) had been sent to England in June to train with the British airborne troops. They would not be recalled home. To create a new 2nd Battalion in a short span of time, the 503rd would incorporate the rifle company and the independent 501st Parachute Battalion, less C Company, which was to stay in Panama. Ridgway decided to send his best rifle company—Captain Ralph Bates' A Company.

As the 503rd PIR and A Company boarded a train heading west to Camp Stoneman, California on October 9, Ridgway drove up in his staff car. He called Lieutenant Colonel John J. Tolson III, the executive officer, over. Tolson was acting regimental commander as Colonel Kenneth Kinsler had been sent ahead to Australia. Their unit history *Bless 'Em All* contains a reconstructed conversation:

> In his direct manner, Ridgway informed Tolson that he was to give this message to the 503rd CO. He knew it was "customary" for another unit to give up their worst unit when ordered to transfer one. "This is not the case here," Ridgway said. "This is the best company I have in the division."
>
> In the event that Tolson had not understood the position with sufficient clarity, Ridgway continued that he also knew it was typical for a senior commander to remove the NCOs and officers and to replace them with those he knew. He instructed Tolson to tell Kinsler he would be keeping an eye on A Company because they had excellent leaders, and "it better not happen." Unfortunately, something may have been lost in the translation, for Ridgway's exhortation appears to have become more of an advisory opinion.[45]

The old A Company of Captain Bates wasn't re-designated in D Company of the 503rd until December 31, 1942. Lieutenant Colonel George M. Jones, the battalion commander of the new 2nd Battalion of the 503rd, decided to replace the first sergeant with a non-commissioned officer from his old 501st Parachute Battalion. Captain Bates refused and, when the matter was raised again some weeks later, he requested a court-martial. Bates was allowed to pick a spot in regimental headquarters and served distinctively throughout the war. The original paratroopers of D Company, 503rd, always kept referring to themselves as "ex A Company 504th."[46]

At Fort Bragg, Colonel Theodore L. Dunn knew it would be difficult to replace his old A Company. Before the original company had been sent away, he had selected a few non-commissioned officers and enlisted men to stay behind as a cadre for the new company. These men included Sergeants Otto W. Huebner and Thomas J. McCarthy and Privates Homer Henry and Robert L. Jones, among others. Four B Company members were made available to reinforce this meagre cadre: Staff Sergeant Jack B. Bishop, Corporals George A. Siegmann and Howard L. Gregory, and Private Albert W. Corey. But where could Dunn find a new company commander to create another A Company that was just as good as the old one, or even better?

Fortunately, that same month, Captain William R. Beall of the 1st Battalion returned from his trip to Hungerford, England. He had observed the training of the 2nd Battalion, 503rd PIR, and the British parachute forces: "I saw them jump one day with the wind blowing as high as 25 miles per hour at times and the only casualties were two slightly sprained ankles. Jumping with full TBA equipment on their persons, they were in action immediately upon reaching the ground. Only 81mm mortars and extra ammunition were dropped in equipment chutes. They jump from 400 feet, less in some instances."[47]

Major William Beall trained the second A Company and commanded
the 3rd Battalion after the Sicily jump. His loss at the Salerno Beachhead
shocked many paratroopers. Courtesy: Mike Bigalke

Upon his return to Fort Bragg, Beall found another even more challenging assignment waiting for him. The tall officer had been a member of the original cadre of the 1st Battalion five months earlier and thus had experience in raising a new unit. He was the right man for the difficult task that lay ahead. Dunn ordered him to reconstitute A Company using the skeleton cadre of non-commissioned officers that had been left behind by the original company and a large bunch of recent jump school graduates. To give him a hand, Dunn made four experienced lieutenants available from other companies.

Twenty-four-year-old Lieutenant William W. Magrath grew up in New York and enlisted in the U.S. Army on August 15, 1941 as a private. Because of his partial college education, Magrath soon made sergeant and applied successfully for OCS. He subsequently qualified for the Parachute School and was assigned to Company B as a platoon leader before being transferred to A Company as executive officer.

The 1st Platoon leader would be 1st Lieutenant James H. Goethe from Jacksonville, Florida. He was born on February 14, 1920 in Varnville, South Carolina. One month after Goethe was born, his father (West Point 1900) received a discharge from the U.S. Cavalry for a physical disability and died in 1936. Goethe had attended college for four years before enlisting for three years in the Air Corps as an aviation cadet on July 29, 1940. In early 1942, he transferred to the U.S. Army as a second lieutenant and was assigned to C Company.

The 2nd Platoon was entrusted to Lieutenant John S. Lekson. He was born on April 14, 1917 in Fairport, Ohio and joined the National Guard in 1940 as a private. After the Japanese attack on Pearl Harbor, Lekson was sent to OCS in Fort Benning and was commissioned as a second lieutenant in May 1942. During OCS, he signed up to see a film about American Parachute Troops but eventually missed it. Despite that, his interest in this new type of warfare had been aroused anyway. He applied for the paratroopers, qualified, and was assigned to Headquarters Company of the 1st Battalion.

Lieutenant Fordyce Gorham was destined to command the 3rd Platoon. He was born on November 10, 1917 in Williamsport, Pennsylvania and dropped out of college after less than a year. Gorham enlisted on February 17, 1941 in the 109th Infantry Regiment of the

Pennsylvania National Guard. He was promoted to sergeant within weeks. That summer, Gorham was sent to Alaska along with a few other non-commissioned officers—all good sharpshooters—to test the prototype of the M-1 Garand rifle under frigid conditions.[48] The tests performed the required results and the M-1 was adopted by the U.S. Army to replace the older Springfield 1903 rifle, which remained as a sniper rifle.

A few months later, in early 1942, Gorham entered OCS and was commissioned as a second lieutenant. He was assigned to C Company after obtaining his jump wings. He was described by one paratrooper, who would later serve under him in Headquarters and Headquarters Company, as "smart, but had no common sense."[49]

Apart from these officers and a small number of original company members, Beall felt that he needed to bring a bit more unit cohesion in the cadre. At around the same time, he learned that three of his former students at the University of Maryland, where he had been an army officer instructor in the Reserve Officer Training Course program (ROTC), were taking up jump training at Fort Bragg. Training in the same jump class were 2nd Lieutenants Robert D. Condon, James E. Dunn, and Mearle D. Duvall. Beall's request to the Airborne Command to have them assigned to his company was readily honored as they had already qualified as paratroopers. Condon was assigned to the 2nd Platoon, Dunn was assigned to the 3rd Platoon, and Duvall was assigned to the 1st Platoon. They all became assisting platoon leaders.

Condon was born in Victor, New York on December 17, 1918 and ran track and cross country while he attended the University of Maryland. Condon knew Beall and his wife Jean very well and visited them often. He even babysat their daughter Linda when the Bealls went out. Condon kept a training diary between the fall of 1941 and the spring of 1942, which he primarily used to record his training and competition. His entry for February 20, 1942 reads as follows: "Find out that Lt. Beall is going in parachute battalion – a break for him but tough on Jean. He leaves immediately."[50]

Duvall was born on March 9, 1920 in Baltimore, Maryland and had played basketball in the Maryland Terrapins while he was a student at the University of Maryland. Due to sports injuries in school, he had surgery on both knees but was still very determined to be a paratrooper. When Duvall graduated from university, he received several offers from professional sports teams, but he gave the U.S. Army priority. Condon, Dunn, and Duvall were commissioned on the same day; Condon had army number 0-463912, Dunn 0-463917, and Duvall 0-463918. During the airborne training at Fort Benning, Duvall tried to land on his rear end. He came down hard on one occasion and broke his tailbone (fracture of coccyx). On September 19, 1942, two weeks before he started his paratrooper training, Duvall married his girlfriend Mary, whom he had met in the university's Education Department.

Lieutenant Dunn had been the Cadet Colonel of the ROTC regiment at the University of Maryland, which means he was the highest-ranking cadet. He was born on September 28, 1921 in New York City and recalled that he, Condon, and Duvall started jump training in Fort Benning in September 1942: "My first jump was a thrill. After jump training, you were eager to 'jump' and you really didn't realize what it was like until the third or fourth jump. Then came getting your wings and joining an airborne unit."[51]

Dunn, Condon, and Duvall were going through jump training with a colonel who was forming a new parachute infantry regiment. The colonel tried to get them to join his outfit, saying that they would get faster promotion. Around that time, Beall showed up in Fort Benning and promised them that they would see action sooner if they joined his unit. Lieutenant Dunn recalled that this appealed to them: "Captain Beall was assigned as Company Commander to rebuild the company and received priority in getting replacements and officers so as to be ready to deploy with the division. Having known Condon, Duvall and me in our college ROTC program, he offered us jobs as assistant platoon leaders in A Company. Afraid that 'the war would end before we got there' we accepted."[52]

Officers from the second A Company before a training jump about late October 1942.
Left to right: Captain William Beall and Lieutenants Mearle Duvall, James Dunn, Robert
Condon, John Lekson, Fordyce Gorham and James Goethe. Courtesy: Robert Condon

Several enlisted men who were assigned to fill the ranks in A Company were recent graduates from Class 38 at the Parachute School. Pfc. Fred J. "Baldy" Baldino was one of the first members of the new 2nd Platoon. Born on February 25, 1922 in a large Italian family in Ashland, Schuykill Country, Baldino grew up during the Depression, and the economy in central Pennsylvania was scarce. He got work as a bootleg miner on the grounds of a coal company.

In May 1941, a close friend of Baldino decided to enlist in the army. Although two years younger, he signed up as well, and both were assigned to the 55th Material Squadron of the Army Air Corps in Florida. Baldino recalled:

> I soon made it to sergeant and was issuing tools out
> to the airplane mechanics. After Pearl Harbor, as we
> sat in the Post Exchange one day drinking beer, with
> about six friends, one of our group said, "You know

we won't get to kill any Germans in the ground crew of the Air Corps. Why don't we join the paratroops?" And so all of us went over to our commanding officer, Lieutenant Ross, and told him we wanted to join the paratroops. (...)

About September 1942 I was sent over to Fort Benning, Georgia, to take the paratrooper training course. On my way over to Fort Benning from Tallahassee, I stopped at a military camp that my brother Tony was training at. When I went into the post and all the guys saw and found out that I gave up sergeant stripes to go to private, just to join the paratroops, they thought I was crazy. Tony and all the guys were going through basic training at the time.

The Parachute School training was very hard to get through. We went through a lot of physical training: running, jumping, rope climbing, training how to fold a parachute, test jumping out of a dummy airplane, mock towers, etc. (...)

On our first jump many of us were so determined and anxious to make that first jump that we didn't mind it so much as to fear. The second jump I hardly remember, but when it came to the third jump and we realized what we were doing, many of us had a lot of fear. But still we persisted and did our third jump. After the third jump we settled down and didn't mind the other jumps.[53]

Private Albert B. Clark from Stockton, California was nicknamed "ABC" after his initials. He was also simply known as "the cameraman," as he seemingly always took pictures, and was drafted in late April 1942: "When I was drafted and interviewed at the reception center by a major, he asked what I would like to do and I said that I would like to join the parachute division. He tried to persuade me to go into transportation and they would send me back to San Francisco, to the motor pool, since I was familiar with the city and had driven trucks. When I insisted, he asked why I had chosen the paratroops. I replied I had made up my mind on the action."

Clark took his basic training at Camp Roberts, California. In late October 1942, he joined "Company A, 2nd Platoon, 3rd Squad. This was the 60mm Mortar Squad which suited me fine as I fell in love with this weapon in basic training. (...) We spent the winter in extensive training and weapons familiarization."[54]

Sergeant Albert "Bert" Clark, known as ABC, was the unofficial company photographer of A Company. He was promoted to mortar squad leader on the Italian mainland. Courtesy: Albert Clark

Essential in training the new A Company troopers was a member of Headquarters Company of Jewish origin, Sergeant Theodore H. "Ted" Bachenheimer. "He was teaching an intelligence section that I was assigned to," recalled Private Baldino. "Ted had in his possession a German Army manual and was teaching us the methods of the German Army."[55]

Born on April 23, 1923 as oldest son of a composer and conductor and a theatre actress, the young Bachenheimer grew up in Braunschweig, Germany. Early in the 1930s, when anti-Semitism became more blatant, the family fled via Prague and France on an ocean liner to the United States. They became naturalized Americans and settled in Hollywood. Bachenheimer began studying drama at the Los Angeles City College. He volunteered for the U.S. Army at the beginning of 1942 and subsequently started jump training in Fort Benning. He was then sent to Camp Robinson, California for a basic intelligence course. Each man was trained to work totally independently in case they would be attached to a rifle company or platoon for special missions. Upon completion of this course, Bachenheimer was assigned to the S-2 Section of the 505th Parachute Infantry Regiment before transferring in October 1942 to the 504th.[56]

"This A Company is about the most disappointed outfit in the military," wrote twenty-five-year-old Private Gordon "Lefty" Gould to his girlfriend Harriet on October 22, 1942. "We are here stationed in our regular outfits but that furlough has been cancelled for various reasons. So I feel bad because we sure earned one and darn it, we expected to be started home by now. Gosh, how I wish that I was on my way home. I feel like going over the hill. I've got my wings and diploma but at present I am not elated over the fact. I am an old grouch tonight. I may get a leave in time, still hopeful."[57]

Gould's opinion changed after he got to know his fellow soldiers. In particular, the company first sergeant who was later demoted to be his squad leader, Sergeant William C. Hauser, earned his respect:

> He was the only first sergeant that I ever met who lacked the proverbial loud voice so often characteristic of first sergeants. Aside from giving orders or explaining military life and tactics he seldom engaged himself in conversations with the other men.

In spite of his sternness and many other faults, Sergeant Hauser earned the respect of every man in A Company. His impartiality, fairness, and physical endurance were the favorite topics of many a story-teller among those who knew him. On one occasion he was called into the orderly room to speak for or against a man being tried under a summary court-martial. Sergeant Hauser saluted the captain and said, "Sir, I have no liking for this man personally, but in my opinion he's a damn good soldier." Because of Hauser's favorable statement as to the culprit's soldiering ability, he received a very light punishment for his misdemeanor.

Sergeant Hauser would never order a man to do something that he could not do himself. If for some reason he punished a man by ordering him to do fifty push-ups, he would usually do them with the one being punished.[58]

Gould wrote to Harriet on November 16, "This time tomorrow night, we have a night jump. But don't shiver, it will be over by the time you get this letter and I'll be saying, 'Now that was easy, fellows.' We even had to work Sunday but I don't mind so much. Before we are through we are going to make Superman look like a sissy! The captain says, 'Men you are going to be tough and if that chute doesn't open, you will run back to the plane and get another one.' (...) I almost like it here but I think I'll like it a lot more after the jump. All we do is exercise, run, use all types of weapons, jump with chutes, learn different tactics, and more exercise. We do this all day and half the night but all the time, I'm thinking of you."[59]

Six days later, Gould reflected on the night jump: "On our last jump (at night) we missed the field. We really had quite the landing, most of us in trees, some in a lake, and a few lucky ones on the edge of the field. It was fun although we were tired and bruised up a bit when we returned to camp. Our next jump will be an exhibition at a nearby town."[60]

Sergeant Otto H. Huebner, an original member, was the A Company reporter for the regimental newspaper *Propblast*. In the third edition, December 1942, he wrote, "There's a collection going on now to buy pencils for the 2nd Looey, who never has one. Can you imagine? The men in the Co. are complaining that their 1st Sergeant [Michael F. Curran] doesn't give them enough work in their spare time. (...) Remember: A Co. is known by the men it keeps, the men are known by the company they keep."[61]

The last sentence not only referred to the pies that had been stolen but also to the few original A Company members who had not been "taken away" by the 503rd. Due to them, an inspiring commanding officer and platoon leaders the new A Company was second to none.

Failing parachutes were not the only reason for some of the pre-combat casualties that were sustained by the regiment. Corporal Roy W. Gray from Charleroi, Pennsylvania died from pneumonia while visiting his parents on November 19, 1943. The news was not only devastating for his parents but also for his close friends in D Company. Gray had been promoted to corporal only weeks before. Staff Sergeant Lacy R. Starbuck, Sergeants Wesley C. Hines and Elbridge H. Wallace, Corporals Woodrow Hinton and John J. Ketterer, and Pfc. James L. Livesay—all friends of Gray—acted as pallbearers on his funeral. The flag at Washington Square in Charleroi was placed at half-staff in respect to his memory. Sergeant Hines wrote a thank you letter to postmaster James Oates on November 26: "Just a line to let you know we arrived back in camp and feeling fine. It is Thursday afternoon and the boys are still bragging about Charleroi. They say after the war is over they are going to make Charleroi their home. On behalf of me and the boys I wish to thank you, Mrs. Oates, Mr. Laclear and members of Post 22 for being instrumental for our having a grand time."[62]

Thanksgiving Day 1942 had been pleasant, and there were no indications that the decision of replacing A Company wouldn't be the only major change in 1942. But then the Regimental S-3, Major Charles W. Kouns, was consulted for his critical view on the leadership in the unit: "One day [Lieutenant Colonel] Tucker asked me if the two Battalion failures could be attributed to the men or to their leaders. He said I ought to know for I was with them continuously. I responded: 'Because of their leaders.' He hastened to say, 'That's all I want to know.' Subsequently, Tucker became the Regimental Commander."[63]

While both Kouns and Tucker had been promoted around the time the Regiment moved to Fort Bragg, the bad performance in the AGF inspections was not forgotten in Division Headquarters. Overall, Major General Matthew Ridgway disliked the way Dunn exercised command of the 504th Parachute Infantry Regiment and that he was often drinking alcohol. He decided to replace Dunn because of his "inability to secure results."[64]

One evening in early December 1942, Ridgway came to Tucker's residence and asked to speak with him privately in the kitchen. They talked for a long time while Helen Tucker stayed in the living room. When they were finished, Ridgway left immediately, and Tucker informed Helen that he would be regimental commander.[65]

As a result of this visit and undoubtedly also due to the earlier conversation between Kouns and Tucker, Major David E. DeArmond, commanding the 2nd Battalion, was relieved from his command and reassigned to the 32nd Infantry Division. He was temporarily succeeded by his executive battalion officer, Major Daniel W. Danielson. A regimental staff officer, Captain David Rosen, became acting battalion executive officer. At a lower level in the 2nd Battalion, more changes were made. D Company received another company commander in the person of Captain Stanley M. Dolezal and a new company first sergeant. Captain William M. Demeritt, Jr., the Regimental Dentist, left at the same time.

Tucker's appointment to command the 504th PIR was welcomed by practically everyone in the outfit. It may have been Ridgway's best decision during the war. "I probably couldn't have fought very well with any other regimental commander or any other division commander," recalled Captain Julian Cook, the 3rd Battalion executive officer. "Because I had known him for a long time. He had been regimental exec under Colonel Dunn, the first regimental commander, and I had been the adjutant and I knew his wife and him very well. I always found that if I didn't like anything either his staff or he said, or orders, or instructions, directions, whatever, I could always talk to him about it. Now, that is not saying that he was going to agree with what I said, but he might then say, 'No, I want it this way' or 'the Division is ordered to do it that way.' At least he was always accessible."[66]

The 1st Battalion Commander, Major Warren R. Williams, Jr., wasn't surprised of the change as he couldn't believe Dunn was "physically able to lead the 504 in combat."[67] Williams had performed well apart from the inspection and was retained as the senior battalion commander. It was a decision neither Ridgway or Tucker would ever regret.

CHAPTER 5

CHANGE IN COMMAND

Fort Bragg, North Carolina

DECEMBER 1942-FEBRUARY 1943

A t higher Army Headquarters, several senior officers raised their eyebrows in early December 1942. Reuben Tucker III was only thirty-one and had been made lieutenant colonel two months earlier. Major General Matthew B. Ridgway's request to promote him to full colonel was therefore not granted.[68] Tucker wrote about his appointment: "No one has been ever prouder or happier to command any unit, than I am to command this regiment. I consider myself very fortunate to have all of you, officers and men, working with me."[69]

"Tommy," as he was known in his younger years, was born in Ansonia, Connecticut on January 29, 1911 to Reuben H. Tucker, Jr. and Clara Booth Tucker. Tucker III was the third out of an old Yankee family of six children. His siblings were Lyman (1904), Grace (1907), Walter (1912), Margaret (1914), and William (1920). Their forebears on both sides had served in the U.S. Army for many generations.

Tucker, Jr. worked as a foreman in the local American Brass Company plant, which was enough to buy a four-bedroom house on 92 Beaver Street that had been built in 1888. Mother Clara wanted to go to college herself after graduating high school, but her parents couldn't afford the tuition as her brother already studied medicine at Yale University. She instead became as tenacious as a drill sergeant to instill in her children the importance of education and persistence.

Tucker won a local Boy Scout award for bravery and resourceful-
ness in saving a younger brother and a friend from drowning in a freez-
ing millpond. At age sixteen, he graduated from Ansonia High School
and worked nearly a year as an apprentice to his father at the American
Brass Company plant, but still his salary and that of his father didn't
stretch far enough to be able to pay preparatory classes for the West
Point entrance exam.

Luckily, Tucker's older brother Lyman was making good profits
with his own business after graduating from Yale University on a schol-
arship. With financial support from his brother, Tucker attended the
Millard Preparatory School in Washington D.C. in 1928. This school
would prepare him for the West Point examinations, and he passed the
intensive course. However, he was turned down in January 1929 when
his appointment was switched with someone else who had come up
with extra credits. That summer, Tucker moved to Wyoming with a
survey gang to make some extra money. A few months later, the Great
Depression started after the stock market crashed on October 29. It
seemed harder than before to obtain an appointment for West Point.

Clara Tucker then decided to call upon her brother whose wife
had a family friend who was a secretary to Representative Thomas
A. Doyle of Illinois. Doyle's lobby worked, and Clara's son received
a congressional appointment to attend the foremost United States
Military Academy.[70]

As a West Point cadet, Tucker performed well in sports like football and hockey, which he had also played in high school, but he had
one Achilles heel: mathematics. Eleven months after entering West
Point, he was on the brink of washing out. Money to pay a math course
was lacking, but again Lyman Tucker was willing to help his younger
brother out. Private tutoring helped to pass for a two-day re-exam-
ination, and Tucker was allowed to stay, but not in his class of 1934.
Instead, he was assigned to the class of 1935. He graduated in the
186th place out of 277 cadets on June 12, 1935.

The day after graduation, Tucker married his girlfriend Helen
McAllister military style at the Catholic Chapel at West Point.
They moved to Fort Sam Houston, Texas where 2nd Lieutenant
"Rube" Tucker was assigned to the 9th Infantry Regiment. Exactly

three years after his graduation, Tucker was promoted to first lieutenant. The family expanded when on February 15, 1939, his oldest son David Bruce was born. Another four sons would be born later, during and after the war.

In October 1939, Tucker was transferred to the 33rd Infantry Regiment at Fort Clayton in Panama. Among the men in his company was the young Corporal Francis W. Deignan, who would later be assigned to the 504th PIR as a platoon leader. The next army post was the 94th Anti-Tank Battalion in Fort Benning, followed by an assignment to the Infantry School at the same place. It was here that Tucker learned about the activation of the Provisional Parachute Group in March 1941 and the plans for activating the 502nd Parachute Battalion. He applied for the paratroops, qualified, and joined the battalion. Lieutenant Colonel George P. Howell, Jr. gave Tucker command of B Company.

With the expansion of the parachute forces, Tucker was transferred to the 504th Parachute Infantry Battalion in October 1941 as Battalion S-3 Officer responsible for planning and operations. The Japanese attack on Pearl Harbor caused a rush of patriotism, and his brothers Lyman and William both signed up. Lyman eventually became a lieutenant colonel, while William would be a Navy Lieutenant in charge of a minesweeper. Their younger sister Margaret joined the 2nd Evacuation Hospital as a lieutenant.

On February 2, 1942, Tucker was promoted to major and attended a course at the Command and General Staff School in Fort Leavenworth, Kansas. He was selected as 3rd Battalion Commander of the newly formed 502nd Parachute Infantry Regiment in March, which was not yet at full strength. Tucker had subsequently been on the original cadre of Colonel Theodore Dunn's 504th PIR in May 1942.

With Dunn's departure, the task of preparing the regiment for overseas deployment now lay entirely on Tucker's shoulders. One of the first decisions he had to make was choosing his regimental executive officer. Instead of selecting Major Warren R. Williams, Jr., a West Point officer who commanded the 1st Battalion, Tucker picked Major Leslie G. Freeman of the 3rd Battalion. Freeman was also an original cadre officer but had no army background like Tucker and Williams.

He was a former member of the Wyoming Central School faculty. The tall Virginian officer was well-respected by the officers and men in his battalion, and Tucker knew he would be an asset to his regimental staff. The new 3rd Battalion Commander, Major Charles W. Kouns, had full confidence in Tucker: "We pressed for more realistic training with live ammunition."[71]

Captain Melvin Zais became the new Regimental S-3 Officer, and his old place was taken by elevating the 2nd Battalion S-2 and S-3 Officer, Captain Melvin S. Blitch, Jr. to Assistant Regimental S-3. First Lieutenant Lewis P. Fern of the 81mm Mortar Platoon was transferred to become 2nd Battalion S-2 and S-3. The Mortar Platoon was taken over by his assistant platoon leader, 2nd Lieutenant Lauren W. Ramsey.

In January 1943, Major William P. Yarborough (West Point 1936) was assigned to the 2nd Battalion by Major General Ridgway and Major Danielson reverted to battalion executive officer. Despite the fact that he commanded a battalion for the first time—an opportunity for which many fellow officers would wish—Major Yarborough wasn't satisfied: "Tucker was the regimental commander and he had been an old friend of mine, but I was so intractable and so impossible that even Reuben Tucker felt that he had a burr under his saddle."[72]

Yarborough was an experienced airborne officer, having been the original C Company commander when the 501st Parachute Battalion was formed. In early 1941, he was assigned to the Provisional Parachute Group Headquarters where he designed the jump boots, paratrooper uniform, and the so-called jump wings. Yarborough was sent along with Major General Mark W. Clark as an airborne observer to London in July 1942. He was involved in the planning of the first American airborne operation in North Africa and was then assigned to the 2nd Battalion of the 503rd Parachute Infantry Regiment.

Yarborough made two combat jumps with the 2/503rd, which later became the 509th Parachute Infantry Battalion. No longer needed as an airborne adviser after the Allied invasion of North Africa, he was sent back to Fort Benning in January 1943. Yarborough "intended to join the 101st Airborne" because his friend and mentor, Brigadier General William C. Lee, commanded the division at the time. But Yarborough had been requisitioned for the 82nd and "felt very dumped on" and hoped "for some kind of recognition as to having already been in a parachute operation and, as is the character of a big outfit, I got none. Therefore my feelings were hurt and I became a sort of a spoiled kind of a brat who wanted out of that outfit."[73]

After the senior officers had been shuffled around and Tucker had finished his command changes, official army pictures were made of each company in the regiment. The C Company executive officer, 1st Lieutenant Albert E. Milloy, had joined the Mississippi National Guard at twenty-one in late October 1940 and was commissioned as a second lieutenant after attending OCS. He was often seen along with his small Cocker Spaniel Honey, whom he acquired when she was seven months old.[74] On the official C Company photo of January 1943, Milloy stood naturally in the front row with his fellow officers and Honey sitting at his feet. Although it was his dog, most of the men regarded her as the company mascot.[75] Honey became a qualified "airborne dog." She accompanied Milloy on training jumps in a large special pocket he had made on his jumpsuit. To be sure she would make happy landings, Honey was equipped with a small parachute—in case of emergencies.[76]

A photo was also taken of all the regimental officers with Tucker and his senior commanders in the front row. Tucker felt happy as it was not only his first picture as a regimental commander, but Helen had also recently given birth to their second son Jeffrey. Each paratrooper obtained a printed yard-long photo of his company, which were all taken by photographer Rell Clements, Jr. Private Fred L. Lanning mailed his A Company photo to his parents in Omaha, Nebraska, along with a list of who was who in the picture. Here is a short extract of the descriptions he put on paper:

Lt. Dunn – Assistant Platoon Leader of 3rd Platoon – millionaire from New York – common as mud – everyone loves him – former wrestling captain in college.

Lt. McGrath – Executive Officer – now acting Company Commander – former long distance runner – rough as a cob – gets along well with the fellows.

Capt. Beall – Company Commander – now acting Battalion
Commander – former track star and coach – a peach of a guy –
fellows all worship him.

Lt. Lekson – My Platoon Leader – Acting Battalion Adjutant
now – former high school geometry teacher – brilliant guy –
well-liked by the fellows.

Lt. Gorham – Platoon Leader of 3rd Platoon – U.S. Champ for
two years at Camp Perry rifle matches – ex-Sgt. And a good
soldier.

Sgt. Rouse – Platoon Sgt. Of 2nd Platoon – 20 years old – been in
the Army three years – odd guy but well-liked.

Sgt. McCarthy – Little Irishman with a great sense of humor.

Roussell – Hillbilly – ignorant as hell.

Baldino – 2nd Platoon – coal miner.

Kleimo – Goldbrick.

Cullin – Was my squad leader – swell guy – New Yorker.

Gould – Old soldier – professional boxer from Massachusetts.[77]

Pfc. Gordon Gould was "picked out to box for the regimental
championship" in early January.[78] He wrote to his girlfriend Harriet on
February 5, "This Parachute outfit is tough on a guy's nerves and we
are all on the verge of fighting amongst ourselves."[79]

In the 504th regimental newspaper *Propblast*, articles appeared
about various companies, sometimes including "complaints" about
other rifle companies. An E Company correspondent blamed their
lack of sleep on F Company in the December 1942 issue: "Pvts Mor-
riss and Day, who once had war officially declared between Georgia
and Louisiana, have decided on an armistice…. We've been getting
hell for talking after lights are out, but how can we go to sleep when F
Co. has its lights on practically all nite?"[80]

In early February 1943, the idea was born among a number of
enlisted men in Headquarters and Headquarters Company to request
a short furlough to a large town to have a nice party. Their company
commander, Captain William Hornby, believed it was a great plan.
Hornby, Lieutenants Virgil F. Carmichael, Jack P. Simpson and William L. Wilson, along with forty-one non-commissioned officers and

enlisted men, received permission from Tucker for a three-day visit to Washington D.C., where they traveled by train.

Their trip was beyond their dreams; senators opened their dining rooms in the Capitol. A reporter recorded that "the trip will no doubt grow with time and the telling and become one of the legendary tales of the Regiment to be retold and relived in the days to come. All agree that it was the fulfilment of their wildest wishes. The only one which can top it will be the Company to lead the 504th down the main drag of Berlin or Tokyo. (...) The highlight of the whole trip was the visit to the White House. Mrs. Roosevelt spent about an hour charming the men with her personality and the tales of her trip to England. Especially interesting was the fact that she had spent some time with Colonel Raff's gang [the old 2nd Battalion of the 503rd Parachute Infantry Regiment] just two days before they flew to Africa. Captain "Wild Bill" Hornby presented a pair of wings and left a note for the president on his desk."[81]

Their trip was not only covered by the regimental newspaper but also by national and local newspapers in and around Washington. That same month, the former 82nd Infantry Division Band was assigned to the 504th PIR upon Ridgway's orders. The twenty-eight musicians, most of them with a professional background, were renamed 504th Parachute Infantry Regimental Band. Originally activated in May 1942, the band was led by Warrant Officer Wilbur Hall and performed on regimental parties as a dance orchestra.[82]

Training continued in earnest and not only for rifle companies but also specialized exercises for the medics and surgeons in the regiment. They had to prepare themselves as much as possible to save lives when the Stateside life would be exchanged for combat situations abroad. "Finally, General [Lesley J.] McNair, [AGF commander,] made a training visit," recalled Kouns, "and overhead machine gun fire was used in a simple indoctrination course. At the end of the realism, McNair shook hands with Tucker. I hastened to tell Tucker that the 'handshake' indicated our acceptance for action. AGF's next directive included our realism for Army-wide use. This led to our snipers laying down grazing fire for some problems."[83]

Captain Zais left when a cadre for the 517th PIR was activated in Camp Toccoa, Georgia. He had been selected as one of the battalion commanders. Tucker then chose Captain Emory S. Adams, Jr. of the 3rd Battalion as new Regimental S-3, although he was quickly detached from the unit. Ridgway knew Adams and his father well and decided to attach him temporarily to his Division Staff as he left in early March to confer with General George C. Marshall at the Pentagon.[84] Therefore, the assisting Regimental S-3, Captain Blitch, would be acting Regimental S-3 all through the next three months.

A drop of a platoon of B Company on Sanford Airport, North Carolina made Major Williams remark that it was "one of the best exhibitions of a tactical jump."[85] An article about this jump exercise was written for the regimental newspaper. First Lieutenant Milton J. Crochet and the 1st Platoon were supposed to land on the airfield and link up with members of the North Carolina State Guard to set up defensive positions around the runway. Although only one man was injured on the drop—with a sprained ankle—the mission turned out different than had been intended: "As soon as the defending platoon landed they were greeted by, it seems, everyone in Lee County. Crochet gave up in despair as he endeavoured to deploy his men around the field. Young boys would try to steal his ammunition. His sergeants would be lost as they were surrounded by admiring local beauties. He spoke over the radio net to see if it was working and to his surprise a girl answered. It seems everyone was doing all right for himself."[86]

Gould wrote to his girlfriend on February 15, "Today we were on a combat problem, we jumped on the out-skirts of a small town, loaded down with explosives, live ammunition and all then we captured it. Of course we didn't shoot at anyone, but at targets. We will probably go on maneuvers soon. Where? No one knows. I am still hoping for a furlough before we leave."[87]

The often-humorous descriptions of units and training made it possible for the officers and enlisted men to contemplate the many months of rigorous training that lay behind them. An unnamed correspondent for D Company wrote in the February 1943 issue of *Propblast*, "D Company has been too busy these last few months to put all the highlights of their experiences on paper. But they are having fun as usual, and with a new C.O., and a new 1st Sgt, plus promotions throughout, the company is united as never before. On the problems it is 'D Company in reserve,' but we're always at the front at the finish... We look forward to making history soon."[88]

Corporal William Connolly and Private Dominic Biello stand in the middle, while Sergeant Joseph Cupples addresses his D Company squad in Fort Bragg. Courtesy: William St. Clair.

D Company marching in Fort Bragg, early 1943. Courtesy: William St. Clair.

CHAPTER 6

PREPARATION FOR OVERSEAS DEPLOYMENT

Fort Bragg, North Carolina

MARCH 1943

T raining accidents caused several casualties, and sometimes they were fatal. Pfc. Stanley J. Daniszewski, Jr. of B Company drowned on March 8 in the Little River in the Fort Bragg Reservation when the boat he was in overturned during a river crossing exercise at 0630 hours.[89] Four days later, tragedy struck again during a training jump, this time at Andy's Field. A private in Captain Jack M. Bartley's C Company died when his parachute failed to open. "The tension mounted as the moment to jump approached," recalled Private Ross S. Carter of the 3rd Platoon. "Our nerves were as vibrating as wind-strumming telephone wires. Suddenly we began leaving the plane. As the line moved fast toward the door I sealed my mind with blankness. My chute opened fast."[90]

Carter came down alright and joined up with a fellow soldier who looked ashen and drawn. "What is wrong?" he asked him. The man told him in a low voice that he saw Private Michael Losyk of their platoon uttering horrible screams as he fell like a rock past him. Carter noticed a group of men gathering on a spot of the drop zone and headed in their direction. "Officers soon broke up the group of enlisted men clustered around [Private] Losyk and screened him from us until the ambulance carried him away. I will not tell you (...) what an 800-foot fall will do to a man. Let your imagination figure it out. We felt very bad in our hearts and in our stomachs as we worked out the tactical problem of storming Old Cooley Conch. Our minds and feeling of comradeship were back there on the jump field with Losyk. It could have been one of us – but it wasn't."[91]

Sergeant Nicholas Bonilla of the 502nd Parachute Infantry Regiment witnessed the funeral for Losyk the next day and wrote to his wife on March 13, "Darling yesterday some parachutist from the 504th Parachute Infantry was killed, and Gee you should have seen the military funeral they had for him. They had the Regiment march behind his casket, they had the casket on top of a wagon, while horses pulled the wagon, and they had the band play the Funeral March. Darling it was beautiful to see, and it was very sad. In fact it was so sad, that a couple of the boys who was watching it, started to cry."[92]

Twenty-eight-year-old Captain Ivan J. Roggen from Maurice, Iowa arrived in March 1943 as the new Regimental Surgeon. He was born on October 12, 1914, the grandson of Dutch immigrants: "My paternal grandfather emigrated from the Island of Terschelling, one of the West Frisian Islands. (...) My father was a minister in the Dutch Reformed Church (a passion that was not passed on to me) and I grew up near Holland, Michigan, graduating from Hope College, a school founded by Dutch immigrants. I joined the Army on October 1st, 1940 at Fort Snelling, Minneapolis in Minnesota."[93]

Upon completion of his officer training, Roggen was assigned as a captain to the 6th Medical Battalion of the 6th Infantry Division at Fort Leonard Wood near St. Louis. In the summer of 1942, he learned about the paratroops and decided to apply for a transfer. He was initially assigned to the 501st PIR upon its activation in November 1942: "My first jump was at Jump School, Fort Benning, Georgia. It was uneventful but thrilling. My only concern was whether or not the parachute would function properly, because we had to pack our own parachute. During training, each trooper was responsible for packing his own parachute. The troopers were of course, very meticulous. Once the Regiment deployed, the parachutes used on combat jumps were packed by supply personnel. Each trooper also carried a smaller, emergency parachute to be used in case the primary parachute did not open. There were some instances during combat jumps when parachutes failed to open and troopers were killed."[94]

After completing his parachute training, Roggen found himself reassigned to the 504th PIR:

> Prior to departing for North Africa, we were sent on two or three field maneuver training exercises, with one or two practice jumps (as I recall). There was also very intense physical training including several forced marches with full field equipment and were very difficult; not everyone was able to complete the marches. I don't recall any significant injuries, but there were numerous cases of blistered feet. I believe our troops departed in excellent physical condition. I know that at the end of this training period, I was personally able to run/jog for an indefinite period of time.
>
> The medical team included the 504th Regimental Medical Detachment and three Battalion Detachments (1st, 2nd, and 3rd Battalions). I was in charge of the Regimental Medical Detachment and my direct staff included the following personnel (may be one or two others I can't recall): the Assistant Regimental Surgeon; a First Sergeant, who oversaw all Regimental enlisted medics; Pfc. Richard Bertolette, the administrative clerk; Sergeant Eddie Migues, the Regimental [Medical] Supply Sergeant; Pfc. [William] Bruggeman, vehicle driver; the Dental Surgeon and his assistant, Sergeant [Joseph] Kisko.
>
> Each Battalion medical detachment included a Surgeon and Assistant Surgeon who were typically Captains, and a certain number of medics (perhaps six per Battalion). Each Company was also assigned a number of medics (perhaps two each). I don't remember the

exact size of these units or distribution of the medical personnel, but it is my opinion that the number of personnel assigned was adequate.[95]

Each rifle company had three medics assigned to them, which were distributed over each platoon. Their individual assignment could differ, however. Private Fred Grainger, for instance, served in both A and B Companies. The two surgeons in the Battalion Detachments could depend on three non-commissioned officers who were each in charge of a small team: a surgical team squad leader, a litter bearer squad leader, and a treatment squad leader. They were in charge of one surgical technician detailed with the sterilization of the medical equipment, a medical technician who took care of the anesthesia, two surgical technicians who worked as operator assistants, two surgical technicians who would plaster broken bones, a surgical technician who would treat patients with "shell shocks," four enlisted litter bearers, and a clerk (usually also an enlisted man) to keep an eye on the records. The surgical section and the treatment section always remained at the battalion aid station, whereas the litter bearer section would move forward to collect wounded troopers.

Medics who were assigned to the 504th PIR were already trained to a certain extent, but they needed to know the other members in the regimental medics' team and the recent methods that had been invented as the training of the regiment progressed. Roggen was not satisfied with the initial training of the novice airborne medics. He said:

> All of the medics arrived at the Division with some level basic medic training already completed. We also provided continued training once they were assigned to the Division including treatment of fractures, use of plasma, treatment of bleeding wounds, etc. There was also training in the process of evacuation of casualties which was generally a tiered process consisting of initial treatment at an Aid Station located very near the fighting, a Clearing Station (typically at Division

level) located far enough behind the front to provide a degree of safety, and then ultimate evacuation to hospitals well behind the front.

However, this training turned out to be less than effective. It is my opinion that this training was based on lessons learned during the First World War where the system of trench warfare resulted in static battle lines and facilitated the establishment of permanent or semi-permanent Aid Stations or Clearing Stations for any length of time. It was not uncommon for us to receive casualties from other units.

In summary, our practice was to stabilize the casualty to the extent possible and evacuate them immediately, as far back as possible. Typically, each Battalion would have an Aid Station and the Regimental surgeons (including myself) would circulate between the Aid Station. I recall seeing jump casualties including a few fractures and a few troopers killed due to parachute failure."[96]

Captain William W. Kitchin and 1st Lieutenant Hyman D. Shapiro served as the 3rd Battalion surgeons. The 1st Battalion medical detachment was led by Captain Charles E. Pack, Jr., and 1st Lieutenant Joseph S. Holbrook. First Lieutenants Hubert H. Washburn and William P. Jordan were assigned to the 2nd Battalion and 1st Lieutenant Francis "Frank" R. Cannizzaro to Headquarters and Headquarters Company. Captains Kenneth I. Sheek and Francis G. Sheehan complemented the doctors who would travel overseas.

First Lieutenant Robert M. Halloran from Bethel, Connecticut served as the Regimental Dental Officer. He enlisted in August 1942 upon graduation from Georgetown Dental School: "We all signed up while students in dental school, hoping to contribute what we could to winning the war." Not long after arrival in Fort Bragg, he became the new Regimental Dental Surgeon. Halloran recalled the medical officers "working incredibly long hours to getting men ready. I looked forward to go overseas. We were young, idealistic, and felt we could contribute."[97]

By March 1943, final personnel changes were made among the officers before the regiment would go overseas: Captains David Rosen and Abdallah K. Zakby were transferred to the 513th PIR. Captain Robert O. Erickson reported on his battalion commander, Major Warren R. Williams, Jr. to Tucker about a certain decision in early March. Erickson could not get along well with his regimental commander, and he was suddenly transferred as an instructor to an ROTC school in Maryland.[98] His place was taken by Captain Edward N. Wellems from Service Company. The Regimental S-4, Major Gerald R. Cox, was transferred out of the regiment and replaced by Captain Julian A. Cook of the 2nd Battalion.

Captain Robert Erickson was transferred out of the regiment to a ROTC unit after criticizing Major Warren Williams, Jr. He had been part of the activation cadre. Courtesy: Ken Thieme

Corporal David Rosenkrantz of the 1st Platoon in Captain Lawrence P. Johnson's H Company wrote a long letter to his sister that month about the training assignments of his outfit:

I can't remember if I told you about one of our companies making a jump in Florida. Anyhow, they had a sham battle against American Rangers, and beat them all to hell, so I guess the Rangers aren't as hot as they're supposed to be.

Last week our battalion made a mass jump. Over 500 men on the ground in less than a minute. It really was a beautiful sight. It was the first time I got air-sick, it's really a terrible feeling, and I had my chute harness adjusted wrong so that I nearly choked on the way down, and my helmet was down over my eyes so that I could only see my feet. It was by far my worst jump.

We are supposed to make a jump set in South Carolina about 150 miles from here. It will be a regiment jumping and capturing an airport. The men will jump on three different sides at once and each company will have its own objective. Ours will be an ordnance plant near the airport. We are to land on a beach so the landing should be plenty soft in the sand.

We have been experimenting jumping with our equipment chutes so that we can fight within a few minutes after we land instead of running all over the place trying to find stuff that the enemy might be covering with fire. We would carry only enough to hold us till equipment chutes could be dropped right to us, with extra ammo and guns and rations.

We intend to do a lot better than the men [of the 509th Parachute Infantry Battalion] who dropped in Africa. We know that they didn't do so hot. They jumped all right but so far from their objective that ground force took it first or surrendered with only a little fighting. (...)

The non-coms in our company were the first ones to jump with equipment in the paratroops in the U.S. Now it has been adapted by our regiment and others as standard procedure. Our jump...will be the first regimental jump, and the jump in Florida was the largest ever made in the U.S. The largest was the one in Africa. (...)

I've been saying we are going to leave soon for the past three months. Well, the officers have orders to be all packed and ready to move at a minute's notice after April 1. So I guess we will go along with them. Will probably get the same order in about a week. Africa, here we come. We are almost positive that's where we'll go. No Japs for us.[99]

The executive officer of H Company, 1st Lieutenant Elbert Frank Smith, recalled:

At that time, the procedure for delivery of equipment to the ground for the parachute jumpers was extremely ineffective. During the training of our men, we had to carry crew-served weapons wrapped in canvas para-equipment bundles with equipment chutes which were attached to the six bomb racks located on the belly of the fuselage of the plane. Before exiting from the plank, the designated trooper jumping would activate the equipment release switch next to the exit door upon the Jumpmaster's command, Go! Between take-off and jump-point, there was potential for one to three bundles of weapons to be lost. Repeatedly, combat soldiers experienced the loss of their equipment and would reach the ground basically defenseless.

No one could explain how or why these bundles would be missing, but we knew a solution had to be found. There were no manuals to reference for ideas to correct this problem. (…) I discussed this problem with Lieutenant Colonel Tucker, the regimental commander; we agreed we must have a solution to this problem so as to have these weapons be combat-ready. Tucker asked me to brainstorm ideas, and I agreed to try to come up with a solution and to keep him informed of any progress.

The success of all airborne missions was dependent upon three factors: all paratroopers to land on designated Drop Zones, all crew served weapons and basic loads of ammunition to be retrieved from para-bundles, and communications to be established. Arriving into H Company, I found a tremendous group of fine soldiers and officers. In our barracks, we deliberated the ways and means of getting these weapons, machine guns and BAR's (Browning Automatic Rifle), out with the men.

During the next few weeks, we planned various modifications to deliver the weapons to the drop zones. We were using C-47's, but the cargo doors were too small to negotiate the bundled weapons through them. Our final idea was to disassemble the weapons and strap the parts to each gun crewmember in a manner in which he could safely jump with it. We rehearsed this modification on the ground and after successful trials decided we should try it from the plane. The commander had been advised that this study was being done, and he requisitioned the planes and equipment necessary for us. We needed eleven planes, two or three of which had to be flown from California to Fort Bragg.

We informed the Air Force of our time schedule. We would be ready at 0800 hours. The designated day we lined up our gear in front of the mess hall by 0600 hours in order to have breakfast. As I came out of mess, the officer of the day informed me that General Ridgway had called and cancelled the training because it would be too dangerous and could potentially lose too much equipment. He mentioned nothing about the loss of troopers. We were not encouraged about this, and we spent the morning discussing our problem. I told my personnel that I would call the division commander and ask permission to continue this training, and I would stand good for the loss of any equipment. All the men raised a "Hoorah!" at that statement and said, "This is our project, and we will all stand good for any loss of equipment." I relayed this message to the general, and he said we could proceed.

We drilled going in and out of the doors for about two hours before take-off. Lieutenant Colonel Tucker came by and asked about our progress in this mission and warned us about the danger of the project. He said we could cancel it, and there would be no actions taken against us, no charges or criticism would be directed toward any man. I told Lieutenant Colonel Tucker that we were going through with it, and he got his parachute. He however did not have the required steel helmet, so I gave him my helmet and put him into the # 2 spot.

We were the first two men out, followed by the rest of the unit. The chutes were fastened to our backs, but the weapons and equipment were fastened to our legs. It was so difficult to move that we could barely get out of the plane. Each jumper had his personal weapons and jumpers worked in pairs or teams to quickly assemble machine guns and heavier mortars. The men and equipment made it to the ground, and we secured our weapons and went to an assembly area in approximately twenty minutes. We had lost one 60mm mortar tube and one sub-machine gun stock. This was a great success, and the morale of the personnel reached a new high.

We were later directed to go to the 2nd Battalion and instruct their troopers in how to do H Company's procedure. We held these training sessions each day after supper. The 2nd Battalion was successful in their training, only losing one man who got tangled in his chute. It was decided that this was the system to ensure success. I was then assigned to 3rd Battalion headquarters as a project officer for the new commander, Major Kouns. There were many projects to complete, as the time was fast approaching for overseas deployment.[100]

On March 24, a major assault demonstration by the 502nd and 504th Parachute Infantry Regiments was carried out in the early afternoon for the British Foreign Secretary Anthony Eden and General George C. Marshall. The two regiments attacked a position under the cover of massive artillery fire by the divisions artillery of both the 82nd and 101st Airborne Divisions and a separate brigade based at Fort Bragg. A lieutenant colonel of the 101st Airborne Division gave the running commentary for the visitors on the grandstand. Foreign Secretary Eden expressed to both regimental commanders his admiration for an impressive demonstration.[101]

By late March 1943, many officers and enlisted men in the regiment became aware that the day of departure for overseas deployment was not far away. Several of the men with girlfriends proposed to their loved ones, as they wanted to be married before shipping out. One of them was Sergeant Ted Bachenheimer of Headquarters Company. While at Fort Bragg, he started corresponding with a young lady in

California, Ethel Murfield, who was a friend of a friend. Through their letters a budding love developed.

On March 23, 1943, they married in Fort Bragg. "We were married in the parsonage of the family I was staying with," recalled Ethel. "The husband and wife and their children were our witnesses and a local minister married us. He was restricted to his camp, so I would go see him each evening until the time came that no one could visit anymore. He put me on the bus one final time and we both said 'See you tomorrow' even though we knew it wasn't true. When you're young like that you never think anything is going to hurt you."[102]

Wedding bells also rang for 2nd Lieutenant Bill E. Fabian of the 2nd Platoon, I Company. His close friend and platoon leader, 1st Lieutenant Henry Baldwin Keep from Pittsburgh, Pennsylvania, decided to give the Buick he bought for his platoon to the newlywed couple. Keep's father, Captain Henry Blair Keep, had been killed in action with the 10th Machine Gun Battalion in France in October 1918. His mother later married Charles J. Biddle (1890–1972), a member of the famous upper-class Biddle family and a Mayflower descendant. Biddle had served with distinction in the Lafayette Squadron in World War I.

Lieutenant Keep was admired by everyone in the 2nd Platoon, including Private Edward P. Haider, who said of him:

> His family was well-to-do, they apparently had a lot of stock in Pittsburgh Steel. One day he noticed that we sure waited a long time for buses to get into town. Fayetteville was about ten miles away and the city busses were our only means of transportation. (...)
>
> According to what we heard, the lieutenant walked onto the showroom floor and shelled out cash for his new black 1942 Buick. He said we could all use it for trips to town whenever we wanted. (...) When you were lucky enough to get some time off, Lieutenant Henry Keep would always make sure you had enough money to cover the fare home and a little extra just for spending money. He was very generous toward the

men in the company. I fondly remember his generosity and kindness.

One Saturday night he threw a company party, a big
dance with all the trimmings, snacks and soft drinks
for everyone. He had several loads of girls brought
in from the local college. The lieutenant arranged for
trucks to transport the girls to the base and then back
again to their school. We got the trucks all cleaned up
and made sure the girls had benches to sit on.[103]

The 505th PIR made a mass regimental jump at Camden, South
Carolina on March 29. The next day, the 504th was supposed to
make a similar landing at Myrtle Beach, South Carolina. "The climax
of state-side training was the Myrtle Beach Problem," recalled Major
Kouns, "a tactical lift of an entire regiment. All went well till the drop
which was [halfway] aborted by the Flight Safety Officer (flying above
the air armada) who judged the fog and visibility too hazardous for
the tight flight formations of a tactical drop. His decision was correct;
however, for many jumpers it was their first landing by plane instead of
by parachute. For others, it was a new dimension of warfare."[104]

Last minute changes in the regimental structure came through on
March 31 as the preparations for overseas deployment drew near and
final promotions were made. For the 1st Battalion, it meant that their
battalion executive officer, Major George W. Rice, was posted out of
the regiment and replaced by Captain Edward N. Wellems. For the 3rd
Battalion, it meant the vacancy of battalion executive officer was filled
by Captain William R. Beall of A Company as a reward for reconstitut-
ing an excellent rifle company in a very short span of time. It was now
time, thought Kouns, "to pack up for overseas shipment."[105]

Beall was informed by Tucker of the regiment's travel destination:
North Africa. He was to travel ahead with a select group of non-commissioned officers to prepare a regimental staging area. Captain Herbert C. Kaufman, the 3rd Battalion S-3 officer, would act as battalion
executive officer until the regiment would catch up with Beall's group
in Algeria. Kaufman's first task was to draft a Personal Affairs checklist

for enlisted men, which was issued on March 30. "Every man should have a will. Send it to your beneficiary," it began as the first of eleven points Kaufman had drafted. "In all correspondence be sure that they give your full name, rank and Army Serial Number" the information sheet concluded. It was a clear signal to each paratrooper that the training period had ended. That meant their regiment would depart for overseas deployment.

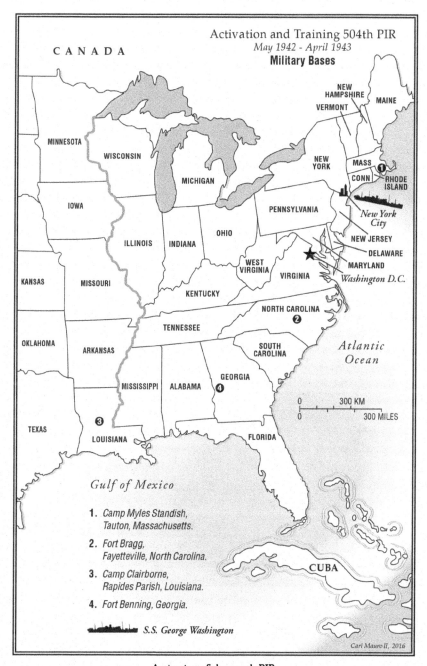

Activation of the 504th PIR

CHAPTER 7

ACROSS THE ATLANTIC

Camp Edwards, New York City, Casablanca

APRIL-MAY 1943

Although the movement orders were first only known to the senior officers, the enlisted men sensed after the cancelled regimental jump that something was about to happen. With the moment of departure for overseas service approaching rapidly, several paratroopers decided to make one more trip home. Private Frank A. Puhalla of C Company travelled first to Chicago and from there to his hometown, Throop, in Pennsylvania. He not only visited family members but also his friends and several acquaintances and said his farewell. "I will not be coming home," Puhalla told everyone. He clearly felt that he would be killed on the field of battle, which would prove to be prophetic as he was killed months later in Italy.[106]

On April 9, Captain William R. Beall boarded a train in charge of the Regimental Advance Party. With him were Staff Sergeant Raleigh E. Malone and Sergeants Willard E. Parker and Carlo J. Pilla of the 1st Battalion; Sergeants Jesse M. Jepson and Stanley G. Smith of the 2nd Battalion; and Sergeants Fred Ueckert and Wayne M. Fetters of the 3rd Battalion. They traveled under sealed orders to Fort Hamilton in Brooklyn. A few days later, Beall sent a telegram asking his wife Jean to meet him at a train station in New York City on April 16. He said he would like to take her out to dinner and go dancing. His wife and their two children were living with her mother at that time, and Jean showed her the telegram.

Beall's mother-in-law encouraged her daughter to go, as she might never get that chance again. Jean Beall got dressed in a beautiful evening gown and caught the first possible train to New York City. Captain Beall met her at the train station, and they went to a dinner club, which had a live performance of Glenn Miller with his orchestra. They didn't eat much but danced to almost every song. The last song played that night was "Sentimental Journey."[107] It was like a premonition for what lay ahead.

Newspapers all over Cumberland County, North Carolina, which includes both Fort Bragg and Fayetteville, featured the article "Army Officer Says AWOL Soldiers Are Impeding War Effort" on April 10. It was arranged by the G Company Commander, 1st Lieutenant Marshall C. McOmber. He asked the newspapers to

> give publicity to men who are AWOL. Citing that those soldiers who fail to return to camp after their leaves are over are subject to severe penalties and at the same time they are endangering the war effort. (...)
>
> A large number of "pick up" notices are received here daily by police, but the names of the service men involved are not published unless an arrest is made. Lieutenant McOmber cited that relatives and friends have a great part in shaping the reasoning processes of service men, and should encourage them to return to duty when leaves expire, for the best interests of the nation and the men themselves. A deserter forfeits his rights to citizenship and in wartime may even be executed, especially if he deserts to escape hazardous duty. The name of the soldier in the officer's letter was also given to police, with a request that he be apprehended.[108]

Shortly after, at 1730 hours on April 12, all communication with the outside world was restricted for the regiment in Fort Bragg by Colonel Reuben H. Tucker. Preparations were made for their overseas shipment and journey to a staging area. Corporal David Rosenkrantz in H Company was promoted to sergeant even though he had lost his carbine on the last field exercise. He explained in a letter to his parents that a new carbine cost sixty dollars. He wrote:

> My lieutenant said he would pay for it but I don't want him to. It really wasn't my fault for losing the thing but I don't want anyone to pay my bills for me, especially when he didn't have anything to do with it.
>
> I have bought a lot of V-mail so that it will get homer quicker after I get across. You ought to do the same thing because you have lots of letters to send too... You should see when we leave here. We will be dressed just like rookies. We will have to cover up the insigna and take the patches off our caps so when we leave no one will know we're special troops.
>
> Last Tuesday nite when I was coming back from Florida I saw guards along the railroad tracks for over a hundred miles so you can see we are getting quite a bit of protection when we leave here. None one from the airborne section of the camp has been allowed to go to town and tell any secrets about when or where we're going, which we don't know ourselves.[109]

The Division Advance Detachment—including Beall's group—of five officers and forty-four other ranks commanded by Major Edwin A. Bedell of the 307th Airborne Engineer Battalion boarded the HMT Andes at 1400 hours on April 18, sailing past the Statue of Liberty early the next morning. Beall and his men knew their destination was Casablanca.

That same evening, at 2010 hours, the 504th PIR arrived after a twenty-four-hour train ride to Camp Edwards, Massachusetts. "I got to see Tucker in a new light," recalled Major Charles W. Kouns. "For the rail trip from Fort Bragg, I had walked through the time-distance intervals. As I waited out the departure time, Tucker asked if I was ready. I told him 'Yes, but it is not time to leave yet.' Thereupon, he ordered me to start with my Battalion. As a result we arrived before the cars were spotted and the premature arrival scrubbed our orderly plans to load. On our subsequent travel legs, he left me alone."[110]

First Lieutenant Elbert F. Smith, Kouns' project officer, remembered that "when orders were received to move to New York City, I was assigned as Train Commander. (...) I was the only person allowed to depart the train to report our movement to Washington D.C., and I was also required to sign for our rations. We remained at the holding area for a few days."[111]

In the middle of a torrential rain, the regiment marched to their temporary barracks. Captain Robert M. Halloran, the Regimental Dentist, recalled "a driving cold rain at the staging area on Cape Cod. No housing planned for our men. Spent hours in rain before we got everyone settled."[112] Camp Edwards near Cape Cod would be their last stop before boarding a troopship in the port of New York City. Equipment was checked and rechecked, and missing items were distributed. All men were to carry a shelter half and two blankets in addition to their own field equipment. "We were there for several days," remembered Private Albert Clark of A Company, "and could not wear our jump suits and jump boots and our uniforms had to have all patches covered and we could not have anything that was connected with paratroops or airborne soldiers. We were restricted to the buildings that we were in and the area around them."[113]

In Camp Edwards, the last letters to their family at home were written before they would depart from the port of New York, as the men knew that the letters that they would write on board of the ship would arrive after a long time. Pfc. Gordon Gould of A Company wrote in his letter to his girlfriend Harriet, "The latest bulletin! Soldiers, write to your folks, relatives, sweetheart and fans. Tell them to use V-mail. So darling, hello and I love you. If possible please use

V-mail. Thank you. Bye. Oh, I guess I'll write a few more lines. Know something, I haven't heard from you in weeks. Maybe they're holding up the mail somewhere. I hope it's that. It's tough not being able to write anything that is happening or get any information. All the other guys are in the same fix and in the same mood."[114]

It was obvious now that the 82nd Airborne Division would not be sent to the Pacific to fight the Japanese. Several troopers "went over the fence" to see their family, friends, or girlfriends without permission. They usually had a few hours before they had to sneak back into the guarded encampment to prevent discovery. On Easter Sunday, April 25, a Division Review was held for Major General Matthew B. Ridgway, who spoke of nearing combat and complimented the way the regiment had left Fort Bragg.

Ridgway's comments were not shared by Kouns, who questioned the quicker-than-planned movements. That night again from Camp Edwards "to ship-side, New York, my Battalion cleared its area prior to departure – and – also one of Tucker's other battalions."[115] The 1st and 3rd Battalions were shuttled by train with blacked-out windows to the ferry of Staten Island to Embarkation Pier 12, followed hours later by the remainder of the regiment.

Here they boarded the troop ship *SS George Washington* on April 26 that would take them to an unknown destination. The greatest adventure in their life was soon to begin. All men received a cup of coffee and a donut by the American Red Cross before boarding the ship. Clark recalled of the trip to the harbor, "We boarded trains again that pulled up on the dock alongside of this huge liner. It was originally a German passenger liner, the *Bismarck*. It was captured during World War One and had been in the scrap yard for a good many years. With World War Two, it was given a million dollar overhaul and it was back in service as a military transport ship, capable of carrying 15,000 troops."[116]

Private Edward Haider of I Company remembered it was night time when the train pulled into New York. "As we got off the train there were two lines of secret service agents that flanked us from the train to the gang plank. These guys kept cautioning us to move quickly and move quietly... At the same time we were being hurried on to the ship and told to be quiet, an army band was playing *Over There*. It was one heck of a feeling – thinking of how we got this far so soon."[117]

Meanwhile, the troop ship *HMT Andes* arrived in Casablanca on April 27, and the advance detail marched to the staging area to be welcomed by the adjutant of the assistant division commander, Brigadier General Maxwell D. Taylor. Already, the next day they moved in motor convoy to Oujda in Algeria, staying overnight in Fez as guests of French paratroopers.

On April 29, the advance detail—as the *SS George Washington* left the harbor of New York City at 0530 hours in the morning—reached Oujda. A temporary bivouac was offered by the 509th PIR, and the engineers started working on establishing some kind of roads from the 509th camp to the new division bivouac area. That work would be followed on May 2 by finding transportation in Oujda for the division to the newly established camp.

On May 1, the first regimental anniversary was celebrated at sea. Pfc. Darrell G. Harris in the Regimental Demolition Platoon believed the troop ship was "not particularly pleasurable. We were served only two meals a day, and we were crammed in like the proverbial sardines with four and five-tiered bunks. The ventilation system on the George Washington was not very effective. With the crowded conditions, the hold was quite stuffy, but we did take turns sleeping on deck. We were glad when it was our turn to go topside. It was early spring in the North Atlantic, and it was still quite cold. However, the fresh air was greatly preferred."[118]

First Lieutenant Lewis P. Fern, the 2nd Battalion S-2 Officer, recalled that on board of the ship "we used to get [Protestant Chaplain] Kuehl and [Catholic Chaplain] Kozak together and let them argue about the Christian doctrine."[119] Private Herbert C. Lucas used his time "watching some boxing matches on the deck. The food was so-so. I did not get sea sick, but many of my buddies did and spent a lot of time in the 'head'. I was absolutely fascinated when I went on deck while we were to offload at the harbor. The sight of the minarets made me realize that I was 'no longer in Kansas'!"[120]

On May 10, 1943, the *SS George Washington*, with Division Headquarters, the 504th PIR, and two replacement groups—EGB447 and

EGB448—on board, arrived at its destination in the early afternoon. Private Clark said:

> Before we got to Casablanca, the convoy split up. A few ships went to Casablanca and the rest went into the Mediterranean Sea and some to Oran and other ports. When we went into Casablanca, the ship weaved way through French war ships that had been scuttled there.
>
> When we got into the port and turned to go into the dock, everybody was going to land side to see whatever they could. The ship hit a sand bar and started to list very heavily to that side. A voice came over the PA system telling everyone to get to the other side before we capsized. The ship soon righted itself and we got to the dock. We soon disembarked and marched through the outskirts of town and after several miles into a dry, dusty and dirty camp area. We were there for several days but couldn't leave the camp.[121]

Major Ivan J. Roggen found it "a long and rather boring trip" to North Africa. "One memorable event occurred: an emergency operation on one of the men in the 504th who developed acute appendicitis (the patient survived). I was not involved in the surgery and I am not sure who performed the operation."[122]

Captain Halloran had no idea where they headed to. "When we sighted Casablanca," he recalled, their destination was clear and Halloran quickly received some "pretty good info about the customs and beliefs of Arabs. Warned of accidental violation of their way of life. Long (15 mile) hike from ship to staging area and very hot."[123]

Kouns, the 3rd Battalion Commander, recalled "the ship-to-shore move at Casablanca jangled a few people. Off-loading was phased and trucks were not on schedule. Troops almost capsized the vessel by concentrating along the shore-side decks. Some last-off ran into the next meal which had no plans except rations in the bivouac area some miles beyond. The ship thus served an unplanned meal to some troops last off. This irked the jangled who declared those on the ship should have abstained from eating if troops ashore had no food. I cite these events as facts arising the fog of war even though an Advance Party had been flown [sic] ahead to smooth the Division's arrival."[124]

Private Edgar D. Stephens of the 3rd Battalion Machine Gun Platoon was disappointed once he got ashore: "We landed at Casablanca, a very modern town but the glamour of the town soon wore off after being pestered by dirty, begging Arabs."[125] Conditions at Camp Leautey were basic: it just consisted of pitched tents and C-rations for dinner.

On May 12 at 0730 hours, six officers and eighty-four other ranks of A Company—minus their 2nd Platoon—left in a motor convoy for Oujda and arrived there the next day. The remainder of the regiment stayed behind until May 14. Lieutenant Elbert F. Smith of 3rd Battalion Headquarters Company remembered they trained "in Casablanca at night because it was too hot to train during the day. We boarded a train known as '40 & 8', because the boxcars could carry 40 men or 8 horses/mules. This train moved us north and east to Oujda, Algeria. Along the way we passed a troop train filled with German prisoners. They were laughing at us because we were going to Berlin and they were going to New York."[126]

Tucker informed Kouns on May 13 "that he would inspect my bivouac before we departed. I called his hand on the mess he had left me at [Camp] Edwards and asked him if he lived by a double standard for his own personal convenience. He did not show his face to inspect my bivouac. However, it had my inspection prior to our departure."[127]

Paratroopers of the 504th Parachute Infantry Regiment disembarking in the habor of Casablanca, May 10, 1943. Courtesy: Mandle family

Paratroopers of the 504th Parachute Infantry Regiment have landed at Casablanca, May 10, 1943. Note the regular infantry boots they wore to fool any possible German spies. Courtesy: Mandle family

Paratroopers of the 504th Parachute Infantry Regiment marching
through Casablanca, May 10, 1943. Courtesy: Mandle family

Regimental Headquarters entrained at 1000 hours on May 14, and the 1st and 3rd Battalions followed at 1430 hours. They travelled over Casablanca to Oujda, a train ride of more than thirty hours. Private Herbert Lucas had little hope that the new bivouac area they were heading to would be better than Camp Leautey. During the trip, he was "observing the landscape, which was fascinating to me. I guess Oujda was what we expected to see in a land of Arabs. The camp was pretty dismal. We slept in pup tents and food was skimpy to say the least."[128]

Service Company and the 2nd Battalion were the last to leave at 0700 hours on May 15 and traveled in a motor convoy. They arrived in Oujda at 2300 hours on May 16. Spartan living conditions combined with hot weather and lack of fruit soon brought out cases of dysentery. An assisting platoon leader in G Company, 2nd Lieutenant John A. Yelverton, became gravely ill and was hospitalized for two months, missing the first combat operation. "Food was mainly inedible," Captain Halloran recalled, it was mainly "C- and K-rations and lots of diarrhea. We learned to make life more comfortable with whatever was available in the area."[129]

The camp conditions were so primitive at Oujda that the battalion surgeons of the 3rd Battalion, Captains William W. Kitchin and Hyman D. Shapiro, urged Lieutenant Smith and other mess officers to do something about it:

> While in training, our troops were again suffering from dysentery because of the filth and very hot weather. Two doctors that were with us suggested that we enclose the mess tent to keep out the dirt, and keep the food cooler. We did not have supplies needed to accomplish these goals. I discovered a Navy base nearby and gathered up some things to use for barter. I traded for oil fired heaters, a large tent, wash tubs, screen wire, lumber, and nails. The Navy was very generous.
>
> We enclosed the mess tent with screen wire. We built a cellar underground inside the tent. It had a wooden floor and ceiling, keeping our food much cooler. The wash tubs were placed at the entrance door of the mess hall so that utensils were washed in hot soapy water before and after meals. We all kissed dysentery "bye, bye." The general was so pleased with our results that he ordered other units to follow our procedures.[130]

Kouns was appalled by the state of the bivouac area, which didn't meet his expectations of a proper setup. The superb handling of Lieutenant Smith to improve conditions made Kouns promote him to executive officer of Headquarters Company. Kouns recalled:

> In the bivouac area units cooked on wood-burning field stoves dug-in a pit in the ground. The fuel wood was inadequate. As normal supply temporized, I requisitioned old wooden cement forms from a local builder. This fuel was shared in our Regiment. The Supply Officer responsible [- Lieutenant Colonel Robert H. Wienecke -] said, "Kouns could improvise

fuel for a Battalion while I could not obtain fuel for a
Division." In due time, Tucker asked me how we were
doing on rations. I told him, "Fine." Then he asked, "Is
it due to Division or to yourself?" I told him it was due
to ourselves – and – as I began to give him details he
did not wish me to elaborate.

Tucker and his Staff had eaten with my Battalion
until a day came when my Mess was saturated and
even bread was one slice to each man or officer alike.
I instructed the Mess Officer of our waiting patrons
and told him to go to Tucker's tent and advise him
just as soon as he and his Staff could be served. After
this incident, Tucker and Staff took their meals with
another Battalion.[131]

CHAPTER 8

EGB447

Oujda, Algeria

MAY-JUNE 15, 1943

T wo large groups of replacements traveled on the *SS George Washington* to North Africa, as it was anticipated that during advance training in North Africa and the first combat operation, a lot of men would have to be replaced. The Airborne Command had calculated that at least 1,200 officers and men would be needed to keep the 82nd Airborne Division at full strength for the greatest part of 1943. "On our surface travel overseas," recalled Major Charles W. Kouns, "our troops contingent included many new faces (and a few old faces) not organic to our home units. If questions were asked, they were described as 'reserves.' It is likely that they comprised casual over-strength to serve as a Replacement Depot."[132]

At Oujda, some three hundred replacements were assigned to the regiment. They all came from replacement packet EGB447. This "unit" had been hastily drawn from the 501st and 513th Parachute Infantry Regiments and some hundreds of recent jump graduates of the Parachute School, who had not been assigned to an airborne unit before. Second Lieutenant James C. Ott from Oskaloosa, Iowa was one of these replacement officers. He was born on November 10, 1921 and left Oskaloosa High School in January 1940. Ott enlisted the same month to join the U.S. Cavalry and was assigned to the 113th Cavalry Regiment.

While stationed in Camp Bowie, Texas, Ott was recognized as a possible platoon leader and sent to OCS in Fort Benning in September 1942. Ninety days later, in December 1942, Ott was commissioned a second lieutenant in the Cavalry. But he had no intention to remain, as a transition was made from horses to armored vehicles. Ott entered the jump course at the Parachute School in January 1943 and participated in a demolition course.

Immediately upon graduation, Ott was sent overseas. On the way to North Africa, he found himself assigned to H Company as an assisting platoon leader in the 3rd Platoon, being the youngest officer: "I joined them alone on board of the ship on the way to Africa. I was proud they accepted me. We played cards to kill the time."[133]

Another replacement officer who joined the 3rd Battalion as Mess Officer to succeed 1st Lieutenant Elbert F. Smith was 1st Lieutenant Thomas E. Utterback. He recalled of the journey across and his stay in Oujda:

> Carrying all of our belongings, we filed from the ferry unto the loading docks and somehow managed to accept the coffee and doughnuts from the smiling Red Cross workers, had our name scratched on the passenger list, and were guided to our rooms. Having gone sleepless for so many nights, I immediately went to bed and was soon asleep. When I awoke in the morning I didn't feel quite right and was a bit unsteady on my feet. When I peeked out of the porthole, it was to see nothing but water and other ships.
>
> Destroyers circled around and through our convoy as protection against German U-boats (on the rampage at that time). Our old tub wasn't in too good condition and quite often broke down. Some mornings we woke up to an empty ocean, because we had broken down and lost the convoy during the night. One destroyer circled us as protection and we wished it well.

About halfway across, tankers moved in to refuel the ships. There was one battle wagon in the center of the convoy which had a catapult float plane on its after deck. During the refueling, this plane was shot into the air and circled the slowed moving convoy to be on the look-out for submarines. With the operation over, this plane was to be replaced on the warship. The big ship would maneuver itself sideways to create a slick for the float plane to land. Twice the plane tried to come in, but had to fly off. The third time, it came in and went end over end. At that point all ships gained speed and went away. I never saw anyone stop to help the pilot. It dawned on me that somebody was going to get hurt in this war.

One day I saw a large oil tank floating off to starboard and watched it long enough to see it spout water; whales are rather shapeless unless seen up rather close. You learned to eat, sleep, and even take a bath with your life jacket on. The wisdom of this was demonstrated one morning when I awoke to the booming of depth charges being dropped by our escort over on the port side, and tho a few miles away it sounded too close for comfort.

I was up on top deck one morning when I noticed doves flying overhead. What a welcome sight that was. Later in the day the cloud bank in front of us took on a queer shape and later became land. North Africa had arrived. As we drifted in closer you could make out the town shimmering in the haze. As the sun came out it became a dazzling white thing with many towers and minarets. (...)

It was almost dark by the time our troops finally got off, and we immediately formed ranks and marched up thru the town to the station. You can't describe the aroma of French-Arabian towns, you must smell them. Camel dung has a flavor all of its own, and it just seemed to hang in the air of the streets. We filed through the wing streets of Casablanca over the cobblestones and just like the tourists that we were we gaped at the veiled women and queerly pantalooned men. That night we finally reached our destination and went to sleep (our first on foreign soil) in Camp Marshall Lyautey.

During the brief stay at Camp Lyautey I managed to get into town several times. Streets of cobblestones just wound around through town. I tried not to stare (as the book said) at the veiled women. But you just couldn't help it when you saw those painted eyes peeking over the veil. Some eyes were pretty, and some of them scared you. Most of the men wore skirts pulled up between their legs to form pantaloons. Most all of them were dirty, though occasionally someone passed who were really duded up—spotless and very colorful. (...)

Now, life in a "Repl-Depl" (replacement depot) is not a pleasant one. You are a soldier without a unit, without a home, and you get to feeling that you are without a country. I commanded a battalion of Repl-Depl's in a parade (good for morale). As I gave eyes-right to the reviewing stand and saw the Stars and Stripes, a lump came in my throat and tears I couldn't deny rolled down my cheeks.

After what seemed like ages, we were ordered onto a French train (40 & 8's) and moved to Oujda, North Africa. Officers in first class compartments, and the men in the old 40 & 8 cars. Cars are coupled together by means of chains and hooks. Plungers are on each side in order for the train to back up. In order to hook the cars together, it is necessary for a trainman, usually an Arab, to stand between the rails holding the hook in his hand, and when the cars have bumped together hard enough to compress the springs on the plungers he may then drop his hook in the ring. I never saw it done, but what I wondered at the casualty rate among trainmen.

On the French lines it is necessary to stop at each station and get clearance up to the next station. Seems that there is a station every few miles, but even then you may have to wait hours for clearance. We traveled for days in such a fashion and it became monotonous. North Africa has plenty of country at any rate. The farming changed from small garden plots to miles and miles of wheat. Not ever getting very far from the coast, the weather was very pleasant. Late one night we arrived at our new location and were trucked out to the station.

The location of the camp had been one of the hot spots in the African invasion, though little remained to show for it. We had trouble getting used to the Franc as a medium of exchange. I think I have been short-changed more and realized it less overseas than any other time in my life. A Franc was worth 20 cents, and making change was quite a job. Here we ceased being replacements and were assigned to our outfits. I was assigned the 3rd Battalion (...) and given the job of Mess Officer. (...)

The U-boats were creating havoc with shipments across the Atlantic, and supply ships bringing us food sometimes didn't make it. Parachute units messed by battalions (three line companies, plus Headquarters and Service Company). The regiment also had a headquarters company and a service company. Sometimes the only food was canned "C" ration, and if the menu called for 50 gallons of canned peaches, we might get three quarters of a bushel of half-gone apricots.

The "C" ration was getting monotonous, as well as tasteless. I decided a good shot of wine would help the situation. We saved up the glass-lined five-gallon GI water cans, and in Oujda found a place which sold wine. It was stored out in the shed in 500- to 1000-gallon wooden barrels.

While I dickered with the French gal in the office to pay for 200 gallons of wine, my boys and the Arab store helper loaded up 500 gallons of good red stuff. We had dug a pit and lined it with straw. During the day the temperature soars in Africa, but being a dry country, cools down at night. So the 500 gallons was left out at night and put into the pit the next morning. At noon, we gave a canteen cup full at the head of the line and they were told to drink it since there was lemonade on the other end. About mid-afternoon I was summoned to the command tent, and for the only time in my time in the Armed Forces was ordered to stand at attention in front of my superior, [Lieutenant] Colonel [Charles] Kouns, the battalion commander.

"I understand you served wine on the GI chow line at noon?"

I replied, "Yes, Sir."

"Did you know that is against Army regulations?"

I said, "No, Sir."

Before the Colonel could pass sentence, the Sergeant Major (bless his heart) spoke up and said, "The men thought it was a great idea, Sir."

The colonel turned to me and asked, "Why wasn't it on the officers' table?"

I said, "I paid for that wine, Sir, and if the officers want wine they can pay for their own."

That night there was a basket in the middle of the officers' table with a sign informing them that if they wanted wine with their "C" rations they must contribute. The basket was full, so I had to go back to the same wine shop (where I had finagled 300 extra gallons) for more wine. Apparently the Arab and the lady hadn't communicated.[134]

Private David K. Finney grew up in Chattanooga, Tennessee where he was born in October 1923. He decided to enlist in the U.S. Army in 1942: "After high school I entered The Kirkman School of Business where I took classes in both business and law. I excelled in both subjects. On week-ends I had a job at the *Chattanooga Times* as a copy boy. This was a part time job but it put a few more bucks in my pocket. This job ended after three months as I wanted something more permanent.

"After leaving I had three different jobs that were short in duration. I quit my first job the same day as I started. The second job I got into a fight with another employee within the first month. We were both fired. The date was October 25, 1942, I was at a job that I had just started the day before. In the middle of the shift I began thinking about a film I had seen recently. The movie title was 'Parachute Battalion' which was filmed in 1941. This film had made a tremendous impression on me. The more I thought about the film I became less interested in this nowhere job I was doing. I turned to the guy I was working with and said, 'I'm joining the Army.' I left and didn't look back as I headed for the Army Recruiting Office which was a very short walking distance from this job."[135]

After a few days, Finney traveled from Chattanooga to Camp Wolters, Texas to commence his six-week basic infantry training with the 58th Infantry Training Battalion: "At the fifth week of training we received word that the men that were interested in trying out to be paratroopers were to be in a certain area the following day. There were about twenty-five men that arrived to take the physical tests for airborne training.

"There were two paratrooper instructors and each took a group of men and explained what they were looking for and showed us how to do particular maneuvers we were to do. (...) A week later a list appeared on the bulletin board with the names of the guys that would be leaving for Fort Benning, Georgia where The Parachute School was located."[136]

A two-day train trip to Fort Benning followed, where the jump training started for Finney:

> Our first morning began with a five mile jog. From our barracks, down the street, for five miles, through the main areas of Fort Benning. This was the routine each morning until further notice.... The first day seemed easy but we all knew from past experience, this would not last. How right we were. Each day was filled with classes on fire arms, mines and demolitions. Some things we had gone over at our basic training at Wolters.
>
> One entire day was with the parachute riggers. In this class, each of us were given an unpacked parachute and told, "This is the parachute you will make your first jump with." Each man was assigned a large table on which he was to pack "this" parachute...
>
> The following week began with a march to the mock-up towers. These towers were about 34 foot in height and

resembled the body of a C-47 with an open door. (...)
We finally made it to the final week in which we were
to make five parachute jumps into an area of the Fort
Benning Military Reservation.[137]

The first two jumps turned out great, but on his third jump, Finney broke his left leg and spent several weeks in the hospital and then three weeks of recuperation leave in Tennessee. He convinced a doctor in Fort Benning to place him back on the jump roster upon his return. Just days later, on March 5, 1943, Finney made his qualifying jump with Parachute Class 745.

Only a few weeks later, the Headquarters of the Parachute School of the Airborne Command compiled a list of recent jump graduates for overseas deployment. Finney was one of them and traveled on the SS George Washington: "As we finished settling in we felt the vibrations as the ships propeller shafts began to resolve. Most of us were off our bunks and onto the deck as we wanted to see the Statue of Liberty as we passed by. It was starting to get dark as we sailed passed her. Most of the men became very quiet. She was soon out of sight as the talking aboard was resumed to a normal sound."[138]

Less than two weeks later, the ship docked in the port of Casablanca. Finney recalled:

> After leaving the ship we marched approximately eight
> miles south of Casablanca to a few stone huts and
> a tent city. This new home was referred to as Camp
> Leautey. No one seemed to know where or how it got
> the name. It had been used by troops before we came
> to North Africa. The tents were already up and so
> were rows of wooden toilets that had no doors. Fortu-
> nately for us that the toilets (latrines) were already fin-
> ished as after a day or two here many men came down
> with diarrhea or as we called it "the G.I.'s." I escaped
> this dreaded condition and would wash my hands as
> often as I could. It became so bad that more trenches
> had to be dug to take care of the shortage of latrines.

During this distressful time several of us managed to get permission to go into Casablanca. We caught a ride on an army vehicle going that way. In fact the driver dropped us off at a bar that was on one of the beaches. This was war? So peaceful and quiet. We sat on the veranda of this bar and had a couple of very cool drinks that the bar tender made for us. They were very cooling but contained very little alcohol. So we were told.

We left him a generous tip and went into the city. An extraordinary city. The old architecture was pleasing to the eye. The people all seemed very nice and smiled as we walked by. We walked many miles admiring this city. In fact we even saw a bar that looked like the one in the movie *Casablanca*. We didn't see Humphrey Bogart or Ingrid Bergman so we knew it was not the same place. The day was a happy one until we got back to Camp Leautey and were again reminded about the diarrhea.[139]

Private John B. Isom was among the first group of replacements assigned to A Company at Casablanca and blended in the 60mm Mortar Squad of Sergeant Jack Bady like he had always been there: "As we arrived in Casablanca we were assigned to our squads and platoons. I was assigned to A Company. I was the ammo bearer in the mortar squad, carrying two 60mm shells on my back additional to my other gear. We got there our first M-1 rifles."[140]

Isom was born on January 17, 1922 in Hodges, Alabama, and enlisted in the U.S. Army in November 1942. One day during basic training at Camp Mackall, Georgia, a group of paratroopers came by recruiting for the airborne forces. "They had shining boots and they didn't look like disciplined soldiers. They were looking out for volunteers. And one came up to me and said: 'Do you want to be in the airborne?' I would receive $50 pay a month instead of $30 dollars a month, so I said 'Yes.' Our group went by train to Fort Benning and as we came in I looked outside the window to our left and saw the three 250-foot jump towers."[141]

The first test came at Lawson Field where Isom and his group had to run around the field for seven miles. He had never run (that much) before. As they started running, Isom noticed that several men fell out left and right. He thought that he wouldn't make it "until I got what they call a second wind and I thought I could run around the whole world. When we came back to the camp I guess I drank half a gallon of water. I was so thirsty. They warned us not to do so, but I managed all right."[142]

After the jump towers came his first jump out of an airplane, the moment of truth for each paratrooper. Would they "freeze" in the door? The first jump was exciting for everyone, but for Isom, it was nearly his last: "I had fear. Everyone was scared, nobody wasn't. But you overcome that fear. We packed our own chutes, they told us how to do so. The second jump I nearly goofed up. They told us to count 1000, 2000, 3000 and then pull the parachute and to look up to see if the canopy above you had deployed. But I didn't do that and when I came down I didn't know that I had a cigarette roll.

"There was a sergeant standing on the ground with a big megaphone yelling to me, 'Use your reserve chute!' So I looked up and I saw that my parachute was only half deployed and I pulled on the ripcord and my reserve chute opened."[143]

Thirty-year-old Private Francis W. "Mac" McLane was another jump graduate who was sent to the 82nd Airborne Division as a replacement instead of a promised furlough. Born in California in July 1913, McLane had originally joined the paratroops in Camp Toccoa, Georgia in 1942 as he became a member of A Company of the 501st Parachute Infantry Regiment. At the time, McLane was acrophobic, overweight, and in a lousy physical condition: "The first introduction was a 'double time' of not more than one or two miles. I died seven deaths on this short run.... Our runs increased in difficulty to a five mile run with full equipment, which meant pack, rifle, bayonet, gas mask, blankets, shelter half, tent poles, tent stakes and toilet articles. By this time, I had lost my excess weight and suffered less than many of the others."[144]

After basic training, McLane was sent to the Parachute School in Fort Benning. On his first jump, he "was enjoying the beautiful view, when I saw a jeep barrelling along below me. I yelled down, 'Stop the jeep!' It skidded to a stop and I landed on the hood, smashing it down on the engine. I rolled over the front end and broke off a wooden lath, which was supporting a flag of rank."[145] Incredibly, McLane wasn't hurt during the incident.

Four more jumps followed, and the last one was made on a Saturday. McLane was promised a thirty-day furlough starting on the next Monday. "I sent a wire home to my parents and went into Columbus to celebrate. Before I could get into any real trouble, I was picked up by the M.P.'s and returned to Fort Benning and placed under restriction – no explanation. To make the story short – Monday morning I was on a troop train bound for a port of embarkation which was Camp Shanks, New York. I found that I had 'volunteered' to go overseas with the 82nd Division. It was all so secret that I wasn't allowed to write home. Some of the boys were from New York City, and they went 'over the fence' to visit their families. I managed to get a letter smuggled out to let my family know what had happened to me."[146]

Both EGB447 and EGB448 were assembled at Camp Shanks and were transported one night to New York City, where the men were herded onto the SS *George Washington*. McLane has "a dim memory of the midnight fog parting to allow a glimpse of the Statue of Liberty as we sneaked out of New York harbor."[147]

Although the ship was on rough water, its length made the trip pitch less than the smaller "Liberty Ships" nearby. McLane was less content with the food, which he considered to be "very grim. Boiled potatoes, fish sticks and coffee. I sneaked into the crew chow line as many times as I could get away with it. About half way across, our engine broke down. We lay dead in the water while repairs were being made. The convoy was out of sight when we heard 'whoop-whoop' and two destroyers were racing toward us. They crisscrossed behind us and dropped depth charges.

"After a couple of passes, they headed back to the convoy. Our repairs were completed and we rejoined the convoy. I never heard what the results were. We came in sight of the shore of Morocco and a P-39 fighter plane buzzed us. We entered the Casablanca harbor and passed the French battleship 'Jean Bart', which had been sunk up to her deck."[148]

From nearby Camp Leautey, the trip continued by railway to Oujda in Algeria. McLane was assigned to a tent with Privates James H. King, Jr. and Allen L. Langdon. The three of them got a pass for Oujda after a rifle inspection. "It really wasn't worth the effort. The only cold drink was Marsala, wine in crushed ice. Not too good. The French beer was not drinkable. We caught the next truck back to camp and wrote letters home.

"Oujda was in a dry lake area. The ground was covered with 'alligator' cracks. Where disturbed, it dissolved into fine dust. We 'double timed' up the side of a mountain (about three miles away), where we had classed in various problems that we might run into combat. The heat was terrible and we sweated gallons."[149]

Pfc. Fred W. Thomas, a soldier in H Company, used the earliest allowed opportunity in Africa on May 20 to write a letter to his parents: "We took a long train trip through Northern Africa about a week ago. I sure did see a lot of country. These people sure are a lot different than they are in the states. We also saw a lot of German prisoners. We passed several train loads of them. We saw and talked to a lot of French soldiers. Guess I could write a book about all the things I have seen here."[150]

In Oujda, the training continued and was even intensified despite the terrific heat during the day. Two fatal casualties were sustained on May 22 and 27, respectively, when Privates Howard W. Morton of H Company and Raymond L. Muston of the 1st Platoon in I Company died as non-battle casualties. Private Donald Zimmerman, a trooper in the 2nd Platoon of H Company, had boxed with Morton in Oujda near some cactus trees that proved to be accidently fatal: "I had a background of boxing and at Oujda I boxed with Private Howard Morton and he landed in a cactus tree that killed him. Captain [Lawrence P.] Johnson, our company commander, took me behind a tent and said, 'One more fight and you will fight me.' Johnson had been with the Rangers before he joined us."[151]

With the lack of sufficient transport planes in Morocco to make a parachute jump, several hours were spent on May 24 to practice rolling on the ground and taking equipment from equipment bundles. Captain Adam A. Komosa, the Headquarters and Headquarters Company commander, believed that "despite the climatic conditions, the camp at Oujda was to become the greatest parade ground the Regiment and Division had graced to date. We were to be the proud recipient of virtually every dignitary in North Western Africa. The proud 82nd paraded before 15 Allied generals in less than a month. The Division colors were dipped for General Mark Clark, Commanding General of the Fifth Army; General 'Tohey' Spaatz, the colourful commander of our African Air Force; General Patton, Commanding the Seventh Army; General [Omar] Bradley, the Division's first Commanding General in World War II, Major General [Alfred] Gruenther, Fifth Army Chief of Staff, [Lieutenant] General Dwight D. Eisenhower, and an impressive row of French and Spanish dignitaries, including Lieutenant General Luis Orgaz [Yoldi], High Commissioner of Spanish Morocco, and many others."[152]

Sidi Mohammed ben Yusef, Sultan of Morocco (left), the French General Charles Noguès (center), Lieutenant General Mark Clark, the Spanish High Commissioner in Morroco General Luis Orgaz Yoldi and Major Matthew Ridgway on the reviewing stand observing the parade of the 82nd Airborne Division at Oujda. Courtesy: Mandle family

The 82nd Airborne Division paraded with fixed bayonets to
impress the Spanish delegation. Courtesy: Mandle family

Lieutenant General Dwight Eisenhower inspecting A Company in Oujda. To his
left Captain Willard Harrison of A Company. Behind them Major General Matthew
Ridgway and Lieutenant General Mark Clark. Courtesy: Mandle family

Lieutenant Generals Clark and Eisenhower along with the Sultan
of Morocco visited the regiment on May 25. Eisenhower and Clark
first inspected A Company and then stood in the review stand to see
the entire 504th PIR march by.

Kouns believed that Lieutenant Colonel Reuben Tucker "was tireless at physical action; he was stingy with words. Once he said: 'Some of you think a guardian angel will protect you. Forget it, you are all equally vulnerable to enemy fire. Learn not to waste your men.' (...) Tucker was obviously a strong, forceful leader and especially a spontaneous brand of soldier. This fact may have prompted Ridgway."

During a surprise visit of Major General Matthew B. Ridgway and other regimental commanders on May 29 to his bivouac, Tucker was promoted to colonel. He received his rank insignia of silver-plated eagles from his colleagues, Colonels James M. Gavin and Harry L. Lewis, under Ridgway's watchful eye. A photographer snapped a photo moments later of Ridgway shaking Tucker's hand. Kouns looked on from a close distance: "When Ridgway shook his hand and left, Tucker said, 'My knees are still shaking!' He was surprised and moved by Ridgway's gesture because as a 'soldier' he knew both reduction and promotion could be dispensed by his peers."[153]

While Major General Matthew Ridgway looks on, Colonels James Gavin and Harry Lewis pin the eagle wings on the newly promoted Colonel Reuben Tucker at Oujda. Major Charles Kouns recalled that Tucker was afraid he would be relieved from command! Courtesy: Mandle family

Major General Matthew Ridgway congratulating Colonel Reuben Tucker.
Promoting Tucker to full colonel was a very wise decision, since he would lead the
504th Parachute Infantry Regiment in all campaigns. Courtesy: Mandle family

On May 30, a three-day training program in the mountains near
Oujda commenced, practicing an assault under small arms fire,
machine gun, and mortar fire and exercising with concussion grenades. The companies were scattered over the mountains during the
exercise to make them familiar with the situation they might find
themselves in on the battlefield.

In the afternoon of June 3, the regimental officers received,
recalled Major Ivan J. Roggen, the Regimental Surgeon, "a very aggres-
sive speech by General Patton, filled with profanity, and urging us to
kill the enemy."[154] Corporal Thomas J. Leccese of the 3rd Platoon, C
Company wrote in his diary: "Parade for General Patton – big affair. I
wonder how many more generals there are."[155]

Several practice jumps were carried out for visiting generals and to
prepare for the coming airborne operation that was being planned by
the Allied High Command. The first regimental jump in North Africa
took place on June 5, the same day the officers and men received their
African Campaign Bars. Leccese was impressed with the scale of the
parachute drop and wrote in his diary that "the sky was full of silk."[156]
One jump was less successful as nearly 30 percent of the 504th, and

the 505th PIRs ended up in the hospital with broken bones and sprained ankles. According to Lieutenant Ott, "the officers made three night jumps in Africa in practice to go into Sicily."[157]

Private Herbert C. Lucas, one of the 3rd Battalion messengers, thought the jump should have been called off. "Physical conditioning was always a top priority in the paratroops. We all remember a 'practice' jump for General Ike [Eisenhower] and other notaries. The wind was too strong and in our opinion it should have been called off. I wasn't injured – as many were – but I was dragged at least a 100 yards before I could collapse my parachute."[158]

On June 9, another mass parachute drop went wrong. The strong wind half inflated some of the nylon parachutes and no less than 120 men of the 3rd Battalion were hurt in the jump. "With intensive training in North Africa," recalled Kouns about Tucker, "he was concerned that over-extension would leave us short of men and equipment on D-Day [of the first combat]. He advised me to employ skeleton units and equipment for late exercises. Late exercises were prompted by unlimited terrain; the cohesion and integrity of power poised for action and, supporting air lift plus field living and mobility. The Division gliders were destroyed by desert wind and inadequate lashing. One massive jump recorded 87 fractures… There were few spare and packing facilities. Same for equipment chutes. There was a rash of freakish training losses."[159]

Unfortunately, fatal casualties were also sustained under other circumstances. Pfc. James C. Powers of D Company died when he fell off a cliff on June 9.[160] Three days later, another paratrooper—Private Floyd V. Quinn from C Company—died an awful death when he was killed by grenade shrapnel during an exercise. It was just four days before his twenty-first birthday. Leccese wrote that Quinn was "a new fellow that got killed by shrapnel from a grenade – as he didn't hug to the ground – between the eyes."[161]

Staff Sergeant Ernest W. Parks of D Company saw in Oujda the first "live" Germans: "A group of our soldiers was engaged in a baseball game when we saw a group of men walking down the road toward us. I could immediately tell they were neither Arabs nor Americans. They seemed to be minding their own business and we thought nothing of it. However, some Arabs, seeing them, and expecting some reward, excitedly told us they were German soldiers. We stopped our game long enough to point out for them the location where they could surrender and sent them on their way. We then resumed our game and disappointed the Arabs."[162]

Leccese's rifle squad was flown to Bizerte and Tunis on June 15 to show the American infantry units how the paratrooper uniforms looked like to avoid friendly fire from ground troops. From the air he was impressed with all the equipment in the desert that had been left behind by the Germans and Italians. "We made a speech to a battalion in the 62nd Coast Anti-Aircraft Artillery Regiment and convinced them to be parachutist conscience," Leccese wrote the next day in his diary.[163]

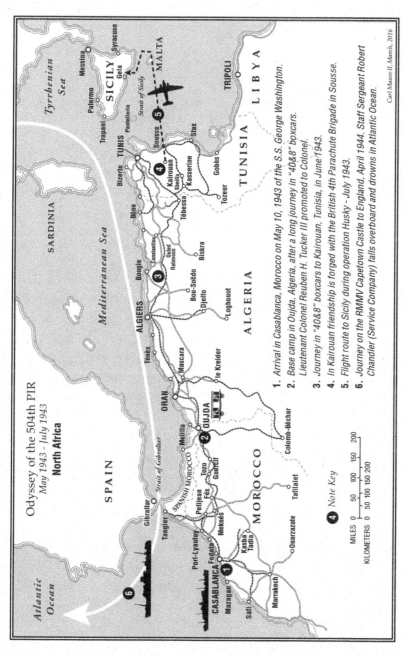

Odyssey of the 504th PIR
May 1943 - July 1943
North Africa

Carl Mauro II, March, 2016

North Africa

1. Arrival in Casablanca, Morocco on May 10, 1943 of the S.S. George Washington.
2. Base camp in Oujda, Algeria, after a long journey in "40&8" boxcars. Lieutenant Colonel Reuben H. Tucker III promoted to Colonel.
3. Journey in "40&8" boxcars to Kairouan, Tunisia, in June 1943.
4. In Kairouan friendship is forged with the British 4th Parachute Brigade in Sousse.
5. Flight route to Sicily during operation Husky - July 1943.
6. Journey on the RMMV Capetown Castle to England, April 1944. Staff Sergeant Robert Chandler (Service Company) falls overboard and drowns in Atlantic Ocean.

CHAPTER 9

TRAINING IN TUNISIA

Kairouan, Tunisia

JUNE 16-30, 1943

On June 16, 1943, advance elements departed by C-47 transport planes "from Oujda to Kairouan in the cool air of 10,000 feet," recalled 1st Lieutenant Moffatt Burriss, the 3rd Battalion S-2 officer. "When we got off the plane, we thought we had stepped straight into hell."[164] Private Edgar Stephens also "left Oujda before the rest of the outfit to help get a new base set up. The plane set us down in a field and even the pilot wasn't sure it was the right spot. The nearest town (5 miles) was Kairouan, the second oldest city in the world. We (the whole outfit) didn't stay there long as we only used it to take off fast for our little trip."[165]

Lieutenant Thomas E. Utterback provided the most detailed description of Kairouan in a letter to his wife, since he was part of the advance detail that had to prepare the new bivouac for the 3rd Battalion:

> I had to load the entire kitchen on planes and we flew to our new station at Kairouan. On the way over we crossed high mountains, and we almost froze in the plane. Then we coasted down off the mountain, out onto a plain. We stepped out of the door and were greeted with air like from a blast furnace. Wind from

the desert wasn't very pleasant. It was with relief that we drove up to the olive grove that was to be our new bivouac area. Thank goodness for olive trees. They should be very cheap—the world has so many of them. Temperature in the daytime was unbelievably hot (into the 100s) though it cooled down at night. The way to endure the heat during the day was to (believe it or not) get into your sleeping bag.

In the distance shimmered the second holiest city of Islam, and the dirtiest. You could smell the town long before you reached it. It was "Off-limits" to troops, but I had to go there to draw rations. Each Arabian city has its inner city of Medina. Here the entire town was behind high thick masonry walls. In there you could just imagine doing something out of line and then just disappearing. Here I first saw the elaborate ceremony of bowing toward Mecca. (...)

Around these parts very stiff fighting had gone on and wrecked tanks and planes were strewn all over the landscape. Large cemeteries of Allies and German were seen everywhere. We were catching up with our war. German graves were usually the better planned and kept. British and American were liable to be found anywhere.

Here the farming consisted of small garden plots and large olive groves. Water for the garden plots was provided by drawing it from wells. Large leather buckets were ingeniously emptied at the top to empty into troughs at the top. Invariably the power was furnished by one oxen and one camel working side by side. Much of our spare time was spent in the irrigation trough letting the cold water run over us.[166]

A week later the rest of division followed by truck or train. Private Herbert Lucas was "selected to travel with a small contingent via a recon type vehicle, whereas the majority of the regiment went by train. So I got to see a number of small towns."[167]

Private Francis W. McLane made the trip to the new encampment by truck. He recalled:

> We passed through the Kasserine Pass, travelling by truck, where we witnessed the scene of the American Army's first real taste of combat with the more experienced troops of the 'Afrika Korps'. We were travelling on a long straight stretch of macadam highway when we came to an old Roman arch. The highway detoured around it, leaving an exposed section of the original, stone block highway about 50 yards long, then swung back and continued as a black top road. (...)

> On a steep hill, about half a mile away, was a destroyed Roman fort. The stone building blocks were all scattered down the sides of the hill. This brought up speculation, from our boys, as to what was all over the hill; boxes, flat boulders, etc. The archaeology aspect was not recognized by many of them. At another time, it would cost a lot of money to see the historical sites that we got to see, for free. (...)

> We settled down near the Arab town Kairouan. The usual Arab stink was added to by our nearness to their cemetery which emitted the over powering stench of the recently departed. I spent most of my spare time developing my marksmanship.[168]

Privates Albert B. Clark and Andrew E. Starling of the 2nd Platoon, A Company, were each assigned to a flat railway car which contained about fifteen or twenty large crates each. They had to guard these crates during the trip to Kairouan:

One day while en-route, the train stopped at a small village for the locomotive to take on water. We were there for some time and some of the troopers were wandering around. Lieutenant Colonel Williams and several others with him, while in town, got into some sort of problem and that night 'Berlin Sally', in her nightly news broadcast told us all about it. She not only identified our unit, but also named Lieutenant Colonel Williams and men with him. It sure alerted us to the German intelligence and their capabilities.

A day or so later, an uneventful one, we were still sleeping on those two cars of parachutes and we woke up one morning and were not connected to our train. Instead we were in the middle of a string of flat cars loaded with wood. Not only that, but a whole switch yard full of cars loaded with wood and we had the only two cars in sight that were loaded with something other than wood. I left Starling to watch over the cars while I went looking for help and found that we were not very far from the station.

After hunting around I finally found a couple of MP's. I then had trouble trying to persuade them that we had been cut out of the middle of a train during the night and had two cars loaded with parachutes and found ourselves in the middle of a yard full of wood and that I left my buddy to watch over them while I looked for help. They acted as though I had gotten drunk the night before and was trying to cover up my problem. I finally got them to go with me and out and watch the cars and they took Starling and me back to their office. After a few phone calls, they decided that we telling the truth. That night there was a hospital train going our way so they arranged for our cars to be attached and take us along.[169]

One night on their journey, their train was parked on a siding of a station when Clark and Starling fell asleep:

> Sometime during the night, a locomotive came through and stopped at the water tower and took off. We never knew if it was French or American. When the locomotive came in, it woke us up and at this time I found that someone had taken my musette bag, near my head, without disturbing me. I had my rifle, pistol belt and camera elsewhere, but there were several rolls of film, both exposed and new and other things in it. I laid there awake for some time listening and finally heard some footsteps in the gravel and after they passed my car, I dropped down and as soon as my feet touch the gravel; there was a flurry of motion and shadows all along the train, heading away.
>
> I pointed my rifle in the general direction of the shadows and fired, emptying the clip. Without any question I think that everybody in the boxcars pointed their weapons and started shooting. After it quieted down then questions were asked. I explained and things settled down and we went back to sleep. I bet that there was one bunch of scared Arabs that night.
>
> The next morning we could not find any traces of blood or sign that anyone had been hit. We did find all kinds of material scattered all over the area. I found my musette bag and the film had been strung out and ruined. There were no parachutes missing. On the other side we found that two large crates of heavy railroad repair tools had been carried several hundred feet away and left. It took 6 to 8 men to carry each one of them back and we put them on the flat cars where they had been. We wondered how they had managed without disturbing someone.

Eventually a locomotive, with an American crew, came along and took us to Kairouan and to our battalion. This camp was set up in a cactus pear grove. It was divided by high walls of cactus plants, loaded with fruit that was covered with tiny spines. Several found out the hard way that they are very painful.[170]

War correspondent Don Whitehead flew along with a stick of H Company commanded by Staff Sergeant William Timson during a training jump. He wrote:

A few minutes later we were over the Mediterranean, A light surf feathered a beautiful beach and the water was startlingly blue. Then the formation of planes swung back inland and headed for our objective. Timson walked down the aisle giving final instructions. The minutes passed slowly. Then far ahead I could see the field which was our objective and this formation of planes driving toward it, dropping lower for the final run. "Four minutes to go!" Timson said. "Check your guns and packs." The men checked over their equipment, straps and 'chute latches. "Stand up and hook up!" the jumpmaster shouted. The troops surged to their feet and snapped the static lines of their 'chutes to the cable running the length of the plane. "Sound off!" "Number eight, okay! Number seven, okay! Number six, okay!" Down the line went the chant.

"All okay!" Timson cried. He stood at the door with his left foot forward, clutching the sides and gauging the distance to the field. The plane was leveled off with a speed of 120 miles an hour. The atmosphere in the plane was electric with a suppressed excitement that was almost suffocating. It was a physical thing that made your heart pound with suspense. Those four minutes seemed interminable. Above

Timson's head glowed a red light. Everyone stared at it as though hypnotized . . .

Then suddenly the green light flashed on – the pilot's signal to jump. Timson took one more look out the door. "Okay!" and he was gone. The others went after him in one great rush (...) If I had a 'chute on, I would have jumped with them even though headquarters had forbidden me to make the jump. You can't sit in a plane when parachute troops rush out the door without an almost uncontrollable urge to follow them.[171]

In Kairouan, several miles south of Tunis and west of the city of Sousse, the regiment was again billeted in a tent city. Enlisted men slept in pup tents while the officers shared two-man tents. It was so hot that there was little or no training at all during the day—only at night when it was cool. Lieutenant Burriss started to realize that the day of battle was drawing near. "We were supposed to continue our training, but couldn't move around during the heat of the day, so we trained a little at night – erecting sand tables (table-sized scale models of target area made in what looked like sandboxes), setting up road blocks, and destroying enemy artillery. We were still playing at war, but here in North Africa, where bloody fighting had already place, the game became more and more serious."[172]

Captain Adam Komosa, the Headquarters and Headquarters Company commander, learned that "Allied Headquarters had us slated for a night airborne operation on Sicily. A night parachute operation had never before been attempted by any army; so organization and training for it offered many new problems. The many intangible and indefinable difficulties of fighting at night in hostile territory, when every object appears to be and often is the foe, had to be overcome. Rapid assembly of the troops and reorganization after landing by parachute appeared to be the greatest problem.

"Training began at night – compass marches by small groups, organizing in the dark, from simulated parachute drops and glider landings, moving across country at night and organizing positions, digging fox holes, laying wire, preparing mine fields by the light of the moon. Emphasis was placed on training in judo, demolitions, commando fighting and the use of the knife."[173]

It was also in Kairouan that the last replacements were accepted into the regiment before the first combat jump. McLane found himself transferred to Lieutenant George Warfield's I Company. His previous tent mates were both assigned to other companies: Privates James H. King, Jr. to D Company and Allen L. Langdon was inducted in the 505th PIR.

"Our camp was an open field on the edge of the desert," recalled 2nd Lieutenant Earnest H. Brown, "where we simply pitch our pup tents. Not exactly the comforts of home, exceedingly hot in the daytime, and cold at night. In spite of the discomfort, our training continued unabated with desert marches, calisthenics and even a practice night jump. In this period I was assigned to (...) the Mortar Platoon of the 2nd Battalion. The 81mm mortar is a support weapon that fires a shell (...) for a maximum range of about four thousand yards."[174]

On June 19, exactly a week after Private Floyd Quinn was killed during an exercise, medic Sande H. Martin died. He was the last fatal casualty before the first combat operation took place. Less than four weeks later the first batch of combat casualties would be sustained. The thought of a nearing campaign was not only on the mind of the paratroopers of the 504th Regimental Combat Team but also on that of the German female propaganda broadcaster, popularly known as "Berlin Betty." She had announced the arrival of the regiment in North Africa, naming Lieutenant Colonel Warren R. Williams, Jr. as one of the commanders. That had unnerved some of the officers. Another broadcast on June 30 seemed to have its effect on some officers, as Corporal Thomas Leccese of C Company wrote in his diary: "The Berlin Bitch is playing merry hell with our division officers, telling us we are in the tough area. The reception waiting for us on the jump, etc. It doesn't bother the men but the officers are jumpy. Nine German prisoners today and a big raid on Sousse in the morning."[175]

Little could Leccese know what some of the officers in the regiment knew; another invasion in the Mediterranean was imminent. The sword had been forged, and now it needed to be tested—on the Italian island of Sicily.

'X BATTALION'

Kairouan, Tunisia

JULY 1-9, 1943

I t was clear to most officers and enlisted men of the 504th Regimental Combat Team that the first combat jump wasn't far away. Unknown to many of them, it had already been decided by Major General Matthew B. Ridgway on May 24 that the 505th Regimental Combat Team would be dropped first on the Italian island of Sicily. Operation Husky, the Allied invasion, would start in the early morning of July 10. The 3rd Battalion of the 504th, commanded by Lieutenant Colonel Charles W. Kouns, would jump as "X" Battalion of the 505th RCT. Colonel James M. Gavin, the regimental commander of the 505th, had been elated to hear that he was to command this task force. Kouns recalled that Colonel Reuben H. Tucker "had suggested that if I were captured, I would probably wind-up in Rome. After this, Gavin looked after my Battalion."[176]

Lack of transport planes meant that the majority of the 504th Regimental Combat Team could not be flown in on the first night. Also, the 325th Glider Infantry Regiment and the 509th Parachute Infantry Battalion weren't committed for the same reason. They were kept in reserve in Tunisia, ready to be deployed on short notice.

Colonel Tucker was furious, as not only would his regimental combat team not be deployed in its entirety, but Ridgway had also decided which battalion was attached to 505th. His senior liaison officer, Major Emory S. "Hank" Adams, Jr.—son of the former Adjutant General of the Army—would accompany the division commander on the American cruiser *Monrovia*. Ridgway could only make an amphibious landing on Sicily, as he was not jump qualified after skipping many opportunities for it in the previous months.

When the decision was made to send the 505th Parachute Infantry Regiment in first, along with its 456th Parachute Field Artillery Battalion, B Company of the 307th Airborne Engineer Battalion, a detachment of the 307th Airborne Medical Battalion, and the 3rd Battalion of the 504th PIR, it was certainly questionable. Gavin's command structure changed drastically in North Africa when he relieved his 2nd Battalion commander and Captain Joseph I. Gurfein of B Company, 307th Airborne Engineers for losing their men's confidence and failing to follow exact orders.[177] Consequently, Gavin's new 2nd Battalion commander and battalion executive officer, as well as two company commanders, were inexperienced in their new capacities. Two of Gavin's three battalion commanders were majors instead of lieutenant colonels.[178]

In the past, it has been said that the 505th PIR was chosen to spearhead Operation Husky because it had a "higher state of readiness" than Tucker's troopers.[179] Considering the amount of command structure changes in the 505th Regimental Combat Team just days and weeks before their entry into combat, one could question that statement. Maybe Gavin's regiment was sent in first to spare the better-trained 504th. The seniority of Gavin over Tucker could have been another deciding factor in the decision to send the 3rd Battalion of the 504th PIR along. Trying to keep the Germans unaware of its parent unit, it was temporarily designated "X Battalion."

The majority of Colonel Tucker's 504th Regimental Combat Team, with a small advance parachute detail of the 325th Glider Infantry Regiment led by 1st Lieutenant Wade M. Meintzer and a detachment of the 307th Airborne Medical Battalion under command, was to reinforce the beachhead of the U.S. Seventh Army and Gavin's task force in the evening of July 10.

One hundred American transport planes were lent to the 1st British Airborne Division, which would leave from the Sousse area in

Tunisia and capture the vital Ponte Grande and Primasole bridges on the eastern side of Sicily. The British Eighth Army of General Bernard L. Montgomery would come ashore from the south with the untried 1st Canadian Infantry Division, the 51st Infantry Division, the independent 231st Infantry Brigade from Malta, the 50th Infantry Division, the 5th Infantry Division, and some commando battalions.

The American invasion force from the sea consisted of the U.S. Seventh Army, commanded by Lieutenant General George S. Patton, Jr., and comprising the U.S. II Army Corps of Major General Omar N. Bradley. Patton had three Ranger Battalions, the 3rd Infantry Division, the 1st Infantry Division, the untried 45th Infantry Division (Oklahoma Army National Guard), and the equally green 2nd Armored Division, which would be used as floating reserve, at his disposal.

Enemy resistance was expected to be light as the British intelligence service had successfully launched Operation Mincemeat, a deception plan that made the Germans believe that Greece and the island of Sardinia were to be invaded by the Allies. The size of the defensive forces on Sicily nevertheless remained impressive, comprising over 200,000 Italian and 30,000 German troops. The Italian VI Army under command of *Generale* Alfredo Guzzoni consisted of the 28th Assietta Division, the 4th Livorno Division, the 54th Aosta Division, and the 202nd, 206th, 207th, 208th, and the 213th Coastal Divisions, plus the Niscemi Combat Group, which included most of the Italian tanks on Sicily and was not surprisingly situated near Niscemi.

The 4th Livorno Division, best equipped of all the Italian divisions on Sicily, had its headquarters in Caltagirone, several miles northeast of Niscemi. According to the intelligence information that was received by the 504th Regimental Combat Team on July 6 and 8, "the 4th Livorno Division is known as an 'assault and landing division', its organization being designed for combined operations. The main difference between this and normal infantry divisional organization being the decentralization of all regimental heavy support weapons...."[180]

German units consisted of the 15th Panzer Grenadier Division of *Generalmajor* (Major General) Eberhard Rodt and the Panzer Division Hermann Goering of *Generalmajor* Paul Conrath. Both divisions were formed in June 1943 out of evacuated remnants of the destroyed 15th Panzer Division in Tunisia and parts of the equally destroyed Division Hermann Goering that were on Sicily as they lost North Africa. The disposition of the latter division, between the American- and British-planned invasion beaches, could not have been better chosen. On personal orders of General Albert Kesselring, the German chief commander in the Mediterranean, Conrath's division had been placed in the southeast and above the edge of the plain east of Niscemi and Biscari. Rodt's 15th Panzer Grenadier Division, on the other hand, was stationed in the northwestern part of Sicily. *Generalleutnant* Frido von Senger und Etterlin, the chief German liaison officer to General Guzzoni, unofficially controlled the German units.

Although Allied code breakers had learned of the presence of the Panzer Division Hermann Goering on Sicily from intercepted German messages, only the army commanders were informed. Ridgway and his regimental commanders knew nothing of the presence of ninety-nine tanks, several of them Tiger tanks, in the division.[181] An intelligence report attached to Field Order Number 1 of June 22, 1943 disclosed the following faulty information: "...aside from Air Force Defence Units noted above – no German field divisions are known to be on the island. It is estimated that two such Divisions might be on the island by D-Day."

Apart from Kouns and a few principal staff officers, no one in the 3rd Battalion knew where the next mission would be, although some speculated that it would be Sicily. Gavin decided to fly with Kouns and Major Edward C. "Cannonball" Krause of the 3rd Battalion, 505th PIR, across the preselected drop zones on Sicily. They requested some RAF Mosquito bombers for the purpose at the Headquarters of the North Africa Air Force (NAAF) in Carthage, Tunisia. In the evening of June 11, they took off from Malta to Sicily at 2230 hours. The parachute identifications on their uniforms had been removed to make the Germans, if they were shot down, believe they were pilots or regular army officers rather than members of an airborne division. Gavin would fly in the leading Mosquito bomber, while Kouns and Krause followed in a second bomber.

They flew over Lake Biviere and course north, passing the western side of Niscemi, circled around the city, and then headed south over the checkpoint, the lake. During the flight, Italian searchlights tried to pick them up, but they were acting too slow to get the Mosquito bombers in sight. Kouns and Krause inadvertently flew over Ponte Olivo at three hundred feet and were fired upon, but no one was hit. The pilots subsequently flew directly back to Malta where Gavin was pleased with the results of the reconnaissance.

"Our training was a hurried up affair," recalled 1st Lieutenant Thomas E. Utterback of the 3rd Battalion, "and we knew that the big day wasn't far away. Training was carried on at night, not only because it was cooler, but it seemed the coming operation was to be a night jump.

"Since it was known that I was a Civil Engineer, I was ordered to prepare a sand table of the drop area and the Major [Kouns] flew over in a pursuit plane one day. He didn't look any too happy about it. It was hush-hush where the drop would be, but from the latitudes and longitudes of the map, I could tell that it was Sicily. Photos were taken of the DZ (drop zone) and brought to me. Right in the middle of the DZ I discovered the existence of an '88 battery' (4 guns) and a tented bivouac area. My report didn't seem to faze anyone."[182]

After the drop zones had been confirmed, the planning stage commenced on July 1. "We studied maps and made sand tables," recalled 1st Lieutenant Moffatt Burriss, the 3rd Battalion S-2 officer. "Intelligence officers briefed us on the enemy's strength. They told us that the mission would be no picnic. They were expecting an attack, and we would probably encounter a good deal of anti-aircraft fire."[183]

On July 2, recalled Kouns, "my Battalion Surgeon was rebuffed by Base Supply for select first-aid items to pack for our drop. Base Supply complained that they had segregated with great effort a combat load of medical equipment for our Division – and – most of it had to be re-consolidated into the general inventory. They frowned on running a small retail store under such experience. Being isolated by dispersal at this time, I justified the 'retail store' support for my Surgeon."[184]

Kouns' 3rd Battalion would be dropped three miles south of the town of Niscemi at approximately 2320 hours on July 9. He had to defend the high ground in the vicinity of its DZ, block the two main roads leading south from Niscemi, act as an advance guard for the 505th Regimental Combat Team, and patrol the area adjacent to the battalion position. Their drop zone would be northeast of the 505th, which had to take a key terrain south of Niscemi. They would construct an airfield there, destroy enemy communications, deny the enemy planes the use of the Ponte Olivo airfield near Gela, block enemy movement from the north toward Gela, capture the important road network labelled "X" south of Niscemi, and take strongpoint "Y"—six concrete bunkers and blockhouses—some three miles east of Gela. Company I of the 505th PIR would light a huge bonfire on a hillside near Gela as a signal for the amphibious forces.

Although some were anxious or nervous to take part in the regiment's first combat mission, most of the men were eager to jump and wanted to move to any other place than the hot African desert. Second Lieutenant Roy M. Hanna, in Headquarters Company of the 3rd Battalion, believed that when they were "to spearhead the initial invasion into mainland Europe, we all knew we were ready for combat and thought we were the best."[185]

The enlisted men and several officers in the 504th Regimental Combat Team were still unaware of the preparations that were made at higher echelons. They tried to make the garrison life and exercises as bearable as possible. Mascots were a perfect distraction for the tension of the uncertain future. Sergeant Edward P. Haider, a squad leader in I Company, recalled his company acquired two mascots in North Africa:

> It seemed like our outfit always had some kind of animal for a pet – from our pig back at [Fort] Bragg; to our monkey and a little jackass, Beanie, that we found in Oujda. Every time a jeep would start up, that monkey was right there hanging onto the windshield. He loved to go for jeep rides. But when we got ready to leave Oujda, we couldn't find the monkey – he must have just wandered off.

We had to carry a lot of equipment when we jumped: mortars, shells, and machine guns. Naturally, we were always looking for an easy way to get the job done. And one day we figured out how we could get out of carrying all the equipment. We visited the parachute riggers and asked them to make a harness for Beanie, and indeed they did. Now, here we are with a parachute for the jackass, so the company commander, Lieutenant Warfield, told us we had to go up and jump with Beanie to see if everything would be okay. We arranged for the jump. Beanie was a white-knuckle flyer and we all had to pitch in to push Beanie out the door. Once that mission was accomplished we went right out after him.

Everything was going great until Beanie looked down and grasped the fact that the ground was rushing up to meet him. Poor thing stiffened his legs and when he hit the ground you could hear his legs breaking. We did the most humane thing we could for him – shot him. Hindsight is wonderful. If we only knew, we would have blindfolded him so he would not be able to see the ground."[186]

A similar test was done by the 505th PIR, so probably Warfield's "experiment" was a division order. Private Darrell G. Harris of the Regimental Demolition Platoon remembered that "one night while at Kairouan, we were alerted because of a report that some German paratroopers had been dropped in the vicinity. Because of this report, I suppose, I dreamt during the night that a German soldier was just outside my tent and that I had grabbed his ankle with my own left arm, which had gone to sleep and was numb to the touch of my other hand.

"That same night, one of our guys on guard duty heard a noise in the cactus hedgerows bordering our camp, and receiving no response to his challenges, he opened fire. Of course the whole camp was alerted by the gunfire, but when we fell out, we discovered he had shot a camel which had been browsing in the area. No German paratroopers ever showed up."[187]

First Lieutenant James Goethe (left) and two other paratroopers of C Company,
either in North Africa or on Sicily. Goethe helped forming the second A Company
and later in the war commanded G Company, Courtesy: Priscilla Goethe Elledge

As Operation Husky drew near, 1st Lieutenant Stuart E. Power, the assisting S-2 (intelligence) officer, shot himself accidently in the heel by his own gun on July 8.[188] "An investigation revealed he had made a mistake," recalled 1st Lieutenant James H. Goethe of C Company. "Seems he called for the medics before he pulled the trigger."[189]

Tucker decided that this incident necessitated the reinforcement of his regimental staff, and 1st Lieutenant Fordyce Gorham, an officer who had previously served as a sergeant in the pre-war army, was transferred to the Regimental S-2 section on July 9. Gorham would at the same time remain in command of the Regimental Reconnaissance Platoon. An additional military intelligence officer, 2nd Lieutenant Jacob S. Brancato, was meanwhile attached as a prisoner of war interrogator.

"The last few days (before the invasion of Sicily) were spent in talking it over and making final checks on our equipment," recalled Pfc. John R. "Jack" Labre, a medic in D Company. "We knew the day we were going to invade and the day before I went to Mass. It was held in a cactus patch and needless to say, the boys were all eager to go. We received Holy Communion and it relieved the tension we were all under."[190]

Time had also come to inform the enlisted men and non-commissioned officers, the last ones to receive information on the operation, and only on a "need-to-know" basis: the more they knew, the more they could jeopardize the operation upon being captured and interrogated by the enemy. Harris recalled that "when we prepared to go into combat, our platoon would be split into squads and attached to the various battalions. Being in the 3rd Squad, I always went with the 3rd Battalion." During the briefing by 1st Lieutenant Carl W. Kappel, Harris learned that "our mission, as demolitionists, was to place charges on a certain bridge and be prepared to blow it in case of a German counterattack. We jumped with twenty-eight quarter-pound blocks in our demolition kits, and more explosives were to be dropped in our equipment bundles."[191]

Kouns lost an officer when he broke his leg during a parachute landing just three days before the first combat jump. "The Battalion Surgeon feared that his patient's transfer to a Base Hospital might compromise the security of our drop," recalled Kouns. "I agreed that the patient be held in bivouac until our drop. Later as a student at the Command and General Staff College, Fort Leavenworth, they described such an option as one of 'Sealing-in the marshalling area.'"[192]

The executive officer of Headquarters Company, 1st Lieutenant Elbert F. Smith, learned at the last moment that he was designated as "commander" of the motorized detachment of the 3rd Battalion that included jeeps and trucks to transport the companies on the island. Although he must have felt some disappointment in being left out for the first combat jump, it signaled at the same time the great trust that his battalion commander had in him: "When the orders came to invade Sicily, I was notified 'at the plane' by Lieutenant Colonel Kouns that I was not to go. I was assigned as the Rear Echelon Commander and the Parachute Maintenance Company.

"While in Kairouan, an engineer group that was moving out gave me boxes of motor oil and grease they could not carry. Later, I would find out why. We took the boxes with us and moved northeast, to meet ships in a port on the Mediterranean Sea."[193]

A few days later, Smith "found that one of the boxes left behind by the engineer group was full of American money—thin sheets of gold which are called gold seal bills. When I arrived in Naples, I took it to the finance officer. He counted it, said it was good money and that I didn't have to turn it in. I told him that I had taken an oath and sworn to protect all government equipment, and that money belonged to the government. I left with an official receipt."[194]

Among the waiting paratroopers of the 3rd Battalion and the air crews of the 61st Troop Carrier Group was a famous photographer who hoped to fly along to Sicily to take some pictures of the drop: Robert Capa. He asked permission to jump with Kouns' unit, but it was denied. Kouns, however, did allow him to fly as an extra passenger on board of his C-47. Disappointed but not deterred, Capa decided instead to take pictures on the ground of the paratroopers finishing their last meal before take-off.[195] One photo of Private John "Jack" M. Fowler of H Company consuming his dinner from his mess kit appeared in Collier's Magazine of September 18, 1943.[196] Another photo of Fowler appeared, along with some close-ups of other troopers and sticks of the 504th PIR inside and outside the C-47s, in the January 15, 1944 issue of Illustrated.

Both Collier's Magazine, for which Capa was working, and Illustrated featured the photos of the 3rd Battalion paratroopers. All over the United States, newspapers printed Capa's pictures for their headline stories, as the U.S. Army had collected several of his photos, which were supposed to be used exclusively for Collier's Magazine, in the Army Public Relations pool. William L. Chenery, chief editor of Collier's Magazine, was not pleased with the publication of Capa's photos in various magazines and fired him. Only through a good friend, writer Ernie Pyle, was Capa able to obtain a job as photographer for Life Magazine.[197]

To Capa, the paratroopers looked fit and bulky as bears in their heavy equipment as they attended a final briefing by Kouns before takeoff. Kouns gave them a refresher talk about the things they had to keep in mind during the jump. Capa would be one of the first American journalists—along with Jack Thompson of the *Chicago Tribune*—to witness the invasion of a part of Europe. Kouns then disclosed their objective: "Your destination is the Italian island of Sicily, and you will be the first American troops to land."[198]

Kouns created the possibility for Brigadier General Charles Keerans to accompany his battalion into action: "I had saved a parachute believing he might wish to jump from my lead plane. At the last minute, he said nothing would please him more; however, Ridgway had emphasized his importance to handle ground duties from the marshalling area in support of the drop."[199]

Utterback recalled of Kouns that "during that day the battalion C.O. was on me all day long. 'Fix up some banquet meals.' Yes, D-day was coming. All day long I had stomach cramps from that old ailment known as the G.I.s. Late in the day, tho early for supper, the outfit pulled out to the various fields and filed out to their assigned planes. As mess officer I was very busy checking to be sure that all men had been fed, including the plane guards, and that the ration for the mission had been issued. The Colonel returned to the bivouac area for the last conference with the Air Corps and picked me up. He made me take some dope for my tummy. I arrived at the plane just in time to adjust my chute and be handed my little book on *Life in Sicily*."[200]

The night of July 9, Haider recalled:

> We were all lying around on the tarmac, under the wings of the various planes we were assigned to for our jump. Lots of courageous talk was going on. We were talking about how we were going to kick some German rear ends since we felt we were well trained and prepared for the fight that lay ahead. We boldly spoke of how we would use our bayonets on those guys. There was no doubt among us that we would all be back in Africa in just a few days for some rest. Some

of us were nervous, but none of us wanted to show it. We just didn't know what to expect or what was about to happen.

We all figured we had plenty of ammo to get our job done. We were loaded down with everything we thought we would need once we got on the ground: pockets full of hand grenades, we each carried at least ten; about ten clips of bullets, each clip had eight rounds in it; two bandoliers with additional rounds, bringing each man's total to about 200 rounds of ammunition. We also carried the Soldier's Prayer Book, a non-denominational book of scripture and prayers; toilet paper and cigarettes. Topping off the equipment list was our reserve parachute and our regular or main chute.[201]

Second Lieutenant Francis W. Deignan, commanding the Machine Gun Platoon, was so engulfed in preparations that he forgot to draw a packed parachute: "There were endless details to attend in order to get my platoon ready and as a result I did not have time to pack my parachute, and took one from the reject bin which had some consequences later."[202]

Deignan's assistant platoon leader, Hanna, recalled that they would jump "at night inland from the coastal town of Gela. The main invasion forces were to hit the coast early the next morning. Our assigned mission was to block off highway intersections leading to the coast, secure a small airfield, and generally disrupt the enemy communications."[203]

Sergeant Haider, on the contrary, had no idea at all what the target would be: "None of us knew for sure where we were going to invade. We didn't find out that our target was Sicily until we were in the air. It was kept a closely guarded secret. There was no doubt, though, that something was up because they gathered up all our bayonets and sharpened them for us. Every night we were going through bayonet drill. We had been told not to load our rifles before a combat jump but to wait until after we were on the ground."[204]

The 3rd Battalion S-2 officer, 1st Lieutenant Moffatt Burriss, was well aware "this was our first combat mission – the day we had anticipated since we began training a year and a half earlier. The mission of our unit, the 3rd Battalion, was to land near the high ground about 15 miles northwest of Gela. The 505th Regiment was to land several miles north of Gela.

"As we took off and Africa fell away from us, we could feel the variety of moods. Some men were anxious, nervous, and sweating profusely, despite the chill in the night air. Others were pumped up with adrenaline and eager to engage the enemy. Still others dropped off to sleep, as if tomorrow were just another day."[205]

After the C-47s had departed from Kairouan Air Base, the rest of the 504th PIR, which remained behind, wondered what they might encounter when they should jump the next night. Would it be an easy, unopposed jump? Or would their jump be cancelled? With these thoughts and thinking about their families back home, the paratroopers drifted asleep in the cool African night.

CHAPTER 11

KOUNS AND THE MACHINE GUNNERS

Sicily

JULY 9-11, 1943

"We were to be the first group in," recalled Captain Lewis S. Frederick, Jr. of the 14th Troop Carrier Squadron, "and had a little farther to go than the others. I had the C.O. of the airborne in the ship, [Lieutenant] Colonel Charles W. Kouns, and also Robert Capa, a war correspondent who was ready to jump but was not permitted. We had an excellent crew: Co-pilot Charles E. Queale. Crew-chief John E. Reilly, Sergeant Hubert D. Green, radio operator; and 1st Lieutenant Jerry, Observer [a Dalmatian dog and mascot of the 61st TCG]. The last one to see us off was the Chaplain and we rolled off in a cloud of dust. Taking off in formation with Lieutenant Colonel Willis W. Mitchell Group Commander in the lead, we flew a tight formation on his left wing until we landed. We flew underneath him near the whitecaps so we could follow his silhouette and the spray kicked up by his props gathered on our windshields. We saw checkpoints so we knew we were on the right course.

"We saw anti-aircraft fire before reaching the coast of Sicily. We hit everything right on the nose with the Colonel doing a beautiful job taking care of us, dodging all the lighthouses and high points. We came in exactly as planned. Coming in there was anti-aircraft fire under our left wing and a lot of flares thrown up to spot us. We flew pretty close but they did not get our exact range so nobody was hit. It was mostly blind shooting in the direction of the sound.

"The Colonel picked out his DZ. We slowed down, dropping our men. The fire did not hit the men. They parachuted down as it was going over their heads. They had only about 600 feet to drop. The Colonel gave us a signal for the drop and I let Colonel Kouns and his men go. They were extremely cool and ready for any eventuality. We let them go right on the spot within a few yards of where they intended to land. About that time we got a burst of anti-aircraft fire on the tail and it shook the ship. Capa, a war correspondent, was just taking a picture. When his flash went off, I thought we were all gone. Had to throttle the left engine as it missed a few times. However, it turned out that we were not hit at all."[206]

Capa remembered that it was only during the flight that Kouns revealed their actual objective: "Well, boys, we are truly the first men of America tonight. We will be the first to land in Axis Europe. For hours and hours we will be alone. There will be enemies all around us and over our heads. We must do our best...we are headed for Sicily."[207] Capa recalled that there wasn't too much flak when the red light flashed on near the door, indicating the time had come to jump. Hunched grotesquely in their bucket seats, the paratroopers slowly raised themselves up and hooked up with the static line. Then the countdown started from the back of the plane after rapidly checking the chute of the man in front of them.

As the green light flashed on, the stick started to go out, the battalion commander first. Capa saw them jump out in a hurry, as any delay would mean a longer distance from each other on the ground. The parachutes seemed to float down "like a string of diminishing pearls."[208] Kouns was one of these "pearls." Kouns recalled:

> After several hours flying while paralleling the south coast of Sicily and still over water, the pilot gave us the red light signal. I stood the men up, hooked up, checked equipment, and stood in the door. I was a bit agitated because water was plainly visible below. After a short while the crew chief came back to the door and stated

that we had about twenty minutes more to go. To avoid confusion in the darkness I kept the men hooked up.

Around midnight, we made a right-angle turn and suddenly I saw the landfall of Sicily; however, I could not see the lake which was to be our landmark and I concluded that we had made our right-angle turn too soon. The crew chief came back again to the door and stated that the flak was light and that we should arrive over the DZ in about ten minutes. Shortly after that we got a red light and I ordered the men to stand in the door. In a few minutes the green light went on and looking back over my shoulder, I shouted "Go!" and went out. The opening shock was rough – my helmet was over my eyes and I felt as though I was being strangled or I had a malfunction. I could not tell how fast I was falling and I opened my reserve chute. Three or four of the suspension lines of the reserve chute fouled in my entrenching shovel and I spent precious seconds trying to get them free. Finally in desperation, I seized the risers of the main canopy and spreading them as far apart as I could, I unwound them so that the main canopy was normal. Directly below, I made out a very large tree and prepared for a tree landing.

As my boots brushed the topmost branches of the tree, I could see that I was being blown rapidly over it to the south and I prepared to land in open ground. Climbing up the risers, I gave a downward pull. I hit uneven ground hard facing the wind, most of my weight hitting on my left heel. My main canopy was draped over the large tree I had just passed and my reserve canopy trailed out beside me. I took out my pistol and lay very still on my back for a few moments. Overhead I could see in dim silhouette aircraft somewhat to the east flying on a northernly course. I got free from the parachute harness, checked my weapons, took out my compass and started moving on the known flight azimuth.

My landing area was crossed by several small trails, a deep gully and scattered wood. I moved from tree to tree, listening for other jumpers and enemy and I seemed to be very much alone. After moving north for about an hour, the moon disappeared and observation was greatly limited. Finally, I arrived at the top of a high hill and saw men of my stick working on our equipment bundles, with what seemed to me, and unnecessary amount of noise. I was challenged and joined the group. All of the men in my plane had not yet converged on the equipment bundles which were dropped in the middle of our stick.

In a few minutes an enlisted man from another plane joined my group and stated that he had located his stick some distance away and, having found us, would go back and bring them up. In about fifteen to twenty minutes we assembled our group which consisted of about a squad and a half, with my radio, three machine guns, several rifle grenadiers, one Tommy gun and several carbines, and held a council. One of the noncoms stated that he had seen the north-south route which we were interested in and could lead us to it.[209]

The group Kouns had assembled consisted of his runner, Pfc. Sterling E. Oberholtzer, his radio operator, Technician 5th Grade Richard D. Kelley, and Staff Sergeant Robert K. Binnix with eleven men from the Machine Gun Platoon. There had been also Lieutenant Francis Deignan—who had acted as jumpmaster—and five other paratroopers in Binnix's plane, but they had not been encountered yet. Kouns had landed without his battalion staff officers, and thus far, there was no trace from any of his rifle companies. Where was his battalion?

The assigned mission of the Machine Gun Platoon was to block a specific road east of Niscemi. It was decided to carry out this mission even though their force was much smaller than anticipated. Kouns continued:

> We moved out in column, retracing the exact route which I had covered in order to reach the bundles and it was obvious that the road the enlisted man had spoken of was not the right road. The time had passed very quickly and I was desperate to get to our objective and get dug in before daylight so I elected to move on trails instead of cross-country for our progress was too slow over the rough terrain.

> Fortunately in the group was one Italian interpreter [- Private Paul D. Papa]. On arriving in the vicinity of the first house in the area, I had the men lie down, except two which covered the house. After destroying the telephone line leading into the house, the interpreter knocked on the door and called the occupants and asked them how to get to Niscemi. The route indicated was a small trail bearing north and west a short distance from the house.

> We moved in 1 column, I leading with the interpreter by my side. A few minutes later we saw pedestrians on the trail and melted into the shadows. There were several civilians moving south and we were undetected. Thereafter, we moved north on the indicated trail and soon came upon another house just off the trail and the interpreter again sought information from the sleeping occupants. They verified that we were headed in the right direction for Niscemi and as we moved a little further along, the interpreter thought he saw an enemy tank parked beside a building. His fears proved to be groundless and we moved on until we came to

a fork in the trails in which there were three or four routes which could be taken. I elected to take what appeared to be the most travelled trail because it was north and west.

After considerable marching, there was a general complaint in the group that they were overburdened and would have to rest. Reluctantly, I allowed a few minutes for the men to catch their breath. At this time I discovered two of the machine guns were not with my column. I concluded that the gunners had lagged behind with their heavy loads of ammunition and guns and had taken the wrong trail or had been picked off in ambush.

We continued our march finally coming out on an east-west, well-travelled, secondary road, high walled on both sides. A few yards west on this road I discovered an opening which led us into a meadow. Daylight would catch us soon in the open. If my calculations were correct, we were on the outskirts of Niscemi close to our objective so I decided to stop and dig-in. Leaving a rifle grenadier on the road to stop any traffic that might move, we entered this meadow and sat down for a few moments to rest.

I got the non-commissioned officers together and explained to them that I was not sure where we were or we could go back and try to locate the rest of our Battalion. The men were unanimous in their decision to remain where they were and fight. On the south side of the road was a hill-mass on which I wished to dig in before daylight. I sent a scout to explore this hill-mass. He came back and stated that all was quiet and there was a house on top of the hill. Taking two men and the interpreter to the house, the interpreter knocked and asked for admittance. The occupants stated they were poor people and asked us to go away. Then we ordered the occupants if they didn't open up in a couple of minutes we were going to come in shooting. Shortly afterwards an old man opened the door. We gained admittance without difficulty and I had the rest of the men come up except for the rifle grenadier who was to guard the road.

The first light was barely visible at this time. I instructed the men to dig in on the west slope of the hill along the fire-crest near the swamp which crossed the east-west road. With the help of the interpreter, I tried to determine our location. According to the map, it seemed that we were in the vicinity of Caltagirone. I attempted to get radio communication with friendly troops with no success.

As the morning progressed, one of my men came in from his foxhole and stated that he saw a civilian shooting birds in the vicinity and asked if he could "bump him off." I asked him if the civilian had seen him and he said, "No" so I told him not to kill the man unless he was discovered. A little later, one of my soldiers brought in a civilian who was very quick to inform us that he was a retired soldier of the Italian Army and produced his discharge papers to prove it. We could get no useful information from him and we held him as hostage against his will.

Then the old man who owned the house stated that on the previous day the Germans had emplaced a heavy machine gun higher up on the ridge we were defending but had removed it. Reconnaissance of the area proved his statement.

Shortly after bright daylight, five or six tanks were seen north and west of our position about 1500 yards moving on a road running parallel to our front. I presumed this was the Gela-Niscemi road which was our mission to cut. The sound of traffic could be heard on a road at a greater range which led me to believe that we were close to the road fork branching south and south-west out of Niscemi. Because of the reported German machine gun on the crest the day before and the tank traffic to the west, I assumed that we were very close to a large armored force assembly area.

With the radio [of Technician 5th Grade Richard Kelley] ineffective, I decided to send a runner south to where I expected my command post would be located. I secured a volunteer [- Pfc. Sterling Oberholtzer], armed with a carbine, for I wished to keep intact my small force armed with rifles and I explained to the soldier that I was sending him on a dangerous mission which he could accomplish in one or two ways. First, by going down the supposed Gela-Niscemi road where the tank traffic was moving. Second, by moving overland cross country along the rail we had just travelled on. He elected to take the cross-country road. I had the interpreter explain to the owner of the house that he was to hitch up his mule cart and convey the soldier as far as he wanted to go. He was to drop the soldier and return to the house and if he made any mistakes he would be shot. The soldier was concealed in the small cart under a pile of straw and hauled away from the house.

Soon the cart driver returned and stated that the soldier had left him back in the woods. Shortly afterwards, I set the discharged Italian soldier at work digging me a foxhole close to the machine gun dug in on the hill. I then took up a position in the stable adjacent to the house to cover any attack that might be made on the house which I was using as an observation post. I also instructed the old man that if anything happened he was to lie down flat on the floor and keep quiet.

A little later, [2nd] Lieutenant [James C.] Ott of my Battalion reported to me in the stable and stated that my runner [Pfc. Oberholtzer], looking for my command post to the south, had told him where I was and I was cut-off. He stated that he had come to help me and that he had eight men back in the hills some distance without arms. They had not been able to find their equipment bundles in the darkness.

About that time, additional tanks were seen moving south on the supposed Gela-Niscemi road. Lieutenant Ott pointed to the tanks and asked if I saw them. Then he said, "Sir, I want your permission to stop those tanks. We may get bumped off but that is our mission to stop those tanks." I said "Alright, you can go. Let me know what happens and we will cover you with fire from this hill." The lieutenant went back to get his men and what arms we could spare.

During his absence several of the isolated paratroopers of my Battalion came up to my observation post, stated that they were lost and asked if they could join my group. One of these soldiers carried a bazooka and two rounds of ammunition. Lieutenant Ott took this man and several others and moved west towards the tank traffic.

As the radio continued to be useless, I then crawled into my previously prepared foxhole. About this time

I began to feel uneasy about our left flank and I sent a Tommy gunner some distance to the left of our small strongpoint and ordered him to let nothing pass.

Shortly afterwards, I heard the explosion of a bazooka rocket explode six or eight hundred yards to our front accompanied with large clouds of black smoke. A few seconds later, I heard a second explosion of a bazooka rocket explode and looking towards this smoke at a greater range across the supposed Gela-Niscemi road, I saw about a platoon of German soldiers grouped closely together under a tree. A little to the west and on the supposed Gela-Niscemi road two black scout scars were parked and some distance west of the scout cars and huddled together on the road was another platoon of German soldiers. I ordered the machine gunners to let them have it and traversing and searching they covered the visible enemy with long bursts of fire. Being the only one with field glasses and the range being great, I instructed as to what targets to fire on. I am sure we got quite a few of the Germans in the road but some managed to crawl away.

At a great range to the north I could hear spasmodic rifle fire [– probably of G Company –] and I assumed my Battalion was committed to action in small groups scattered all over the countryside. About this time the enemy fire became intense and I tossed my field glasses over to the machine gunners and instructed them to pick their own targets. We fought for some time and suddenly Corporal [Frederick J.] Ferguson, my machine gunner, was hit and slumped over the gun. I asked him if he was hurt badly and he seemed somewhat dazed.

About this time a runner from Lieutenant Ott crawled up to my foxhole and stated that Lieutenant Ott had just destroyed two German motor lorries, had killed a number of high-ranking Germans officers and that the Germans were awfully mad. He also said that there were too many of them for us and we would have to get out. I asked the runner where Lieutenant Ott was and he pointed back to the southeast.

I told the runner that we were dug in where we were, we were killing the enemy and that we could not leave. We had obtained complete tactical surprise and I reasoned that the enemy would have no immediate knowledge of our strength and disposition. Also it seemed that we might be supporting mutually other friendly troops. I told Lieutenant Ott's runner to take the radio and get out and try to get back to Lieutenant Ott.

Soon we were getting considerable fire from automatic weapons. Our tracers in the machine gun plus the muzzle-blast and long bursts had identified our position. I checked the machine gun ammunition and found we had about a belt left. I decided that we would withdraw after a little as my plan was to move the machine gun to the rear and cover the withdrawal of the riflemen from my right. I asked Corporal Ferguson if he thought he could crawl out from his position and get behind the house and that I would meet him there. I instructed the machine gunner to stay with his gun for about three minutes so that Corporal Ferguson could get out and then he was to move straight to the rear.

Corporal Ferguson and I met behind the house in the cover of a small bluff just below the crest and I started to dress his wound. We must have been spotted for we were taken under fire and pinned down. I told the Corporal that we would have to get out of that spot and for him to follow me. By crawling and running, hitting the ground and rolling we managed to elude many bursts of machine gun fire. Corporal Ferguson fatigued quickly and said he didn't think he could make it, but I encouraged him to follow me at each rush.

A short distance from the position on an adjacent crest was an armored vehicle which probably had us in their sights. We moved back a little distance further behind another house. I removed a shell from Corporal Ferguson's elbow and gave him first-aid. Then I gave him my pistol and I took my carbine, guarding one side of the house and he the other. I presumed we would be overrun and that we would exact the highest toll possible. There was considerable smoke and confusion due to a surrounding stubble field being on fire. The machine gunner did not appear.[210]

Corporal Frederick Ferguson of the 3rd Battalion Machine Gun Platoon was wounded and captured while fighting with Lieutenant Colonel Charles Kouns on Sicily. Courtesy: Margaret Ferguson Holland

Kouns' runner, Oberholtzer, recalled that it was at this moment that Private Paul D. Papa was ordered to investigate an objective behind some trees, but he refused to do so. Oberholtzer then volunteered in his place, and they came to a road where they saw a German sentry, probably standing there to prevent the Americans from approaching a column of Tiger Tanks. They called out to the German to surrender, but he resisted and was subsequently shot by the paratroopers. A short firefight broke out in which Papa took off and was not seen again. Records show that he wasn't captured, so he must have joined friendly forces at some point.[211]

Further along the road, they encountered a German tank and German infantry, most likely from the 2nd Company 504th Schwere Panzer-Abteilung, which we will encounter again in other chapters. Kouns led the men to a house, which looked deserted, but as they entered, there were three Italian civilians inside. Oberholtzer recalled that two of them were permitted to leave; the other was kept as a hostage. Binnix, who remembered that they had left their position at the house on the hill around 1200 hours, was also with them.

Kouns continued

> After a short interval half a dozen or so men withdrew from our strongpoint and joined us and we took refuge in a thick-walled stone house. I decided that with the small group and the limited ammunition (enough for one more sortie) that our best bet would be to try to hide out until darkness and then rejoin any other elements of the Battalion we might find. I kept as hostage in this house one Italian civilian. One man was slightly shot-up, the remainder of the group (four or five) was somewhat dazed and extremely fatigued. I took guard in a doorway of the house and a short while later an Italian patrol surrounded the house. I forced our civilian hostage out for we could not cover him and fight too.

Two live grenades were thrown in with no damage. We threw out several grenades and began a new fire-fight, which went on for sometime until one by one my soldiers complained that their weapons were jammed. My carbine too had jammed and I presumed this was from dragging them in the dirt in the get-away from our first position. However, I was able to force-load with some difficulty. One of my soldiers armed with a '03 rifle and bayonet suggested that we rush the enemy by leaving the house but this not seem feasible.

A short time after that I was struck in the shoulder with what I believe was a concussion grenade and I didn't remember anything until I came to and saw all the men quiet except the man with the '03 rifle who was waving a white flag on his bayonet in the doorway. Intense fire was coming in the house and ricocheting about the walls. The soldier with the white flag then discharged his weapon through the doorway. A wooden shutter covering an iron grill window in the room we occupied was blown off and it seemed as if the next grenade that could be thrown in the window would wipe us all out. I took the soldier's rifle and attached a pillow-case to it and jammed it in the grillwork. I turned to the soldiers and told them I was going out first with my hands up.[212]

Binnix said that "at 1700 hours were surrounded by Italians under a German officer. After withstanding heavy fire (...) were forced to surrender."[213] After the war, Binnix told his platoon leader, Lieutenant Deignan, that he believed they could have held out much longer.[214] It is questionable whether his view is fair, considering the fact that he carried far less responsibility than Kouns and there had been no radio contact at all with other groups. Besides, in a March 1944 interview with *The Bayonet* newspaper in Fort Benning, Binnix stated that their group expended virtually all its ammunition and was then forced to surrender. [215]

Oberholtzer recalled that the Germans and Italians stripped their prisoners to the waist and thoroughly searched them. All military equipment was taken from them, and they were marched to Niscemi.[216]

Kouns recalled:

> We were taken prisoners by about a platoon and marched down the east-west road west towards where I had seen the black smoke from the two bazooka rockets. This road could be classed as a secondary road. The road lay in a deep cut, the shoulders were higher than our heads, and it would have been impossible to turn a heavy tank around.
>
> Two German soldiers appeared from the brush and made motions with their rifle to murder the prisoners. The Italian soldiers thereupon threw two contact grenades at the Germans who made a hasty retreat. Nearby on the road lay one dead German officer. Shortly beyond the swamp, which I had previously covered with rifle grenadiers, we came upon the tail-end column of a German armored column of heavy tanks. In the last tank in the column was a lone German soldier who menaced a bayonet at the prisoners as they marched by.
>
> After passing six or eight abandoned heavy tanks hub-to-hub we came to the head of the column where lay in ruins two motor lorries completely burned out. I presumed this was the damage that Lieutenant Ott had done with his patrol earlier in the day. A few hundred yards further we were taken off the road into an Italian garrison heavily wired in.

It was this garrison that Lieutenant [Francis] Deignan of my Battalion was brought in on a stretcher, his head swathed in bloody bandages. We were loaded onto a lorry and taken into the town, which I believed was Caltagirone [Niscemi], about a ten or fifteen minute drive, and locked up in civilian jail. Lieutenant Deignan presumably was taken to a hospital.

The next morning an Italian officer took me to a window in the jail building and from a small balcony pointed out a large green valley to the south in which many tanks were engaged. Being the only officer present, some distance further inland, in what I believe was the town of [Piazza] Armerina.[217]

This time Kouns was taken before the Italian XVI Corps Commander, *Generale di Corpo d'armata* Carlo Rossi, for interrogation. He recalled, "He wanted to know my unit. I told him I was a Prisoner of War and could tell him only my name, my rank and serial number. He smiled and sent me off to a nearby garrison where I was locked up for several days and then moved to Capua, Italy. Along the roads the Germans were using U.S. Paratroopers they had captured as work details to repair bombed-out roads. The combat jump in Sicily injured my left heel temporarily but I did not feel it noticeably until after my capture. The grenade wound in my left shoulder was superficial."[218]

In the last chapter, the prisoners of war stories of Binnix, Kouns, and Oberholtzer will be recounted. It will be remembered that they had seen Lieutenant Deignan wounded on a stretcher at Niscemi. For Deignan, his first combat jump proved to be more chaotic than he had expected. He said:

The flight from Africa took approximately eight hours, I believe, and being very tired I prepared to get some sleep, instructing my runner to wake me one hour from the drop zone. Being nervous he forgot and I woke to find the red light on. I quickly struggled into my equipment and on standing in the door, I was the jump master. (...)

I had a fine opening, and a fine landing. However it developed that there wasn't anyone else on the ground and no other planes flew overhead. I was beginning to wonder if the invasion had been called off. Later I was to discover that I had landed on the edge of the escarpment and the rest of the stick and battalion had dropped far below in the valley.

Not realizing at the time that I was some five miles behind the German-Italian lines I decided to continue on with the mission hoping something would develop on the way. After about one hour I suddenly came across a 90mm AA gun. These guns were rare and valuable in that theatre and I thought I must have walked through its local protection. I hit the ground and thought, "What to do?" I knew the rest of the 504th were coming in the next morning and if they flew near this gun there would be hell to pay, so I decided to attack it and try to put it out of commission. I slung my carbine and pulled pins on two grenades to drop one in the pit and then leap into the pit and try to put one into the gun's breech.

On crawling closer I was much relieved to discover it was a dummy emplacement, but now I had two live grenades in my hands and my fingers were becoming cramped. If I exploded them in the pit it would alert the enemy. Finally, I maneuvered them under some flat rocks making booby traps and continued on with the mission, which was to proceed some five miles from the drop zone and either secure or blow some bridges that were there to keep the tanks from the

Hermann Goering Division from coming down to the beach the next day.

When dawn began to break I found myself in completely open country so I decided it best to capture a house that I could fight out of if necessary and soon did. On approach I heard voices and discovered two soldiers on guard duty at the house. I captured and disarmed them and used them to gain entry. Inside were a few old men, women and children. We settled down to wait for darkness, however for the next few hours soldiers in twos and threes kept returning to the house. I would let them in, disarm them and herd them into the large front room. I had apparently captured some small kind of small headquarters and these men were out on patrol. Soon I had some fifteen prisoners.

About 2100 hours some of the children began to cry. One of the women pointed to the water pump and indicated the kids needed water. I realized there was a chance she would run off if let out, but if the children kept crying someone would come to investigate. I let her out and she ran off. I prepared for trouble. It was a fine house to defend: on a slight rise, clear fields of fire, heavy stone construction with slate roof, bars and wooden shutters on the windows.

In about an hour the enemy arrived and began firing and advancing on all four sides. I rushed from window to window thinking, "This is like some crazy Western movie." We fought a long time with the troops moving closer and closer until they were at the walls and on the roof. They would pop up, fire through the window and I would fire out. Those on the roof were trying to chop through. By this time my carbine, a lousy infantry weapon, was so hot that each time I would fire the bolt would freeze home and I would have to kick it free with my heavy boot. It being very short when I would do this it was pointing right at my chest and I thought, "I am going to end this war shooting myself?"

Of course the prisoners whom I had failed to tie up observed all of this and soon rushed me and we began a great rolling fight on the floor. The troops outside used this to break in the door and rushed in. Somehow I managed to break free of the pile of bodies, but this exposed my head and someone shattered a rifle across my skull and the last thing I remembered were pieces of the rifle flying about.

When I regained consciousness the troops, who were Germans, took me outside to march away. The path was lined with women who all had long sharpened grape arbour stakes and they tried to jab out my eyes. The Germans, who hated Italians, drove them off with rifle butts, and took me to be interrogated. However sometime later I began to go blind so they took me to a hospital, which was a castle on a high ground nearby. By nightfall I was completely blind.[219]

On July 14, Deignan's vision slowly returned, and he began to plan his escape. His jaw and legs had been smashed in the fight, so he saved most of his food ration each day. From the balcony, Deignan spotted two cruisers down in Gela harbor about twelve miles away. He also noticed Tigers below:

...hidden in the castle hospital grounds and every once in a while they would clank out and fire down the valley, then retreat back behind the hospital walls. However the U.S. Navy had parachuted some gunnery observers to the high ground behind the hospital and they began to call in the Navy gunfire. Two huge Tiger tanks were hurled upside down and the rest clanked away.

The heavy 6-inch shelling continued and soon the hospital was filled with screaming civilians for the shells were hitting into the tile roofs of the town houses and the wounded looked like they had been run through a giant meat grinder. I quietly removed the Stars and Stripes from my jump jacket.

The shelling finally stopped and I found the doctor in charge of the hospital and told him I was taking over and he was to have all the arms brought to me. Italian hospital personnel were armed. He did and also brought an Air Force lieutenant who had been a patient there too. We destroyed the arms in case we had to retreat from a German counterattack.

About an hour later heavy fighting broke out in the village [of Niscemi] below the castle and I could see troops moving in. I turned the hospital over to the lieutenant and went to join the fight. Much to my surprise it was the 505th Parachute Infantry Regiment and I ran into a Captain Edwin Sayre who was engaged in house to house fighting. I joined up with him and he got me an M-1 rifle and we proceeded to clean up the houses and streets. However, we had only gone a few blocks when I found I was wounded much more severely than I thought, both my head wound and legs gave out. Captain Sayre propped me in a doorway and said he would be back when he could. He did and I was loaded onto a jeep and brought down to an evacuation station on the coast, loaded onto a ship and ended up in the 29th Station Hospital in Algiers.[220]

Deignan's assistant platoon leader, Lieutenant Roy M. Hanna, was more fortunate:

We had already received the red light indicating that we were 10 minutes before jump time. I was the jumpmaster, standing in the open door of the plane with my men standing up behind me ready to jump. And, as any dummy should have anticipated, the enemy anti-aircraft guns began firing as we approached the coast. I helplessly stood in the door watching our planes full of paratroopers being shot down and watching tracers and flak going all around us. As far as I know, nothing hit our plane.[221]

At this time, I didn't realize that between each tracer there was a stream of invisible bullets. A few minutes later, the green light came on, and I took my eleven machine gunners out the door. It was the highest jump I ever made – well over 2000 feet. I watched as the 400-pound machine guns and ammunition bundle, with their 24-foot chutes, went directly down, while I – with my 200 pounds, including my equipment and my 28-foot chute – floated around in the night sky. I did watch the blue lights attached to our guns and ammo and got a general idea where they landed.

I finally came down in an olive tree – my first tree landing. After cutting myself and my Tommy gun loose (glad to have the switch blade in my jumpsuit), I dropped about two feet to the ground. The only sound on this beautiful moonlit night was a dog barking about a mile or two away. I started walking in the direction of the equipment and then heard a meek voice saying, "George," and I answered, "Marshall" – our passwords for the mission. "Man, am I glad to see you," the soldier said. "I can't get this M-1 together."[222]

The strange part here was that he wasn't one of the men from my plane; he was a new replacement that joined H Company in Africa. I put his gun together, put a shell in the chamber, and sent him to try to collect my men while I went to look for our machine guns that were dropped separately from the belly of the airplane (being heavier and having smaller parachutes the guns probably dropped straight down). A short time later I heard one shot, the only one I heard that night.[223]

Shortly, I was halted by my runner, Private [Winford H.] Salter. He immediately asked if I came through there a few minutes earlier. As it turned out, our stranger, when challenged, fired one shot and took off for the hills. We never heard from him again.[224]

Private Winford H. Salter reported he had found six other members of their stick, plus two paratroopers of I Company. The machine guns, however, were all missing. Hanna continued:

After trying unsuccessfully to locate the rest of my original eleven men, I led my new combat team up a rather large hill. Because we had no idea where we were and heard no gunfire to direct us, we all just stretched out on the ground and took a nap. I must have forgotten my previous training, because I didn't establish an outpost or make any other security arrangements.

At dawn, we heard some shooting, and all nine of us grabbed our equipment and went to investigate. We came to a small olive grove and joined two paratroopers (I believe from H Company) who were flanking a German barracks. They told me a couple of their buddies were attacking the other side. As a German machine gunner began sweeping the area with fire, I ended up behind a tree about 10 inches in diameter, directly behind two men firing from a prone position. As the machine gun strafed the area, one of the prone men was shot in the side of the neck and the other through the thigh.

Before the machine gun again swept our way, I jumped over a hedge, ran opposite the machine gun, which I couldn't see, and lobbed a hand grenade in that direction. I was either lucky enough to make a direct hit or I scared the Germans into running. In any case, the machine gun quit firing. At this point, I looked through a broken-down section of a stone fence and saw many German soldiers running from the barracks.[225]

Hanna made his way back to the hedgerow and collected his nine men. They withdrew and at a later moment ran into an officer and nine enlisted men of the 505th PIR. He said:

A first lieutenant (a mess officer, I believe) outranked me and so was in command. He decided we would cross a field about a mile wide and set up a defensive position in a large stone building located at the bottom of a hill. And, like trained soldiers, we started across the field in a skirmish line, with me on the extreme right flank.

We hadn't gone far before we started drawing machine gun fire – my first experience with a "buzz" [sound of passing bullets] and a "snap" [bullets hitting an object].

Two other men and I jumped into a ditch that ran all the way to our proposed defensive position. One of the men was my platoon sergeant, Sergeant [Alvin L.] Yocum, and the other a bazooka man from the 505th with a bazooka and three rounds of ammunition. The three of us stayed in the ditch all the way to the proposed defensive position. I lugged the bazooka ammo for the 505th man, but when we arrived at our destination, I found he had left his bazooka behind. We waited for some time, but no one else showed up.

We investigated the stone building and found it to be a large Italian-style home, with many people gathered there. None spoke English. The three of us climbed the hill, and, from there, we could see Gela. After wandering around for two and a half days from the time we landed, we got back to where Colonel Tucker was trying to reorganize the badly scattered 504th. I was the senior commander [of the 3rd Battalion] for a short time.[226]

Back in the United States, Mrs. Marion Putnam Kouns had a thrilling novel experience as she walked in Irvington, New York, on Monday morning and glanced at the front page of a New York newspaper. She saw on the first page a picture of her husband with a group of paratroopers on a transport plane, which the caption said was involved in the invasion of Sicily. The date of the newspaper was July 14, just five days after the drop had taken place. The picture by Capa had been wired in and was not very clear, but she recognized her husband's face right away.

Marion Kouns was startled and felt both proud and worried; her husband was leading one of the finest paratrooper battalions into battle.[227] Seeing his picture kind of bridged the long distance of thousands of miles from the island of Sicily. The question was what happened to his battalion during this invasion? Were they dropped on their target, or were they scattered? She was luckily unaware of the fact that Lieutenant Colonel Kouns and part of his battalion, especially G Company, had landed almost right on top of the Hermann Goering Panzer Division.

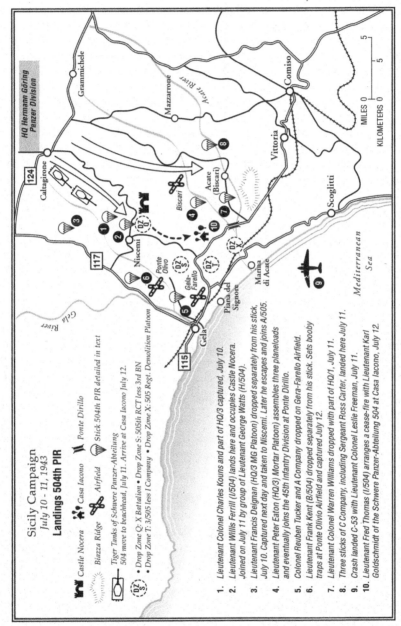

Sicily Campaign
July 10 - 11, 1943
Landings 504th PIR

Castle Nocera   Casa Iacono   Ponte Dirillo
Biazza Ridge   Airfield

Tiger Tanks of Schwere Panzer-Abteilung
504 move to beachhead, July 11. Arrive at Casa Iacono July 12.

• Drop Zone Q: X Battalion • Drop Zone S: 505th RCT less 3rd BN
• Drop Zone T: 3/505 less I Company • Drop Zone X: 505 Regt. Demolition Platoon

HQ Hermann Göring
Panzer Division

Operation Husky

1. Lieutenant Colonel Charles Kouns and part of HQ/3 captured, July 10.

2. Lieutenant Willis Ferrill (I/504) lands here and occupies Castle Nocera.
   Joined on July 11 by group of Lieutenant George Watts (H/504).

3. Lieutenant Francis Deignan (HQ/3 MG Platoon) dropped separately from his stick,
   July 10. Captured next day and taken to Niscemi. Later he escapes and joins A/505.

4. Lieutenant Peter Eaton (HQ/3 Mortar Platoon) assembles three planeloads
   and eventually joins the 45th Infantry Division at Ponte Dirillo.

5. Colonel Reuben Tucker and A Company dropped on Gera-Farello Airfield.

6. Lieutenant Frank Kent (B/504) dropped separately from his stick. Sets booby
   traps at Ponte Olivio Airfield and captured July 12.

7. Lieutenant Colonel Warren Williams dropped with part of HQ/1, July 11.

8. Three sticks of C Company, including Sergeant Ross Carter, landed here July 11.

9. Crash landed C-53 with Lieutenant Colonel Leslie Freeman, July 11.

10. Lieutenant Fred Thomas (I/504) arranges a cease-fire with Lieutenant Karl
    Goldschmidt of the Schwere Panzer-Abteilung 504 at Casa Iacono, July 12.

CHAPTER 12

SAGA OF HQ AND G COMPANIES

Sicily

JULY 9-11, 1943

For nearly eighty years, a myth existed about what happened to the planeload of Captain Herbert C. Kaufman, the 3rd Battalion S-3 Officer. Kaufman was standing at the door of the C-47 as it approached the shore of Sicily. Enemy flak guns opened fire, and suddenly, a piece of shrapnel tore through his throat, supposedly causing him to fall out of the plane. His stick of paratroopers, thinking it was time to jump, followed him out the door. This story was believed by many veterans of the 3rd Battalion. However, it was based on hearsay.

"I was assigned a plane with Captain Kaufman as jump master," remembered 1st Lieutenant Thomas E. Utterback. Kaufman would jump first, followed by Technician 5th Grade Roland K. Manley, 1st Lieutenant John S. Messina (the Headquarters Company commander), 1st Sergeant Albin S. Topczewski, then Utterback, a cook, Sergeant Carlo J. Pilla, Technician 5th Grade Myron F. Labinsky, and finally medical corpsmen. Flying not far from them was the plane carrying Major William R. Beall and the battalion surgeon.

Utterback continued:

> Between Kaufman and Manley was a large bundle
> of medical equipment that was to be pushed out the
> door. I don't remember much of the ride over. The

dope had gotten in its work and I was very sleepy. I remember Captain Kaufman pointing out Malta, and since we were flying just above the waves the going got rather rough. A queer feeling, and I just made the relief bucket in the rear of the plane. It was getting dark but much too light to suit us. The Captain's orderly pointed to a balloon flare to our left and yelled, "Captain, the bastards done see us!" It suddenly dawned on me that we might get shot at. Then we were over Sicily and anxiously searching the landscape for landmarks. The sky became lit up with star shells and rows of tracer shells. Knowing that tracers were only one round per 15-20 rounds in firing, you realized that a lot of stuff was being thrown up at you.

As we approached the DZ the order was given (red light) to stand up and hook up. Just then all hell broke loose. Apparently an 88 (remember the 88 battery?) was working on us. The plane was suddenly thrown into a steep dive. This was enough to throw us all down into the bottom of the plane. Cordite smoke was so thick you could hardly breathe. I thought we had been hit and were going down. (There I found it's not too hard to die if you once accept it.) Then the plane straightened out and we managed to get up and untangle. Looking out the window we saw only water. We had gone back out over the Mediterranean Sea.

The red light (warning) was still on. The plane slowed and the green light (jump) came on. There was no anti-aircraft fire, and we were out off-shore. Kaufman and Manley struggled to push the medical bundle out the door. After they went out, we followed. If Captain Kaufman had a shrapnel wound in the neck he got it over the DZ in the first pass and had said nothing about it.

I was carrying an assembly light, one of these crazy kind that blinks and you can't shut off. I thought it best to hold this against my leg so it wouldn't show so much. Below, a warm reception awaited us. One fortified building had several machine guns throwing tracer around until it looked like you were landing within the red ribs of an umbrella. Couldn't do much about that, but was worrying about hitting that blacktop road. Just then a wave splashed over that "blacktop" and I dropped the "flasher" to climb the riser almost to the silk in order to stay out of the water. That blacktop road was a coral rock seacoast. I was slicing so much that I hit the ground very hard, and lost the blinker light and my helmet. It was a mad scramble to get out of my harness, find my helmet, and get that blinker light turned upside down. And all the time the machine guns chattered merrily along. I had (...) landed between the defensive barb-wire and the water, right beside a pillbox built into the barb-wire line.

The parachute harness was of the old style; it required undoing a buckle in order to get out of it. Excitement, tension, and fatigue ruled and I could not undo the buckle. I took out my parachute knife and cut myself out of the harness. The only cover was where a workman had dumped a load of dirt, so I got behind that. Then two soldiers approached: the two communication sergeants, [Sergeant] Pilla and [Corporal] Labinsky. They had also landed inside the wire. There was no fire coming out of the pillbox. As a matter of fact, it was very quiet. Fortunately, Pilla was a wire-man and had a pair of lineman pliers. While I watched behind, those two cut our way through the barb-wire entanglement and we got into a bomb crater. Apparently, some Allied bomber had tried to take out the pillbox earlier and fortunately had missed.

It would be known later that we had been dropped at the edge of the small seaside village of Marzamemi with the city of Pachino visible inland up on a hill. I had been heavily doped with morphine to combat a bad case of dysentery before the drop. Because of this, I think I actually had slept on the plane en route to Sicily. Being safely down in a shell hole on the ground felt good. Pilla and I were looking down on the pillbox and quietly discussing whether a hand grenade thrown at night left a trail of fire (light) when Pilla looked around and said, "That damn Polack Labinsky is a grudge fighter and he is gone. I had better go find him."

Left by myself, so help me, I must have taken another nap. I was awakened when a squad of Italian soldiers filed by me and entered the pillbox. They must have been the assigned crew, and were up in the village when we dropped. Shortly after that, a sticky grenade hit the side of the pillbox and its flare lit up the whole area. A boatload of British commandos rushed the pillbox and rapidly eliminated the Italian crew. Thank goodness we hadn't considered capturing that thing, or we very easily could have been eliminated instead of the Italians. When this was over, the British started throwing big stuff along the shore, apparently to not only take out shore defense, but to cut the barbed wire. It started coming in down by the village and progressed in my direction. It advanced to the point where one more round would have hit where I was. Again, you can cross the bar, but that last round never came.

Shortly after the bombardment, the British landing force stormed ashore and into the grape vineyard. It became obvious to me that it was no time to stand up and get acquainted, since every time I looked up some Limey poked a rifle in my direction. Finally, I saw a medical corpsman and yelled "Medic!" and he came running over pulling at his first aid kit. I stood up by him and explained the situation and asked to be taken to his commanding officer. He took me to a British captain in a house by the vineyard. The officer had no weapon, but was popping a riding crop. He conceded that they had two paratroopers over in the barn. There I found Pilla and Labinsky, both knocked out and terribly shot up.

I roamed the troop area and found one of our medics between the barbed wire and the grape vineyard. The medic himself had a broken leg. He had splinted it with a stick and then knocked himself out with the morphine which was strapped to our ankles in our first-aid pack. I found my cook (the sixth man out of the plane) still in the water by the beach. He hadn't sliced his chute, and had gone in the drink. His legs were horribly scraped by being dragged up and down by the tide. He was still in his chute, but was still alive.

The British attack in waves, which are given target destinations. The first wave went to the railroad tracks, and the second wave went to the highway. I got among the third wave going up a hill. There I found [Sergeant-Major Herbert C.] Carney who had been captured by the Italians and released by the British. A bullet had come close enough to take both buttons off the neck of his jump jacket. We also met one of our GIs who had landed in an artillery battery area and had heaved a grenade into the area. (I don't remember hearing this battery firing a single round; he must have boogered the whole outfit).

As I roamed the battlefield in the middle of the afternoon, I was challenged by a Limey soldier with the password "George Marshall," and I counter-signed with "Kill It-alians". He quickly had a rifle barrel in my stomach—since the British say "Eye-talians," my answer didn't work. So, with the barrel in my back, he paraded me all over the battlefield. Finally, an Intelligence Sergeant declared me a bona fide officer in the U.S. Army. I then turned and demanded a salute from my barrel-wielding persecutor. I got it.

Of the three planes (instead of 10) that I saw as I went out the door (each plane held 18 men which meant 54 men had jumped), I collected 21 men. As senior officer, I reported them to the British for ration and duty. They were supposed to return us to our unit as soon as possible, but we were 60 miles from where we were supposed to be. We made the most of it. The ration given us by the British was a gunny sack with rice in one end and coarse sugar in the other, one tin of Bully beef, and a tin of crackers. For 21 men, it hardly was a feast.[228]

First Lieutenant Thomas Utterback of the 3rd Battalion was among the fortunate ones in his plane to survive the landing on Sicily. He later commanded Headquarters Company in the Salerno Campaign. Courtesy: Laurie Utterback

Unknown to Utterback, 1st Sergeant Topczewski landed in shallow water and broke his legs.[229] Messina jumped a little ahead of him and sadly drowned along with Manley and Kaufman. Messina, a graduate of Rhode Island State College, had trained his company for many months. He lost his life without the opportunity to see how his paratroopers proved how valuable his leadership had been.[230]

Lieutenant Utterback was eventually sent on a ship back to North Africa. He said, "That night the *Luftwaffe* paid us a visit in strength, and dirt was flying everywhere. Between each visit I added another foot to the depth of my hole. One night we were loaded onto a boat full of prisoners, as guards, and left the island behind for Tripoli."[231]

The 3rd Battalion S-2 Officer, 1st Lieutenant Moffatt Burriss, recalled that

> ...just as we reached the coast of Sicily, we ran into extremely heavy antiaircraft fire. The nervous guys sweated more profusely, the gung-ho types quieted down, and the sleepers woke up. We saw bursts of smoke all around us and heard the explosions. As a defensive maneuver, the formation split up. Our plane banked eastward instead of westward, and suddenly the red light came on. That meant ten minutes until jump time. I gave the order, "Stand up and hook up."

> Then, only a minute later, the green light flashed. I hadn't even given the command to check equipment, which was normal procedure, but we had no time. The green light meant that we were over the target area. If we didn't jump immediately, we would be too far away to carry out our mission. "Go!" I shouted.

> "Hell, I'm not even hooked up!" someone in the back shouted.

> Ordinarily, it took ten seconds for the entire stick of seventeen men to bail out the door. Because we

had no real warning, however, it took us longer. As I
jumped, I knew that my men would be scattered over
a very wide area, rather than bunched together. That
would make reunion more difficult and would jeopardize the mission. (I later learned that three men
couldn't jump because they were over water. One,
Lieutenant [Herbert] "Rosie" Rosenthal, made the
pilot fly back over the jump area, but they still landed
15 miles from the rest of us.)

As soon as my chute opened, I looked around. It was a
beautiful moonlit night, and I could see the landscape
below almost as clearly as if it were the middle of the
day. No one was moving down there, and I heard no
gunfire as I dropped silently into a vineyard.[232]

Burriss landed between two rows of vines, stood up, and checked
himself for injuries. Not finding any, he disentangled his parachute and
laid it flat on the ground, so no Germans would spot his chute from a
distance during the day. He then set off through the vineyard to find
the other men of his stick. After twenty minutes, he located 1st Lieutenant Forrest E. Richter and Private Harry W. Gough. But where were
the other jumpers in the stick?

Burriss recalled:

We looked up the moonlit road adjacent to the vineyard but saw nothing. Crouching behind a two-foot
rock wall, we looked at our map with a pin light. (...)
As we were discussing our position in whispers, we
heard voices down the road. A detachment of men
was approaching. We couldn't tell whether they were
Germans or Italians, but we knew they weren't Americans. We lay flat on the ground beside the wall. They
were stumping along and talking in normal voices,
their weapons slung over their shoulders. They had no
idea we were in the area. "Get your hand grenades," I

whispered to the other two. I already had my grenade in my hand. "When I give the order, we toss them!"

As the troops were passing on the other side of the wall, I whispered, "Now." The three explosions came almost simultaneously and pieces of shrapnel rained down on the vines behind us. We heard screams of pain and frightened yells from the wounded and dying men. Just by listening, we knew we had gotten a number of them. What's more, the survivors didn't know where we were located.[233]

The three paratroopers kept still until they heard some Italians returning to help their moaning comrades. They tossed three more grenades and dispersed the enemy for good. Some four hours later, Burriss gave the order to dig foxholes. While they were digging, an enemy machine gun opened up, and they dove in their partially finished foxholes. Accompanying rifle fire made it obvious that they were pinned down.

Just as Burriss believed there were only two options left—fight and be overrun or escape and be gunned down—shells landed on the enemy positions and the firing ceased. The Italians jumped up and ran wildly through the vineyards, looking for any affordable cover. Behind them came a shouting group of British infantry soldiers.

They raised themselves up and called out that they were American soldiers. A British sergeant and two enlisted men approached with weapons trained on them. Burriss, Gough, and Richter promptly raised their hands above their heads and shouted, "We're American paratroopers!" The British disarmed them and led them to their lieutenant. Burriss tried to reason with him, explaining they had jumped on the previous night. Consulting his own map with the aid of the lieutenant, he suddenly realized why the British were so apprehensive: he was in the southeast part of Sicily, over fifty-five miles from the drop zone!

Burriss offered to join the British with Richter and Gough, as they could then probably rescue or find some of the other members of their stick. The British officer gladly accepted the offer and had their weapons and grenades returned to them. While Burriss received his weapons back and loaded them, the sergeant stated, "If you had said you was Yanks, I would have believed you." This remark came like an insult to Burriss. "I am a Rebel from South Carolina," he said. "Before I would call myself a Yank, you would have to shoot me."[234]

The following days, the three paratroopers stayed with the British infantry. Burriss remembered that "for us, the next few days became a mopping-up operation, though there was fierce fighting elsewhere in Sicily. We moved on with the British and joined up with a couple of men from our stick, as well as with men from another stick dropped in that area. Eventually, we constituted a small band of displaced Americans, ready to engage the enemy aggressively, anxious to rejoin our own units, and sick of British tea."[235]

On July 14, a British major informed them that they could not be taken to the American sector to rejoin the 504th Regimental Combat Team. Instead, they were to escort Italian prisoners on British ship to a POW camp in Tripoli. From there they were flown back to Kairouan.

Technician 4th Grade Edward Kanapkis and Privates George R. Amaral and Henry F. Conley of Headquarters Company jumped in the vicinity of Spaccatorno, Sicily. They were not seen on the ground by the others and are still missing in action. Elsewhere, Corporal Russell F. Looney of Headquarters Company came down so hard that he sprained his ankle "and was knocked out in the landing near a cactus plant. An Italian soldier shot at me and I killed him with two hand grenades."[236]

The Mortar Platoon led by 1st Lieutenant Peter J. Eaton was more fortunate and landed approximately two miles northwest of Biscari just minutes before midnight. "We flew in so low it seemed the wings would almost touch the water at times," Pfc. John C. Turner recalled. "On sighting Sicily, our pilot climbed to an altitude permissible for drop. Flak was so heavy you could see the tracers through the tail of the plane."[237]

After his descent, Turner was "caught on a fairly large tree limb, which broke dropping me into a ravine... I disengaged my harness, checked my weapon (my rifle had dirt in the breech and bore, noted by grinding sound when I loaded it). I checked my pistol and loaded it... One of the troopers from my stick, [Private] James Buskirk, landed on the bank above me, heard my commotion, and challenged for identity. I gave the password. We proceeded to the plateau, where we assembled with other paratroopers."[238]

On the plateau, Lieutenant Eaton gathered three planeloads that had all landed intact, including his own. He gathered their equipment, and they set out in a westward direction toward Niscemi with scouts placed in front. Around 1200 hours on July 10, the scouts signaled the group to halt about three miles west of Biscari and eight miles southeast of Niscemi. They sighted an Italian truck carrying one and towing another 47mm anti-tank gun. Eaton ordered his men to open fire, and they killed all the occupants except one. Turner recalled of this engagement, "At that location, an enemy truck loaded with a 57mm [sic] anti-tank weapon, and towing one, which also had soldiers aboard to operate those weapons, came up to our position. We attacked the truck, killing all except one man who escaped. We took the weapons and set them up in an olive grove alongside the road coming out of the village. Troopers were placed in a perimeter of approximately 300 to 400 yards on each side of the road on top of the mountain."[239]

Sensing the Italians must have been part of a larger detachment, Eaton ordered his men to set up an all-round defensive position. Sergeant George H. Suggs and seven other men manned the two captured Italian guns and bore-sighted them, even though they were unfamiliar to them. With the roads mined and the anti-tank guns displayed, the group waited for things to come.

Half an hour after their first engagement, a much larger Italian motorized column was observed moving across the Niscemi–Biscari Highway 115. They moved in a single file for about 2200 yards long, so Lieutenant Eaton estimated they were battalion strength. An eleven-ton Italian tankette was preceding the column. Using the two anti-tanks guns, the tankette was knocked out, and the 81mm mortars were used on the motorized infantry, which became scattered and retreated in confusion.[240] Turner, however, recalled there were two light Italian tanks instead of one, and both were disabled. One man escaped.

Late that afternoon, the paratroopers heard the rumbling sound of a German Tiger tank. Eaton believed the Italians had requested strong German reinforcements that would be virtually no fair match for the lightly equipped American paratroopers. Apart from his 81mm guns and the two Italian guns, his troopers only had carbines. Eaton then ordered Sergeant Suggs to destroy the captured enemy equipment. Turner remembered that "Lieutenant Eaton suggested, 'We had better get out of here,' so we advanced toward Niscemi. We came to a creek, and, at once, all hell broke loose above us."[241]

At a bridge across the creek, the group contacted the 1st Battalion of the 180th Infantry Regiment commanded by Lieutenant Colonel William H. "King Kong" Schaeffer. Eaton offered the services of his small airborne force. Schaeffer gladly accepted his help, as he had been tasked to capture Biscari airfield. Eaton, having landed near Biscari, knew part of the route from his own experience.

In the morning of July 11, as Turner recalled, "the battleship *Savannah* was shelling the river bridge, still held by the Germans. A shell ricocheted off and landed approximately 80 to 100 yards from our location. We moved to the western end of the bridge and secured it. We crossed the bridge in an easterly direction, turned left up the river highway toward Biscari, and on up the mountain where we had disabled the two light tanks. We noted the plateau was clean of the olive grove previously there, and considered ourselves damned lucky that we had moved our position. We proceeded north through the village, composed of few houses which were gutted and deserted."[242]

The 1st Battalion of the 180th Infantry Regiment encountered heavy enemy resistance as they neared the Biscari airfield. Suddenly, seventeen Tiger tanks of the 2nd Company, 504th Schwere Panzer-Abteilung, and two motorized infantry battalions of the Hermann Goering Panzer Division counterattacked. Schaeffer ordered his task force to make a stand, even though they were clearly outnumbered. Artillery, machine gun, mortar, and tank fire raked the American position, and a number of officers of the 180th became casualties.

The Germans forced them back to the southern side of Highway 115. In the process of retreating, Schaeffer, one of his officers, and a first sergeant were cut off in a culvert and became prisoners for the duration of the war.[243] The fighting got so intense that Lieutenant Eaton ordered his mortar crews to destroy the 81mm mortars and withdrew with the elements of the 1st Battalion, 180th Infantry. Late on July 12, he learned of the location of the temporary 3rd Battalion CP and rejoined the 504th Regimental Combat Team near Gela.

The 3rd Battalion Section of the Regimental Demolition Platoon had been scheduled to destroy a tactical bridge between Niscemi and Gela. They jumped three miles south of Niscemi. Pfc. Darrell G. Harris remembered that "we all were new at combat on that first jump, including the air crews, and the jump did not work exactly as planned on the sand table. Very few of us landed on our intended drop zone, and we were not able to accomplish our primary mission."[244]

In a statement Harris made nearly a year later, when his fellow squad members were still missing, he recalled that the five others of his planeload assembled after the drop: "For about two hours we looked for equipment bundles. It was dark so we decided to wait until daylight."[245]

Private Forrest E. Humphrey remembered, "We spent some time looking for our equipment bundles and found one shortly before daylight. At about 0630 hours on 10 July 1943 decided to try to locate the rest of our unit. Private [Robert E.] Ray and myself left. At about 1030 hours we made contact with the crew of an enemy anti-aircraft battery. A fight started in thick brush and I did not see Private Ray again, but could hear him firing about fifty yards from me. I was surprised by five enemy who came up behind me and opened fire. I was hit in the right arm and began to bleed freely. As we were greatly out-numbered I decided we should withdraw and called to Private Ray three times but received no answer, and believed he had stopped firing. I made a break and ran."[246]

Harris was shocked by the wounds of Humphrey: "This was the first time I had actually seen a battle wound, and though it was an arm wound, it looked terrible, especially where the bullet exited. The victim had lost a lot of blood, and he was unable to keep up. We dressed his wound with Sulfa powder and bandages and continued to search for our bridge. We later found that we had been dropped several miles off target."[247]

To this day, Ray is missing in action. Humphrey was later collected by medics after the American beachhead was enlarged. But in order to get to the coast, Harris recalled, they "elected to hide by day and travel by night while making our way back to the beachhead. After two nights without sighting any enemy troops, we decided it was safe to travel by day. On that day we did encounter some German troops and we had a brief firefight with them. (…) However we did manage to evade them without further losses, and we broke through to the American side of the beachhead."[248]

Probably the most isolated landing inland was made by 2nd Lieutenant Floyd E. Fry and another part of the Regimental Demolition Platoon. Fry flew with seventeen troopers in his stick and suffered two casualties in the plane from enemy flak. The green light came up, and he jumped out with the fifteen remaining paratroopers. While assembling in the dark, it turned out that six men were missing in action.

Early the next morning, Fry was able to orientate his small force and realized he was dropped in the central part of Sicily, no less than 150 miles from the original drop zone and cut off from friendly forces. Two of his men exposed themselves too much and were killed outright by enemy sniper fire. "When we ran into an enemy detachment which was too large and too much fire power for us to fight," recalled Fry later, "which most of them did – we avoided them. We lived off the country most of the month which we spent behind the enemy lines. About the only food we had was bread and wine."[249]

One of these six missing men was Private William R. "Buffalo Bill" Grisez of Tulsa, Oklahoma. He recalled that in the evening of July 10, he was wounded in the back by a German bayonet, and they were taken prisoner by soldiers of the Hermann Goering Panzer Division. Grisez made the trip to Stalag II-B at the same time as Sergeant Edward P. Haider and worked on three different farms. From French forced laborers, he obtained a white towel and, using a red and a blue pencil, worked for several nights by candlelight to create an American flag. Grisez carefully stored it under his clothes in case the Germans would search his bunk or barracks. He planned to use it when the liberation came to identify himself.[250]

The Communications Platoon leader, Lieutenant Calvin Campbell, wasn't so lucky when he was erroneously dropped about ten miles northeast of Pachino. As he was struggling out of his parachute harness, another paratrooper landed on his chest, causing several broken ribs. However, the story Campbell told to *The New York Times* in September 1945 was more fiction than truth, as he supposedly was "the first paratrooper to jump in the invasion, landed on the back of a bayonet-wielding German soldier and began an immediate fight for life, which he still recalls with a shudder (...) The 190-pound, six-foot-four lieutenant killed his man, but only after the German had broken two of his ribs with his bayonet."[251]

According again to his official statement on Operation Husky, Campbell did not see any other paratroopers than the man who had literally landed on him. They hid in a grape vineyard when after daylight they were subjected to continual machine gun fire by a group of Italian soldiers—so far from the "bayonet-wielding German" he invented in 1945! Later that afternoon, a Canadian patrol drove off the Italians and set up camp in the adjacent field. Toward dusk, Campbell and the other paratrooper approached the Canadian outposts, and after proper identification had been established, he was treated for his injuries. He was eventually evacuated from Pozzallo to a ship. Campbell checked the position where he had been dropped with the ship's captain on naval charts of the district, and together, they determined that he had been dropped over forty miles from the actual DZ.

"Just before I went out of the door of the plane," recalled Staff Sergeant Richard F. Long, Campbell's platoon sergeant, "my watch said 11:30 p.m. It was still July 9. We were flying low and there were tracer bullets on both sides of the plane as we jumped. When I landed everything was quiet except for the fire of the anti-aircraft batteries about 500 yards away. I saw only one other chutist and the two of us traveled together that night and the next day. We cut quite a few communication lines and were fired upon as they were in search of us. However, we finally rejoined our regiment safely several days later."[252]

Major Beall, the battalion executive officer, jumped near an Italian garrison. He was soon joined by another member of his stick, Captain William W. Kitchin, the 3rd Battalion Surgeon. They quickly withdrew to a nearby vineyard and tried to orientate themselves. Beall realized they had not landed on the spot they were supposed to be dropped. The landmarks were all different, and they couldn't see any other parachutes in the area. Their attempt to find more men failed. At around 0200 hours, they could hear Italian machine gunners some 200 yards away firing at another target, which had to be American paratroopers judging by the M-1 carbine fire that for nearly one hour was intermittently returned.

Around 0730 hours, a Canadian advance patrol of the Royal Canadian Regiment of the 1st Canadian Infantry Division showed up, and Beall and Kitchin met them and asked their exact location. A Canadian lieutenant pointed the position on Beall's map: they were on the southeast part of Sicily, not far from the town of Pachino. They were almost sixty-five miles southeast of their assigned drop zone! Beall informed the patrol leader that there was an Italian garrison nearby and asked their assistance to attack it. The request was denied, as the patrol had orders to move elsewhere. Beall decided not to waste any time arguing and headed with Kitchin to the beach where they received the required assistance.

After the garrison had been taken, one Italian officer and twenty enlisted men were captured, and one American paratrooper and a Canadian soldier were killed in the process. Eight Americans paratroopers, including a wounded lieutenant, were liberated. The officer and a wounded enlisted man were evacuated to a Canadian hospital while Beall continued his search for more stray paratroopers. They spent the night on the beach.

With the break of dawn on the morning of July 11, Beall had assembled two officers and eighteen enlisted paratroopers. He arranged a visit by boat to visit Major General Guy Simonds of the 1st Canadian Infantry Division aboard a battleship and request transportation. Simonds provided a RAF crash boat to transport the paratroopers to the American sector.

The next day, Saturday, July 12, Beall's group set out on board the RAF crash boat and landed at Scoglitti on Sunday, having picked up Lieutenant Rosenthal and thirty stray paratroopers from different units along the way. At the bivouac area west of Vittoria, Beall found himself in command of the 3rd Battalion, numbering only three other officers—Kitchin, Rosenthal of Service Company, one other officer, and ninety other ranks.[253]

What exactly happened to G Company on Sicily has never been put on paper thus far.

A reason for it might be that about forty were captured. One of them was Sergeant Peter J. Ranti of the 1st Platoon. Ranti recalled:

> Our objective was a hill 10 miles on the other side of Gela. It controlled the main road inland. Our mission was to keep all enemies away until our own motorized units would come along. We took the hill, and armed only with rifles, machine guns, mortars and the new bazookas we held it but because of a hitch in operations our boys didn't get there. We landed during the night of July 9, a day before the boys stormed Gela, and were taken prisoners by a German motorized section four days later.
>
> I guess the Germans could have finished us off easily right there and then but they needed information so they contented themselves in just capturing us. We were taken to Naples, questioned at length but all we knew was our names and serial numbers. An Italian officer there, on learning that I was of Italian extraction, put on a show for the Nazi officers by calling me a "traitor" and I was immediately thrown into solitary. During my solo sentence, I learned the other boys were taken to Germany.[254]

Most of G Company had come down widespread—from the vicinity of Gela to Caltagirone, Niscemi, Biscari Airfield, and further away to the southeast. Private Wallace G. Telford and a fellow paratrooper wandered around in Sicily for two weeks before they were captured. Before that time, being behind enemy lines, he had discarded his rifle. Telford later stated to his family that he had made up his mind that "under no circumstance I would take another life."[255]

The 2nd Platoon sticks were led by 2nd Lieutenants Louis W. Otterbein, Jr. from Bloomfield, New Jersey and Charles R. Witt from Southtown, Minnesota. Otterbein was twenty-nine years old, the older officer of the two, and the platoon leader. They came down separately, and Otterbein recalled that he landed near a German command post; the supply bundles also fell almost directly into enemy hands. Otterbein was flown in a German Junkers-52 transport plane to Naples for interrogation. His story in captivity is continued in the final chapter.

Lieutenant Louis Otterbein of G Company was among the first
to be captured on Sicily. Courtesy: John Otterbein

Although the 2nd Platoon drop turned out unfortunately, it did create sufficient confusion among the Hermann Goering Panzer Division that was beneficial to the 505th PIR and enabled them to take up position at Biazzo Ridge. Likewise, strongpoint "Y" could be taken by Captain Edwin Sayre's A Company of the 505th. We saw in the chapter about Lieutenant Colonel Charles W. Kouns and the machine gunners and how they had set up a position on a hill overlooking the road from Gela to Vittoria. Further to the southeast, the 3rd Platoon of G Company had landed with two sticks closely together. The twenty-nine-year-old platoon leader, 2nd Lieutenant Clyde F. Baley from Hillsboro, Wisconsin, quickly joined forces with his assistant platoon leader, 2nd Lieutenant Harry E. Evans from Harrisburg, Pennsylvania. Evans had also gathered several paratroopers, and the two lieutenants set up a pre-planned roadblock northwest of Vittoria with small anti-tank mines near a bend in the road to Gela.

By daylight, Baley and Evans were ready for whatever would be thrown against them by the enemy. The only aspect that hampered their mood was the lack of radio contact with other elements of the 3rd Battalion. Where were the 1st and 2nd Platoons and their company commander, 1st Lieutenant Marshall C. McOmber? During the morning hours, they could hear the sound of tank engines that seemed to approach in great numbers, but the bushes on each side of the road prevented their sight. Both Baley and Evans expected to encounter only small Italian tanks and were astonished to see six huge Mark VI Tiger Tanks appear down the road. These were fifty-six ton masses of steel armored with an 88mm canon. The small anti-tank mines had some effect on these heavily armored structures, as one or two seemed to stop. But their tank machine guns effectively suppressed the paratroopers in their foxholes. Accompanying German infantry and some Tigers rapidly fanned out over the area. There was practically no way of escape for the outgunned paratroopers; they would either be shelled by 88mm tank fire, machine gun fire, or enemy close-range small arms fire. Before long, Baley was among the several wounded, and there wasn't any option left than to surrender.

Second Lieutenant Clyde Baley of G Company was captured on Sicily
after his men had placed anti-tank mines. The "few Italian tanks" proved
to be German Tiger tanks... Courtesy: Nancy Baley Kapke

One of Baley's soldiers captured in the same skirmish was Private
William T. Bodnar, who had jumped right after his good friend Private
Aubrey Mann. He didn't see Mann after the drop. Bodnar recalled they
were captured by the Hermann Goering Panzer Division. There were
some tense moments during the disarming of the paratroopers when
the Panzer grenadiers found trench knives with brass knuckle handles.
Bodnar eventually spent his POW time on Stalag II-B Hammerstein.
The bodies of Corporal Harry L. Johnson and Mann were not located
until August 28. Strangely, their date of death was after the war and
never corrected to July 10, which is far more likely the day they were
killed in action.

The suddenly appeared Tiger tanks belonged to the reserve platoon of *Oberleutnant* Hans Hummel's 2nd Kompanie, Schwere Panzer
Abteilung 504. Ironically, the Germans shared the same unit number.
Twenty-one-year-old *Leutnant* Karl Goldschmidt recalled that with
the arrival of his platoon:

> ... we got determination in our attack, and (...) *Ober-*
> *leutnant* Hummel stopped and ordered to refuel and

bring up ammunition. He himself carried out a reconnaissance maneuver with HQ Troop on the right side
in the direction of Gela. He shortly received an anti-
tank shot through the safety-hatch. *Leutnant* Heim
took command of the company, because the leader's
tank drove itself stuck due to a penetrated shell. It
could not be pulled free again.

At that time an enemy attack on Vittoria [by G Com-
pany] was reported. *Leutnant* Heim gave me the order,
to secure three dropped out tanks with my platoon.
He himself attack with the HQ Troop in the endan-
gered direction. We took several American soldiers
prisoners while combing the area.[256]

Lieutenant Baley was adamant not to give away any more information than necessary. His POW filecard therefore has "*Verweigert—
refused*" on several questions. Perhaps this was the reason he was sent
from a military field hospital in Caserta to Stalag Luft I and did not
end up in Oflag 64 with other captured officers. The Germans incorrectly assumed he was a pilot instead of a member of the U.S. Army—
all because Baley had given them so few details (not even his date of
birth) to his interrogators. His family was first notified of his capture
through the Vatican in the fall of 1943, and it was later confirmed by
the War Department.

Some G Company troopers who were dropped well within ene-
my-held territory were more lucky than Lieutenants Baley and Evans.
Another miraculous escape was experienced by Pfc. James L. Gann,
who landed a few miles from Biscari Airfield. Gann found five other
paratroopers after the drop, but they soon realized they had landed
amidst a far larger group of Germans. They hid in a mausoleum in
a village cemetery that was not locked. They closed the door and
remained there for thirteen or fourteen hours. It was raining toward
evening, which enabled Gann to put his helmet up and get water for
their canteens. At several moments, they could hear the Germans

searching the area for them, and it was obvious that their planeload landed near a garrison.

The next day, they could leave their less favorable hiding place toward the invasion beaches. Gann and his fellow troopers finally encountered infantry troops of the 45th Infantry Division and were later directed to the regimental assembly area. Here they learned that their Canadian-born G Company Commander, twenty-five-year-old 1st Lieutenant Marshall McOmber, was said to have been killed while charging a German machine gun position. His company executive officer, 1st Lieutenant George W. Cline II, was also killed along with Private James R. Frazier. Both jumped from the same C-47, and their bodies are still missing to this day. One soldier later stated he sighted Cline's body in a ditch near Biscari Airfield.

Also missing are Pfc. Marquis E. Davis and Privates Roy N. Heaton and Edman Roberts. The big question remains: Where were they killed? Heaton was supposedly killed by rifle fire and buried in a field grave by fellow paratroopers about eight miles north of Gela. This information came from one G Company lieutenant who was imprisoned in Oflag 64.[257] Post-war searches revealed no bodies. It is believed that Davis and Roberts were captured and died on the railroad tracks outside Naples on their way to Capua. The diary of Private Elmer C. Kaberlein, quoted extensively in the next and in the last chapters, reveals that he saw Davis wounded after Allied bombers had accidently bombed their POW train.

Privates First Class Harold C. Eisenbruch, David C. McEwen, Dean W. Vangilder, Arlos A. White, Privates Joseph R. Durendo, Joseph J. McEachern, and Albert E. "Woody" Miles were also killed in action. By far, G Company sustained the highest number of fatal casualties and captured paratroopers, which necessitated later a large influx of replacements. They had lost more than one-third of their company strength. But their actions had not been in vain; it confused the Hermann Goering Division to a large extent.

Second Lieutenants James G. Breathwit and Harry G. Stewart of the 1st Platoon were the only two company officers to report at the regimental assembly area at Biscari. Stewart received as Regimental Personnel Officer the sad duty to write the next-of-kin of the killed paratroopers. Twenty-two-year-old Sergeant Milton F. O'Quinn was wounded in Sicily and evacuated to a field hospital in North Africa. Once back with G Company, he wrote on September 23 to his wife Betty, "I have more time to myself now so I can write my sweet gal more often. (...) I guess you know by now that [Private Kenneth R.] Crawford is missing in action. Rae came to see me at the Company but I was in the hospital. I missed him by a matter of days (2). I guess you know that Captain Kaufman was killed."[258]

The planes carrying G Company Headquarters dropped their human cargo in the area of Vittoria and Biscari Airfield. Lieutenant George J. Watts of H Company wrote to Francis McOmber, the widow of his best friend, on October 10 and told her what he had learned: "They landed at a place called Vittoria in the midst of the enemy. Entirely surrounded and hopelessly outnumbered. Mac and some of his men held back the Germans while a couple of men escaped and went for help. It didn't get there for two days – they couldn't hold out that long."[259]

After being hospitalized in North Africa with malaria for a month, Watts returned to Sicily on August 11:

> Since I had been told Mac was missing in action, I went up to Vittoria. The army cemetery had no record of him so I went to the civilian cemetery. It was then I found his grave. I got the rest of the story from the medical card that had been on his body. It said he was wounded on the 10th of July and an Italian priest brought him to an aid station at Vittoria. He died on July the 11th and was buried by an unknown parachute sergeant on July 12.
>
> The civilian cemetery could not compare with the army cemetery at Gela, Sicily, so I left orders at Gela to have the body moved. It is much better that way, where Cal will be taken and if ever any remains are shipped home they will know where he is.

You may be not be notified for sometime by the War Department. They check everything carefully and have to be absolutely sure. For that reason please do not contact them or the Red Cross until you are notified. I would lose my official head if they knew I wrote you first. I don't care much though – it is the least I can do for you. Please write if there is anything more I can possibly do. Offer my deepest sympathy to Mr. And Mrs. McOmber.

Since the Battle of Italy I have again landed in the hospital – this time with malaria and yellow jaundice. While in the hospital the first time in Africa I was given my promotion. I asked for Mac's old company. I lead them here in Italy and believe me Jerry is paying for killing Mac. He will continue to pay as long as I can get near him.

Once more let me tell you now sorry I am and let me say Mac did die like an officer and a gentleman. It was in the service of his country and he was doing the job in the best way he could. He and others like him made the Sicilian invasion possible. You feel justly proud to have been his wife. Be brave. Yours, Geo.[260]

Sadly, two months after he had written this moving letter, Watts was killed on Hill 950 in December 1943. His death is mentioned in the subsequent volume of this regimental history, *Spearhead of the Fifth Army.*

CHAPTER 13

SAGA OF H COMPANY

Sicily

JULY 9-11, 1943

Right after 1st Lieutenant Frank J. Kent, the H Company executive officer, leaped out of the C-47, the man behind him became jammed in the door, which delayed the jump of the remainder of the stick. Kent descended separately from his group and observed heavy enemy fire nearby. It was obvious that he was pinned down when combing patrols of Germans started to swarm the area. Kent threw hand grenades and ran back each time before they exploded, but small grenade fragments and German machine-pistol bullets wounded him in the leg.

When dawn approached, Lieutenant Kent camouflaged himself on a hilltop overlooking Ponte Olivo Airfield a little more than a mile north of Gela. He decided to hide during the hot July day, observing German tanks and infantry between him and the airfield. Dusk fell before Kent snuck out of his heading place and crawled down the hill in the direction of the American lines, which he assumed to be near the airfield. He managed to infiltrate through the German sentries and decided to place his last remaining grenades as booby-traps.

Luck ran out when a sentry challenged him in German and upon his refusal to answer, fired. The shot missed, but Kent had seen the flash and returned fire, wounding the sentry. More shots were fired at the paratrooper, and he was struck down and captured. A German officer interrogated Lieutenant Kent and told him that his sentry had been severely wounded. "If the sentry dies, you die," he told Kent sternly. Anxious moments followed until a German medic reported that he believed the sentry would make it. For Kent, this meant a transfer to the field hospital of the Hermann Goering Panzer Division and having a prisoner of war status.[261]

One stick of the 3rd Platoon led by Sergeant Michael J. Kogut landed near Niscemi. Kogut assembled his men and at 0200 hours sent them off in different directions to search the equipment bundles that had been released from their plane. Pfc. Hugh A. Sheridan failed to return and was never seen again. Although no fight took place, Kogut and the other stick members heard the sound of gunfire in the distance. Sheridan is still missing in action.

Second Lieutenant Herman Littman, the twenty-four-year-old assisting platoon leader of the 1st Platoon, was wounded in both legs after a firefight. With two of his men, he hid a short while in a vineyard near the command post of the Hermann Goering Panzer Division, but they were eventually spotted by a German sentry, who told them, with a heavy accent, "For you, the war is over." They were taken to a German field hospital. A doctor warned Littman that he had to amputate his legs. "No, you are not taking my legs. You just want my jump boots," Littman replied. Another surgeon operated and saved his legs.

Several days later, Littman and another walking wounded were allowed to "walk around the hospital ground. The guard would sit on the steps with his rifle and we would double time around the hospital. He still sat and waited there. I thought 'now is the time', so when we got behind the hospital we just took off across the field to a wooded area.

"We got to the hills and came across an Italian worker walking on the road. He took us to his cottage to rest there. He gave us white bread and fresh milk. Then he disappeared and we thought he was getting out to get some help. About half an hour later we heard "Achtung, Achtung! Heraus mit hände hoch! – Come out with your hands up!" He had given us in to the Krauts. This time they took us to a prison camp in Capua, Italy. From there to Stalag 17 in Germany and then they separated the officers from the enlisted men and put me in the only officers camp they had in Poland. That is how I got into Oflag 64."[262]

Several other H Company troopers were also captured, like Private Elmer C. Kaberlein, who kept a diary. He wrote:

Took off at 1915 for combat jump in Sicily. Made jump at exactly 11:25 p.m. somewhere near Gela. July 11, 1943 – Captured by German and Italian soldiers about 6:00 p.m. Taken to a German Headquarters and questioned. Then taken to a small prison camp.

July 12 and 13, 1943 – Remained at prison camp awaiting to go elsewhere. Had soup and 1/5 loaf of bread each day.

July 14 thru 18, 1943 – Began walking to another prison camp. Walked each day thru southern part of Sicily, trying to catch rides on German trucks. Very little water and small rations of food. Slept in fields each night. Very cold.

July 19, 1943 – Went thru Messina in trucks. Town was in total ruins. Crossed body of water by ferry to Reggio, Italy. Sweating out P-38's all the time riding in German trucks.

July 20, 1943 – Began walking again thru southern Italy. Came to small town and here we boarded train for Naples.

July 21, 1943 – Train and nearby airport strafed and bombed. Jumped out of window and laid in ditch. Three killed and nine or ten injured. Two injured paratroop buddies of mine were left behind (Elwood Strouse and M. E. [Marquis] Davis). Arrived at Capua prison camp late at night, very hungry. Were fed bread, cheese, and tea (very good).

July 22 thru 31, 1943 – Stayed in Capua—buddied up with Sgt. [Burl E.] Merrill. Had three Red Cross boxes (appreciated very much).

August 1 thru 5, 1943 – Left Capua via train for Germany. Forty-four men in one box car, plenty crowded and a very rough trip. Again sweated out being bombed. This time we were locked in the boxcar.

August 6, 1943 – Arrived at Hammerstein, Germany prison camp, Stalag II-B. Lived in large barracks, 500 men to a barrack. Daily food ration here was 1/4 loaf bread, small piece of butter, spoon of jam and soup once per day. Each morning roll call was had, sometimes lasting quite long, and in the rain. Received one Red Cross Box here.[263]

While Littman and Kaberlein were among those who remained prisoner until the end of war, Sergeant David Rosenkrantz, a squad leader in the 1st Platoon of H Company, and Corporal Lee Black, the company's medic, experienced a much shorter captivity. Both were captured on July 10 in the southern Sicilian town of Scicli by approximately two hundred Italian soldiers of the 206th Coastal Defense Division. To their astonishment, the Italians held a conference the next day about who was going to surrender—them or the Americans? The outcome was unbelievable: they decided to dine with their "captors" until the first Allied ground forces would show up.

After a magnificent meal with plenty of wine supplied by the town mayor, an infantry platoon of the Canadian Loyal Edmonton Regiment supported by a troop of tanks from the Canadian Tree Rivers Regiment arrived the next morning. The troop leader, twenty-three-year-old 2nd Lieutenant Jack Wallace, wrote in his diary that day:

Later in the afternoon, the commanding officer of the Edmonton Regiment requested tank support for an attack on Ragusa. A platoon, which my tank

accompanied, was also dispatched to accept the surrender of a small town called Scicli. The town had
offered to surrender, but the commanding officer
didn't want to take any chances so he had us lob shells
over the town as a precautionary measure.

When we entered the town there were no sheets or
white flags about to indicate surrender. The streets
were also uncomfortably quiet. Twenty minutes after
we arrived, an American paratrooper approached us
from another section of town and told us everything
was under control. He and a few others had parachuted on the night of the invasion, but had been
dropped on the wrong spot, captured and jailed. They
talked themselves out of jail by telling the mayor that
if he didn't surrender his town shortly, fleets of bombers would blow the place off the map.[264]

The American paratrooper described in the diary of Wallace was
undoubtedly Rosenkrantz. A reporter for the United Press wrote their
story down, and by the next day, an article appeared in the *Los Angeles Daily News* in Rosenkrantz's hometown. It was a great relief for his
family to learn that he had landed safely and was still alive.[265]

"We were dropped at 2330," recalled Rosenkrantz's platoon leader,
1st Lieutenant William H. Davidson. "At the time of the drop the
flight was to the Northeast. Opening shock was normal. There was an
anti-aircraft burst about 15 seconds before the drop. The wind drift
was from 15 to 20 miles per hour. I would guess the height of the drop
to be between 400 and 600 feet. Landed normally in a vineyard. I was
the No. 2 man out of the airplane and two enlisted men landed near
me joined me during the night. By 1100, fifteen men from my aircraft
reported back to Marzamemi. Two of the 15 were wounded by enemy
fire. We got the red light before we hit land. At the green light, some of
the men said they were not hooked up so all of the men did not leave
the aircraft. It is believed that three men remained onboard and were
carried to be dropped later as an aircraft was seen to pass over as I was

unhooking my parachute on the ground. We were able to locate all of the bundles that were on the aircraft."[266]

Private James H. Legacie, Jr., a twenty-two-year-old paratrooper from North Dakota, had joined the 2nd Platoon of H Company as a replacement not long after a demonstration jump for General Eisenhower had necessitated a transfer from EGB447. "I landed in a grape vineyard," Legacie recalled, "and the first thing I did on the ground was reaching out for a big old grape which tasted wonderful. We had received a password to use – 'George Marshall' – to identify ourselves. I heard someone about twenty yards away and figured I had to be the next man of the stick so I said, 'George,' expecting to hear 'Marshall.' But nothing happened. So I repeated, 'George, George!' Suddenly I heard a voice calling, 'Jesus! Don't shoot! I am Crawford from H Company.' I found it funny at the time so I started laughing."[267]

In the same plane as Privates Legacie, Willard Crawford, and Lawrence Dunlop was Pfc. Walter R. Huckins, a bazooka gunner from Fanwood, New Jersey. Huckins recalled that he found his squad leader, Sergeant Robert A. Tague, and Sergeant Kenneth E. Brady with some others. Two days later, his group had grown to about fifteen men with 1st Sergeant Edward W. Sneddon in charge. Sneddon sent Huckins and a man from Alabama to an earlier discovered well to fill their canteens. But while they were at the well, a German halftrack manned by eight men arrived on the scene. Huckins and his comrade concealed themselves behind some bushes and waited until the Germans had filled all the containers on the truck and then stepped out and shot them except one blond soldier—a medic.

With their prisoner, they drove the truck back to the American position on a hill. When questioned as to why they waited before shooting the Nazis, the Alabama trooper replied, "Well, I didn't see any sense in us having to fill all those cans." Sneddon then decided to move on, and they finally reached Castle Nocera.[268]

During the fight at this castle, which will be told in more details in the next chapter since a part of I Company was involved as well, Huckins was hit in the right side of his head as he tried to rescue a wounded man under German tank fire. He lost his right eye, his sense of taste and smell, and became deaf in one ear due to the tank shell explosion.

Eventually, Huckins made his way through various hospitals in the Mediterranean Area and a hospital ship back to the United States. He stated during a Red Cross drive tour in 1944 to promote the sale of War Bonds: "When I buy bonds I invest in my buddies who are still over there pitching," said Huckins while speaking at a rally for the Sixth War Loan in Ambler.[269]

One of Huckins' fellow soldiers, Corporal Chester H. Aszklar, "got a piece of shrapnel in my arm. While we were firing at the Germans they throwing ack-ack up there and finally mortar shells. We lost seven people up there that got killed. (...) Next morning we were relieved by the 1st Infantry Division."[270] Aszklar was patched up in a field hospital and rejoined his platoon.

"As a member of the Battalion Communications Platoon," remembered Private Herbert C. Lucas, "I and Bill Wheeler were assigned to jump with a platoon from H Company headed by a sergeant. There were no officers on our plane. I was not injured on the jump, but I landed in an olive tree. My toes barely touched the ground and my weight pulling against the harness, made it difficult to unhook the harness. Finally, after about ten to fifteen minutes, I managed to squirm around enough to get my feet firmly on terra firma, and was able to get out of the harness.

"First time in combat, you think that the enemy is all around you. You are going into the unknown. You don't know what is going to happen. Fortunately, there was no enemy in the immediate vicinity. Eventually the members of our stick assembled. We had no idea where we were, but later found that we were far off course. The next morning, from the advantage of a high hill, we observed enemy soldiers below. Our sergeant decided we were probably outnumbered and decided not to attack. So we stayed away from the village and after several days we finally caught up with the regiment."[271]

First Lieutenant George J. Watts, the 3rd Platoon leader, had landed some one and a half miles southeast of Niscemi. "I was in X Battalion with 'Mac' [McOmber]," he recalled, "but he was to take some hills, and protect me while my men and I laid a minefield. Coming in over Sicily we ran into heavy anti-aircraft fire. The planes spread out in an effort to avoid the flak and some of the ships were lost. (...) I landed in the right places and gathered my supplies."[272]

By 0830 hours on July 10, Watts had assembled fifteen paratroopers and moved to a strategic hill where they set up an all-around defensive position. During the night, his force grew as 2nd Lieutenant Edward C. Digan of Headquarters Company, and some thirty-five enlisted men from various companies joined him there.

At around 1300 hours, the radio operator got through to 1st Lieutenant Willis J. Ferrill, a platoon leader of I Company, who had assembled some sixty officers and men at the nearby Castle Nocera. Watts spoke with Ferrill and agreed to lead his group to Castle Nocera, where he assumed command as ranking officer.

Some sticks landed close together near the intended drop zone, including a stick from the 3rd Platoon with the assistant platoon leader, twenty-one-year-old 2nd Lieutenant James C. Ott, as jumpmaster. Ott recalled that "a lot of the men got sick. We received quite an amount of flak as we flew over Sicily."[273] His planeload came down in an orchard near the scheduled drop zone and assembled. There were fifteen men, of which four were injured. Ott had received the instruction in Kairouan to cover the right flank of the 3rd Battalion with his platoon, and despite the fact that his group was isolated and understrength, he decided to set out to accomplish this mission.

While they made their way north, a house was sighted, and Ott knocked on the door and talked to the civilians. He found they were friendly and decided to leave the four wounded behind. They would only hinder the advance and could be collected at the earliest possibility. The civilians pointed him in the correct direction of Niscemi. At around 0200 hours, Ott found the exact bearing for the road to Niscemi. Their group moved east and after about two hours, they ran into Lieutenant Colonel Charles W. Kouns, who had gathered nine men and positioned them on a hill. Kouns was glad to see Ott, as he hadn't been able to make contact with any other planeload of his battalion either.

Not long afterward, after dawn, they sighted a large column of German infantry, estimated to be a regiment of the Hermann Goering Panzer Division, moving along the road toward Niscemi. The column turned left on a by-pass toward Gela, obviously to repel the beach landings of the 1st Infantry Division. Kouns ordered Ott to move to the road and observe from a closer distance. Covered by the rifles of Kouns and several paratroopers, Lieutenant Ott moved out with Privates Bill Barbour, Sidney A. Jahay, William P. Woodworth of Headquarters Company, Pfc. Richard W. Rozzell, Pfc. Nicholas N. Stampone, Privates Abraham Gurley, George M. Harrison, Paul G. Kichman, and Elmer E. Lindsey of H Company. The group included a two-man rocket-launcher team. They reached the vicinity of the road, a distance of some six hundred yards, unseen.

Although the Germans had set up machine guns in the area dominating the road, they failed to spot the paratroopers. This was about to change when Ott peered through the opening of a cactus hedge and observed the Germans taking a break and their men being scattered. Suddenly, a German officer spotted Ott, but it was too late for him, and he was shot on sight. Ott then took a rocket-launcher from one of his men and fired a shot on a German staff car. The grenade blew the car to pieces and in the process killed the driver and three officers. All hell broke loose as the German infantry started to respond.

The group ran back through a vineyard and got scattered along the way. Ott made his way to a house with Stampone, Gurley, and Harrison. They managed to remain undetected. Eventually, his small group joined other 3rd Battalion paratroopers at Castle Nocera.

Most of the remaining men, including Kouns, were less fortunate—they were captured. Their actions distracted enough attention to keep large, roaming German patrols inland to hunt for more paratroopers and thus away from the beaches. All nine enlisted men with Ott were later awarded Silver Stars for their actions that were similar in text: "Private Lindsey, with eight other privates and one officer, crept to within close range of an enemy column which had halted for rest. Discovered by the enemy, the officer used a rocket launcher to destroy an armored car in which all occupants were killed. Private Lindsey and his comrades effectively covered the withdrawal of the rocket launcher team with rifle fire and created such confusion among the enemy that it refused to exploit its numerical superiority. In this action Private Lindsey displayed high courage and devotion to duty that gave not thought to self in the performance of his task. Since this action Private Lindsey has been reported missing in action."[274]

Private Donald Zimmerman, a twenty-year-old trooper in the 2nd Platoon of H Company, "had volunteered to jump into Sicily with a .30-caliber machine gun" in his arms. His platoon leader, the short 1st Lieutenant Richard D. Aldridge of Toledo, Ohio, was the stick's jumpmaster. Zimmerman recalled that when the enemy flak guns opened up nearing the Sicilian coast, their pilot received the order by radio from his group commander to swing to the left because of the anti-aircraft fire. But the pilot was a squadron leader and decided to fly straight on, passing right over Gela, and gained height at the same time.

When the red light came on, Aldridge ordered his stick to stand up and hook up to the static line. "Aldridge jumped when the light changed," remembered Zimmerman, "and his radio operator was between him and me. He refused to jump. [Private Lawrence W.] "Bucky" Neumeyer was right behind me with the tripod and two or three bandoleers. With the people behind me and using the weight of the light machine gun we knocked the radio operator back in the plane. He returned to North Africa with it."

As the way had been cleared, Zimmerman quickly leaped out of the door, directly followed by Neumeyer, who, according to Zimmerman, "landed in a vineyard and I landed outside the vineyard some twenty or thirty yards away. He had a compound fracture of his right leg and so we couldn't move out to find any others. We were on our own as the rest landed far away from us. We were north of Gela in a kind of valley and there was a highway right where we landed. All the equipment (of the supply containers released from under the plane) landed on the road. I tried to keep our equipment out of the way, concealed."[275]

During the day, a mixed column of Germans and Italians approached down the road. Zimmerman decided not to engage them: "I didn't feel to attack them with our machine gun as they were retreating west. Some soldiers came by the equipment bundles on the road, but they didn't touch them. I guess they thought the bundles contained explosives."

Over the next three or four days, Zimmerman removed all the equipment from the road to avoid drawing attention to the vineyard. He said:

We were there three or four days until Lieutenant Aldridge showed up by himself on foot. He had moved on himself between Gela and the drop zone. The next day Lieutenant Ott came in with a small group down from the highway.

That same night a group of Italian soldiers appeared on the top of the hill to our east. I had the machine gun set up on the side of the road. I heard Aldridge and Ott talking and you could hear the Italian mess kits rattling as they came closer. I was lying behind the machine gun and I opened up and used about half a bandoleer up the hill. They threw up flares to locate us. I could hear some screaming on the hill. Everything went quiet and we all hid as the flares lit the countryside. We ended up retreating through the night down to a dry creek bed about 100 yards behind the road. Lieutenant Aldridge got us back there.

The next morning I woke up and I had lost my machine gun and everything. I was so sleepy then as I hardly got any sleep since we had landed. There was a bridge at the creek and that is why the Italians and Germans who came by earlier thought that the bundles contained explosives for blowing up the bridge. From that time on we travelled back to the bivouac area where we rejoined other men of H Company.

I got booby-trapped at the bivouac area and they took me to a forward hospital with American, German and Italian wounded that was being run by Catholic nuns. It was in a town. They took me there in a jeep and they

couldn't do anything for me there so they gave me
some sedation and I when I woke from the anesthetic
I was in a field hospital.[276]

The assistant platoon leader of the 2nd Platoon in H Company,
2nd Lieutenant Warren E. Tobias, Jr., recalled that at exactly 2242
hours, "we bailed out approximately 18 miles north of Gela and about
ten minutes later reaching our given destination (...) six miles southeast of Niscemi. I know that [2nd] Lieutenant Richard H. Briggs also
bailed out safely, for my company was assembling and orders being
issued. A runner (a Sergeant, but name unknown) of Lieutenant
Brigg's company, came to our company and shouted that Lieutenant
Briggs wanted all members of his platoon – which was I Company, 3rd
Platoon – to return to their correct company for further orders from
Lieutenant Briggs."[277]

The 3rd Battalion Supply Officer, twenty-three-year-old 2nd
Lieutenant Rudyard M. Swagler, gathered several men of his stick and
joined forces with Lieutenant Tobias and some paratroopers of his
2nd Platoon, H Company. They numbered twenty-five paratroopers
in all and captured and killed several Italians and Germans during the
first night.

In the early afternoon of July 11, the group was augmented by fifteen infantry men who had landed on the beaches. They encountered
an Italian fortified position around some pillboxes—presumably the
"Strongpoint Y." Automatic weapons fire pinned the group down, and
even though he was wounded in both arms by rifle bullets and in the
side by mortar fragments, Swagler charged ahead of his men toward
the pillboxes.

While leading his men forward, Lieutenant Swagler was shot
in the back of the head by enemy fire and left for dead in a ditch. "I
received a bullet in the right rear part of my brain," Swagler later tes-
tified for a medical board. "I saw the man [who shot me] after he hit
and spun me around (...) I shot him before."[278] By a miracle, the bullet
had been deflected by his helmet, and after some hours, an American
medic located him and supplied blood plasma. The blood transfusion
saved his life, and Swagler was transported to the 9th Station Hospital

in Oran, Algeria, where the rifle bullet was removed from the right occipital region. He first awoke on July 15 in the hospital.

After several weeks in the 9th Station and 12th General Hospitals in Oran, Swagler arrived on August 30 at the Halloran General Hospital in New York City. Further treatment followed a month later in the Hoff General Hospital in Santa Barbara, California near his home. For Swagler, the first combat jump had proved to be his last, but his friends in the 504th PIR were still unaware of his remarkable rescue.

First Lieutenant Rudyard Swagler served as S-4 Officer of the 3rd Battalion and was left for dead in a Sicilian roadside ditch. Medics saved his life with blood transfusion. Courtesy: Leslie Swagler Fligg

CHAPTER 14

SAGA OF I COMPANY

Sicily

JULY 9-13, 1943

P ilots of the C-47s transporting 1st Lieutenant George M. War-field's I Company became disoriented over Sicily, and as a result, their sticks were more widely dispersed than any other airborne unit. The paratroopers came down from southeast of Niscemi to Noto and Pachino. But this had one large advantage: the commanding general of the Hermann Goering Panzer Division, *Generalleutnant* Paul Conrath, didn't dare to commit all his forces toward the American beaches. Their unit history mentions the invasion: "In the night to 9 July the alarm phases II and III were ordered. This time it was serious: American airborne forces landed in the immediate proximity of the bivouac area near the airfield Grammichele [Biscari Airfield]. The battle for the *Fortress Europa* had started! In the early morning hours of 10 July 1943 the Hermann Goering Panzer Division, with its balance in the area of Caltagirone, received orders from *Generalfeldmarschall* Kesselring for an immediate counterattack."[279]

Meanwhile, a large sub-unit of the division, Brigade Schmalz of *Oberst* Wilhelm Schmalz, was stationed in the vicinity of Catania. His signalmen received the following report in the early morning of July 10: "Enemy landings near Syracuse, Ispica and Noto."[280] They were unaware that the last two towns were accidental drops.

Lieutenant Warfield landed with his stick eight miles west of Noto. They were dozens of miles off the correct drop zone. First Sergeant Wallace Ritch of Cordova, Alabama was also aboard Warfield's plane, but he was never seen again. The paratroopers heard a tommygun being fired in the distance; Ritch was the only one in their planeload who had carried that weapon. Warfield wrote to his widow in April 1944: "Your husband was my 1st Sergeant at the time of the invasion of Sicily and was also in my plane at the time of the mission. He was jumping last man in the plane, but no one ever saw him again after leaving the plane over Sicily. I accounted for all other men in the plane, but Sergeant Ritch is still missing. We landed about 8 miles west of Noto, Sicily and after the end of a week I returned to our land place, but no trace was every found of Sergeant Ritch. We all hope against hope that he will turn up when this is over. Sincerely, G.M. Warfield."[281]

Warfield discovered they were much closer to the British invasion beaches on the east coast than the American beaches in the west. He recalled that the British 1st Parachute Brigade was to capture the Primasole Bridge, so he led his men to the bridge. Here they made contact with the British airborne troops. Warfield's group was ordered to board a troop ship with his men as improvised prisoner guards for the large number of Italian prisoners that had been taken and were bound for POW camps in Egypt.[282]

"We were in the third flight of airplanes in plane No.7," remembered 1st Lieutenant Donald L. Holmes of the 3rd Platoon, "the next plane behind Lieutenant Campbell. Our airplane became lost from the formation and upon approaching the mainland of Sicily, flew inland and turned around and came out over the ocean and then back inland. There were no other airplanes visible. When we left the airplane, I immediately focused all my attention toward locating other airplanes that might be dropping in the same locality. Even after hitting the ground, I did not see or hear another airplane.

"When it became daylight, I discovered that I was on high land and could see the sea when I looked to the east or to the south. I estimated my position to be 30 miles north and slightly west of Pachino. There were 18 of us together and we immediately set up a roadblock and occupied that area for two days and two nights. One of our men was wounded and one was captured by the Germans."[283]

Holmes' group eventually ran into the elements of the 152nd Infantry Brigade of the 51st Highland Division. He received instruction from that them that "we were to proceed to the British beachhead at Portopalo." Holmes was glad to find Lieutenant William Watson of the 2nd Battalion who had been brought there by Canadians. "I also saw Captain Wagner of the 505th," recalled Holmes. "He had about 350 men with him who had been dropped between Avelo and Noto. He said that some men from I Company of the 504th had attached themselves with his outfit."[284]

The body of his assisting platoon leader, 2nd Lieutenant Richard H. Briggs, was never found. On the same plane were Staff Sergeant Charles T. Massey and Private Joseph S. Pappalardo. Massey's field grave was uncovered in 1955 near Ragusa, and he was surprisingly reburied at the American Cemetery at Colville-sur-Mer in Normandy. The names of Briggs and Pappalardo are still on the Wall of Missing at the Sicily–Rome Cemetery at Nettuno, Italy.

Sergeant Louis E. Orvin, Jr., of Savannah, Georgia, a squad leader in the 3rd Platoon, was dropped with his stick near the town of Noto some sixty miles east of the intended drop zone. Orvin was the jumpmaster of his plane, and after landing in a vineyard, he first hid his parachute under a vine tree. Then he set out to "roll up" his stick. Orvin could only round up seven of them, including Corporal Herbert "Herby" H. Kendall, the radio operator, Private Russell J. McDermott, and Pfc. Chester J. Botwinski. Botwinski, who was one of the company runners, got separated from his stick after he had been sent forward as a scout. For about five days, he encountered no friendly troops until he reached the British lines at the southern coast of Sicily.[285] Orvin's group also linked up with the British invasion forces and was sent as prison guards on a ship to Egypt.

"It was dark as hell," recalled twenty-six-year-old Private George Ourganian of Bloomfield, New Jersey, who sat in another plane. "When I hit the ground I threw away my parachute and got all my weapons ready. I couldn't find my companions, so I headed south by the compass.

"Around midnight, I met an Italian in a vineyard. He let go with his tommygun and we started to shoot it out. I heard a moan. Guess I clipped him. Then eight more Italians ran up, some in civilian clothes and I turned the gun on them. I felt a shot in my arm. The Italians dumped me in a pushcart and took me to a stable. Then we heard shooting, and they all ran out. I crawled out and hid in a ditch. The Canadians found me. They took me to a hospital ship."[286]

The 2nd Platoon of I Company sustained the highest rate of casualties with I Company. Their platoon mission was to take a strongly defended hill about five miles south of Niscemi. One planeload led by their platoon leader, 1st Lieutenant Henry B. Keep, landed many miles from their assigned DZ. The pilot of his plane followed several other C-47s carrying the 3rd Platoon and Company Headquarters of I Company and flew too far east. By the time the green light at the door flashed on, the stick was about five miles south of Noto, Sicily. Keep as jumpmaster leaped first out of the door and was followed by his platoon radio operator, Technician 5th Grade Augustine Kettren from Lalmer, Pennsylvania. Sergeant William D. Hartgraves was the last man in his stick, which also included Private George B. Hill.

Upon landing, Lieutenant Keep couldn't locate any other members of his planeload. He wandered around almost all night in totally unfamiliar terrain, only to be wounded by a tank and eventually captured at dawn. Keep was liberated a few days later by Allied troops who overran the field hospital he was in. His radioman Kettren was also wounded and found by friendly troops. Kettren's combat days were over, while Keep's wounds were less serious and only kept him shortly out of action.

Sergeant Hartgraves was captured according to some I Company veterans, but it is uncertain as his body is still missing and he is not in any POW records. He may have been taken as POW by train to Capua, Italy, where all prisoners were first registered. There was a bombing raid on the railroad tracks outside Naples as the train with POWs neared the town. It could be that he was killed in this bombing raid. However, it is still unsure until his remains are located. Another paratrooper, Hill, was killed, and his remains were located five miles south of Noto. He was eventually reinterred in the American War Cemetery in Florence.

The other half of the 2nd Platoon consisted of the assisting platoon leader, 2nd Lieutenant Bill E. Fabian, seventeen paratroopers that included the I Company medic, Technician 5th Grade James L. Snodgrass, Privates First Class Robert P. Dean, Angelo M. Delloto, James P. Haire, Jr., James H. Hennessey, James J. Jeffery and Joseph S. Kacala, and Private Lucian A. Evans. All these men would be captured shortly the landing.

Twenty-one-year-old Sergeant Theodore F. Macauley from Brooklyn, New York was the second ranking paratrooper aboard Fabian's planeload. It meant he was placed in the rear of the stick. "If I ever get home I'll stay put," he had written to his mother from Tunisia. "I've seen all the countries I want."[287] Macauley recalled their plane came over the coast at Gela and got some flak. This caused Fabian to jump a little late, and instead of south of the hill, they went out the door either directly over or north of the hillmass. Enemy troops on the hill shot off flares and fired with machine guns and anti-aircraft fire at the C-47 and the paratroopers as they descended from an altitude of 350 or 400 feet into the brightly illuminated sky.

Macauley jumped last and believed that several men had been hit during their descent. Upon landing, he assembled his gear. He then moved in a southern direction to "roll up his stick" and encountered Snodgrass, the medic. Shortly afterward, they were joined by Sergeant Walter V. Ott from Service Company who had landed on the east side of the Gela–Niscemi road. Ott had jumped from another plane and was immediately brought under machine gun fire upon landing. He had assembled his M-1 rifle and began to crawl to the highway to the west, knowing he should have landed on the other side.

Together they met under some trees and started to elude the enemy while heading for the highway. Twice they crossed communication wire—on the ground and strung from trees—and cut them hill mass through. Then the enemy opened fire, and while Macauley and Ott both dropped to the ground, Snodgrass turned to run back and inadvertently stepped on the bayonet of Ott's rifle. It cut his foot through his shoe. Snodgrass gave himself a morphine injection but immediately became groggy. He begged to be left behind, but Macauley and Ott decided to carry him to a safer place.

Once over a small rise some three hundred yards from the highway, they came in full view of a German garrison and a group of Italians covering a road block. The Italians instantly opened fire, and the paratroopers hugged the ground and crawled in the long grass in a circle to the north to avoid the road block. But a German patrol went after them and pinned them down with machine gun fire. They crawled to a shallow ditch in the ground and returned fire until four Germans crawled closer and tossed a hand grenade. Fragments hit Ott in the legs. Macauley, Ott, and Snodgrass decided to surrender to the four Germans, as their position seemed surrounded and pinned down.

Their German captors were members of the Hermann Goering Panzer Division that handed out cigarettes and chocolate and allowed Snodgrass to bandage his own foot. Then the Germans escorted them to the Italian roadblock before departing into the countryside to find more paratroopers. They were stripped of their weapons, watches, and food. Macauley had hidden some money under his rank patch that was not discovered. Their hands and feet were bound with telephone wire, and stops were made at an Italian garrison on the northeast side of Niscemi and in the town for interrogation.

Sergeant Macauley was first questioned in the garrison for about five minutes by an Italian officer. He asked where his unit had been stationed in North Africa, how long they had been on Sicily, and whether or not any of the three paratroopers could speak Italian. Macauley answered all questions only with his name, rank, and army serial number. This irritated the interrogator, who threatened to shoot Macauley.

During Ott's interrogation, he was shown a rifle with the name and serial number of Private Howard K. Blevins, Lieutenant Colonel Kouns' jeep driver. The interrogator stated that Blevins had been killed (which wasn't the case) and asked if Ott knew him. Ott repeatedly refused to answer the questions and only gave his name, rank, and army serial number. He was finally escorted back to his cell and not threatened as expected.[288]

Later in Niscemi, Macauley, Ott, and Snodgrass were questioned together for about an hour, and again they answered only with their name, rank, and serial numbers. They were then taken to an assembly place for POWs about sixty miles away on Sicily, where they encountered the captured group of Staff Sergeant Robert Binnix of the Machine Gun Platoon. The experiences of Macauley and Ott as POWs are told in the final chapter.

Sergeant Edward P. Haider of Company Headquarters found the information received at the briefing false from the start: "We had been assured that it was going to be a dark night. Who were those weather forecasters anyway? It was anything but dark! The moon was out and it was shining about as bright as ever. (…) We knew as soon as we were over Sicily because the antiaircraft fire was unbelievable. It was something else. As the plane bounced along, we did our best to stay put in our seats which were no more than small aluminium trays fastened to the fuselage."[289]

A German flak shell hit the right-side engine and set in on fire. Another shell fragment created a large hole in the bulkhead, and smaller fragments ripped through the fuselage and hit various paratroopers in the back of the stick. Haider recalled:

> By this time, the guys were being blown right out of their seats. The floor of the plane was already covered with bodies. Strange, but after months of training with these guys, I don't recall any of the names of those who were lying in the plane before we jumped… There was plenty of fear to go around in the plane as we waited for the jump signal. But it was sort of surreal – there was no real panic.
>
> After what seemed like an eternity to those of us still lucky enough to have dodged the shell with our name on it, the pilot turned on the light that signalled us to stand up and prepare to jump… our jumpmaster, some other fellas, and I hooked up to our static lines. The plane was really going wild by now – rolling and pitching all over… so many of our guys in the plane

had already been hit or killed. When we got the green
light – out the door we went...

I was so relieved to get out of that flying disaster. We
could not have been much over 100 feet high when
we bailed out, for just as my chute popped open my
feet were scratching the grass. Our plane fared no better than most of the soldiers, for as soon as we were
out of the door it flew straight into a nearby rocky
outcrop of mountains.[290]

As Haider tried to unbuckle his parachute, he noticed that there
were several German machine guns firing in the area. It almost seemed
like he had landed right in the middle of the entire German army! He
crawled away for about a mile until he ran into two (and later, a third)
members of I Company. They had jumped from another plane. Not
long after they moved on, they heard an American paratrooper calling for help. He had broken his leg and was in great pain. His shinbone
seemed shattered. Haider gave the injured paratrooper a shot of morphine and left him under some bushes.

Several skirmishes with German patrols took place during the
night. It seemed they couldn't escape them as "at every turn we were
running across small German patrols. These troops were the elite Hermann Goering Division."[291] Haider's group kept engaging or evading
them successfully until one of them was killed by an 88mm shell as he
crossed an open field. There was nothing left of him.

Later, they sighted an airfield on top of a hill. They decided to
move up there as it seemed to be a clearly defined landmark. Maybe
they would run into other paratroopers on the way. As quiet as possible, the three paratroopers crept toward the hill. The airfield looked
desolate, and there were no other Americans in sight. Using a bazooka
and one round they had found in an equipment bundle, they knocked
out a German fighter plane that was concealed under camouflage net-
ting. The explosion alerted the German guards and Luftwaffe crews,
as Haider remembered: "They started heading in our direction and
we took off down the hill as quick as we could. We could hear them

yelling and knew they were looking for us, but luck was on our side this night."[292]

After two days and nights of dodging and engaging German patrols, they ran into Captain Lawrence P. Johnson and two troopers Haider recalled were named Don and Bill.[293] Johnson asked them if they had seen any other members of his H Company; Haider said no. Although they had no idea where they were on Sicily, Johnson decided to keep moving around to harass the Germans and Italians as much as possible until other paratroopers or Allied land forces showed up.

It was July 12, and after patrolling through several vineyards, they came upon a large farmhouse on the side of a hill. Slowly, as Haider recalled, the group moved closer: "As we approached the house all hell broke loose. They were trying to kill us as we walked up to the house. We returned fire, not knowing if a German patrol had holed up in the house or what we had run across. The shooting didn't last long and a group of Sicilians, all in Italian Army uniforms, came out with their hands in the air, shouting, 'Don't shoot! Don't shoot!' They were very poor soldiers by our account.

"The captain queried the folks about anyone else being in the house. One of the men, who appeared to be their spokesman, assured us that the house was now empty. Instead of checking the premises, the captain and the rest of us just started walking away. A shot rang out and hit Bill in the stomach. Without saying a word, the captain grabbed the group's spokesman by the hair, pulled his head back and cut his throat from ear to ear – almost cutting off his head. We tossed some grenades in the house and got out of there."[294]

Johnson decided to split up again to search for more paratroopers. He headed off in one direction with Don while the three I Company troopers went in another direction. Johnson is officially listed as being killed on July 10, 1943, but this should at least be corrected to July 12. His parents received a letter from one of his friends, a certain Lieutenant Norman Moseley, who informed them that he heard that Johnson was killed by enemy machine gun fire while trying to accomplish his company's mission—blowing up an enemy ammunition dump.[295]

On July 13, the I Company troopers were positioned in a vineyard when they spotted a company-sized group of Germans coming in their direction. At a few hundred yards distance, the paratroopers fired their rifles. Soon, all three were wounded by machine gun fire. Sergeant Haider recalled:

> We were not in the greatest of positions – lying between the rows of small vines that made up this particular vineyard. A German machine gun, that was way up on a hill overlooking the vineyard, kept us pinned down. The guy firing the gun just didn't let up. Then the artillery started to land all around us – they had zeroed in on all of us. The artillery just wouldn't let up until the ground troops got close. We were not letting up either, firing at them and throwing hand grenades... (...)

> We could hear the Germans moving up on us. I could hear one of the Germans ask his captain if they should shoot us. When the soldier asked this I figured – this is it. As I said, we were good, we had shot and hurt so many of the German soldiers that mercy was something we were not anticipating. The words of the soldier, "Should we shoot them?" rang like a bell in my head. Boy did I sweat. I told Tony and Len what the soldier had asked their captain. The captain said, "No, these men are wounded so we will take them in." Oh, what sweet relief![296]

First Lieutenant Fred E. Thomas, the executive officer of I Company, landed about five miles southeast from Niscemi and gathered five men from his stick. They reached the southern edge of the town around 0330 hours but couldn't spot any other paratroopers. Thomas assumed the battalion was west of Niscemi and led his small group in a westward direction.

At around 1000 hours, Thomas's force encountered a German group that was being fired upon. Seven Germans were killed, but in the ensuing fire, two troopers were killed as well, while a third paratrooper was wounded. Thomas and the remaining two men were forced to withdraw, leaving their casualties behind as the unknown friendly force on the other side of the Germans had disappeared. Later during the day, they ran into eight troopers of H Company commanded by Private Henry E. Ferrari. Ferrari's group hadn't met any other paratroopers, so Thomas decided to move in a southeastern direction to the landing beaches.

An EGB447 replacement in I Company, Pfc. Albert C. Haggard of the 1st Platoon, recalled that "as we crossed over the coast of Sicily, we came under fire from German anti-aircraft guns. Now flying over land, we headed toward our dropzone. Within a few minutes, the pilots passed the word back to stand up and hook up. (...) Clicking noises could be heard all over the plane as we snapped our lifelines onto the cable running the length of the cabin. The red light turned to green, and troopers ran for the door. The middleman in the stick tripped the switch to release the equipment bundles, and then it was my turn. With my break cord attached to the static line, I stepped out the door into nothingness, and fell into a war. (...)

"The moon was brightly shining and from this lofty position, it was easy to see everything in the sky, but the only aircraft I saw was the C-47 I had jumped from, easily visible with sparks flying from the exhaust. I saw other parachutes, but they had also come from my aircraft. Where were the other planes? Were we all alone?"[297]

Haggard unbuckled his parachute and had just cautiously started to walk when he was challenged with "George" by a nervous voice. "Washington," he replied as fast as possible. He recalled:

> Sergeant [Lloyd V.] Engebretson swiftly rushed to my side. (...) "I am sure glad to see you," he breathed heavily as we both rejoiced in the fact that we were no longer alone. "I am sure glad to see you," I said, as the panic I felt earlier subsided. I was still uneasy and scared. (...)
>
> Together, we proceeded to lower ground. (...) We had congregated almost a whole planeload of paratroopers and each and every one of them had an

assembled and loaded weapon, although we had yet to see an officer! (…)

Feeling braver with our increased numbers, we set out to find the houses and Italian troops we had been assigned to destroy. For hours we searched the hills, but never found our assigned target. Finally, giving up on finding the Italian barracks, we backtracked, searching for our heavy equipment bundles. We found some of them, and armed ourselves with M-1's while keeping the Thompsons as our primary weapon. We also retrieved a machine gun, although we never found the bundles containing the mortars. As daylight approached, we formed a circle and dug in.[298]

Sergeant Lloyd Engebretson of the 1st Platoon in I Company made it through several campaigns. He would become a well-respected platoon sergeant and was cited for bravery in the Waal River Crossing. Courtesy: Gary Engebretson

In the same plane as Haggard was twenty-three-year-old Private Alfred Burgreen, who "landed in a sloping olive grove and sprained my ankle. I was loaded with my M-1 rifle. I didn't see anyone [at first]. I saw a nearby hill from the village of Niscemi. My instinct was to get on

top of the hill."[299] There Burgreen met their platoon leader, 1st Lieutenant Willis J. Ferrill, who came down approximately six miles southeast of Niscemi. At 0900 hours, Ferrill had assembled twenty enlisted
men from both H and I Companies at Castle Nocera. There he found
nineteen-year-old Private Shelby R. Hord of Kalamazoo, Michigan and
three other men of H Company who landed practically on top of it.
They gathered their own machine gun and two 60mm mortars from
equipment bundles.

Hord recalled a year later that

> the trip over the water had been very rough and all of
> us were sick as pups. We had come through a lot of
> flak and tracers over the coastline, but everything was
> nice and quiet where we jumped. I landed hard, but
> this didn't surprise me – I always land hard I guess.
> Our fellows were strung out all over the place but six
> of us got together and secured our bundles, which
> contained two light machine guns and ten boxes of
> ammunitions, some land mines, a bazooka with shells,
> and a lot of other stuff. This was too much for us to
> carry so three of us stayed to guard it while the other
> three searched in different directions for the rest of the
> bunch. We searched from midnight until just before
> dawn. It was getting light when we saw we were in a
> small valley. On one side above us was a castle. It
> looked like a good place so we crept up there and cap-
> tured it.
>
> The castle was filled with about 100 people from the
> nearby town who had sought refuge there with the
> Sicilian baron who owned the place. They made a
> great fuss over the "Americani" and helped us retrieve
> our equipment from the floor of the valley. Later that
> morning we were joined by a lieutenant and 12 more
> troopers. We dug in around the hill below the castle
> walls and asked the baron to send the townspeople

away and go with them as there was likely to be fighting. The baron agreed and asked our men to use what we needed but to protect his many valuable possessions in the castle if possible.[300]

The high ground of Castle Nocera, three miles south east of Niscemi, provided an excellent field of fire on the surrounding area. Lieutenant Ferrill sent out a contact patrol to find the rest of the 3rd Battalion while a radio operator tried in vain to reach other units. The patrol encountered a German 88mm anti-aircraft battery on a hill 1000 yards to their rear, killed two gunners, captured two, and was forced to withdraw to Castle Nocera.

At around 1400 hours that day, a motorized force of about twenty Italians attacked the position; fourteen of them were killed and two were captured. The others retired to a safer distance. Hord received the Distinguished Service Cross for his extraordinary heroism: "Private Hord, a machine gunner, alone and upon his own initiative, courageously advanced three hundred yards under intense machine gun and rifle fire toward an enemy machine gun position. From a distance of about fifty feet he threw four hand grenades into the position, then attacked the enemy with his carbine, killing four and wounding three. The enemy force was completely disorganized and routed, enabling his unit to advance and use the captured machine guns against the enemy."[301]

Hord remembered that

> I was pretty nervous because I wasted three of my grenades, throwing them at trees and rocks before I was sure of hitting some Germans. Anyhow, I only had two left when I stuck my head up over a small ledge right at three Germans behind a machine gun. They were so busy firing they must not have seen me, so I tossed my next and last grenade right into them. One got up and started to run, and I don't know what happened to him because I was busy finishing off the other two with my carbine.

Then I kept going up the hill and ran into a German officer standing in a small path. I tried to shoot him but my carbine jammed, and for what reason the Lord alone knows, he just stood there without saying a word while I stuffed a round into the chamber with my fingers and shot him. Then the gun started to function O.K. again, so I let him have a couple more. I started looking around then. I could hear other guys yelling to each other on the other hill that I was over there with the Germans and not to shoot me. (…) I don't ordinarily swear, but all during this time I was going up the hill, shooting and throwing grenades, I heard myself yelling and cursing. Looking back on it, I guess I was pretty keyed up.

I heard a lot of firing up the hill, so I kept going and found six Germans behind two machine guns in a small gun emplacement they had dug. They saw me right off, but by this time I was firing and they didn't have a chance to kill me. That stopped the reaction, except for some scattered rifle fire from Germans in the bushes around the rim of the hill.

Five of my buddies came over and finished them off and then we carried the German machine guns and ammunition back across the valley to our position under the castle. That's how I got the Distinguished Service Cross.[302]

After this engagement of four hours, in which Private Thomas E. Lane of H Company killed four Italian riflemen who were protecting their machine guns, the number of paratroopers grew bit by bit, including some machine gunners from the Machine Gun Platoon. Lane also "provided water to the soldiers of his company" in these hours and was later awarded a Silver Star: "During most of this time he was exposed to heavy machine gun and small arms fire of the enemy and was sniped upon on many occasions."[303]

Meanwhile, Ferrill's force grew to about sixty officers and men, which enabled him to put up a listening post on the evening of July 10. Hostile patrols were driven off during the night, and in the morning of July 11, they were reinforced by Lieutenant George J. Watts and his mixed group of paratroopers from H and Headquarters Companies. Watts, being a first lieutenant longer than Ferrill, assumed command of the castle defenders.

On July 13, the paratroopers sighted a large column of the Hermann Goering Panzer Division below Castle Nocera. Ferrill recalled that out of "the valley came a column of Heinies. That was Tuesday. We were dug in and everyone had drawn a bead when the column fell out on the roadside for a 20 minutes break...

"We held our fire until they started struggling to their feet, then let them have it with everything, including four Italian field pieces we had captured. By that time we had more enemy ammunition and guns than we had of our own.

"Toward evening they sent two runners up to negotiate a surrender. When they learned that we were paratroopers they would have none of it. We kept on fighting and I thought they would rush us at night, but under cover of darkness they pulled out. We later counted more than 50 dead Germans, all from the Hermann Goering Division."[304]

A large German infantry column with two Mark IV tanks was spotted around 1330 hours on July 13 moving northeast toward Niscemi. On Watts' orders, the roads leading to the castle had previously been mined with Hawkins anti-tank mines. Two 60mm mortars of H Company, machine guns (both American and captured ones), and three bazookas provided enough firepower to engage the column. Under exposure of heavy enemy machine gun and rifle fire, Lane managed to carry water to over a hundred of his comrades during the battle. For his actions, he would later be decorated with the Silver Star.

In the fierce ensuing fight, the Germans lost seventy-five; the paratroopers also had fatal casualties. Second Lieutenant Edward C. Digan of the 3rd Battalion Headquarters Company was mortally wounded and posthumously received a Silver Star: "Lieutenant Digan was in command of a rocket launcher platoon. The position was being attacked by an enemy infantry battalion supported by tanks. The entire area was subject to intense crossfire by enemy machine guns from the flanks. Lieutenant Digan, without regard for his own safety and exposing himself to enemy gun fire, carried reserve ammunition to the forward machine guns on the hill several times. While attempting to carry ammunition across open terrain to a machine gun position, he was seriously wounded in the neck. During treatment of his wounds, Lieutenant Digan made several attempts to get up and carry ammunition to the gun, but was too weak to do so. He died an hour later."[305]

CHAPTER 15

BAPTISM OF FIRE

Sicily

JULY 11-JULY 12, 1943

T he Regimental liaison officer, Major Emory S. Adams, Jr. (West Point 1940), was aboard the American attack transport *Monrovia* as the 3rd Battalion and the 505th Regimental Combat Team were dropped on Sicily. The ship had made an uneventful trip from Algiers to the island. Adams, along with several other officers of the advanced Division Headquarters group, was eager to go ashore after the amphibious landings had started. Word came back that the Ranger Battalions and the 1st Infantry Division had successfully landed at Gela, the same place the *Monrovia* was headed for. Once in the area, Major General Matthew B. Ridgway went ashore on a landing craft along with his aide. They first visited the command post of the 1st Infantry Division east of Gela. There was no news there about the reinforced 505th Regimental Combat Team. No one had either seen a paratrooper or received any radio calls from them.

Borrowing a bodyguard, Ridgway and his aide walked further inland until they encountered a lone company commander of the 505th Parachute Infantry Regiment, Captain Willard R. Follmer, who sat against a tree with a broken ankle. Follmer had no idea where Colonel James Gavin or any of the battalion commanders were. Ridgway's group moved on for a few more miles, encountering only a few stray paratroopers, whom he directed to join patrols of the 1st Infantry

Division instead of taking them along, which might have been the wiser thing to do.

Finally, at the end of the morning, Ridgway returned to the 1st Division CP and tried in vain to raise contact with a paratrooper detachment. He chose to remain on the *Monrovia* for the night and told his staff officers, including Adams, that he was unable to find his battalions. He then contacted Lieutenant General George S. Patton, Jr. by radio and advised him to call off the 504th Regimental Combat Team drop for that night.[306]

The next morning, July 11, Patton sent orders to Ridgway to arrange a drop of the remainder of Colonel Reuben H. Tucker's 504th Regimental Combat Team at an abandoned airfield called Farello three miles east of Gela. Patton could use the remaining part of Tucker's force as the opposition seemed to increase, especially near Biscari and Biazzo Ridge where the 45th Infantry Division was having a hard time.[307] This was transmitted to Tucker in Kairouan, who ordered his troopers to prepare for their first combat jump.

Many of Tucker's troopers had been disappointed on July 10 when they learned their planned drop was cancelled. That evening, 2nd Lieutenant Robert D. Condon of A Company was reminiscing about his life and the paratroopers in his 2nd Platoon. He became platoon leader in January 1943 when Lieutenant John S. Lekson was transferred to the battalion staff. Condon now bore the burden of commanding his men in their first taste of combat. He felt that

> the big day had come. We had been conditioned physically to an extent that approaches perfection. The night before was spent as though it might be the last night on earth. For some, it was! You were continually awakened by nothing at all and lay there in the ground until the mind became dulled with the thoughts of home and mother; the days at college; your first job; summers at the shore; the very enjoyable summer the family spent together in New England. Until finally you are again asleep.

Morning came early, but you found everyone up and excited about the big deal that would materialize that evening. You saw men standing, quietly, just watching the sun rise. You overheard someone jokingly remark to them, "You better take a good look, it may be the last one you will see."

We moved to the airport and the day was spent busily preparing the final details for the coming night's work. Before you knew it they were serving supper and surprisingly everyone had enough good food to eat. The past weeks had been spent in the desert and the food had not been too palatable.[308]

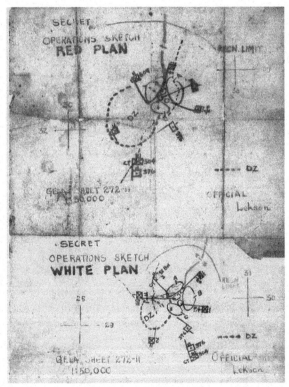

Sketches that were kept by 2nd Lieutenant Robert Condon of A Company of the Sicily invasion. Neither plan was executed due to the friendly fire disaster... Courtesy: Robert Condon

Lieutenant Colonel William P. Yarborough, the 2nd Battalion commander, felt disappointed that "I had no part of the planning of Sicily."[309] He believed his participation in earlier airborne operations of the 509th Parachute Battalion in North Africa qualified him for advice on the battle plan. Yarborough had previously arranged camouflage paint for his paratroopers so they could paint dots on their helmets and khaki-colored jumpsuits. This example was soon followed by other units within the 504th PIR.[310]

"We painted green and brown spots on our jump suits, web equipment, and helmets," remembered Private Ross S. Carter of C Company. "Some of the boys even painted spots on their Tommyguns. Two little death's heads were put on our company's helmets for identification. Later on we discovered that German SS troops wore the same emblem but did not give a damn about that.

"We were issued water-purifying pulls, Atabrine pills to prevent malaria, anti-fatigue pills, emergency rations consisting of K-rations and D-bars, the latter being concentrated chocolate, one of which sufficed to keep a man fed for a day."[311]

Sergeant Ken Nicoll of the 2nd Battalion Mortar Platoon made it through all campaigns. His uniform clearly shows the painted dots, an idea of Lieutenant Colonel William Yarborough before Operation Husky. Courtesy: Allen Schoppe

The Regimental Reconnaissance Platoon, commanded by 2nd Lieutenant Harold M. Gutterman and the Regimental Demolition Platoon of 1st Lieutenant Erwin B. Bigger, would be flown in piecemeal; many planeloads included two scouts or demolition men. This way, most parachute sticks would have specialists with them. The parachute riggers of the 504th Parachute Maintenance Company were equally divided over the planes.

Captain Ted M. Wight's C Company of the 307th Airborne Engineer Battalion and Lieutenant Colonel Wilbur M. Griffith's 376th Parachute Field Artillery Battalion were divided over separate serials. The only exception were the forward artillery observers: Major Robert H. Neptune was in the same airplane as Colonel Tucker. Neptune's task was to serve as Tucker's artillery liaison officer. Another forward observer, Captain Frank D. Boyd, jumped in the same stick as Lieutenant Colonel Warren R. Williams, Jr. of the 1st Battalion.

As the evening of July 11 drew near, Yarborough found to his dismay that "I didn't have a map as the battalion commander. Reuben Tucker had one, he had the only one in the outfit so far as I know. The briefings consisted of drawing on the ground with a stick. 'We're here; they're there. You're going to do this and they're going to do this,' you see."[312] Yarborough felt he wasn't properly prepared for the mission that lay ahead.

First Lieutenant Lewis P. Fern, the S-2 officer, flew with his intelligence section: "Colonel Tucker discovered that Lieutenant Colonel Yarborough had his entire staff in one plane. You don't do that, as the battalion is leaderless in case the plane is shot down. Tucker sent word about one hour before we took off to break down the staff on several planes."[313]

Second Lieutenant Lauren W. Ramsey, the platoon leader of the 81mm Mortar Platoon, had joined the 2nd Battalion only a few weeks before along with four other officers: "I joined the 504th Parachute Infantry in North Africa. Most of us weren't even long with the 504th when we went to Sicily. I didn't know all my men." Ramsey considered the 2nd Battalion was ill-prepared for the invasion, and overall that "our leaders were inexperienced. They hadn't been in a war. Everything we did was new. None of our men had any combat experience."[314]

Protestant Chaplain Delbert Kuehl remembered "the colonel spoke to our group. He said, 'I want you now to be the kind of soldiers you were trained to be, and I know you will be.' Prior to that we had gone through the sand table exercises in preparation for the drop. We expected that we would receive opposition, but we didn't except to have any unusual opposition. Before we went, I had a service around a large cactus, and we boarded the planes."[315]

Lieutenant Condon of A Company recalled that "at the signal from the CO we moved to the planes to await zero hour. At the planes we made a final check on the men's equipment and weapons. We made sure that the extra machine guns and ammunition on the bomb racks were securely fastened. Then we just sat and waited. It was interesting to listen to the men and the subjects they discussed at this thoughtful hour. Some described in lengthy detail the prettiest girl they had ever seen. Others expressed a wish for a good drink, or a dish of ice cream, or a good cold bottle of beer before they would go. All the men enjoyed the questions and complimenting remarks of the ground crew that would be left behind.

"The signal came at last. We took our places in the plane and checked to make sure that we had all our men and that they were in the correct places. We also made a final check on the equipment. Whether we knew it or not we were about to begin the most exciting night of our lives."[316]

Carter of C Company remembered that "extra water was to be dropped in plastic water bags in case we couldn't find any. We also had gas masks and first aid packets containing bandages, sulfanilamide powder, and eight pills of sulfadiazine to swallow with water to keep down infection. In addition, we each had a little kit with morphine and Syrette to give it with. Each platoon had a first aid man who jumped with it. He carried blood plasma and knew how to give it. We were walking arsenals. Bandoleers of rifle ammunition crisscrossed our chests, Tommygun ammo hung on our sides, and grenades bulged our pockets and canvas bags."[317]

Some officers of the 504th PIR climbed aboard a transport plane unauthorized, as they didn't want to miss this "milk-run" combat operation. Their task was to remain in North Africa and wait to come to

Sicily on a later detail or to operate the base at Kairouan. The invasion of Sicily had started early on the previous day, so there would be less resistance than the 3rd Battalion and the 505th Regimental Combat Team experienced, they reasoned. Captains Harry J. Cummings, the Regimental Personnel Officer, and Otis A. Danneman of Service Company found a seat in C-53D 42-68708, piloted by 1st Lieutenant Raymond O. Roush and 2nd Lieutenant David E. Mondt of the 62nd Troop Carrier Squadron, 314th Troop Carrier Group. Staff Sergeant Raymond J. Butler was the radio operator on board, and Sergeant Fielding J. Armstrong served as the plane's crew chief.[318]

As the pilots did not check on the passengers, the jumpmaster of each stick was responsible for accounting for the paratroopers inside the plane. The pilots and crew focused only on flying.[319] Therefore, it could happen that Captains Cummings and Danneman overruled Master Sergeant James E. Byrd and arranged to fly along. Brigadier General Charles L. Keerans, Jr., the Assistant Division Commander, thought the same, and his staff car pulled up near the airplane as the engines were already running in preparation for take-off. The pilots were astonished to see him board the aircraft holding a folded parachute pack in his hands.

Mondt, the co-pilot, had barely comprehended what had taken place when Captain John M. Gibson of his squadron ordered him out of the airplane. Gibson was not scheduled to fly the mission at all, but he pulled his rank and ordered Mondt to leave the aircraft, which was already set up to depart right behind the leading airplane. "Where do I have to fly?" asked the agitated lieutenant. "Kick someone else off another plane," came Gibson's laconic reply. Gibson directed Roush to the co-pilot seat and took over the controls from him. Mondt could do little else than leave the C-53 and walk to the edge of the runway, viewing his colleagues depart on what was supposed to be his second combat mission.[320]

Brigade General Maxwell Taylor, Assistant Division Commander, with Colonel
Reuben Tucker just before take off at Kairouan Airfield, July 1943. Tucker would
lead his regiment in all WWII combat operations. Courtesy: Mandle family

A last handshake is given to Captain Julian Cook, Regimental S-4, as he boards the C-47 that
will take him to Sicily, July 1943. Cook would rise to assistant battalion commander in the
Italian Campaigns, and later lead the epic Waal River Crossing. Courtesy: Mandle family

Paratroopers of Colonel Tucker's plane climbing into the C-47 at Kairouan, July 1943. They would have to make their first combat jump amidst friendly fire. Courtesy: Mandle family

As darkness fell, the 144 airplanes droned across the Mediterranean Sea toward the island of Malta and turned left. The lead serial of the 52nd Troop Carrier Wing was formed by the 29th Troop Carrier Squadron. Captain Willard E. Harrison and a stick of A Company headquarters personnel flew in the leading aircraft of the squadron with the remainder of the company flying right behind him. Although A Company had been reconstituted only months before, they were now to lead the main force of the 504th PIR into combat.

Condon, who didn't fly far behind his company commander, recalled:

> After circling in the air for about an hour the armada of planes was in line. As I leaned out the door and looked to the rear I saw a sight that I shall never forget. The large C-47s were in flights of three in a "V" formation as far as the eye could see. It was immense almost to the point of being unnatural. It was the beginning of the African July and the sun was just setting. (...)

As we flew north toward Tunis and the coast I continued to stand in the door. The Arabs were finishing up their evening chores. But as the great spectacle passed over their quiet evening they stopped to stare up at us in wonder. The ground itself looked like a little kid's garden that he has under his Christmas tree. And I thought of Christmas and wondered if I would ever see another one. I looked at the men, who sat quietly smoking and wondered if they were thinking the same things that I was. I tried to read their faces but they were lacking in all expression. They just sat and smoked.

As I looked from one to the other I thought how young they looked; how proud their mothers would be if they could see them. They must be thinking the same things that I am, – Will I be afraid; Will I get killed – I hope to hell I don't! Then I noticed the sun. It was in the final stages of setting and the sky seemed to be more beautiful than ever before. I wondered if I would see it set again.

By the time we flew over Tunis and reached the north coast of Africa it was dark. Although the city was blacked out you could distinguish the network of streets and the shadow of the taller buildings in the light of the three-quarter moon. We were over the blue Mediterranean. I went forward to check the course and time. We were flying a check-point course. We had flown on a certain azimuth a certain mileage to Tunis. Now we were to change azimuth and fly to the south-eastern tip of Malta. Then northeast to the southeast tip of Sicily, and in across the island. Then – well time will tell.

It was two hours or more flying time before the objective would be reached so I sat down on the floor of the plane and rested my back against the chute. I thought that if this was the night that there would be a lot of things that I wanted to do that would never be done. Anyway I felt great. At a time like this a man is carried forward by a feeling inside himself. A feeling that seems to make him swell up and tell himself that no sacrifice is too great for the country and family that he has left.

The men were relaxed, some even asleep. The task ahead did not seem to be worrying a one of them. The navigator came back and said that he wanted me to check the ground wind. After careful check we found that there was practically no wind at all.[321]

Private Albert B. Clark sat probably in the same plane as Condon and thought that the "flight to Sicily was uneventful until we were almost near Malta. The crew chief and I were sitting in front of the door talking and watching the night. When I said, 'What the hell, did we get an escort tonight?' He said, 'What do you mean?' I replied, 'There's a fighter out there right behind those three planes on our left.' He took off for the pilot and returned a few minutes later and said that the pilot said that they weren't ours but Jerries – German fighter planes – flew in our formation.

"We watched them for a while and they took off. Why they didn't shoot us down we could never figure out, but we were very happy that they left us alone. We continued on and around Malta and back to Sicily. We got the signal to stand up, hook up and check equipment."[322]

Lieutenant Condon did not see the fighter planes as he dozed off for a short while:

I must have fallen asleep, for the next thing I knew we were over the island fortress of Malta. The aircraft batteries on the ground flashed recognition signals to the lead planes. The island rose out of the water; a solid mountain of rock. It truly looked its reputation as a perennial fortress. We circled the island and headed for Sicily.

I checked the time with the navigator. We were in the lead planes of the whole regiment and we would hit the island on the second. We were on the nose. I told the men that we would have to be ready in two minutes as it was only four minutes to the island. They smoked a last cigarette. I closely watched my watch. The red light came on and seemed to fill the plane with a feeling that something beyond even our imagination would happen soon. I was nervous, nervous to the point of wondering whether or not I was afraid.

So when I "stood the men up" I had to concentrate on not letting any of what I felt show in my voice. They were depending on me, I could not let them down. I had worked with these men for a year now. Had taken them direct from "Jump School" and had done my best to train them.

I walked to the rear of the line, carefully feeling my way in the dark. I checked from front of the plane and the rear of my "stick" to the front of it and the open door of the plane, slapping each man on the back and wishing him good-hunting. "Stand in the door." I hooked up my own static line and took my place in the door.[323]

Captain Harrison tried to follow the flight route "in the leading plane of the first serial and reached the coast of Sicily near Punta Secca at approximately 2230 hours, thence flew in a northwesterly direction along the coast toward Gela. The left wing flew just over the water line, and the squadron of nine planes continued perfect formation up the coast at an altitude of approximately nine hundred feet.

"We encountered no fire of any kind until the lead plane reached Lake Biviera when one .50-caliber machine gun, situated in the sand dunes several hundred yards from the shore, opened fire. As soon as this firing began, guns along the coast as far as we could see toward Punta Secca opened fire and the naval craft lying offshore, both towards Punta Secca and toward Gela began firing antiaircraft guns."[324]

Unaware of the fact that the German Army didn't use red tracers, Lieutenant Condon believed enemy gunners were firing below:

> In a minute we would be over Sicily. One moment the sky was as clear as any I have ever seen back home. One moment the moon was setting in a pale, dusty white. The next moment the sky was filled with the reddish, hellish death of war. I sucked in a deep breath. I could hear my heart pounding like a large drum, even above the roar of the engines. This is the end. I will die tonight. I know it.

> There was a sheet of tracer from one end of the earth to the other. It rose like a sheet of death as far as the eye could see. German anti-aircraft batteries. They came through the wings, the floor, the tail – those little red messengers of death. Those German bastards! If we could only get on the ground.

> I watched our left wing plane. How could it stay up? They had it in a complete cone of fire. The stuff was like rain. If we had been flying upside down I would have sworn it was the fire and brimstone that is mentioned in the Bible. There was another spray toward us and it sounded like nuts and bolts rattling around on the belly of the plane. The navigator screamed.

The plane gave a jerk. I looked out the door and saw our equipment chutes heading earthward. The bastards had shot off our extra ammunition and guns. We were in the cone again. I was scared to death. Every damn thing I had ever done, good and bad, slid by before me like the fastest motion picture I have ever seen. I thought of Mom, and all the times I could have been home with her and wasn't; of Dad and how hard he had worked for us kids, grown old before his time doing things for us; of that kid brother in the Air Corps, much too young for this stuff. I promised God that no matter what I had done if I ever lived through this, I swore I should be better.

A big red one came in the door over my shoulder. It was foot from me but I thought I was dead. Christ did I pray. I wanted to get behind my men, between them and the firing. I couldn't do it. Something held me in the door. I have often wondered what it was. Discipline or pride perhaps? And then it stopped. I checked my men. By some miracle none of them were hit. I thanked God again. We were close to our objective now. And I was waiting for the green light.

As I hung out the door I could see the DZ ahead and damned if they didn't have bands of fire [on the drop zone]. The green light. I turned to my men. "This is it," I shouted and with a very deep breath I hit the silk. Downward, earthward, our silken banners flowed. I could see those Germans trying to hit the men on the way down. I grabbed the front two risers and pulled them to my knees. We were only in the air ten seconds but it seemed like eternity.[325]

Corporal John Savage of A Company recalled that "as we crossed the coastline, I was impressed by the quantities of smoke from the exhaust that the plane was throwing out. Later I discovered it was fire from the ack-ack guns. About the same time, hot metal began pelting the plane like hail on a tin roof. I was glad to jump that time. We floated down just like a practice maneuver, with sound effects. I thought for a while I was going to land on a burning Nazi tank, but didn't."[326]

On July 13, Lieutenant Colonel Williams had assembled part of his Headquarters Company, including 2nd Lieutenant Calvin J. Billman and the majority of the 81mm Mortar Platoon. He arranged rifle protection for his mortar crews from a major of the 180th Infantry Regiment while they fired mortar shells on the tanks. One light tank was knocked out, and the others withdrew. Billman was awarded the Silver Star: "The unit to which Lieutenant Billman had become attached withdrew from its position in the face of artillery and mortar fire. Lieutenant Billman remained at his post of observation and directed mortar fire which destroyed two 20mm ammunition carriers."[327]

Corporal Harry A. Gordon of the Machine Gun Platoon was also posthumously decorated with the Silver Star for fighting at the same location: "Corporal Gordon held his position and kept his light machine gun firing to cover the withdrawal until his position was hit by mortar fire. Corporal Gordon was killed in this action."[328]

Captain Charles W. Duncan's B Company came more widely spread down than A Company. "As we reached the coast," recalled Staff Sergeant Henry P. Paquet of the 2nd Platoon, "order came to stand and hook up. Then we started climbing and, after what seemed an hour, the order to jump came. (...) I could see tracers all around me and several went into my canopy after it had opened. I loaded my Tommygun and tried to draw a bead on a machine gun which was shooting too close for comfort. But I found my oscillation was too great, but that made me just that much harder to hit. A moment later I struck the ground and as I did so someone started firing at me. I cut myself loose from my parachute and took off. Later I met some of our men."[329]

In the early morning hours, Paquet's group was ambushed on a bridge and blown off the railing by the explosion of a German hand grenade. Paquet injured both ankles: "The next morning about an hour before daylight we were ambushed and I was later captured by the Germans. An hour later I managed to escape."[330] Probably in the same plane were Pfc. T.J. Crockett and Private Ralph C. Hall, who were also captured upon landing at the German-held Biscari Airfield. Crockett's landing was extremely painful as, to his horror, he came down upon a strand of barbed wire.[331] They were both incarcerated in Stalag II-B Hammerstein.

A radio operator in B Company, Technician 5th Grade Lawrence W. Stimpson, recalled that "just before we got to Sicily, they had us stand up and hook up to get ready to jump. I guess they figured if there wasn't any trouble, we were going to jump, which we did. I know I was about the third man. I could see the door real clear that I was jumping out of and pretty soon I could see these sparks flying. And I thought, 'Didn't they put a shroud over that exhaust point of that C-47 so it wouldn't show sparks at night?' Then it dawned on me – those sparks weren't going parallel, they were going directly towards us.

"About that time, we got the signal to jump, and that sky looked just like the 4th of July with the fireworks and it was not the enemy that was firing on us – it was the Navy... I understand that there were bombers bombing the beachhead at the time. They kind of got mixed up in our formation. One of the guys said he saw a bomber go underneath us just about we were getting ready to jump."[332]

Pfc. Edwin E. Decker jumped with a 3rd Platoon stick of B Company and wrote to his parents a few weeks later: "I came down in an olive orchard the night we landed. Everything seemed pretty strange. There was a stone wall going through the orchard with a ditch filled with running water on top of it, for irrigation I guess. This is the way lots of the water is moved short distances here. The wall seems to be built of mortar and stone and then a little ditch hollowed out on top. Let me know what you hear from the others of our section who were in North Africa."[333]

Twenty-four-year-old Sergeant James O. Eldridge of C Company wrote to his sisters that on

> the day of the jump everyone was up real early in the morning and seemed to be in high spirits. Just after we

had finished breakfast (...) our company commander gave us a talk, then we checked and packed our gear and moved to the airport. We stayed there all day and were supposed to jump that night but just as we were putting on our chutes we got word that a lot of activity was taking place in the area where we are supposed to jump. Several of the fellows were pretty burned up about the matter but others said they were sure the Germans didn't expect us this early or they certainly could not have been so rude as to be maneuvering around in our landing sector at a time when we needed it most. Anyway the officers got together and decided that since the Germans were already there that rather than cause hard feelings we would stand by and take what was left.

Well, we stood by on alert all through the night and the next day. Then about six o'clock that night we got the word to get into our 'chutes. But first we took about 20 minutes to exercise, then put on our gear, including our 'chutes, and got into the planes.

We circled around for about 40 minutes, getting flight information and then all the planes turned noses out across the Mediterranean Sea. Everyone seemed to be feeling great and I might stress that "seemed," because if they were like me, you could call it "whistling in the graveyard." Not near as much was said about the jump we had ahead of us as you might think. The talk was about band leaders and it was pretty well agreed that Harry James was tops as far as we were concerned. And the talk finally drifted around to baseball and boxing, of course. (...)

As we neared Sicily everyone felt it more and more. About 15 minutes before we were supposed to jump we got the command to put on our helmets. As time grew shorter we got the commands, "Stand up" and "Hook up." Well, I would like to tell you that I walked up and down that plane floor with a big grin on my face, feeling like I was about to enter the Friendly Tavern. But the way it was, it was quite different. The jump master gave the command, "Stand in the door." (...)

I must have stood in that doorway about eight minutes while the pilot was trying to locate our area. I kept trying to convince myself that my feeling came from something I had eaten, but I knew I was wrong. I was the number one man and was supposed to go when I was hit on the leg by the jumpmaster. I remember him asking, "Is everybody ready?" Everyone says, "Yeah." Then he asked, "Is everybody happy?" Everyone says, "Yeah." Then he said, "Okay, men. Let's give them hell!" Then the light turned green and he hit my leg.

I jumped – and the next few seconds seemed awfully long. We got together all right and started clicking in great order, but maybe I can tell you more about it next time. All I could tell you this time was about the jump.[334]

Sergeant James Eldridge of C Company was part of the Regimental Boxing Team and made it through all campaigns, later in G Company so he could easier train with other boxers. Courtesy: Jimmy Eldridge

Technician 4th Grade Robert W. Lowery of C Company, Captain Albert E. Milloy's radio operator, remembered that "we took off in the late afternoon to be able to jump after dark. Everyone was uptight. It took about three hours to make the flight. We were in two-engine C-47s that carried fourteen men in each. We were supposed to jump on an airfield inland.

"As we came near the shore and were flying over the invasion fleet one of the ships opened fire on us. We were supposed to be flying at about five hundred feet at that time. The fleet had been notified that we were coming. Some of the reports say that one of the ships had not received the message. When the first one opened up, they all started shooting. Captain Milloy, our Company Commander, was to jump first and I was behind him as his radio operator. When I got out the door and saw all the tracers coming I thought, 'Is this what battle looks like?' It did not sink in at that moment that they were shooting at us."[335]

"I got airsick," recalled 1st Lieutenant Francis W. Payne, commanding the 1st Platoon in C Company. "Some of my men were snoring. I felt like hell. Finally we hit the island, flew over the coast and everything on the island began shooting at us – just looked like the 4th of July. We stood up and hooked our static line. The time had come! There is the red light. Tracers are sizzling by us. Green light! Go!

"Crack! My parachute opens. More tracers zip by singing like hell. I saw one chute on fire. Some of our planes have been shot down. Wham! I hit the ground."[336]

In another plane, Payne's assistant, 2nd Lieutenant James E. Dunn, thought "the Sicily jump was a mess. En route to the Drop Zone the air column got broken up and flew over the landing ships as a German night bomber attacked. Our ships opened fire hitting some planes, ours and enemy, and further disrupting the approach to the drop sites. My plane load was dropped approximately 25 miles from the drop zone (off our maps). Through an interpreter we asked some locals where we were and how to get to the drop zone. We got there the next day."[337]

Another platoon leader, 1st Lieutenant James H. Goethe of the 2nd Platoon, noticed the German bombers as well: "A group of

German bombers decided to unload on the unloading convoy off Gela, Sicily. I know for when they turned on the green light for us to jump a German bomber crossed beneath us. How I managed to hold 16 people in the airplane until the bomber cleared beneath us I will never know."[338]

Carter of the 3rd Platoon landed in a vineyard: "Stunned and breathless, I lay on the ground tangled in my chute and fighting equipment, expecting German infantry to pounce upon me any second. I put my rifle together and got on my feet. Fifteen yards distant a double stream of red tracers bubbled skyward over a stone wall about eight feet high.

"New at the fighting game, I never considered that I was watching *red* tracers, whereas the Germans use silver tracers. With a grenade in hand, I sneaked up to the wall. At that time the gun quit shooting and I heard, 'Man, we gave it to them Nazi bastards.' I realized then that our own men had been shooting at us. I had been on the point of killing some of our soldiers, who must have killed some of us."[339]

During the night, Carter ran into more platoon members, until they were nearly all assembled: "We spent the day watching our first dogfights, listening to rumors and wondering what next. My platoon was together again."[340] His platoon sergeant, Staff Sergeant William Walsh, recalled how "we flew through intense fire from our own and enemy forces. Our flight became very disorientated and the pilots had radio orders to jump their loads at their discretion. My platoon was scattered over a wide area. (...) We were jumping new nylon parachutes and there was considerable stretch in the body harness. My own chest strap and reserve chute were right tight against my chin after the opening shock. It was at night and a difficult landing at best."[341]

Private Keith K. Scott of 1st Lieutenant Richard F. Mills' Machine Gun Platoon flew in the same C-47 as his platoon leader. He recalled:

> We first received the order to stand up and hook up just off the coast. Just over the beach we ran into anti-aircraft fire. Our plane kept diving and banking. The pilot passed the word down the line to jump on the red light. At the time the word reached Lieutenant

Mills the red light flashed on. We started out. Just as I got to the door our plane was hit. I was knocked back against the opposite side of the ship. I finally got out. Where we landed there were a couple of pillboxes burning from the bombing raid.

We started to assemble in an orchard where the artillery opened up on us. That didn't last long. We assembled and found out that (...) Corporal [Stanley J.] Len had broken his leg. We wrapped him in a chute and hid him in a vine patch. We left him with two riggers.

Lieutenant Mills got his bearings and told us what the score was. We had dropped 15 miles from the right DZ in enemy territory. We got our weapons and marched down the road. We heard somebody yelling and a whirring sound like an auto stuck in the mud. I don't know why but we marched right into them. We walked across a bridge.

As we reached the end we heard someone yelled, "Halt!" It was the Heinies. Lieutenant Mills said, "Ground equipment and jump over the bridge." He no sooner said that than they opened fire on us. We ran into a vino patch and hid. They shot flares in the air and tried to pick us off. They tossed grenades and fired their guns into the patch.[342]

In the confusion, Privates Scott, Alvin H. Boggs, and Arthur M. Wright were cut off from the platoon. They were chased by Germans, losing track of Wright along the way, who found his way back to the platoon. Scott and Boggs hid for two hours before they worked their way back to the DZ. Scott said, "I had a compass and we started towards what we thought was Gela. About noon we saw a German patrol. Just two men. We were afraid to fire on them because the range was too great for a carbine. We ducked them and later came across a gun set upon a hill. We looked it over but couldn't make it out so we avoided it and started up the railroad tracks. I saw someone on the skyline and started up the hill. (...) He had me covered with a .50-caliber so I started yelling. It was a 1st Division man. They took us to the assembly area."[343]

Lieutenant Mills was evacuated and classified for the "Zone of Interior," or the United States, for further treatment. He rejoined his platoon in the summer of 1944. The platoon sergeant, Staff Sergeant Cecil W. Anderson, earned a Silver Star when the platoon "withdrew from its position in face of artillery and mortar fire. Staff Sergeant Anderson held his position and put out of action two 20mm gun carriers with 81mm mortar fire."[344]

The 1st Battalion surgical assistant, Technician 4th Grade Frank X. Gorniak, landed just behind the German lines and was greeted on the ground by a hail of machine gun fire. Within minutes, the Germans took him prisoner, but it didn't take long before the German position was attacked by fellow troopers from Gorniak's plane.

Grenades were thrown by the Americans, and a piece of grenade shrapnel wounded Gorniak in the side. Despite being wounded, he was allowed to tend the wounded of both sides once the attack had subdued. But while out in the open, a sudden barrage of Navy shells came down, since the American warships were shelling the German lines. Gorniak used the opportunity to crawl forward but was once again wounded by shrapnel. Luckily, he was found by friendly troops and taken by ship to a hospital in North Africa. Gorniak was awarded the Purple Heart and Silver Star and recovered quickly.[345]

CHAPTER 16

FRIENDLY FIRE

Sicily

JULY 11-JULY 12, 1943

B ehind the serial of the 1st Battalion came the serial carrying the officers and enlisted men of Captain Adam A. Komosa's Headquarters and Headquarters Company. Private David K. Finney realized that they

> headed for our first combat experience. Some of us closed our eyes in hopes of catching a few minutes of sleep, others smoked cigarettes or tried getting a view from the small windows of the plane. Speaking for myself, I was nothing but a bundle of nerves and very jumpy. Nothing seemed to help our anticipation of the things to come.
>
> The planes were flying about fifteen feet above the whitecaps on the waves. As we neared the coast of Sicily the pilots gained their normal altitude of about one thousand feet. A naval vessel began firing at the planes, then all the ships followed suit with small arms and anti-aircraft fire. The planes broke formation trying to evade the flak. We could see the flashes from the guns and the exploding shell around the plane.

As bullets and exploding shell fragments hit the body of the plane, every man was standing trying to hook his chute onto the static line. We were being thrown around as the pilot tried keeping the plane under control. We could smell smoke which smelled of electrical wiring then another loud cracking sound somewhere on the body of the plane.

As we pushed our way to the open door we could see one of our planes burning as it dived towards the watery grave below. Suddenly we were over land and out of the flak. Our first Baptism of Fire was from our own Navy. As we jumped into the night the air seemed to have a strong acrid smell. The sounds of planes, bursting shells and men screaming is what I will always remember of this night.

I began trying to open my eyes but nothing happened. My first thought was, "I am blind." I felt my face and as my fingers touched where my eyes should be I felt dirt and a wet feeling. I took my canteen and cleaned off my eyelids with a handkerchief. I was happy to know I could see again and there was only a slight cut on my forehead. I next noted that I had landed in a grape vineyard but no one else was around me. I slowly stood, trying to decide what my next move would be and to hook-up with some of my outfit.

I could hear the sound of a "burp" gun in the not too far distance, then I saw the silhouettes of two people walking in my direction. I dropped down by the grape vines and waited. I was happy to hear them speaking English. One of the guys had a southern drawl that certainly couldn't be coming from a "kraut" or a "dago."[346]

In another plane, C-53D 42-68720 of the 62nd Troop Carrier Squadron, carrying part of Headquarters and Headquarters Company, sat medical officer 1st Lieutenant Francis "Frank" R. Cannizzaro, 2nd Lieutenant James B. Beld, 1st Sergeant Carl O. Smith, Staff Sergeant William W. McPhail, Technicians 4th Grade John W. Eide and Ralph Kerns, Technicians 5th Grade Jack Andreas, Clayton F. Conover, Clarence G. Hawkins, and John W. Turner, Corporal Floyd I. Ricketts, Corporal Ira K. Comstock Jr. from Service Company, Privates First Class James C. Conklin, Daniel V. Denton, Galen W. Dugan, and James M. McNamara, and Privates William E. Chapman, Arthur E. Collins, Russell K. Dixon, Joseph H. Hart, and James R. Warren. Hart and McNamara were both members of the Regimental Reconnaissance Platoon.

Without waiting on the green light to come up, the jumpmaster of McNamara's plane decided they would jump. Machine gun bullets and 20mm gun fire were raking the hull of the aircraft as it flew some five hundred feet above the water. McNamara and Hart were positioned in the back of the stick and jumped last. Both landed on the beach. The realization set in that their fellow planeload members had drowned in the sea. They took position in a ditch and decided to await daylight in order to determine whether there were Americans or Germans in the area.[347]

According to Komosa:

> Approaching the Sicilian coast, the plane formation was suddenly fired upon by one American machine gun. At first it appeared as a flare. Then the fire suddenly became very intense. Immediately, as though a prearranged signal, friendly anti-aircraft and U.S. Naval vessels lying offshore fired a devastating torrent of anti-aircraft fire. The plane had no slit trench to get into, nor can it assume the prone position to take cover. We felt like trapped rats. It was a most uncomfortable feeling knowing that our own troops were throwing everything they had at us.

Planes dropped out of formation and crashed into the sea. Others, like clumsy whales, wheeled and attempted to get beyond the flak which rose in fountains of fire, lightening the stricken faces of the men as they stared through the windows.

More planes dived into the sea and those that escaped broke formation and raced like a covey of quail for what they thought was the protection of the beach. But they were wrong. Over the beach they were hit again – this time by American ground units, believing the planes to be German. More planes fell and from some of them, lucky men jumped and escaped alive; the less fortunate were riddled by flak before reaching the ground.[348]

Baptism of fire started for Captain Robert M. Halloran, the dentist: "When tracer riddled the plane, the sky lit up and it seemed exactly the way Hollywood portrayed combat. Later discovered it was our Navy shooting at us."[349]

The C-53 transport plane of Captain John Gibson and Lieutenant Raymond Roush was shot down before the coast of Gela. It was even more vulnerable than a C-47, as the C-53 was a less modified airplane. Instead of a metal reinforced floor, there was a just a wooden floor and no cargo door in the rear of the plane. This made it more difficult to rapidly clear the passengers from inside in case of an emergency landing.

It all happened quickly. Gibson got disoriented because of the heavy anti-aircraft fire and flew up and down the south east part of Sicily. Suddenly, the red light flashed on while the plane was still flying through a hailstorm of machine gun and anti-aircraft fire. Master Sergeant James E. Byrd, the jumpmaster of the stick, ordered the men to take off their Mae Wests (life jackets) and shouted, "Stand up and hook up!"

While waiting on the green light to come up, Byrd was killed by tracer fire as he stood in the door. Troopers were milling about, dragging the lifeless body of Byrd away from the door opening. Men in the rear of the airplane asked with tense voices what had happened. Another trooper, Pfc. Richard R. Wagner, was wondering if this really was the "milk-run" operation they had been promised. Who was firing on them if there wasn't supposed to be any enemy opposition? Wagner and Pfc. Albin V. Rozman both belonged to the Regimental Reconnaissance Platoon and had been assigned to this mixed stick. They didn't know many of the other officers and men in the airplane.[350]

Apart from Brigadier General Charles L. Keerans, Jr. and Captains Harry J. Cummings and Otis A. Danneman, the paratroopers in this stick further included Lieutenant Colonel Leslie G. Freeman, the executive regimental commander, Major Ivan J. Roggen, the Regimental Surgeon, 1st Lieutenant Eugene R. Cohen of Service Company, and others. "The Sicily jump was a memorable event for me," recalled Roggen, "because I never had a chance to jump. It was a beautiful night and the anti-aircraft tracer rounds looked like the Fourth of July fireworks celebration in the USA – then reality set in."[351]

Sergeant Fielding J. Armstrong, the crew chief of the C-53, shouted to Gibson, "The port engine is on fire!"[352] A 20mm shell struck the cockpit and severely wounded Gibson in his arm, while Roush was wounded as well, although less seriously. Both pilots stayed on the controls but realized that with their starboard engine on fire, they had little chance of finding the drop zone while they were still near the shore. The pilots called out to their passengers that they would make a ditch landing and that everyone had to take in ditching positions. With a loud splash, the C-53 hit the surface of the sea and was soon making water. Paratroopers were entangled between the arms and legs of their comrades, while their static lines were still hooked up to the anchor cable. It took a few moments before the men realized the crash landing had been successful. Unknown to them, they had landed just a few hundred yards of the shore at the southwestern town of Scoglitti.

In the sinking airplane, the paratroopers tried to cut their static lines, undo their parachutes, and discuss their options. They still believed Germans or Italians were firing on them. A paratrooper pulled out his .45 and fired some shots toward the shore. "Cut that firing!" a voice rang out, fearing the shots would attract more fire. The paratrooper stepped back and replaced his pistol. Around that time, machine gun fire raked the fuselage—red tracer fire, so obviously Allied bullets as German tracers were white.

Lieutenant Cohen unbuckled his parachute and decided to leave the airplane. Presumably he carried along the heavy canvas bag containing gold seal dollars, which Freeman could use to bribe assistance from local civilians. In any case, Cohen sank as a rock just after he had passed through the partially submerged door.[353] His superior officer, Captain Danneman, became entangled in the twisted wreckage of the C-53. He pleaded for help, but the troopers near the door could not see him. Danneman's frantic calls ceased as he slipped beneath the sea level.[354]

Roggen nearly drowned inside the aircraft as he couldn't unbuckle his parachute. He recalled:

> Our aircraft was shot down and crashed in the Mediterranean Sea about several hundred yards from shore. Once our aircraft was in the water, we took a considerable amount of machine gun fire from the shore. When the aircraft crashed, the 16 to 18 troopers in the aircraft were thrown forward and the aircraft began to sink. I was under the water and was unable to reach the buckle which would disconnect my parachute. I was also unable to reach my knife to cut the straps on my parachute. I was on the verge of drowning when a friend of mine, Captain [Harry] Bob Cummings, pulled me to the surface and cut loose my parachute.

> As soon as I was freed, Captain Cummings moved to the door of the aircraft and was shot, falling out of the aircraft into the water. I inflated my Mae West life preserver and exited the aircraft. Each trooper made it to shore as best they could. The water was about five feet deep and the machine gun fire stopped by the time I made it to the shore.

By the next morning, we regrouped as we could and I saw three of our troopers (including Bob Cummings) dead on the shoreline. (...) Captain Cummings was the Regimental Personnel Officer (an administrative assignment) and was not scheduled to jump on this mission. He requested permission to go with us and was allowed on board, but would have returned with the aircraft to Algiers. Of the survivors, we had several casualties, including a badly wounded pilot. I was also wounded by machine gun fire; a minor wound in the knee. We were never able to determine who was firing at us."[355]

Unknown to Roggen, it was Private (later Pfc.) James R. Brooks who risked his life to drag the dying Cummings to the shore. He was posthumously awarded the Silver Star in June 1945: "After the C-47 in which he was riding had been shot down over the Sicilian coast, Pfc. Brooks, whose right arm had been fractured by a .50-caliber bullet, unselfishly risked his life in an effort to save that of a mortally wounded officer. Under heavy fire from .50-caliber machine guns emplaced on the beach, Pfc. Brooks dragged the dying officer from the plane and valiantly struggled against the current and surf until he reached the shore approximately 150 yards away. Only after being assured that the officer was being cared for did Pfc. Brooks permit himself to be evacuated."[356]

Cummings was posthumously awarded the first Distinguished Service Cross within the regiment: "Captain Cummings accompanied a fellow officer [Major Roggen] with a serial of his regiment in a transport plane, which crashed off shore, and while rapidly filling with water, was under continuous heavy machine gun fire. Captain Cummings freed himself and was in the plane door prepared to leave when he saw that his fellow officer was wounded and unable to free himself from his main and reserve parachute and full combat equipment. Captain Cummings returned and assisted the officer, enabling him to leave the plane, but was himself mortally wounded by machine gun fire. Captain Cummings' courageously and selflessly saved the life of a comrade, reflecting the finest traditions of the military service. His action has been an inspiration to his regiment."[357]

Wagner decided to put on his Mae West after he had discarded his parachute. He then made his way, half-walking and swimming, to the door where he found his exit blocked by a body. Wagner leaned over to find out who it was and in the faint rays of the moon made out it was his friend Rozman riddled by machine gun fire. He pushed Rozman's body aside after he had put himself together again.

As he tried to get out, Wagner felt a slight breeze as two bullets whined past his neck and legs. He quickly slipped out of the plane and was debating what the best option would be. To wait until he would be picked up by a boat at daylight, or to make it to the shore, maybe two hundred yards away? At that moment, a voice called out from the beach, "It's okay to come in now. Whoever the bastards were that were here are gone!" Wagner swam to the shore and ran into the wounded pilots of the airplane. He had made it.[358]

The crew of the C-53 made it safely to the shore. Gibson's wounds were so severe that he would not return to the 62nd Troop Carrier Squadron and was sent back to the United States for further medical treatment. Roush did return to the 62nd and flew for another couple of months.[359] On the shore, Armstrong, the crew chief, ran into Keerans: "He apparently had escaped the ditching and subsequent machine gun shooting unscathed. While we were talking, the general spoke to a number of passing people he apparently knew. He asked me to go inland with him, and I said no, that I was trying to get back to my outfit."[360]

Lieutenant Colonel Freeman managed to make it to the shore as well, but he was severely wounded. His commander, Colonel Reuben H. Tucker, fared little better. Captain Julian A. Cook recalled:

> The pilots really weren't expecting it and they depended upon the ability and initiative of each one, but our pilot was flying the regimental commander and he was pretty good and he had a lot of determination and so did Tucker. I remember they flew over the area once and there was so much smoke and Tucker

said, "Let's go again." And on that one, we jumped. But the plane had been hit. I had been told that there was no water in Sicily and since I was Regimental S-4, I had a canteen on each hip.

We were standing up, ready to go when the plane got hit. I felt it and knew I was hit. I could feel all this blood running down into my boots and I thought, "Oh, my God! I can't live long this way." I thought I should start feeling weak from the loss of blood and I started to hold myself up with both hands. Nothing happened, of course, this all happened real quick.

Then it came to me and I realized that the cold water, flying over the Mediterranean is kind of cold and it cools that water off. They hit both my canteens and that water just gushed right out and down my legs and I was bleeding too. The cold water and the warm blood, it all seemed the same. That is why my boots were filling up and I couldn't see how I could live very long with that.

But then, the fellow right behind me who was later killed, Captain [Robert R.] Johnson, the Adjutant, he had beautiful wavy hair. Of all things to be carrying in his jumpsuit, he had some hair tonic and that had been hit and smashed and it ran out on the floor. A little bit of my blood got into it. So people who came out later on saw all this gooey, reddish stuff that was conjelled, like hair tonic did when it was dried out, and they thought, "My God, Cook can't be alive." So they thought I had been killed.[361]

As soon as he landed on the ground, Colonel Tucker ran despite a slight leg wound to five American tanks. The crews were firing their .50-caliber machine guns on the transport planes. Tucker banged on the tanks and threatened to shoot the gunners if they didn't cease fire. They stopped firing.[362] Cook came down nearby and noticed the shrapnel had not only hit him in the side, but "also got me in the thigh and when the doctor finally opened it up, the artery would pulse right out and he couldn't understand how I jumped and didn't break it. If it have been an 1/8 of an inch deeper, I would have been gone."[363]

The last serial with the 376th Parachute Field Artillery Battalion suffered the greatest losses. Twelve transport planes carrying sticks of this battalion were shot down, crashed in the sea, or exploded in mid-air. Twenty-four officers and men were killed, eleven were missing, and eight were wounded.

Captain Ted M. Wight's C Company was dropped in three different places instead of one. Only the planeloads of 1st Lieutenants John M. Bigler and Lloyd M. Price (2nd Platoon) jumped on the right place. Two soldiers, Privates James W. Denkins and James R. Edwards, died of friendly fire at Farello airfield.[364] "All of the paratroopers were hooked up and ready to jump as we neared the objective," recalled 2nd Lieutenant Delor M. Perow with the third stick of the 2nd Platoon. "I was at the door, the first to jump. The red signal, meaning 'prepare to jump' was on and we were awaiting the green light when a shell exploded nearby and a piece of flak caught me in the neck. The wound was bleeding profusely and the sergeant came up and said that he would lead the men down. I was taken back to North Africa on the transport for hospitalization, keenly disappointed over my bad luck."[365]

Near Perow's stick at Biscari landed the planeloads of Captain Wight, 1st Lieutenant Wesley D. Harris, and that of 1st Lieutenant William W. Kellogg. Wight injured his leg upon landing, but remained in command. The 3rd Platoon sticks under Lieutenants Ernest H. Campbell, Vernon P. Ellis, and Patrick J. Mulloy came down between Santa Croce and Cosimo, several miles southeast of Biscari. The engineers joined each other on the 13th at the 505th PIR bivouac area between Victoria and Biazzo Ridge. A day later, they reverted to the command of the 504th PIR near Gela.[366]

On the ground, Major General Matthew Ridgway met Tucker at the edge of the emergency landing field at Farello, three miles east of Gela. They both tried to stop the nearby anti-aircraft gunners firing as best as possible, but it was already too late. During the previous afternoon, Ridgway had personally visited six pairs of coastal artillery anti-aircraft weapons several hundred yards from the beach, but now it seemed it had all been in vain.

CHAPTER 17

"THE MOST ANGUISHING EXPERIENCE"

Sicily

JULY 11-JULY 12, 1943

The transport planes carrying Captain Melvin W. Nitz's F Company formed the leading element of the 2nd Battalion serial. Second Lieutenant Edward J. Sims, the assisting 1st Platoon leader, landed with his stick over twenty-five miles from the drop zone. Sims wrote:

> As we approached Sicily, I was standing at the open door of the aircraft and could see land as it appeared under the port side wing. The night was calm and the light from the quarter moon reflected off the white caps of the Mediterranean Sea below. Suddenly, against the dark background of the sky, a gradual build-up of fire red tracers from below was engulfing our formation. I felt a shimmy go through our plane and then pandemonium reigned as anti-aircraft guns of our own forces, at sea and on the beaches, were blasting our slow flying aircraft.
>
> As my plane flew through the heavy flak, I could hear the hits as they penetrated. From my door position, I scanned the sky for other planes, but could see only

those going down in flames. My plane developed a distinct shudder and banked away from the flak with one engine starting to sputter. I had my men stand up and hook up then, before going forward to talk with the pilot I instructed my platoon sergeant to get the men out fast if the plane started to go down before I returned.

From the pilot I learned he had lost the formation and had a damaged starboard engine. We decided, since there was land below, that he would stay our present course and allow me a few seconds to return to the door, then turn on the green (go) light when in jump altitude. We both realized that with the heavy load he had, it would be difficult for him to fly back to North Africa. I rushed back to the door yelling to my men to get ready to jump. As I arrived at the door, the red (warning) light came on followed, within seconds, by the green light just as I hooked up. I immediately released the equipment bundles from under the plane, then jumped into darkness with my men following.

Landing was quick and rough, my parachute had just opened seconds before landing. The plane must have been less than 300 feet above the ground. When assembled, I learned that one man had been injured when he hit a stone fence. I sent patrols in opposite directions on a nearby road to look for signs and landmarks. One patrol located a road sign indicating that Augusta was 40 kilometers. This was sufficient to allow me to locate our general position on the map as being south west of Augusta, Sicily and about 25 miles from where we planned to land in the vicinity of Gela. (…)

I had 14 men with me so we moved in a south westerly direction, on roads and cross country, toward Gela.

At one point, we had a short fire fight with a small German force, but they soon fled. Later, we spotted a company size German force moving north, but since they did not see us, we held our fire and let them pass.

Our next contact was with advance elements of the U.S. 45th Division. They opened fire on us and for a few moments the situation was dangerous. We had a tough job trying to convince them that we were U.S. paratroopers.[367]

Chaplain Delbert A. Kuehl flew with a stick of F Company Headquarters led by 1st Sergeant Nelvis M. Lee. His stick was one parachute short, but the crew chief could offer Kuehl one used by the air crews. "They told us that we would be coming over Sicily and that we would drop amber flares for recognition to the Navy and other units signaling that we would be dropping in. (...) We were flying very low. I saw the amber flares drop. Shortly after the amber flares dropped, somebody got trigger-happy in the Navy, and it looked like a mammoth Fourth of July celebration. The sky was full of tracers."[368]

The pilot and crew chief of the plane were both killed and the co-pilot took control of the aircraft. While flying over rocky hills, the co-pilot flashed the red light on, and Lee ordered the men to stand up and hook up and then positioned himself in the door, ready to go. Kuehl stood right behind him as the green light flashed on. "Sergeant Lee was first out of the door. I soon followed him and I heard someone saying, "No!, No!, No!" The next fellow behind me saw a ridge coming up."[369]

The warning came too late for Kuehl, who landed hard on the top of the ridge. He later learned both kidneys were dislodged by the impact. For an indefinite time, he was knocked out: "I was bleeding in several places and my jump suit was torn. There was a rock wall in front of me. So I made my way down the rock wall and met the fellow who jumped behind me and he had two broken legs. The next fellow I encountered had one broken leg."[370]

Kuehl then heard a machine gun firing nearby that reminded him of the .30-caliber "life fire" exercises. Two shadowy figures approached the wall, conversing in English. Kuehl called out the first part of the password he had been issued, "George!" He waited to hear "Marshall," but it remained silent. Kuehl called out "Hold your fire, I am an American! Don't shoot! I am coming over the wall." But once he stood up one of them fired and missed. He became livid with anger, pointing on the American flag on his uniform. How was it possible the two Americans fired on him when he used the password? "Eventually we linked up with the 45th Division men without shooting each other and got medical attention to our men that needed it."[371]

First Lieutenant Charles A. "Hoss" Drew of the 3rd Platoon arrived at 0200 hours on July 12 at the regimental area with over forty F Company paratroopers. He recalled:

> The pilot of my plane gave me the warning twenty minutes out from the DZ. After the red light came on, he had to give me the green light in about one minute, due to the plane being on fire. We jumped into a steady stream of anti-aircraft fire, and not knowing that they were friendly troops. About seventy-five yards from where I landed, plane Number 915 was hit and burned. To my knowledge, only the pilot and three men got out. The pilot was thrown through the window. Another plane was shot down on the beach, and another plane was down burning about one thousand yards to my front.
>
> There were four men killed and four wounded from my platoon. Three of these men were hit coming down, and one was killed on the ground because he had the wrong password. After landing we found out this had been changed to "Think" – "Quickly." The anti-aircraft fire we jumped into was the 180th Infantry [Regiment] of the 45th Division. They also were not told we were coming. We tried to reorganize, but found

we didn't have but forty-four men, including three officers. We searched all night for the rest of the men. After accounting for them we took care of the dead and wounded and started toward our objective.[372]

Private Richard H. "Dick" Gentzel of Drew's platoon wrote in a letter to his best friend:

Everyone was excited about the $10,000 jump. That's what we call all of our combat jumps. Finally the day did arrive. We had a good breakfast and dinner and a K-ration supper.

We got into the planes about dusk and took off. While flying across the Mediterranean Sea we could see a convoy of boats going to make the invasion. It really looked swell. I guess my thoughts were mostly of home, or at least I did a lot of thinking about it. Finally we hit Malta and turned south. We knew then that it wouldn't be long before the old light would go on.

When he hit the coast of Sicily I thought all hell broke loose. Here the anti-aircraft was firing at us, plus .50-caliber machine guns. It looked like the Fourth of July, but we were on the receiving end and I didn't like that. Finally the lieutenant told us to stand up and hook up.

When I got to get up it seemed as though there were weights holding me to the seat. I was the third man in the string and could also see the tracers coming up at us. The lieutenant and the man in front of me, [Private Charles K.] "Chuck" Flaville, stooped over to kick the equipment bundles out. When they did so a stream of tracers came right through the door and you could hear all of them splattering into the tail of the plane. Just then the ship put its nose down a little and the green light went on.

The lieutenant and Chuck knocked the bundles out and went out after them with the rest of us right after them. As I was falling through space waiting for the chute to open I could see these tracers hitting other planes and knew how those fellows felt. When the chute opened it brought me back to my senses. I looked down and was surprised to see an olive orchard under me. Some Joe was trying to pick us off as we were coming down. You could hear the slugs tearing through the chute.

I managed to go tearing through the top of an olive tree and came to a sudden stop when I hit the ground. I lay there for a minute trying to get my breath back but the shooting started again, so I just took my knife and cut my way out of the harness and started to crawl away from the chute. Just then Chuck hit the ground about 50 yards away. I ran over to him and helped to get him out of his chute. Together we moved towards one of these machine guns.

Before we got there the whole sky became lighted up. We looked up and here was one of our transport planes on fire [the airplane carrying half the 2nd Battalion Communications section]. It came down through that little orchard, tearing up the trees and everything else it hit. The whole plane burst into flames when it finally came to a stop. We didn't have to bother with the machine guns we were after anymore; the plane took care of that.

That night was horrible. Firing was all around us and you didn't know if the other man was a "Jerry" or not until you were right on top of him. It was too late to shoot him then; you had to depend on your bayonet or trench rifle. We used them quite a few times that night.

Dawn found us on the outskirts of a small town. Can't tell you its name. There we met the rest of the outfit and we marched about 10 miles down a road to another olive orchard. We were going to rest there for awhile. We were in the orchard for three days till we reorganized and we also waited there for any stragglers who might have gotten lost the night of the jump.

Later I found out that the two men back of me [Pfc. James M. MacDonald and Private Leonard J. Cope] had been killed by anti-aircraft fire. Also we lost three more men [Staff Sergeant Paul M. Roepke, Pfc. Arthur McNally and Pfc. William H. Schrack] when we got on the ground. All were good buddies of mine.[373]

First Lieutenant Zigmund C. Lutcavage of the 1st Platoon came down safely and joined up with several of his planeload, including Roepke. In the early morning of July 12, they encountered soldiers of the 45th Infantry Division and called out their password. A stream of fire came back, which killed Roepke, McNally, and Schrack.[374]

The shot down C-47 of the 53rd Troop Carrier Squadron viewed by Gentzel and Drew carried half the communications section of the 2nd Battalion. On board were 1st Lieutenant Mack C. Shelley, the 2nd Battalion S-3 Officer, 2nd Lieutenant Hugh A. Henderson, the assisting platoon leader, 1st Lieutenant Hubert H. Washburn, the 2nd Battalion Surgeon, Staff Sergeant Clinton G. Stevenson, Technician 4th Grade Delmer G. Morrow, Technicians 5th Grade Richard A. Bartow and Adrian J. Fillion, Corporal John G. Guba, Privates First Class Charles A. Clevenger, Henry J. Kobak, Joseph Kopstein (one of the *Propblast* editors), and Wilbert D. Sheffield, and Privates Robert E. Barnes, Russell W. De Vore, and Clarence W. Schwark. Also flying along were Private Alex I. Hardridge, a medic, Pfc. John C. Durham of Headquarters and Headquarters Company, and Technician 5th Grade Newton L. Crane of Service Company.

The airplane was hit by anti-aircraft fire and caught fire. Shelley, the jumpmaster, was standing in the door and was thrown clear as the aircraft spun downward in a fast rate and tore through some trees. He landed into a nearby haystack, which cushioned his impact, but he was knocked unconscious.[375]

When he came to, Shelley realized his comrades were still inside, unbuckled his parachute harness, and crawled with difficulty and in great pain to the burning wreckage. He pulled himself inside the cargo door and started pulling at the limp bodies inside. A few moments later, an explosion blew Shelley away from the plane, and he again passed out. His next memory was of two armed Italian soldiers who were discussing what they would do with him, but he passed out. Eventually, Allied troops located him, and he was evacuated by ship.[376]

Major Ivan J. Roggen, the Regimental Surgeon, received the unwelcome task of identifying the bodies in Shelley's planeload. "Washburn, the 2nd Battalion Assistant Surgeon, was aboard an aircraft that was shot down and crashed ashore. I later saw the aircraft and identified his body, which had essentially been cremated in the ensuing fire."[377] The remains of the passengers and crew are buried at Jefferson Barracks National Cemetery in St. Louis, Missouri.

"Riding in the plane on our left wing was half of my platoon," recalled 2nd Lieutenant John J. O'Malley. "In its frenzy to escape the lethal inferno, their C-47 veered sharply to its right and almost struck our plane. I watched in horror as their C-47 then tilted and plunged to earth, where it exploded in a huge ball of fire. Those were my boys. That was the most anguishing experience of my life; one that I would never forget."[378]

Lieutenant Colonel William Yarborough flew in the same airplane as O'Malley. He recalled:

> We flew past the Island of Malta as the search lights were beginning to come up for the evening's pasting that they always go. I remember standing in the door

there, the door was off, thinking about what a gallant
bunch of guys there were (...) and all of a sudden we
got a burst - a burst of what appeared to be flak. And
we couldn't understand it, I thought maybe a German
aircraft has gotten to into the formation.

Then we passed over some Navy ships and we got
some more of it (...) But darkness came really quickly
and the flak became worse and worse and worse and
we were flying through a solid wall of this stuff.

When we got land-fall at Sicily, you could see fires
burning all over the place and the stuff was just coming
up in sheaves. The airplane that I was in was piloted by
a young fellow who was obviously as scared as everybody else was and I went up to tell him that we were
going to hook up then and if it got any worse, we were
going to get out wherever we were as long as it was
over land. So, I fought my way up through two rows of
guys hanging there and found this young fellow scared
to death, and I told him what I was going to do and he
agreed because he wanted to get out of there and get
back to North Africa if he could.

I fought my way back to the door again and in the
meantime the airplane on my left was shot down and
hit the ground in flames and it had my S-3 in it and
part of my communication section. Other airplanes
were being hit. We could see around them and ours
was hit several times with small stuff.

As I stood in the door ready to get out of there, the
crew chief lying on his belly, said, "Colonel, it's a hell
of a lot safer out there then it is in here." I said, "You're
damn right and that's why we are going out, see." Well,
the reason that we got out is because the formation

was being broken up and I think the pilot had lost his orientation by that time, anyhow, on the DZ.[379]

Yarborough's stick dropped near the city of Biscari. He only found half of his planeload in the dark before he marched in the direction of the west coast. His S-2 officer, 1st Lieutenant Lewis P. Fern, jumped from the lead plane in the battalion serial. He wrote these short sentences in the unit journal:

2000 – Take off for Sicily. Planes circle field, pick up formation and we are on our way.

2205 – Rounding the Island of Malta; very short time we should be over our objective.

2330 – Have run into "flak" twice; once over the water and the other hitting the coast. Plane "3" in the Hdq Co group acted out of control, then nosed down, crashed and burst into flames. It is hard to tell at first whether we were being strafed or shot at from the ground.

2344 – We're about a minute out from our DZ, can see "flak" all around us. Cannot see any other ships.

2355 – Plane #1 jumped over some city.[380]

The executive officer of E Company, twenty-nine-year-old 1st Lieutenant Walter S. Van Poyck from Wilkes-Barre, Pennsylvania, watched in horror as the aileron, a small hinged section on the outboard portion of a wing on the left wing of his plane, was shot away. "As the coast was crossed all hell broke loose. We were fired upon by our own Navy and shore troops. When I saw both red and yellow tracers hosing toward us, I knew we were in for it. The two German night fighters strafing us didn't bother me nearly as much as the knowledge that the 'friendlies' were giving us such a rough time.

"Standing in the door, I watched with incredulity, our entire left aileron blown away. Everything from .30-caliber to 90mm hit us. With our plane out of control, we jettisoned some 7000 yards from our DZ. My best estimate is that we jumped from about 400 feet. My scattered Company was among the 400 of the regiment's 1600 men who reached the Gela DZ the next morning... Upon return to Africa after the Sicilian operation, I checked my plane, the 'Red Dog,' and was informed it was among the missing."[381]

Second Lieutenant Chester A. Garrison, the assisting platoon leader of the 2nd Platoon, landed hard. He remembered that

> ... we enplaned and were lifted away from the dreary training on a grim terrain into the light of a full moon and toward fearsome adventure. The coolness of the evening entered through the open doorway of the C-47, and the thinning of the oxygen put the sixteen troopers, almost immobilized by their equipment, to sleep in their bucket seats.
>
> As jump master, I sat opposite the door opening. Midway through flight, when the Air Corps attendant asked me if I would like to see Malta below; I waddled to the doorway and looked straight down. There it was: a grayish island fortress seemingly lifeless without a glimmer of light. It too slept, as it silently went by.
>
> As the pilot used the island for a checkpoint, he veered the plane to the left. Alerted to get ready, my men formed a line, hooked up to the cable stretched like a clothesline above our heads, and waited. I stood in the doorway waiting for the green light from the pilot to flash. Looking out into the night, I was startled to see a swastika-marked plane glide by in the opposite direction only about 50 yards away. It moved like a shark cutting silently through the dimness.
>
> I saw fireworks below – actually flak. Since I was new to the war scene and did not know that allied and axis tracer bullets were different colors, I assumed that waiting Germans were firing at us. In fact, the tracers

were from American forces, both Navy and Army. Only minutes before, German planes had attacked the American fleet just off the Sicilian coast at Gela; the Navy fired back at them and, since we arrived at such an inopportune time, turned their anti-aircraft guns on us thinking we were more Germans. The ground forces followed suit....

Soon after, the green light flashed on, and Garrison jumped from the C-47 and saw a plane nearby plummeting earthward in flames. He landed sideways on his right knee on an uphill slope: "I peered about for companionship: the Army field manual hadn't accounted for a solitary solution. Presumably, I was in enemy territory – but without friend or foe. (...)

"Out of a copse not far away stumbled a figure. (...) I waited breathlessly until I recognized the person as an E Company trooper, but not from my plane. He kept shaking his head to clear his brains, as he had banged his head from landing on a swing-back of his oscillating. Realizing he wouldn't be much help, I told him to fall in line behind me, which he was barely capable of. So two of us stumbled on as I acquired three more troopers until we met one who was directing strays to a collecting point that was not anywhere near or at all like the sandbox mock-up we had studied in Africa."[382]

Garrison was shocked to learn that no one had seen Colonel Reuben H. Tucker. That afternoon, his planeload walked into the assembly area. They had jumped moments later after an anti-aircraft shell had exploded near the fuselage.

Private Paul A. Kunde served as a sniper in E Company Headquarters and was armed with a '03 Springfield rifle with a scope on it: "We all assembled in a grape vineyard and we moved out of there with 1st Sergeant Henry Griffin in charge. He had been our heavy weight boxing champion in Fort Bragg. The next morning we met up with others from different sticks. You would run into three or four people at a time and we finally found our company commander, Captain Ferguson."[383]

At the airfield, Staff Sergeant Ernest W. Parks of D Company found Sergeant Wesley C. Hines from Belle Vernon, Pennsylvania. He was

reading a New Testament. I chided him somewhat for using the moment to do something I had never seen him do before. I will never forget his reply: "Ernie, my girlfriend sent this special New Testament to me. It has a metal covering on the back. She wrote a letter to me, saying, "Wear this over your heart in combat. It will save your life."

We were approaching what we thought was our drop zone when the red light came on inside the plane signalling us to prepare to jump. We had just a very short period of time to stand up and hook our chute lines for jumping from the plane. That time period, if memory serves me correctly, was approximately four minutes.

Suddenly we were being hit by small arms fire coming directly from beneath us. Tracer bullets, which are bullets that are clearly visible as they fly through the air toward their targets, seemed to light up the sky around us for our jump was in the darkness of night. Sometime later we learned that those bullets were, in fact, friendly fire. Those on the ground had mistaken us for the enemy!

One of the bullets from the ground fire entered through the open door of the plane as we prepared to jump. That bullet struck Wesley precisely where he had stored the metal-backed New Testament in his uniform. Miraculously or not, the metal caused the bullet to ricochet and enter his shoulder instead of his heart. (...) My first memory of war was landing within a few feet of a burning tank. It was, more than likely, hit directly by naval guns. For the first time in my life I experienced the smell of burning human flesh.[384]

Second Lieutenant Arthur W. LeSage, Jr. stood in the door of the C-47 when he saw to his horror how Hines caught a .30-caliber bullet in the chest. The impact knocked Hines backward into the plane and simultaneously the green light indicating that they had to jump flashed on. Believing his sergeant had been killed instantly, LeSage gave the order to jump. Rapidly, the paratroopers leaped from the plane, leaving Hines behind on the floor of the C-47.

The crew chief of the plane came over to Hines and noticed to his amazement that he was still alive. In the left breast pocket of his jump-suit, the sergeant carried the New Testament sent by his girlfriend, Doris Jones. The bullet had hit the metal cover just above the inscription "May The Lord Be With You" and had glanced off under his arm instead of penetrating his chest.

Hines was flown back to North Africa where he was hospitalized and the bullet was extracted. He sent it to his mother along with the Purple Heart he received. Hines also wrote a letter to the chaplain urging him to write Captain Stanley M. Dolezal of D Company and request decorations for the brave men of his stick.

The 1st Platoon leader, 1st Lieutenant Wilfred Jaubert from Opelousa, Louisiana, recalled:

> When we approached the coast we were standing up as was customary as the red light was on. The fire works began and being in the door I was watching the tracers go by. I thought that it was the Italians and I turned to the Sergeant behind me and remarked that we would get the S.O.B.'s when we got on the ground.
>
> The pilot of the aircraft, Captain [Thomas C.] "Doc" Cargill [of the 14th Troop Carrier Squadron] took no evasive action and continued on course and as far as I would make out we landed at or very near the

designated drop zone north of Gela near Niscemi. One other plane from my platoon dropped at the same time.

The plane that I dropped from was one of the old DC-3's from the airlines and had a small oval shaped door and was difficult to exit from. Most of the aircraft in the formations were the "luxury" C-47's with wide square doors. We landed in the midst of destroyed German tanks still smoldering which was really weird as the only sound was me trying to assemble two planeloads of men. After assembly we headed south towards the tracers and fires.[385]

Jaubert met a cannon company commander within the 1st Infantry Division: "He told us that the anti-aircraft firing which shot down so many C-47s was done by the U.S. Navy and army anti-aircraft units. He directed us to the nearest headquarters which was Division Artillery Headquarters 1st Infantry Division. The Commander, Brigadier General [Theodore] Roosevelt, [Jr.] (son of Teddy) was very kind to us and attempted to contact Colonel Tucker. We finally received orders to move to an assembly center where we waited for the surviving troopers to assemble."[386]

First Lieutenant Wilfred Jaubert of D Company led a patrol into Albanella before the regimental advance towards Altavilla. Jaubert commanded the regimental pathfinders during Operation Market Garden. Courtesy: Jack Jaubert

Captain Dolezal flew with part of his D Company headquarters group and recalled "we had flown in low, like stupid ducks. Hell broke loose. (…) I landed so hard my right knee came apart. As I lay on the ground, I could see fiery wreckage falling around."[387] Dolezal assembled five troopers, all injured because of their low altitude drop, and led them hobbling to a farmhouse. He knocked on the door and an old man finally opened. Using pidgin Italian, Dolezal asked the terrified Sicilian farmer if they could rest in his living room. The timid man smiled and led them in, where his wife and daughter produced sticks for canes.

At dawn, the farmer's wife went out to the barn to milk their cows, but she suddenly rushed back. There were German soldiers patrolling the dirt roads near the farm. Dolezal and his men hid in closets and under the beds. Luckily, no house search was made. For two days the group stayed in the farmhouse to recuperate and, after seven more days of hobbling cross-country, reached Allied lines.[388]

First Lieutenant William L. Watson of Headquarters Company realized that the men in his stick "were under fire from our own U.S.

Navy. We came down near the town of Gela." Although he landed in a tree, Watson felt more secure on *terra firma* than in the sky. Having freed himself from his parachute and standing on the ground, he looked up and could see red tracer fire illuminating the sky. Soon he ran into a number of other men from his plane.[389]

Second Lieutenant John S. Thompson, the assisting platoon leader of the Machine Gun Platoon, sat near the door of his C-47: "The 2nd Battalion was flying in a tight V-of-Vs as we flew over a calm Mediterranean Sea. As we neared the island of Malta we would see a long convoy of ships edging their way toward the coast of Sicily."[390]

Suddenly, Thompson saw

> a sea of red tracers wound their way up through the formation and we wondered why and of what origin they came. Some of the planes had been hit and the formation scattered in many directions as we flew over the coast. We were flying very low now and one plane on our left went down in flames. Looking out of the door, I found that there were no other planes in sight and we were all alone in the air.

> The pilot sent back word that he thought we had just flown over our DZ and wanted to know if we should return by circling around and coming in from the water over the east coast. I told him to circle around and as soon as we hit the coastline to give us the green light. (...)

> We hit the ground very quickly, and with no casualties, assembled and immediately sent out three groups of four men each in different directions to gain information and find out where we were. Two hours later, the three groups had returned. One group had six German prisoners. These prisoners were part of thirteen Germans who were surprised down near the shore and seven had been killed in resisting. With no one able

to speak German, we decided to take them along with us. Knowing that we were on the eastern part of the island, and knowing that our objective, in the vicinity of Gela, was on the central part of the island, we decided to head west along the coast, moving at night and resting in the daytime. Travelling was difficult, having to climb over one stone wall after another, and the terrain was mountainous.[391]

Some of Yarborough's paratroopers landed even in the designated British or Canadian beachheads on Sicily. First Lieutenant Carl L. Patrick from Columbus, Georgia and his stick of the Mortar Platoon, for example, were dropped some seventy miles from their drop zone. Of his planeload, only 1st Sergeant Tommy D. Moreland showed up. They had landed only a few paces from a German observation post, and while crawling away to find cover, Patrick received multiple wounds from machine gun fire. They slowly started to crawl away from the German position and by dawn saw a large Canadian patrol approaching in the half light, who took them to an aid station. Patrick was eventually evacuated back to the United States where he trained replacement paratroopers at the Parachute School.[392]

Second Lieutenant Earnest H. Brown recalled:

> Our stay in Tunisia had not been very pleasant, and it was with mixed emotions that we prepared to leave on our first combat mission. One thing a soldier never forgets is his first combat mission – it is faced with a mixture of fear and self doubts. Our training had been thorough and tough but every man on the mission had to wonder if he would be emotionally prepared for what was to come. The real problem was that no one was sure exactly what we were facing.

> We loaded on the planes a little before midnight and took off for Sicily. Our flight over the Mediterranean was quiet and uneventful, the formation of C-47's

flying about 800 feet above the sea. We had a bright full moon, and a beautiful view of Malta, our check point where the formation made the turn to head to Sicily. We were flying along with only the hum of the plane engines when suddenly all hell broke loose.

As we had approached the coast of Sicily one of the ships in the invasion fleet fired on us and then the whole of the British and American fleet joined in the firing. The planes that were not shot down scattered to escape the anti-aircraft fire, and the plane I was in found itself over Sicily with only one other plane with it.

Standing in the door of the plane I could see nothing that looked anything like the sand table we had studied so diligently back in North Africa and I realized that our pilot was lost. About that time the red light by the door came on – this was our order to get ready to jump. Taking a deep breath to calm my misgivings, I gave the order to stand up and hook up, and we prepared to jump. Just as we got the green light and started to jump, one machine gun fired at us from some distance, but we all got on the ground without injury. On assembly of the men we found we had the Mortar Platoon of the 2nd Battalion and nothing else. Our first problem was to find out where we were and whether we were in friendly or enemy territory. As found out later we were about twenty miles from where we were supposed to be dropped, and in what is referred to as no-mans land – that is the area between the American and German forces.

Before daylight we managed to make contact with a unit of the American 45th [Infantry] Division, and since it seemed to be going in the direction we wanted to go, we became a part of it temporarily. The next evening the company we had temporarily joined moved out of the line and travelled all night for the purpose of blocking a road out of a little town to prevent the escape of the German units believed to be in the town. Shortly before dawn we arrived at our objective – a small gently sloping hill cresting a few hundred yards from the town and overlooking the road. I found myself and one of the mortars on the crest of the hill, with the rifle company on the reverse slope behind me. I would have preferred a different arrangement, but as a visitor, I could only make the best of the situation as I found it.

We dug our foxholes along the crest of the hill, and I was sitting by my foxhole eating my breakfast of K-rations when we got our first sign of trouble. It was just after daylight when a German command car with a single occupant came out of the town at high speed straight toward us. Of course fire from the rifle company stopped the vehicle and killed the occupant, then for a few minutes things became quiet again.

The quiet didn't last long. Suddenly, from positions near the town, a 20mm gun opened fire from our right front, and a machine gun fired on us from the left front, both guns sweeping the entire area. We managed to get the mortar fire on the 20mm gun, but at that time from a wooded area near the town a line of German infantry emerged and headed directly at us. My attention had been focused on the front and trying to silence the German guns, so I was surprised when I found that the rifle company had disappeared. I later was told that someone started a rumor of German tanks, and the unit spooked and retreated. But that left me with about a dozen men of the Mortar Platoon on the crest of the hill looking at a line of German infantry coming at us.

We simply moved away from the road to a wooded small area, and watched as the German unit called up its trucks, and took off. Fortunately for us the Germans cared of a couple of wounded soldiers, and (...) it took us about three days to rejoin our regiment.[393]

CHAPTER 18

UNFOLDING THE FIASCO

Sicily

JULY 12-JULY 14, 1943

After the anti-aircraft fire had died out and the transport planes were out of sight, time came to assemble. At the drop zone near Farello Airfield, Colonel Reuben H. Tucker was taking stock of the planeloads that had reported to him so far. The situation was far from good—all of his battalion commanders were missing, all company commanders of the 3rd Battalion were absent, and countless sub-units were incomplete. Captain Willard E. Harrison's A Company, minus a few men, was the only rifle company that was present.

At 0715 hours on July 12, Tucker reported in Division Headquarters that he had assembled only four hundred of his paratroopers. During the day, more men showed up in small groups or individually. That evening, the first Division G-1 Report counted thirty-seven officers and 518 enlisted men present for the 504th PIR.[394]

At 0930 hours on July 14, Major William R. Beall's group began its march from the assembly area near Vittoria to Tucker's bivouac area near Gela. Both Beall and Tucker could only hope that more 3rd Battalion paratroopers would "dribble in," since no other had reported in so far. Luckily, more stray groups appeared that same afternoon. The first group to arrive was that of Lieutenant George J. Watts' from the Castle Nocera that was contacted by a motorized patrol of the 16th Infantry Regiment of the 1st Infantry Division. "On the afternoon of our third day at the castle," recalled Sergeant Shelby R. Hord of H Company, "the first of our advancing amphibious troops came up this same road from Gela and we were able to retire. We went down into the city and reformed with the rest of our outfit."[395] The patrol leader asked Watts to hold out some hours while the American wounded and prisoners were evacuated.

One of these wounded was twenty-three-year-old Private Alfred Burgreen of Lieutenant Willis J. Ferrill's 1st Platoon. He had been wounded on July 13 and was hospitalized for a month: "They started shooting shells and bullets at our hilltop. Foolishly, I hid behind a bush. A soldier near me stood up and I believe died. Then a bullet sideswiped my neck and I was bleeding. I crawled backwards to a hut with open windows. A shell burst outside. I was prone and a shell went into my leg. There was a medic there who bandaged my bleeding left foot and neck. (...)

"Finally American troops landed at Gela and the Hermann Goering Division retreated. I was put on a hospital ship at Gela and went across the Mediterranean Sea to Constantine, Algeria. In the American hospital there, shrapnel was taken out of my foot."[396]

An infantry company moved forward and relieved the 104 paratroopers, who were directed to Beall's 3rd Battalion group near Vittoria. To his astonishment, Watts learned that he was acting company commander of H Company as Captain Lawrence Jordan and Lieutenant Frank Kent had not yet reported in. The captured material by Watts' force "included German recon cars, valuable medical supplies, three 240mm Russian mortars, eight German machine guns, and a large quantity of ammunition."[397]

Beall was shocked to hear from Lieutenant James C. Ott that Lieutenant Colonel Kouns had been captured and that he was thus the new battalion commander of a little over two hundred officers and men, still less than half of its normal strength. The loss of Kouns was not only felt by his officers. "I admired Lieutenant Colonel Kouns and was sorry that his combat career ended almost before it began," recalled Private Herbert Lucas of the 3rd Battalion Communication Platoon, "as he became a prisoner of war shortly after the jump into Sicily."[398]

Next to arrive was Lieutenant Fred W. Thomas's group of ten H and I Company troopers. For two days after landing, they had been through small firefights and artillery barrages. Thomas's group finally came upon a large winery known as Casa Iacono in the late morning of July 12. The winery was about ten miles east of Gela and contained two seriously wounded and three uninjured soldiers of the 1st Battalion, 16th Infantry Regiment. They told Thomas that their regimental aid station was a few miles away. Mrs. Iacono, meanwhile, helped take care of the wounded.

Meanwhile, two Mark VI Tiger tanks of the 2nd Kompanie, Schwere Panzer-Abteilung 504, retreated from the Gela–Niscemi crossroads on the order of their platoon commander, *Leutnant* Karl Goldschmidt. He was unable to raise contact with three missing tanks, and the Allied naval gunfire threatened to knock out his last two tanks. The tank drivers had barely retreated their steel structures out of sight of the U.S. 1st Infantry Division and the invasion fleet when one of the Tiger's engines started to drone loud and suddenly stopped.

Gefreiter (Lance Corporal) Werner Hahn climbed out of the tank when he realized that the driver couldn't get the engines working. With amazement, he watched a gap diagonally across the turret: an American shell had almost pierced it completely. Had the shell been fired from a shorter distance, it would have penetrated the thick armament of the Tiger tank. The driver discovered the Tiger's cooling systems were without water. Goldschmidt's tank pulled up next to them on the road. Where to get water? They noticed a large grey winery villa a short distance away, and Hahn and radio operator Eugen Grün walked over to the building, each carrying a twenty-liter canister to collect water.

The large winery villa was the very Casa Iacono where Thomas's paratroopers had taken their wounded. Still unaware, Hahn was impressed by the medieval-like structure of the winery with several towers flanking its lower outer wall. He took his pistol and knocked on the door, and finally, the frightened Italian owner, Mr. Iacono, opened it. He reluctantly led the Germans to a water pump on his farmyard. Hahn also spotted a cattle trough nearby and decided to wash some of the dirt off his face. While splashing water on his face, he suddenly felt someone was tapping on his shoulder. Hahn turned around and looked straight into the face of an American paratrooper. He quickly asked the paratrooper in school English if he had any chocolate. To his amazement, Hahn received a chocolate bar, and both he and Grün started to munch on it while more and more paratroopers gathered around them.

Hahn decided to impress the paratroopers by mentioning that there were two Tiger tanks a little further down the road, uncamouflaged. They would form perfect targets for the Allied dive bombers and—when attacked—they would probably also strafe the Casa Iacono. "You must help us camouflage the tanks," he insisted. The paratroopers consented, and some accompanied Grün and Hahn to the tanks. Goldschmidt approached with his MP40 ready to shoot. Hahn calmed him down and convinced his officer it was wise not to fire. He explained that there were more paratroopers in the farmhouse.[399] Thomas addressed Goldschmidt through Hahn, and they agreed to camouflage the Tigers.

While the tanks were being camouflaged with branches and twigs, the Germans proudly showed all the hits that the tanks had endured but that hadn't destroyed them. The mixed group of Americans and Germans then walked back to the farmhouse where they exchanged cigarettes and chocolate and drank wine together. Thomas and Goldschmidt were surprised to learn that they served in a unit with the same numerical unit number. They promptly exchanged addresses and promised to contact each other after the war. With both sides not knowing where their own forces were being positioned, they decided on a status quo and try to obtain medical aid. Meanwhile, Mrs. Iacono and Hahn redressed the wounds of the wounded American soldiers and a wounded German.

Thomas was informed of the Germans' previous engagement at the Gela–Niscemi crossroads and decided to head down there himself to locate the regimental aid station, leaving his men as "hostages" behind at the Casa Iacono villa. Thomas found the 1st Battalion aid station of the 16th Infantry Regiment a few miles away and asked for help. Staff Sergeant Earl Wills, the chief assistant, and a couple of medics declared they were willing to come along. They set off in two jeeps guided by Thomas. Within minutes, they arrived at the front door of Casa Iacono.

"I couldn't understand why there was no hostile air," recalled Wills of the farmhouse. "We patched up the wounded. All were litter cases. One of the American soldiers had a shattered arm. Another had been shot in the body. One German had shrapnel wounds in his arms, legs and buttocks."[400]

As soon as the medics started to load up their wounded on their jeeps, two of the German tank crew members walked forward and started to cry, knowing that their wounded comrade would end up as a prisoner of war in the American aid station. "I told them I would be glad to take them along too if they cared to come," Wills commented dryly, "but they told me they couldn't. As we started to leave Lieutenant Thomas told us, 'You know you're in hot water?' I asked him what he meant and he said there were two German Mark VI Tiger tanks outside in an orchard with their guns trained on the villa. 'I have to get their okay before you can leave,' he said. He came back a few minutes later and said it was all right for us to go."[401]

Growing impatient, Wills asked Thomas what it was all about. Thomas explained how his group had found five infantry men in the villa and how the Germans had arrived. He had struck a bargain with Goldschmidt when they both realized that they were in a bad position. One of Goldschmidt's men was severely wounded, while one of his two tanks were immobilized. Goldschmidt had promised to disable his tanks and was willing to withdraw his force but only after Thomas would arrange the evacuation of his wounded soldier to a first aid station behind the front lines.

That evening, the Germans left the area after sabotaging their Tigers and retreated on foot. Exploding ammo in the Tigers caused a mortar barrage in the Casa Iacono area, but it halted the pursuing American forces for a while.[402] The paratroopers remained in the villa and, as agreed, didn't pursue the German tank crews. Soon after, Thomas learned of the assembly area near Gela and moved there with his group.

Last to appear that day was the 3rd Battalion Mortar Platoon led by 1st Lieutenant Peter J. Eaton, which brought the battalion to a strength of about 250 men. Thomas became acting battalion executive officer, Ott assumed the duties of S-1, and 2nd Lieutenant Herbert Rosenthal became the new S-4. Eaton received command of HQ Company.

"We held out for five days and then were relieved," recalled Watts, who was devastated to learn his best friend Lieutenant Marshall McOmber of G Company had been killed. "I had gone in with malaria and due to the lack of food and poor water I was terribly ill when I was relieved. I was sent back to Africa to a hospital. It took me a month to get back to Sicily. (...) While in the hospital (...) I asked for Mac's old company."[403]

Watts' wish to command G Company was apparently also shared by Beall, who temporarily shifted 1st Lieutenant Richard Aldridge of H Company to lead G Company in his absence. This meant that 2nd Lieutenant Warren E. Tobias, Jr. would be acting H Company Commander and Ferrill the acting I Company commander. All these "companies" were each little more than one platoon strong as many plane loads were still missing. Beall also informed his unit commanders that it could be temporary since little was known about the company commanders that had jumped on Sicily days before.

On July 16, the 3rd Battalion received a new commanding officer when Major General Matthew B. Ridgway placed the Regimental S-3 officer, Major Emory S. Adams, Jr., in command. Adams, as we have seen, had earlier served in the 3rd Battalion as executive officer before serving as S-3. He was the perfect choice to inspire and lead his depleted battalion.

Back in North Africa, 1st Lieutenant Elbert F. Smith had commanded the 3rd Battalion rear echelon for over a week until 1st Lieutenant Thomas E. Utterback, the Mess Officer, returned from Sicily: "Three planes flew down and returned us to our olive grove near Kairouan. I was informed that I was now the Battalion Rear Echelon Commander. I had 33 men, plus the cooks. (...) I was named Headquarters Company Commander, replacing 1st Lieutenant [John S.] Messina, who died in the water jumping from the same plane I had."[404]

On July 21, he wrote to his wife Pauline and children Tommy and Jeanny, "Before we went over I prayed for just a little luck and have occasion to give thanks many times over for how lucky I really was. (...) One is surprised how calm and cool one is under fire. Good training becomes evident and machine-gun bullets just don't seem to be built for you. Now that the first part is over—the whole thing seems like a rather unpleasant dream or a wild Western scene while half asleep. (...) Right now I'm about as homesick as ever. Hope Mussy throws in the towel (the fat so-and-so) and we really start putting pressure to bear on Germany. Believe we have a good start."[405]

Unknown to Tucker, Lieutenant Colonel William P. Yarborough set up a regimental bivouac area near Biscari in the early morning of July 13. His stick moved twenty-five miles in two nights before they had an unlikely reunion with West Point classmate Lieutenant Colonel Charles "Chuck" Billingslea: "We moved during most of the night. We slept under the leaves and then cautiously moved in the daylight. We didn't find any more of our people. I believe it was the second day we hit the coast and were able to identify where we were on the lateral road. By this time, we were tired of walking and we decided the next vehicle that came along was going to be ours. Whether it was American, German, Italian, whatever, Sicilian. So, we heard a noise down the road and here came a jeep moving along and who should it be but my friend Chuck!"[406]

Billingslea had jumped as an airborne observer on the first night and told Yarborough to head for Biscari. "Driblets of our outfit began to come in from all over the place," recalled Yarborough, "[but] Tucker was unreported for quite some time."[407] Rumors circled around that Tucker's plane had been shot down. Yarborough, being the ranking officer in the bivouac area, became acting regimental commander with Captain Melvin S. Blitch, Jr. of the regimental staff as his executive officer. 1st Lieutenant Lewis P. Fern recorded in his journal on July 13:

0900 – The strength of the Regt was as follows:

| 1st Bn ----------221 | Commanding | Lt [Edson R.] Mattice [C Company] |
| 2nd Bn ---------187 | „ | Capt [Stanley M.] Dolezal [D Company] |

3rd Bn -----------59	„	Lt [Harry G.] Stewart [G Company]
Hq & Hq Co ----67	„	Lt [Carl W.] Kappel
Medics -----------21	„	Lt [Kenneth I.] Sheek

The remainder of the day was given to collecting rations and equipment and preparing."[408]

The Machine Gun Platoon stick of 2nd Lieutenant John S. Thompson had also been misdropped. He recalled:

In our two days of walking we observed many more enemy troops, at a distance, moving north. On the third day we came across a field strewn with parachutes. These parachutes had been used by members of the 505th Combat Team and some men were lying quite still in their harnesses, evidently not having a chance to get out of them.

Upon coming to a crossroad, we saw three pillboxes commanding all the road entrances. There had evidently been a stiff fight here, for there were about twenty bodies of paratroopers in the vicinity of the pillboxes, also many enemy dead.

Later in the afternoon we came upon a battalion CP and were informed that it belonged to the 45th Division. Here we turned over our prisoners for interrogation. We found that these Germans were part of a force who had the mission of laying mines along the coast. At this CP we were able to find that we were fifteen miles southeast of Ragusa (...)

Later that night we arrived at Ragusa and met several paratroopers from the 504th CT who were on their way to Vittoria, where the 2nd Battalion was assembling. We took these men along with us, and early the next morning we arrived at the 2nd Battalion CP, where we met [Lieutenant Colonel] Yarborough and Jack Thompson of the *Chicago Tribune*. They informed me that only one third of the battalion had reported in so far and it was believed that the rest of the regiment had landed on their designated DZ at Gela.[409]

Chicago Tribune reporter John "Jack" Thompson—no relation to Lieutenant Thompson—spoke with Yarborough and wrote later, "I found Lieutenant Colonel William P. Yarborough, who had headed a battalion. His plane had been hit repeatedly. He was not hurt, but several of his men were wounded. His eyes dark with fury, his voice almost uncontrollable. Yarborough said: 'They all jumped. Every man in my plane jumped altho some could hardly stand up. I haven't found them all yet, but every man jumped.' That night we did not know the full extent of the tragedy. Scores of the planes in the flight had passed over our bivouac to drop their loads safely farther inland."[410]

In the bivouac area of Yarborough's part of the regiment, only fifty-four of the 2nd Battalion paratroopers were assembled on July 14, recalled Fern: "Everything has quieted down considerably, rumors of all sorts are in the air. Seems that the planes jumped us from the southeast tip of the island off Biscari. Most of the 3rd Bn never got near their objective. This may account for the one day delay in our jump.

"Late in the afternoon, Lt Col Williams came in with about 100 men. He is in command of the 504th as senior officer. There was a bit of fighting about one mile down the road in which remnants of this outfit were in. Unable to get particulars. Still a few unburied dead in the area, both German and American. There is a parachutist's grave close by."[411]

On July, 15 Fern wrote:

1030 – Lt Col Williams returned from a meeting with Col Tucker, who is bivouacked on the outskirts of Gela. Therefore, Col Tucker is still in command of the 504th. The Regt is reorganizing here, moving out at 1100 on foot.

1100 – The 2nd Bn followed by the 1st and 3rd Bns moved out toward Gela on route #115.

1730 – The head of the column pulls into the bivouac area at Gela. Here we find most of our missing men. Company E is intact, also parts of Hq Co, D and F Co's, now the only planes we can't account for are Lts Patrick's and Shelley's – the latter we saw go down in flames. Find it hard to get an accurate strength report with men still coming in.[412]

With the merging of Lieutenant Colonel Warren R. Williams, Jr.'s force and Tucker's group at Gela, the strength of the 504th Parachute Infantry rose to about 1,300 officers and men. Eight pilots had turned around on the night of July 11 and headed back to North Africa with their full planeloads, a total of 107 paratroopers. They figured it was suicide to fly on, and in doing so, saved the lives of the men on board. The personnel included two planeloads of Headquarters and Headquarters Company, one planeload of F Company, two planes carrying C Battery of the 376th Parachute Field Artillery, two planeloads transporting D Battery gunners, and one battery with Headquarters Battery, Division Artillery personnel.[413]

"On our flight into Sicily on July 11, 1943," recalled Lieutenant Edward J. Sims of F Company, "there were 144 planes carrying the 504th Parachute Infantry Regiment, less 3rd Battalion. A total of 23 planes never returned to North Africa. Of the 23 planes, six had been shot down before the men could jump. Another 37 planes were badly damaged. Eight planes aborted the operation and returned with their load to Tunisia. All together, 229 casualties were sustained."[414]

In all, at least fifty-five paratroopers of the 504th PIR were killed in the friendly fire incident. This number might be higher, as some of the killed paratroopers were given a date of death when their bodies were located instead of the date they were actually killed. Of the 376th Parachute Field Artillery Battalion and C Company, 307th Airborne Engineer Battalion, no soldiers were captured. Their sustained losses were nevertheless high: thirty-five officers and men died because of the friendly fire incident in the 376th and two soldiers of the 307th Airborne Engineers. Statistically, the death of ninety officers and men is a blow, and it was devastating to their families and friends. Several of the 131 wounded paratroopers could never fight again and were eventually sent home. Another sixteen paratroopers were reported missing in action. Gaps had been punched into the 504th Regimental Combat Team that were impossible to heal and difficult to replace.

"General Dwight D. Eisenhower, Allied Commander in Chief, landed in Sicily today (July 12) from a British destroyer and drove to the front," wrote a *New York Times* correspondent, "where he visited American invasion forces. General Eisenhower found that all was going well."[415] This news bulletin could not have been further from the actual truth.

Eisenhower ordered Ridgway to investigate the disaster that had taken place. This "investigation" raised many eyebrows. Why didn't he choose a neutral senior officer, like Major General Joseph M. Swing of the 11th Airborne Division, who had jumped as an observer with the 505th Parachute Infantry? Swing would be less prejudiced than Ridgway, who had reason to write positively about his own actions related to the disaster.

Ridgway concluded in his report that it was impossible to find out who was to blame. He thought that

> not only was friendly fire the cause of the destruction of many of our transport planes with loss of life, but that such fire was delivered from the ground upon descending parachutists, who were killed before or upon landing. Positive evidence also indicates that elements of the 45th Infantry Division had a different countersign from that officially furnished to our parachute personnel. This, too, I verified from Colonel Tucker within a few minutes of his landing, for he had the same countersign (ULYSSES GRANT) as I. It was incorrect. At this time in the operation each division ashore was authorized to designate and actually did designate its own sign and countersign… The delivery of friendly fire upon our own aircraft, in the light of all this and all other past experience, can be guaranteed

only by positive orders that during the anticipated
hours of airborne movements fire of all kinds against
all aircraft must be prohibited in a zone sufficiently
large to insure that even planes that go astray shall not
be subjected to this hazard.

The responsibility for loss of life and material resulting this operation is so divided, so difficult to fix with
impartial justice, and so questionable of ultimate value
to the service because of the acrimonious debates
which would follow efforts to hold responsible persons or services to account, that disciplinary action is
of doubtful wisdom.

Deplorable as is the loss of life which occurred, I
believe that the lessons now learned could have been
driven home in no other way, and that these lessons
provide a sound basis for the belief that recurrences
can be avoided. The losses are part of the inevitable
price of war in human life.[416]

Sims felt bitter about the outcome of Ridgway's report: "A full-
scale investigation was ordered immediately, but it was inconclusive. In
my opinion, the investigation was a shameful cover-up."[417] Major Ivan
J. Roggen, the Regimental Surgeon, believed the real reason for the
friendly fire was "poor coordination between the U.S. Navy and the
Airborne."[418]

The 52nd Troop Carrier Wing stated in their report that the U.S.
Navy is to blame for "the turkey shoot":

This second mission, after the Mission on the night
of 9 July, was almost considered a "milk run", because
this time the drop was to be made behind friendly
lines. (...)

The airplanes took off the night of 11 July 1943 at 20:45. They followed the prescribed route to Malta and on toward the coast of Sicily, maintaining good formation. Weather was good until they rounded Malta; visibility then became slightly poor and grow hazy as they approached Sicily. This haze continued along the coast of Sicily and over the DZ.

All went well until the airplanes began to enter the designated corridor. There shore batteries opened fire on the airplanes and the entire corridor became alive with deadly machine gun fire and heavy flak. The fire became so intense that the formations broke up, each airplane seeking openings through the heavy curtain of fire. The situation became more acute as the planes approached the area of the DZ. (...)

Six of the airplanes failed to drop their paratroopers. They felt it suicide to drop them through such concentrated fire. One ship made three attempts to approach drop zone but could not because of the impenetrability of the anti-aircraft fire. Another plane, trying to escape hostile fire, was going at such an excessive speed, it could not jump its troops. All the airplanes that were able to survive the intense accurate fire dived through the barrage and headed out to sea, over the coast in the vicinity of Gela and Licata. There another tragedy confronted them: our own Navy.[419]

It is virtually impossible to ascertain who is to blame for firing the first round. No action was undertaken after Ridgway's report came out to relieve one of the admirals, or generals, from their command. Eisenhower, as senior Allied commander, could have stepped down, but he didn't. Moreover, war reporters were instructed to remain silent on the subject.

On March 16, 1944, the news of the tragedy first appeared in the American media when Sergeant Jack Foise, a correspondent for the *Stars and Stripes* newspaper, mentioned in a speech in San Francisco that 410 American airborne troopers had been killed by friendly fire. Foise further stated that some twenty planes had been shot down. Journalists immediately inquired more information and confirmation of the story from Secretary of War Henry Stimson, who said he "did not recognize the figures" that Foise had mentioned.

Several hours later, the War Department printed the following memorandum on the matter: "This force, consisting of 170 aircraft, received anti-aircraft fire from enemy ground forces and from friendly naval and ground forces with losses of 23 aircraft and 410 personnel. The flight arrived in the battle area immediately following an enemy bombing attack and while their flares were still in the air. The combination of circumstances involving the approach immediately in rear of a hostile bombing attack at night at a relatively low altitude were the responsible factors in the loss of the planes. This action was made the basis of careful study designed to improve identification and timing and prevent similar losses in the future. The Navy concurs in this statement."[420]

Two American Air Corps officers, Major General Paul L. Williams and Brigadier General Mike Dunn of the 52nd Troop Carrier Wing, both recommended to the War Department shortly after the Sicily jump that the C-47 airplanes should be equipped with self-sealing gas tanks to reduce the chance of causing a transport plane to become a great ball of fire after it would be hit by flak. For nine months, the War Department undertook no action.

In March 1944, some generals decided otherwise and took the matter up to General Henry H. Arnold, the commander-in-chief of the U.S. Army Air Corps, but his chief of staff blocked the order to have self-sealing tanks installed in all troop carrier planes. Senator Harley M. Kilgore of West Virginia then wrote a letter to Stimson to urge him to undertake action. Only in late March 1945 was the decision made to install these tanks on all troop carrier aircraft. By that time, the measure was too late to influence the last airborne operation of the war.[421]

CHAPTER 19

CHARGE AT TUMMINELLO PASS

Sicily

JULY 17–JULY 22, 1943

Although Colonel Reuben H. Tucker's command was still under-strength, Major General Matthew B. Ridgway decided have them spearhead the move up the western coast of Sicily. Lieutenant General George Patton, the Seventh Army commander, had sensed that the Germans had pulled the bulk of their forces together against the British Eighth Army on his right flank, whom he had to support. Not willing to sit aside, Patton guessed the Italian opposition north of the city of Agrigento could be neglected. While his II Corps supervised the operations of the 1st and 3rd Infantry Divisions and the 2nd Armored Divisions, he created the Provisional Corps and gave Major General Geoffrey Keyes the order to advance along the coastal road from Agrigento to along Sciacca and Castelvetrano airfield and finally up to Palermo. This route, Patton figured, would be easier to march on than the rugged hills further inland.

Keyes organized three different columns: the 504th and 505th Regimental Combat Teams and X Force, comprising Colonel William O. Darby's Rangers and the 39th Regimental Combat Team of the 2nd Armored Division. The 504th was to lead the way (mainly on foot) along Highway 115 until they had reached Sciacca, then they were to swing east toward San Margherita and Alcamo, while X Force and the

505th would turn west to take the coastal towns of Marsala (X Force) and Trapani (505th).

At 0600 hours on July 17, the 504th Parachute Infantry Regiment spearheaded the coastal drive of the 82nd Airborne Division from the assembly area near Gela toward the line of departure near Realmonte some twenty-three miles away. The 2nd Battalion, led by Lieutenant Colonel William P. Yarborough, was up front, followed by the 1st and 3rd Battalions. Along the way, Yarborough's men crossed the Platani River using a quickly built bridge by the 307th Airborne Engineers and brushed aside the few opposing Italian infantry with a few rounds of small arms fire and some artillery rounds.

Early afternoon found the leading elements nearing the Verdure River when an Italian anti-tank gun, concealed in a concrete pillbox on the other side, opened fire. It missed the leading American vehicle—a 75mm gun mountain on a halftrack—which backed into a ditch. By sheer luck, the gun barrel pointed directly on the enemy pillbox, and the gunner fired several rounds. American machine gunners and mortar crews joined the barrage, and before long, seventy Italian soldiers came out with their hands up.

First Lieutenant Lewis P. Fern, the 2nd Battalion S-2 officer, wrote in the battalion journal on July 19, "Broke camp at 0400 and marched to point 15 kilometres outside of Ribera. Here we got a fragmentary field order from Colonel Tucker to enter Ribera. Seems they expect to get some resistance. 2nd Battalion is to act as the advance guard for the division.

"At 1300 we entered Ribera; no opposition. Cleared the town of 300 prisoners. Numerous road blocks at all entrances to the city. Lieutenant Colonel Yarborough setting up military police system. At 1700 we were strafed by 7 ME-109's which we probably from Sciacca, which is a short distance from Ribera. Three men of D Company were hit; nothing serious. E Company which was covering the west road, ran into a mined road block and some MG fire, which lasted about 10 minutes. No casualties, 50 Italian prisoners."[422]

The executive officer of E Company, 1st Lieutenant Walter S. Van Poyck, recalled that "one of the many Sicilian towns entered first by our troops was Ribera. I remember rounding the bend in the road and witnessing the fresh paint still dripping on the wall of the northern-most building. The ever present Viva Il Duce had been crossed out. In its place was scrawled Viva Churchill and Viva Velt (they just couldn't spell Roosevelt or hadn't enough time for the complete sign)."[423]

The hot Mediterranean sun together with the dry, dusty road made the ride unpleasant with dust billowing up by the moving vehi-cles. Suddenly, a couple of German ME-109 fighter planes came roar-ing in. They spotted the long-stretched column and opened fire with their two machine guns and two 20mm guns. Second Lieutenant Edward J. Sims of the leading F Company saw how "enemy planes strafed our column. We did take up dispersed positions and opened fire, but all of the planes continued to fly south. It was obvious there were no serious hits."[424]

The 1st Battalion was less fortunate than the 2nd Battalion. Cap-tain Willard E. Harrison's A Company rode in trucks in the central part of the column, which advanced in a long file along Highway 115. "We had probably been on them for about an hour," recalled Private Albert B. Clark of the 2nd Platoon, "and were going through a grove of trees when two ME-109s started strafing us. Being in the trees we didn't know they were around until we heard them and a stream of bullets started hitting the pavement and coming towards us."[425]

Paratroopers leaped out of the trucks and dived into the ditches, trying to find some cover in the low brushes. Some men opened fire on the airplanes, but they "made one pass and took off," continued Clark. "So did our trucks – they turned around and took off before we could do anything. Most of our equipment, including ammo bags, mortars and rifles, was gone. Some of us did take our rifles with us when we bailed out. Since we didn't have any transportation, we took off on foot to try catching up to our company. I don't know how far it was but we finally caught up just as it was getting dark. (...)

"This incident brought about the first combat injuries that we had. One man, [Private] James [F.] Gaygan, took a bullet through the shoulder and his combat days were ended. There were a couple oth-ers with serious wounds but I don't remember their names at this time. There were several that had minor wounds and, after a short stay in the hospital, returned to duty. One that I remember was [Private] Fred Baldino. Luckily we did not suffer any fatalities."[426]

Pfc. Joseph Hirsch and the platoon leader, 2nd Lieutenant Robert D. Condon, were also hit. Condon was treated with sulfa drug by Major Ivan J. Roggen, the Regimental Surgeon, for a mild wound to the right eye incurred from a bullet. He could stay with his platoon and did not receive any lasting damage. Baldino suffered from a flesh wound in his arm and spent a week in the hospital.

"We saw a variety of casualties," recalled Roggen, "but I cannot cite any official statistics. It seems to me the most common casualties were caused by shrapnel wounds. I can say the German 88's made a definite impression on us and were seen as a major threat throughout the war. The survival rate of the casualties we received at the Aid Stations depended greatly on the specific circumstances of each battle. The quicker we could evacuate them to the better equipped medical facilities in the rear, the higher the survival rate. Throughout the Sicily Campaign I had personal use of a captured German halftrack which we used extensively to evacuate casualties."[427]

The leading elements had reached the outskirts of Ribera, some one and a half miles from the airport at the coastal town of Sciacca, at 1800 hours. Bivouac was set up for the night two hours later, after some enemy fire from the airport was received.

At 0800 hours on July 20, the 2nd Battalion preceded once more the 82nd Airborne Division's advance some nine miles to a point just south of Sciacca, where they were ordered to set up another headquarters. A lieutenant colonel from division headquarters showed up around 1100 hours and stated a reconnaissance had been made of this area and that the road until a road junction south of Santa Margherita was clear. Lieutenant Colonel Charles Billingslea, the tall regimental executive officer, came by a few minutes later, announcing that he had scrounged up three trucks for the movement. Using the trucks, he said, about a company at a time could be shuttled forward.

Captain Melvin W. Nitz's F Company was first to move, but suddenly, the leading truck stopped. "I was leading with my platoon when I noticed smoke rising from the road ahead," Sims recalled, "so I dispersed my platoon into firing positions and went forward to check out the smoke. The road had been mined with anti-tank mines and a two-wheeled cart, driven by an old man with a young child, had set off one mine killing both of them and the mule that was pulling the cart. To our left on the crest of a small rise were a number of pill-boxes with white flags being waved from the gun ports. We advanced cautiously and flushed out a large group (about 100) of Italian soldiers who wanted to surrender. After disarming them, they were sent, under guard, to our rear. I will never understand why they allowed the old man to drive his cart into the minefield."[428]

The time was around 1415 hours. Unfortunately, as Fern recorded, the engineers of the 307th Airborne Engineer Battalion who had been attached were called away on division orders to Menfi, where the 1st Battalion had run into another mined road. Engineers of Captain Ted M. Wight's C Company were ordered to remove the mines. Second Lieutenant Vernon P. Ellis was killed and Private George B. Phillips was wounded when one of the German mines exploded.

In the 2nd Battalion column, Fern learned that

> our demolitions men were back at camp waiting for transportation and weren't available. In the meanwhile Lieutenant [Jack P.] Simpson and a few of F Company's men removed enough mines to allow a truck to pass through the road block. This delayed movement for some three hours.

> Just as the road block had been cleared, the 82nd Recon showed up, saying they were to precede us. With the 82nd Recon in front, we proceeded to our objective. Three miles out of Sciacca we sighted an abandoned tank park (German); nothing but oil drums and a few spare parts laying around. About half miles further we found a destroyed searchlight battery, also German. After questioning a civilian, who was the caretaker of this land, we found out that the night before some 15 Germans had destroyed all equipment

and burnt all papers before leaving by truck. This installation had been in some two months.

Some 500 yards further we found an abandoned artillery park with other than paper strewed around the area. Then 800 yards further we found a battery of 75's still intact; across the road was a deserted headquarters and bivouac area. At this point it was near dark and we still had to get three of our remaining companies up. This bivouac area was about 7 miles out of Sciacca. At 2300 we had all companies in the area with an outpost established in front of our positions. The battalion intelligence had found an airfield some 600 yards west of our bivouac area.[429]

Private Richard H. Gentzel of F Company remembered that "one night we pulled up to an olive orchard and they said we would stay there until morning. Well, we all dug in and went to sleep. That was just as it was getting dark. About two o'clock we were very rudely awakened by our sergeant, who told us to get up as we were moving out. We started to walk again."[430]

It was now the early morning of July 21. The ultimate target for the 2nd Battalion was the town of Santa Margherita, only some eight miles further down the road and just short of the Belice River. F Company commenced the advance as planned at 0300 on foot followed by the 2nd Battalion staff, Headquarters Company, D Company, and E Company in the rear. Yarborough sent the battalion intelligence section up front, but Nitz sent them back as he did not think he needed them.

As far as Yarborough knew, there were "no plans for supply that we could see. Our food was what we had on us. No way to carry wounded or whatever, we were just on foot, see. With the battalion in pretty good shape, we began this march and the first action that we ran into was at a place called Tumminello Pass. Tumminello was high ground with a very distinct military terrain feature surrounding it."[431]

Already five miles had been traversed in advance guard formation when at 0515 hours what seemed to be an outpost was spotted. "As we neared our objective," wrote Fern, "we ran into what appeared to be an outpost. They waved a white flag. A few men were sent from the point to investigate but just what they found was never reported."[432]

Almost exactly fifteen minutes later, just before dawn, the point of the 2nd Battalion column received point blank artillery fire from a battery of Italian 77mm guns. Several troopers in F Company were hit and the column immediately deployed to both sides of the road. Gentzel was one of the leading scouts as the artillery shells came in: "About daylight we hit this pass which was our objective. This became the Battle of Tumminello Pass. I was on the point with one of the other fellows watching this pass. As we got closer to it – we were within 600 yards of the pass – I saw a big ball of fire, then heard a swish and then [an explosion] right behind me. (...) We were caught right in the open. All hell broke loose. Machine guns and artillery were firing at us. Once I looked at Butch, the fellow who was on point with me, and he grinned and said, 'Pretty hot here. We'll get the hell back a little.'

"He had no sooner said that when a shell hit on the road between us. It lifted both of us off the ground and scared us something.... The concussion had knocked off my helmet and it made my nose bleed. We were running backwards with machine gun bullets running up and down the road. It seems as though they were saying, 'We will get you, we will get you yet.'"[433]

Fern, behind F Company, recalled that "during the first dozen rounds, men were scattering and taking positions. Enemy MG fire opened up on the men moving up. Their fire was effective enough, stopping the point right where the 77's had caught them. It took about four minutes before the companies were able to organize."[434]

Yarborough called his mortar crews forward "and they did what I thought was an excellent job of maneuvering under the overhanging terrain so that the artillery couldn't get to us."[435] Only two 60mm mortars were initially available—one with E and one with F Company—until the larger 81mm mortars of 2nd Lieutenant Lauren W. Ramsey's Mortar Platoon could join after a fifteen-minute set up. The 4.2-inch chemical mortars of the attached 83rd Chemical Mortar Battalion were supposed to arrive at dawn, but Major David Meyerson didn't want to put his trucks on the road in the darkness. They were still miles away.

Fern noticed that

> the enemy was so well camouflaged it took some time before it was possible to discover where his fire was coming from. As it grew light, it became easier to pick them out. Our LMG's then started opening fire; their targets were caves which we found out later to be very effectively situated. The road leading to the pass was a dog leg to the right. The right side before the turn was a high ridge about 300 yards off the road before the slope began. The ridge itself was 700 yards long. The left side of the road was generally flat and sloping away from the road. As one made the turn, one entered the pass with high vertical cliffs rising on both sides some 250 to 300 feet. The pass further on became a bottle-neck. On both sides of the approach was a tree-strand wire which up to now has always meant the presence of mines. On the road as usual was a well prepared road block with mines intact. (These were removed by the Demolition Platoon.) There was a house on the cliff on the left which overlooked the whole area.

> The enemy fire was coming from both sides of the pass, the ridge, house on the left and the mouth of the pass. After some 10 [more] minutes of fighting, D Company on order sent one platoon up on the east end of the ridge. As soon as this took place, fire from this sector stopped. E Company went through the saddle on at the east end of the ridge for a flanking movement. There was a flanking movement [of an F Company platoon led by Lieutenant Drew] on the left also. Shortly after this, the 81's opened up, zeroing on the house with two rounds.[436]

An attached artillery observer of the 62nd Armored Field Artillery Battalion directed his guns to fire on some pill boxes and the Italian battery.[437] First Lieutenant Charles A. Drew and his 3rd Platoon paratroopers made use of the covering fire to move up a hill on the left flank of the Italian position. Drew ordered his men to fix their bayonets and led them in a bayonet charge. Gentzel, a member of the platoon, recalled that minutes after the first Italian gunfire was received, F Company

> got organized and started firing back. Such a noise I never heard in all my life. The machine guns our boys were manning shot down the enemy until we had a flanking fire and movements that gained the hill and pass after an hour and 40 minutes of fighting.

> On our way to charge we were running across this open field when the lad in front of me turned around and dropped. At the time I didn't realize just what had happened to him. When we were half way up the hill the enemy pulled out a white flag. We finally had taken it.

> We rounded up the prisoners. There were about 250 of them. I forget the exact amount. We started to look for some who would be hiding and went all through their dugouts. All that were in the dugouts were dead and wounded. We overran the hill a little then to assure ourselves that we wouldn't get a counter-attack of any kind.

> After everything was quiet, I went back down the hill to get my helmet. Then I looked at the fellows who were hurt. I saw a close buddy there that never knew what hit him. I knelt down and said a little prayer of thanks. I sure was glad to be alive and all the rest of the boys that survived that battle were too. All I got

out of it was a stone off the road which struck my leg and back. Just enough to make me miserable. A more seriously wounded got panicked. I went and had them take the stones out of me.[438]

Pfc. James C. Turner of F Company would be awarded a Silver Star in September 1945 while being a Staff Sergeant when he "volunteered for a five man combat patrol to destroy enemy machine guns holding up the company attack from emplacements near the pass. He crawled up the hill under intense machine gun fire and knocked out one gun with a grenade. The patrol was thus able to reach the top of the pass, destroy other positions and disrupt the enemy defenses. In the confusion, Staff Sergeant Turner ambushed and killed with grenades six officers on motorcycles who attempted to escape."[439]

Private Abraham Bloomfield received a Silver Star for the same action: "Bloomfield, a battalion clerk, volunteered for a patrol to eliminate enemy positions dominating approaches to the battalion objective. He dashed across three hundred yards of open ground with the patrol under a hail of rifle, machine gun and 77-mm fire to one of the machine gun positions. There he disabled the gun, killed two enemy and wounded one. Continuing the climb with two remaining members of the patrol, he grenaded another machine gun position, putting it out of action and uncovered the command post of the enemy strong point, which resulted in the surrender of the command post and the strong point. Elimination of the strong point permitted the battalion to seize its objective with a minimum loss of time."[440]

The F Company medic, Technician 5th Grade Levern H. Miller, also earned a Silver Star at Tumminello Pass when they were "pinned down by heavy machine gun, rifle, mortar, and artillery fire, at a range of approximately four hundred yards. During this firefight, four men of Technician 5th Grade Miller's organization were seriously wounded, requiring immediate medical attention. These men were exposed with no cover nearby. Technician 5th Grade Miller, with complete disregard for his own safety, exposed himself, and braving enemy fire, moved to the position of the wounded men and gave them the necessary medical aid."[441]

The Italian garrison of Tumminello Pass were shocked by the unexpected bayonet charge, and one colonel, thirteen of his officers, and more than 1,500 enlisted men surrendered. They had lost over one hundred dead and thirty-five wounded, a sheer contrast to F Company's eight wounded and six killed in the entire action—Staff Sergeant Henry J. Wilczynski, Sergeant Joseph L. Lockhart, Technician 4th Grade Louis F. Fattore, Technician 5th Grade Alfred Secondine, Pfc. Edward Coen, and Private Dan I. Paulk.

Fern took stock of the salvaged Italian equipment: "Fifteen vehicles (motor bikes), two damaged and non-operating tankets, medical storehouse, three cars (not running), all kinds of machine guns, one mortar, all kinds of ammunition, five 77's intact with sights, and large amounts of communication equipment."[442]

Chicago Tribune reporter John "Jack" Thompson wrote about the battle at Tuminello Pass: "This outfit ran into some trouble yesterday evening at a crossroads. The Italians there had several guns in good position and opened fire on the front column, landing a burst which killed six men. The boys dug in and went to work and in half an hour a white flag went up. As our men came out the enemy opened fire, so our men fixed bayonets and went in, killing 30 before the enemy surrendered legitimately."[443]

By 0830 the fighting at Tumminello Pass had ceased. The battalion was still some miles from their final objective, Santa Margherita in the northwest. Yarborough, however, was pleased with his battalion's first combat engagement as a unit and realized his men needed some rest and a meal before they could continue their advance. Also, the more than 1,500 prisoners needed to be searched and separated. He decided to concentrate his battalion inside Tumminello Pass with road blocks on the roads leading to it. Ridgway arrived and asked why Yarborough stayed there. "Sir, we've just taken Tumminello Pass," he replied. "If you stay in the area here, you are going to be shelled. This is no way to do it. Keep moving, get going," Ridgway stated. Yarborough was disappointed: "I felt that he should have patted me on the shoulder and said, 'Say, you guys did a good job here. You took this place, see you captured a battery of artillery.' He didn't do anything of the kind."[444]

At around 1300 hours, Colonel James M. Gavin's 505th Regimental Combat Team and Company B of the 83rd Chemical Mortar Battalion passed through Tumminello Pass on their way to Trapani in the west, while the 2nd Battalion was relieved by the 3rd Battalion and proceeded to its previously assigned bivouac area near Santa Margherita. Captain Adam A. Komosa, commanding Headquarters and Headquarters Company, remembered that "at the end of the day the 2nd Battalion was occupying Sambuca, and the remainder of the Regiment was moving from Menfi to Santa Margherita. The gruelling Mediterranean sun, however, told on the foot-weary paratroopers; it was march, march, march, day and night. They prayed for the enemy to make a stand so that they could stop and fight – and rest. Five days and nights this continued and in an outstanding tribute to the physical stamina of parachute troops, men of the 504th walked and fought their way from Agrigento to Santa Margherita – a distance of 150 miles."[445]

From the Belice River line, which had been reached, the final phase of the conquest of the western of Sicily was to start. With the 1st Battalion and various regimental units at Menfi, the 3rd Battalion near Tumminello Pass—moving up to Santa Margherita—and the 2nd Battalion in Santa Margherita and Sambuca, July 22 brought the stirring news that the Italian garrison of Palermo had surrendered to an advance unit of the 2nd Armored Division. The 2nd Battalion spent the day resting, cleaning their weapons and equipment, and listening to Yarborough's critique on the first combat engagement of the previous day. Many troopers took the chance to trade their M-1 carbines for M-1 rifles when the opportunity arose, as the M-1s were much better for long distance shooting.

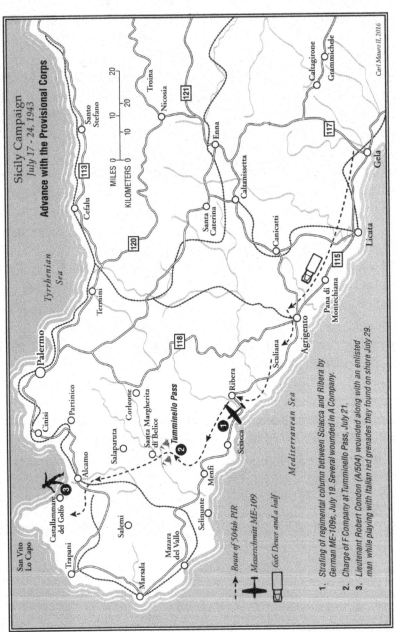

Sicily Campaign
July 17 - 24, 1943
Advance with the Provisional Corps

Carl Mauro II, 2016

Route of 504th PIR

Messerschmitt ME-109

6x6 Deuce and a half

1. Strafing of regimental column between Sciacca and Ribera by German ME-109s, July 19. Several wounded in A Company.
2. Charge of F Company at Tumminello Pass, July 21.
3. Lieutenant Robert Condon (A/504) wounded along with an enlisted man while playing with Italian red grenades they found on shore July 29.

Sicily Campaign

CHAPTER 20

GARRISON DUTY

Sicily

JULY 23-AUGUST 11, 1943

On July 23, Lieutenant Colonel William P. Yarborough received the order to capture Castellammare del Golfo, a city on the northern coast of Sicily, a little more than thirty-four miles from his bivouac. Word came through that seventeen trucks would be sent up at 1600 hours after the 505th Parachute Infantry Regiment had been moved up to Trapani. Not willing to sit back and await things to come, Yarborough decided to press on with an Italian interpreter and his S-3 officer by commandeering a jeep that brought some rations up: "We ran into a road block which was garrisoned by Italians who came out of the road block with their hands up, but their weapons were still in place (...) We said, 'Well, there's an airborne division coming people up the road and the best thing for you to do, would be to surrender now and save the trouble, you see. Otherwise they are liable to come in here shooting.' (...) Fear predominated in their hearts and they said, 'All right. We'll do what you say.' I said, 'Well, take those guns now and take them apart and lay them alongside the road and get the ammunition out here, where we can see it. Take your side arms off and put them here.' And they did all that."

Yarborough then queried the Italians about the location of their main position. "It's just a little way down the road," answered an officer. Taking the Italian in his jeep, the Americans drove down to the

Italian headquarters building. Outside the stone structure, an Italian officer wearing two berettas came out of the building, inquiring what was going on. "You better lay down your arms alongside the road here," Yarborough had his interpreter say, "because an airborne division is coming up the road and it is going to be tough for you if you show any fight." The officer seemed impressed and complied to Yarborough's orders to gather all his weapons in a huge pile. No man was to wear any possible weapons like rifles, pistols, knives, or even clubs. Some of the younger Italian staff officers started to cry and expressed their uncertainty about seeing their families again. The paratroopers tried to calm them down, assuring them that if they put their pistols in the jeep, they would be all right.

After the weapons and the "prisoners" had been gathered, they waited for the remainder of the battalion to arrive: "Hours went by and hours went by and then these guys began to look at you (...) It was not until just before dusk in the evening that the first elements of the 82nd began to arrive up there. And by this time we had gone out of the defensive position and gotten one for ourselves alongside the road with our ammunition around us."[446]

It took until 0330 hours on July 24 before the seventeen trucks that had been previously promised arrived at the bivouac area near Santa Margherita to take the 2nd Battalion to Castellammare del Golfo via Alcamo. There the battalion was reunited with Yarborough and his three companions.

The capture of Trapani and Castellammare del Golfo ended the battles in the western region of Sicily. Colonel Reuben H. Tucker, on higher orders, sent out various elements of his force on policing duties in the adjacent villages and towns around Alcamo, Castellammare del Golfo and Santa Margherita to keep the places civilized. Engineers of the 20th Combat Engineer Regiment were ordered to clear a path to nearby beach. Lieutenant Walter S. Van Poyck of E Company believed "one humorous sidelight of the Sicilian campaign was the offer of many POW's to join us and fight the Italian mainlanders. To prove their loyalty, many displayed civic, fraternal and veterans organizations membership cards which they had carried since their younger days in the U.S. Returning to the old country they had been impressed into the army."[447]

Yarborough became mayor of the larger town of Alcamo and suddenly had to set up the civil structure. Italian police personnel came and asked what to do with the political prisoners in the town prison. Yarborough ordered them to be released. Then they asked if the fixed price for bread could be dropped. "I sat at the mayor's desk in Alcamo for about three days," he recalled, "passing on things like that, using the best judgement that I could muster but feeling completely inadequate in the light of the human problems that surround uncovering of an enemy city by an Army."[448]

The following days, the situation changed little: policing duties were carried out, and minefields were cleared by C Company of the 307th Airborne Engineer Battalion and E Company of the 20th Combat Engineer Regiment. Lieutenant Lewis P. Fern located a 208th Coast Artillery Division headquarters of fifty Italian officers and three hundred enlisted men, who pointed out that a Colonel Kimball from the infantry had drawn a treaty for them. Tucker was informed, and he dealt with the situation: over two thousand prisoners of the 208th were sent to POW stockades.

Passes were issued to the officers and enlisted men in limited numbers to go to the beach or the towns of Alcamo and Castellammare del Golfo. Newly promoted Corporal Paul C. Mentzer of the 3rd Battalion Communications Platoon wrote to his parents on July 25, "We are having a lot of fun here in Sicily – swimming and lying on the beach. This is a very beautiful country and I lot better climate than North Africa."[449]

That same day, D Company medic Jack Labre wrote to his parents:

> My combat jump the night we invaded was my seventh jump and I did not have any trouble. The parachutists did a good job in softening up the island for the other troops. As you probably know, we landed in southern Sicily. Yes, there were plenty of bullets to dodge but none had my name on it. I am now in northwestern Sicily living in an old mansion we use as

headquarters. It's devoid of all furniture but sleeping on a smooth floor is a pleasure, after many nights in orchards and vineyards.

The people of Sicily for the most part are friendly towards us and give us hearty welcomes. They seem glad to be out of the war. The towns and cities are all old and the people are packing in them like sardines, making very unsanitary living conditions. I'm afraid I could never get to like this country. Many fruits and vegetables grow here, affording a welcome change of diet. Watermelons and grapes, especially. I had a sample of their spaghetti, but can't say I enjoy it.

I just took time out to watch wave after wave of bombers and fighter planes go over. I pity the Germans and Italians who have to dodge them.[450]

Labre's view on the Sicilian population was shared in an August 10 letter by Private Fred W. Thomas of H Company, who was stationed elsewhere: "The towns in Sicily are all very old. They don't have hardly anything to sell. The people are all poor. They wear old ragged cloths. Some of them don't even have shoes. They say Mussolini has taken everything they have. They sure hate him. The only transportation they have is horse and cart. They have some good farms, but they have to pay so much tax that they don't make anything. The only ones that make anything is the big land owners, and some of Mussolini's gang. The people of the U.S. don't know how lucky they are."[451]

The 2nd Battalion was moved to the Salemi area on July 28, while the 1st Battalion moved to Castellammare del Golfo. While it meant a relatively easy duty for the latter, the 2nd Battalion received a phase-line plan to comb the area around Salemi. Fern wrote in his unit journal on July 29, "Found it a bit difficult to locate our pre-designated CP's according to the maps we have. The only map supplied is 1:100,000 and about thirty years old. It was 2200 before D Company reached their phase line; E Company got in about 1830; and F

Company about 2000. The progress reports from D and F Companies were negative. E Company found quite a bit and the information was handed to Regiment about 2300. Our CP is located on the outskirts of Castelvetrano airdrome."[452]

That same afternoon, an unfortunate incident occurred near Castellammare del Golfo. The 2nd Platoon of A Company was swimming when someone came up with the idea to use small, red Italian grenades to play a ball game near the sea. "They all knew what they were playing with," recalled Private Fred J. Baldino. "The Italians dumped a whole truckload in the sea near where we were camped for a couple of days. I saw them playing with the grenades and I ran the other way and soon afterwards one exploded..."[453] One enlisted man lost an eye, and 2nd Lieutenant Robert D. Condon was wounded in his left leg. Both were quickly taken to a hospital in Salemi and later evacuated to the States.

Second Lieutenant Robert Condon of A Company photographed in his hometown Baltimore, Winter 1944. Condon was injured after the Sicily Campaign had ended. Courtesy: Robert Condon

Another tragic incident took place two days later concerning 1st Lieutenant Zigmund C. Lutcavage of F Company near Marsala.

"Lutcavage was accidentally shot in the left elbow by one of his own men," recalled Lieutenant Edward J. Sims, "who was shooting at wine barrels. His elbow was shattered and he was evacuated through medical channels to the U.S. for treatment."[454] These incidents overshadowed the subsequent peaceful days that were spent on Sicily.

On August 2, as the 2nd Battalion had returned to Salemi, Yarborough received orders to report to Tucker. He was told to proceed to Division Headquarters to see Major General Matthew B. Ridgway in person. Yarborough correctly sensed that it wouldn't be a pleasant conversation as he had argued with Ridgway at Tumminello Pass. Ridgway greeted him sternly and said, "Your services are no longer required. I want you to go back to Lieutenant General Mark Clark and tell him that he should find another job for you."

A plane took Yarborough back to the Fifth Army Headquarters in North Africa, where he earlier had been an airborne adviser. Clark promised him that in due course he would get another command. To Yarborough, it came as a blow: "I wanted to die. I felt that if I could only get into combat someplace and get an honorable slug or whatever, that I would have paid the price for my high spirited stupidity, you see. Challenging authority in a way that no outfit can just work on that basis. You can't have that kind of thing and I recognized where the deficiency lay. It was with me and not with Ridgway or with Tucker."[455]

Major Daniel W. Danielson, the executive officer, replaced Yarborough. Tucker brought in Major Melvin S. Blitch, Jr., his S-3 officer, to take Danielson's old position. Captain Robert R. Johnson, the S-1 officer, was also sent to the 2nd Battalion to take command of Headquarters Company, as Captain Malcolm A. Nicolson was made Battalion S-3 in place of the missing 1st Lieutenant Mack C. Shelley. Second Lieutenant Chester A. Garrison of E Company, who was still limping after his unfortunate landing, was made Battalion S-1 officer to reduce the double duty of Fern. S-1 officers were also added in the 1st and 3rd Battalions. In the 1st Battalion, it was 1st Lieutenant Gus M. Gerard.

Garrison felt distraught with his transfer:

> The staff was where the bastards were! From what I had seen of adjutants, I didn't want to be one (...)

A battalion adjutant keeps track of personnel, as well as communication with the four companies of the battalion and with regimental headquarters: he is an in-between man. His primary output is paper, although he can also be vocal. He keeps the commander informed and sometimes acts as his aide. In the absence of the commander, the adjutant is the commander's voice about personnel – not touching on supply or tactical matters. (...)

I rapidly discovered that the job was not designated for a limping lieutenant. It might sound like a strictly desk job to take care of complaints, questions, and policies, but I found I was checking with the medics and circulating in the companies in search of individuals. I was also involved in parades and changes of location. Despite my vigorous activity, my knee healed by itself, but occasionally it still gives hint of a coming change of weather. The irony of my dislike for my assignment is that I adjusted to it well enough to remain an adjutant for two years. I soon realized that I was probably doing what best suited me in a combat unit. Among its advantages was that I was not in line for patrol duty.[456]

August 5 brought another transfer of the 2nd Battalion headquarters to the castle in Partanna. While D Company was billeted in Santa Margherita and Montevago, E Company remained in Salemi, and F Company was sent to control Gibellina, Salaparuta, and Santa Ninfa. "My platoon," recalled Sims, "was assigned to police an area near the small town of Salaparuta, which was the milling center for a larger area. (...) We immediately set out to search the surrounding area for hold outs and soon found a large building that had been used by the Germans for food storage. The large amount of food supply remaining was confiscated. I then arranged with the local clergy to distribute the food to the most needy in Salaparuta."[457]

First Lieutenant Ned E. Wall, the executive officer of A Company, wrote to his parents:

> Since landing in Sicily the time has passed very rapidly although the days have been hard and long. The rations have reached us each day and we've had plenty of fresh fruits and vegetables that are produced here. We are being issued by 5-in-1 rations now. One box of rations which serves 5 men for one day. We prepare it ourselves over open fires. Speaking of food, just this morning I had three fried eggs. I purchased from a civilian yesterday, bacon, oatmeal, grapefruit juice and coffee. The army is certainly good to us.
>
> I was in a church service a few minutes ago. It was a make-shift affair as no chaplain was here. I had Lieutenant [Stanley J.] Whitman take charge. We sang a few songs and he read a Psalm. All in all it was pretty nice.
>
> You know the way we came into this operation. We carried very little with us. As a result we wash our clothes (jump suit) and put them on wet or if time permits wait for them to dry. Just last night Captain [Willard E.] Harrison, Lieutenant Whitman and myself went to a well near our bivouac area and washed our clothes.. (...)
>
> Just had a little conversation with a couple of Italians which I didn't get much out of. The people in Sicily seem happy to see American soldiers. As we march through the towns we take, the people crowd the streets and clap and cheer. They seem to think the Americans will take Sicily and make it just like the United States in no time.[458]

First Lieutenant Ned Wall of A Company was killed on Hill 424. His close friend,
Lieutenant Stanley Whitman, named a son after him. Courtesy: Gary Wall

One hundred and nine officers and men of the 504th PIR were captured on Sicily. Most of the enlisted men also belonged to the 3rd Battalion, with the exception of one planeload from D Company and at least two from B Company. In comparison, fifty-one officers and enlisted men of the 505th PIR were taken prisoner. The number of fatal casualties was even higher: 114 officers and enlisted men of the 504th were killed versus seventy-one officers and men killed in the 505th. H Company needed no less than four replacement officers and forty-six enlisted men to rebuild it strength in August. The 3rd Battalion had nearly one-third killed, wounded, and missing. All these men had to be replaced.

CHAPTER 21

EGB448

Oujda, Algeria
Kairouan, Tunisia

AUGUST 12-AUGUST 24, 1943

I n North Africa, the yet-unassigned soldiers of EGB448 waited impatiently during the Sicily campaign until they were called upon to join their new parent unit. Gathering 1,200 officers and men for EGB448 in April 1943 had proved to be difficult as the composition of EGB447 had almost drained out the Parachute School in Fort Benning. So, unlike the many jump school graduates that had been assigned to EGB447, the majority of the men in EGB448 came from existing parachute regiments that had been activated in late 1942 or early 1943. Especially Colonel Howard R. Johnson's 501st Parachute Infantry Regiment, Colonel Albert H. Dickerson's 513th Parachute Infantry Regiment (for the 504th PIR), and Colonel Robert F. Sink's 506th PIR (for the 505th PIR) were called upon to provide replacements.

They had arrived in Casablanca on the *George Washington* and remained in Morocco until June 7, 1943. Twenty-nine-year-old Private Earl S. Oldfather from Galveston, Indiana was one of the older replacements. He managed to keep throughout his army time a unique diary of which interesting extracts follow:

> May 10 – Docked at 1206. This is quite a harbor. Saw the mast of
> a ship that was sunk – others that had been damaged. Saw a

couple of native guards – dressed poorly and their rifles are quite long. The fellows threw candy and money at them. (...) From the boat this looks like a very modern city. We are going to be the last ones off – wait and wait. I was up and down from deck to hole several times. (...)

We marched to the train depot. Told not to give the Arabs money or cigarettes. There were several along the way begging. They came right up to you and ask. Saw palm trees and very modernistic buildings. The train cars were different – electric engine. I had to sit on the arm of a seat – plenty crowded. Rode 12 miles out of Casablanca. Marched quite aways from the train to bivouac area. Deckman and I pitched together. Oh yes – we were issued 5 rounds of ammo on the boat – turned it in here.

May 11 – Three lieutenant colonels spoke – welcomed us to this camp – Marshal Lyautey. Our stay here may be days or months.

May 13 – We're on schedule now. Had close order drill and exercises. Came back in – gave us tablet salt. The lieutenant gave a talk – telling us how to recognize Navy officers and French officers. One of the sergeants passed out. This old sun sure is hot. This p.m. more drill – exercises – obstacle course – tumbling and a run.

May 17 – Fell out for drill. Went on run and little hike. Stood retreat. Lieutenant announced there was a water shortage. Each Company will have a certain time to shower. No more washing clothes or shaving in the wash houses.

June 7 – Got us up at 0430. (...) Finished packing – made a rol – changed to khaki and boots. Waited. Had a physical. After chow we were issued 6 pair of celluloid glasses – nice to keep dirt out of your eyes. (...) Lieutenant took our names. Marched to the train tracks. Had markers from 1 to 33 – we were 28 – that's the car we board. Waited a half hour. We are being transported in old French box cars – 30 men each. (...) Stopped outside of Fedala for half hour. Told to save our water in our canteens – must last 24 hours. Don't buy anything from the Arabs. Don't yell at girls. Don't leave car without permission. Don't throw paper out.

June 9 – Arrived in Oujda about 0230 a.m. Fell out about 0730 with pack, etc. Marched to the station out far. Trucks took us to the camp about 8 miles out – 29th Replacement Battalion.

June 14 – New system in eating – do it by platoons. We were last this morning. More squad drill – settle on the M-1. Marched over to the hangars – jumped out of a plane door. This plane had been shot down in combat. Second at chow. Fell out in G.I. shoes and shorts for physical. Then a talk on military information and cover and concealment.

June 19 – The Captain and a Lieutenant Colonel gave us a pep talk – also a personal message from General Clark – commander of the Fifth Army. The General is very fussy about the salute. When he passed by here (29th Replacement Battalion) he wasn't saluted as much as he thought he should be – he wanted to know why. He was told we hadn't been paid for a long time – we had been shoved around and felt like orphans. He then ordered the ordnance officer to close up shop and work on our payroll only until every man was paid – in all (I think). He also ordered Fifth Army insignias to be made and sent to us. We are no longer orphans.

June 29 – Lieutenant General Clark and other brass came around. He watched us jump once. This was out of the small door plane – then we went to the large door plane.

July 14 – Lieutenant Baggs picked different fellows to give the rifle exercises this a.m. I gave one. He said, "Very good" when I got thru. Ran obstacle course. Then platoon tactics – 3 problems – lots of mistakes. Lieutenant Rolak made a speech that didn't go over so good – Lieutenant Kemble stepped in.

July 16 – Last night was the first time since arriving in Africa that I have slept without coveralls. Had to pack my bags and roll up shelter half. The first roll call as at 0730 – then another and then the final by the Colonel. We're going by truck – 13 men and 1 officer to a truck. I'm with Lieutenant Hutton on truck #27.

July 20 – Arrived at destination about 1100. Had roll call – picked up bags – waited in the hot sun. Names were called for different outfits. Gregas went first – field artillery. Then Pasbrig, Deckman and I to the 504 Parachute Infantry. (...) Loaded on trucks and taken to our new homes. Living in pup tents again. Each area is surrounded with cactus. (...) The 504 is in Sicily – expected back anytime.

July 21 – No reveille. They marched 200 of us – we three included – to Service Company for breakfast – the rest stayed here to be fed by the 509 [Parachute Battalion]. (...) We were divided into 4 companies and taken to our new area. (...) In Company B Essig joined us. The four of us put up quite a tent. Squads were formed. We are in 2nd Squad, 3rd Platoon. Essig is squad leader. Got dinner. C-rations for supper. The Colonel of the 509 welcomed us. Showed on a map how the battle of Sicily is progressing. Had a concert – swell popular music.

July 28 – A sergeant who had been in combat in Sicily gave us a little talk.

July 30 – Repacked the 'A' and 'B' bags belonging to the fellows in Sicily. Their 'A' bags are being sent to them.

August 2 – Issued an M1 rifle #1098376 – took most of the afternoon to clean the thing.

August 5 – Exercises in G.I. shorts and boots – double timed to and from the field. The rest of the morning was on maps and compass. (...) Those who missed formations dug latrines. (...) Compass problem this evening. We were divided into 6 combat patrols. Each man had an azimuth to remember. The course wasn't long but tough – over a lot of ravines. The officers said we did good.

August 7 – Exercises in G.I. shorts and boots. Then squad tactics with rifles.

August 18 – Have a new Lieutenant – from the 504 and has seen combat.

August 19 – Fired on the range (...) The purpose of the firing was to zero your rifle – no scores kept. (...) I fired 40 rounds there – kept 8 rounds for myself. Late getting in for dinner.

Cleaned rifle – hot soapy water – then bore cleaner. Shaved. The 504 is returning.

August 20 – Went thru infiltration course this morning and threw a grenade.

August 22 – No reveille – ate at 0700. Boy – getting all we can eat and all the sugar we want. Must be fattening us up for the kill. Went to church at 0900. The 504 chaplain is back – a young fellow.[459]

When the 504th PIR returned from Sicily, the EGB commander received the order to release a few hundred officers and enlisted men to augment the losses that had been sustained. "We paraded for Colonel [Reuben H.] Tucker, commander of the 504, this morning," wrote Oldfather in his diary on August 24. He continued:

The entire Regiment was there. We were dressed in khaki with insignias attached – got those last night and sewed them on. Rifles with bayonets carried at sling arms. Ate dinner at 1100 after which we got our parachutes – adjusted them. We are jumping with equipment – rifle – musette bag – bayonet – canteen – first aid pouch – pistol belt with harness – steel helmet – jump suits. (...) Landed forward right on my face – hard – steel helmet protected my nose.

August 25. We missed out on the Bob Hope show last night. He was here in person. Slept till almost 0700. (...) We signed the payroll – no amount entered. Getting back jump pay for November 21 to April 20 – cheating me out of some. About 0920 we were told to pack up, be ready to move at 1000. After a while told to drop everything – marched over to mess area. Colonel Tucker gave us a pep talk and welcome to the 504. Then we were assigned to Battalions and

Companies. I'm in the 3rd Battalion, Company G. (...)

Marched over to the 3rd Battalion – its near the water point. The Major [Emory S. Adams, Jr.] – Battalion CO – welcomed us – introduced [the] officers. Roll call. Marched to Company area – assigned to platoons and squads. I'm in 3rd Platoon, 2nd Squad. [Private James C.] Woods is in the same. Marched to the platoon area.[460]

Oldfather's platoon leader was 1st Lieutenant Frank J. Lavis with 2nd Lieutenant Chester A. Smith as his assistant. Other replacements were also assigned to their platoons at the same time. Private John J. Foley, Jr. trained with the 3rd Battalion of the 506th PIR at Camp Toccoa, Georgia: "The 506th was an experimental regiment as it wasn't part of a division and we received our basic infantry training in the regiment. We went from Camp Toccoa to Fort Benning where I qualified as a paratrooper and when I heard they needed replacements for the 82nd Airborne Division I applied for a transfer and was placed in a replacement group. We landed in Casablanca and I remember the demolished French battleship *Jean Bart* in the harbor."[461] Foley was assigned to the 3rd Platoon in H Company.

Another replacement in EGB448 was twenty-two-year-old Private Thomas J. Zouzas from Ellsworth, Kansas. He took basic training in Camp Wolters, Texas before attending The Parachute School. Zouzas learned about the need for replacements and "volunteered to go overseas immediately." He found the train journey in boxcars to Oujda unbearable:

They were so crowded that we had to lay down in shifts as there was no room enough for all to sleep at the same time. They were hot, dirty and very uncomfortable. After two such trips that lasted about eight days each, I declared that I would never make another such trip.

It was not long before they decided to take us for the third time. Being a man of my word, at the first stop I failed to go aboard. At first the officer of our section waived me to board the train. I just waved good-bye to him and shook his fist at me and I'm sure he was thinking 'COURT MARTIAL'. I was thinking the same thing but decided it would be worth it.

I spent a week in Oran, having a ball. I then caught a C-47 from Oran to Bizerte which took three hours and not eight days. (...) The only problem was that I had to go through Bizerte and in doing so, I was picked up by the military police and jailed. It was the worst jail I was ever in. It contained Arabs, Italians, Americans, British, etc. They were airmen, Navy, infantry, etc. They pushed a tin of Spam under the door and it was grab with your fingers as much and as fast as you could or you missed your lunch. The floor was made of cold tiles and we had no blankets. I begged and pleaded for them to let me out and I would go to my outfit. They let me go after three days.[462]

Upon his release from the prison in Bizerte, Zouzas joined the regiment in Kairouan: "The food was so bad that the troops demonstrated with a sit-down-strike outside the mess hall. (...) I decided to volunteer to work in the kitchen for the purpose of getting more chow."[463]

Private Francis X. Keefe's assignment to EGB448 was his second unit transfer in less than five months. He was born on September 16, 1924 in Jersey City and moved to Manhattan, New York City when he was eight years old. He had entered military service in 1941 after lying about his age and served for a year in C Battery of the 244th Coast Artillery in Camp Pendleton, Virginia. They fired old French 155mm guns from the World War I.

In May 1942, Keefe decided to rejoin the U.S. Army along with his best friend William McKeever. Again, he lied about his age and said he was twenty-one instead of seventeen. Both were sent to Camp Croft, South Carolina for basic infantry training. Some weeks later, McKeever and Keefe applied for the paratroops, and their entire platoon was transferred to the 507th PIR at Camp Toccoa, Georgia.

It didn't take long before Keefe's unit was filled with volunteers: "F Company went through jump training together and we all made it, except one guy. He refused to jump. The first day, a Monday, it rained, so we had to make two jumps on Tuesday. We had to pack our chute again after the first jump. They examined our packs before they sent us up again."[464]

In January 1943, a new PIR, the 513th, was pre-activated. Several officers and men were selected from the 507th to serve as cadre members for the 513th. Each company contributed two enlisted men, and Keefe became a member of Headquarters Company, 3rd Battalion of the 513th PIR. His new battalion commander was Major Henry B. Frank.

Unlike the 507th, the 513th was a training outfit. Lieutenant Colonel Albert Dickerson, the regimental commander, had received the order to prepare as many trained paratroopers as possible for the Parachute Replacement Pool at Fort Benning, Georgia. They moved to Alabama in early March, and several enlisted men left to join replacement group EGB447. Later that month, Dickerson received orders to administer the Parachute Replacement Pool with another few hundred paratroopers. Keefe was among the men who were selected for the replacement group EGB448. Frank was placed in command of this detachment.[465]

In August 1943, Keefe assisted in an infiltration obstacle course run by 2nd Lieutenant William D. Mandle from Wichita, Kansas. Mandle had been S-3 officer in the Provisional Parachute Replacement Battalion composed of EGB447 and EGB448 personnel and was assigned to I Company. Like Keefe, Mandle had served previously in the 513th PIR and in North Africa. According to Keefe, "Lieutenant Mandle was in charge of the infiltration obstacle course. A squad of us were assigned to him. They had two men on machine guns and they fired above the barbed wire. Some 25 to 30 guys would crawl very low under the barbed wire during each course. Our job was to set explosives off for effect behind a barrier. One of the men holding up the barbed wire was wounded by the machine gun. At first no one knew what happened, but an older Arab of about 60 years old saw that the bullet hit a pole, riccocheted and hit a guy in the side. We were there for three or four days."[466]

In Kairouan, Keefe was assigned to the 1st Platoon of I Company, which was commanded by 1st Lieutenant Willis J. Ferrill. Private Francis McLane was promoted to Corporal and received Keefe in his rifle squad: "I had been part of the EGB replacement pool and during our stay in North Africa, from Morocco on, there were two characters who wore big 'P's on their backs. They were escorted to chow, to the latrine, to the shower, to Mass, etc., by an armed guard. They made a great show of double timing around accompanied by flapping elbows, flailing arms, staggering gait and generally screwing everything up.

"When I was finally assigned to I Company, who would unload from a truck but these two yard birds. They walked up to me with big smiles on their faces and had chosen me for a buddy, meet [Privates Leo P.] Muri and Keefe. Of course, we turned out to be great friends. We argued about everything possible. Keefe was always collecting rumors and believed them until a new one took its place. These two were very different and interesting. I think they found me to be a little odd. The difference between east coast and west coast upbringing."[467]

Replacement officers flowed in to complement the junior officer gaps caused by the sustained losses and transfers within the regiment. One was twenty-three-year-old 2nd Lieutenant Reneau G. Breard from Monroe, Louisiana, who joined the 1st Platoon in A Company. Breard was a graduate of the University of Louisiana before he received a reserve officer's commission in June 1942. He recalled, "Paratrooper training was very rough physically and only fifty percent of the class of 100 finished the four week course."[468]

Being new to the platoon, Breard was placed in the rear by 2nd Lieutenant Stanley J. Whitman during "night problems." These were planned marches or combat situations that took place after dark as it was cooler then and combat jumps would also be at night. Breard did not like it at first that Whitman or the platoon sergeant led the platoon on these night problems, but he soon understood they were more experienced and learned a lot.

"I am at liberty to tell you that I have seen Casablanca (the town where the important conference took place) and Rabat," wrote 2nd Lieutenant Edward W. Kennedy from Holyoke, Massachusetts on June 17 to his sister Rose. Kennedy joined H Company from the 29th Replacement Battalion as an assistant platoon leader. He "had an enjoyable swim 'somewhere in the Mediterranean.' (...) Gradually from the day we left Fort Benning things are getting tougher. I think of nothing of going to sleep on rocky ground now nor of eating more sand than food."[469] Kennedy was awarded the Soldier's Medal in July 1943 by Lieutenant General Mark W. Clark of the Fifth Army for saving a French soldier from drowning in the coast of Algeria.

The regiment had a special tradition for new officers who were assigned to the regiment prop blast. They had to drink from a big silver beaker, Tucker's Tumbler. It was designed by Sergeant Sam D'Crenzo of the 1st Battalion, and small silver cups were engraved with the name of each officer. The medics filled it with a mixture of liquids and alcoholic drinks. One of the officers in charge of the ceremony would indicate when the "green officers" could stop. When it was Breard's turn, he had to drink almost the entire beaker. It made him sick, and for three days, he lay ill in his tent.

"Individual replacements were surely needed," recalled Captain Robert M. Halloran, the Regimental Dentist, "after being almost decimated by our own Navy in Sicily. They were integrated easily, although some weren't assigned where they were best suited. We learned to sort them out. To get medics with medical background, instead of assigning them to a rifle company for example."[470]

But replacements sometimes blended in like they had always been there. "After the Sicilian campaign was over we flew back to Africa to prepare for the jump into Italy," recalled Sergeant James O. Eldridge of C Company. "We had to have replacements and one of them was a young, nice-looking fellow from a small town in the West. He had a funny sort of name, [Private Warren W.] Zumwalt, so we naturally called him 'Zoomie.' Well, 'Zoomie' had only been married about four months before he had to come overseas, but since he had been across he had become a proud father. He was a good all-around athlete and had a wonderful personality."[471]

First Sergeant Regis J. Pahler of Headquarters Company, 1st Battalion remembered that "we were always happy to receive replacements as they were replacing veterans who were either killed or wounded in combat and we needed them badly to bring our unit up it fighting strength. We welcomed them with opened arms and did as much as possible to prepare them for the forthcoming combat. After the first 88mm shell hit near them, they were seasoned troops, and worked well in what ever unit that they were assigned. The first sergeants of each company were called to report to Battalion Headquarters to pick up their replacements. From there on, it was up to the first sergeant."[472]

CHAPTER 22

CANCELLED JUMP ON CAPUA

Tunisia and Sicily

AUGUST 25-SEPTEMBER 12, 1943

O n August 25, Pfc. Fred W. Thomas of H Company wrote to his parents that he still hadn't received "an answer to any of my letters since the invasion July 9th. Bob Hope and Frances Langford put on a show here for us last night. They were very good. Frances Langford is the only American girl we have seen here since we left the States. She sure looked good. Bob Hope looks and acts the same as he does in the picture show. (...) I'll be glad to get out of this place. I've seen enough of Africa."[473]

Unknown to Thomas, plans were being made at the highest echelon to take bring the war into a new phase. At Fifteenth Army Group Headquarters, two follow-up operations were prepared for the invasion of Italy. While General Bernard Montgomery's British Eighth Army would cross the Strait of Messina to land at Reggio on September 3 (Operation Baytown), Lieutenant General Mark W. Clark's newly formed Fifth Army—consisting of the British X Corps and U.S. VI Corps—was to capture a beachhead in the Gulf of Salerno on September 9 (Operation Avalanche). Although the capture of Rome, the Eternal City, would mean a decisive blow to the Italians, it was far beyond the range of fighter squadrons based on Sicily.

This meant no protection for the vulnerable troop carrier planes above the drop zones. The Gulf of Salerno has the advantage that it is situated some 160 miles south of Rome and almost halfway up the boot-shaped Italian Peninsula. But there were also two disadvantages: the proposed landing beach was split in two by the Sele River and dominated by a range of steep cliffs and hills. Clark's Fifth Army had to await the advance of Montgomery's Eighth Army in a northern direction to join forces with them. Once this link-up had taken place, they would attack on a broad front from the Tyrrhenian coast to the Adriatic coast toward Rome.

Afraid that the broad Volturno River, forty miles north of the Salerno Beachhead, would form a major barrier once the bridges were blown, Clark ordered the 82nd Airborne Division to land near Capua. Major General Matthew B. Ridgway briefed his regimental commanders on this mission. It was such a bold plan that Colonel Reuben H. Tucker could hardly believe it: an airborne landing of the 504th and 505th Parachute Infantry Regiments near the city to capture Capua and its local bridges across the Volturno River. About 130 gliders with the 376th and 456th Parachute Field Artillery Battalions, elements of the 80th Airborne Anti-Aircraft Battalion, 307th Airborne Medical Company, and signal units would follow. Colonel Harry L. Lewis's untried 325th Glider Infantry Regiment was to make an amphibious landing at the mouth of the Volturno River and advance fifteen miles inland to Capua. Ridgway accompanied this force as he still wasn't jump qualified. The Fifth Army would attack from the Salerno Bridgehead up north and contact them in a few days' time. This airborne mission had been codenamed "Giant I."

Ridgway further informed Colonels James Gavin and Tucker that they were under extreme time pressure: in the following two days, the U.S. 51st and 52nd Troop Carrier Wings were to shuttle the 504th and 505th Regimental Combat Teams back to Tunisia. Throughout the night, staff officers and quartermasters worked on to assemble widely spread components in time at the departure airfields of Borizzo and Castelvetrano. Although only twenty-five trucks and fifty jeeps were available, they managed to concentrate all the officers and men on schedule.

Four night jumps were arranged for the replacements in Kairouan to get in shape for the coming battle. Ridgway also requested a number of volunteers from Gavin and Tucker and Lieutenant Colonel Doyle R. Yardley of the 509th Parachute Infantry Battalion to try a new concept—pathfinders—already in use by the British Airborne Forces. They were to jump ahead of the main force and mark the DZ or possible LZ and clear the immediate surrounding area. Lieutenant Colonel Charles Billingslea, the airborne adviser of Clark, and Lieutenant Colonel Joel L. Crouch—a troop carrier officer—would be in charge of this experiment at Comiso airfield on Sicily.

Tucker decided to send 1st Lieutenant William S. Jones, 1st Battalion S-2 officer, and his S-2 section, augmented by 1st Lieutenant William W. Magrath of B Company, several non-commissioned officers, and some riflemen from A, B, and C Companies. At Comiso, the volunteers of the 504th, 505th, and 509th were organized into two pathfinder teams per unit. One team would be setting up the electronic devices to guide in the main force, while the other group would act as a security team to clear the area of enemy soldiers.

Holophane lights—available in amber, green, and red—were mounted on adjustable tripods to mark a large "T" on the drop zone. Each team was to carry eight lights with them—seven for the drop zone plus one spare light. The 504th Regimental Pathfinders also received one "Eureka" sending unit that Sergeant Regis J. Pahler would jump with. Eureka was the codeword for the British designed transmitter beacon AN/PPN-1A. The Eureka beacon, weighing seventy-five pounds, was carried by a pathfinder on the jump and would be set up on the pre-designated drop zone to home the transport aircraft to the correct area. It could both transmit and receive on five different frequencies.

To pick up the signals of the Eureka beacon, a counterpart called "Rebecca" was installed in the aircraft of group and flight leaders and operated by the navigator. He could transmit signals to the beacon and read off his distance and compass bearing to the drop zone. British instructors at the Provisional Pathfinder School stressed that under no circumstances the Germans should be able to get their hands on the Eureka. Once their secret communication device would be studied by German scientists, it could have disastrous results for future airborne operations—and give them a valuable tool. Each Eureka therefore contained a self-destruct explosive device to destroy if the pathfinders would be forced to surrender.

After the initial training on the operation and set up of the pathfinders, two tests were carried out in Tunisia with a selected number of air crews under command of Crouch. The first test took place in the night of August 28–29 when the equipment was set up on the ground and the Eureka guided some C-47s, outfitted with the Rebecca transmitters, to the selected location. A second test took place on August 30 when a small number of pathfinders jumped on the drop zone, set up their equipment, and guided the planes in without any problems. Satisfied with the results, Ridgway decided that these teams would be used in their role as pathfinders during Operation Giant I.

On September 1, three war correspondents were assigned to the 504th Regimental Combat Team for the invasion of Italy: Paul Green of the *Stars and Stripes*, Cy [Seymour] Korman of the *Chicago Tribune*, and Richard Tregaskis for the *International News Service*. Tregaskis had previously covered the Guadalcanal battle of the 1st U.S. Marine Division and wrote in his diary, "We reported to regimental headquarters on a sun-baked, dusty plain near Kairouan. The glider-borne troops with which we will be travelling will be attached to the 504th. We met Colonel Reuben H. Tucker of Ansonia, Connecticut, C.O. of the 504th, and listened while the blond, barrel-chested parachutist briefed his officers on the mission to Capua.

"The colonel was enthusiastic: 'This is truly airborne operation; one that's never been tried before. We used to think about something like this and dream about it. And it's not goin' to be easy; it's goin' to be rough. We're goin' in there and we're goin' to hold this place and we're goin' to stay there.' The deep-voiced colonel was discharging his words like volleys."[474]

First Lieutenant Wilfred Jaubert recalled that "we were briefed very thoroughly for an operation at Capua and we were issued explosives so that the battalion demolition officer would have enough to blow up the very substantial bridge crossing the Volturno. I think that it was at this jump site that we were to free allied prisoners in a nearby camp."[475]

The next day Private Earl S. Oldfather of G Company wrote that in the afternoon his platoon fell out "with full combat equipment. Went to the beach. The Lieutenant explained that we were going in by boat this time. They drew the boat in the sand and we practiced loading and unloading, then dashed across the beach."[476]

First Lieutenant Thomas E. Utterback, the Headquarters Company Commander, recalled that "the 3rd Battalion 504th (we seemed to always become detached) was to be in LCIs (Landing Craft Infantry, the kind with a ladder down each side) and to enter Rome up the Tiber river. We were to go as far up as possible, even to the point of ramming some of the locks.

"The 82nd was moved to Licata, Sicily. The lonely 3rd Battalion was left behind, and moved to some sand hills near Bizerte, in northern Tunisia. Those sand dunes were full of scorpions and caused much misery. (...) Our LCI training didn't materialize, so we were ordered to saddle up and be flown to join the rest of our outfit at Licata."[477]

Unknown to the members of the 504th Regimental Combat Team, the political situation changed drastically on the following days when the Italian *Generale di brigata* (Brigadier General) Giuseppe Castellano, a member of the Italian High Command and a close friend of Benito Mussolini's son-in-law, met General Dwight D. Eisenhower's chief of staff near Syracuse. Castellano acted as emissary of the new Italian Prime Minister, *Marescialle* (Field Marshal) Pietro Badoglio, who had succeeded Mussolini after his arrest on July 25 on orders of King Victor Emmanuel II. He promised the Allied negotiators that the Italian Army and government were willing to talk about the conditions to surrender. There was one thing, however, they worried about—the German response once they would find out of any agreements between the Italians and the Allies. To prevent any possible German retaliation in Rome, Castellano requested an airborne drop near Rome.

Ridgway, meanwhile, felt uneasy about the Capua mission and complained about it to Clark. To his surprise, Clark reduced the contribution of the 505th Regimental Combat Team to two battalions and cancelled the involvement of the 325th and 504th Regimental Combat

Teams. Lewis's 325th would be a floating reserve for the Salerno land-ings, while Tucker received no assignment.

The next day, Ridgway learned why the 504th Regimental Com-bat Team had been so easily withdrawn from Giant I. Eisenhower had earmarked Tucker's men for an airborne operation near Rome, known as Giant II. Brigadier General Maxwell D. Taylor, the assisting division commander, received orders to plan this mission in detail. That same day Castellano and Major General Walter Bedell Smith, Eisenhower's chief of staff, signed an armistice agreement aboard the HMS Nelson. Montgomery's 8th Army had a few hours earlier crossed the Strait of Messina almost unopposed.

While these events occurred at higher levels, Tregaskis learned of the cancelled Capua drop and began guessing for the real reason behind that cancellation other than "lack of transport planes," the Germans had been warned and waiting at on the drop zone or other explanations. On September 5, he wrote in his diary, "We took off this morning for Sicily for the attack on Italy. Colonel Tucker, his staff offi-cers and some of his troops had flown to Sicily in other planes. I joined them at the bomb-wrecked airfield near headquarters of the 504th. I discovered that even the battalion commanders still have not heard about the attack on Rome – if that's what it's going to be."[478]

Tregaskis clearly wasn't the only one who was still left in the dark as to what the next combat terrain would be. Jaubert of D Company recalled that "we were air transported to Trapani, Sicily and camped on the airfield. We knew that we were going some place but didn't know where."[479]

The following day, September 6, Tregaskis seemed to obtain evi-dence for his assumption that Rome might be the objective: "This afternoon I flew with Colonel Tucker to Airborne Headquarters. At the intelligence tent, he was given his envelope of orders. He took the envelope to a deserted corner of the olive grove where the camp was set up. Then he secretly read the final details of a mission that may be the hottest in the history of this war.

"Tonight the colonel's room in the barracks was darkened. Flash-lights were directed at the door to see if anyone was listening. The colonel was confiding information to his closest intimates. I heard the concluding words: 'Now you fellows know, and I know what I'm talkin' about. But if anybody so much as mentions the name of *that town*, so help me, I'll have him court-martialed and shot!'"[480]

By September 7, the entire 82nd Airborne Division was concentrated on Sicily after a three-day shuttling operation. "From scraps of information which I have been able to pick up," Tregaskis wrote in his diary, "I am now certain that the Italians will co-operate on this mission, to the extent of lighting the airfields near Rome, turning over trucks to the troops for transport, and actively supporting our airborne division with two Italian divisions now bivouacked near Rome. I heard that the guards in our camp area have been instructed that anyone leaving the camp without permission will be shot. That order gave rise to many wild rumors amongst the men: that we were destined to jump on Genoa or even Berlin."[481]

Rumors reached division headquarters as well, and Taylor was afraid that Giant II would be comprised by them. Ridgway received permission at 15th Army Group headquarters to send a few officers to Rome to assess the military situation, the firmness of the Italian promises, and any awareness of Operation Giant II. Taylor and Colonel William T. Gardiner, S-3 of the 51st Troop Carrier Group, set off in the night of September 6 to 7 on a British PT boat for the island of Ustica forty miles north of Palermo. Here they rendezvoused with an Italian corvette and were carried to the port of Gaeta. Aboard they wet their pilot uniforms and were "roughly" escorted as "prisoners" in open view to an Italian Naval car.

On the outskirts of Gaeta, Gardiner and Taylor climbed in an Italian ambulance and were driven to Rome, entering the city after dark. They first met some high-ranking Italian generals before they were taken to Badoglio's villa. Gardiner and Taylor, who both spoke several languages fluently, inquired about the German strength around Rome. They were informed that two divisions, including the 3rd Panzer Grenadier Division, had been concentrated around the city, along with some anti-aircraft units. Their armament included one hundred flak guns, 150 heavy, and fifty light tanks. The total strength of the German forces near Rome was estimated by the Italians to be over 30,000. Their own Italian Motorized Corps was fairly immobile and could not support the required number of trucks and ammunition to mechanize the 504th Regimental Combat Team.

Badoglio seemed in no hurry at all to announce the armistice that night as had been earlier agreed by Castellano. Taylor urged him to reconsider this as the major invasion of Italy would be in a matter of hours instead of days. He didn't tell him any specifics of Operation Avalanche or the landing locations. The seventy-one-year-old Badoglio was shocked by this news and promised military support only when an Allied amphibious landing near Rome, followed by an airborne drop on Rome, would take place.

By 0121 hours on September 8, Taylor sent two radio messages—one from himself and one from Badoglio—through Italian clandestine channels to Eisenhower. He stated that there wouldn't be an armistice announcement and there would be no support from the Italians for the 504th Regimental Combat Team. He sent another message at 1135 hours with his own portable radio transmitter, using the pre-arranged code word "innocuous."[482] Gardiner and Taylor were flown to Algiers later that day in an Italian airplane.

Meanwhile, Tucker gathered his battalion commanders and Captain Robert L. Dickerson, acting commanding officer of the 2nd Battalion, 325th Glider Infantry Regiment. He told them that his entire order should be memorized so no plans could fall into enemy hands. Dickerson's battalion would be air-landed in the eastern part of Rome and move as rapidly as possible to St. Peter's Square, while the 504th Regimental Combat Team—less H Company—would be dropped on Stazione di Furbara and Cerveteri airfields twenty-five miles northwest of the city. They would link up with Dickerson's men at St. Peter's Square and await the arrival of Major Teddy Sanford's 1st Battalion of the 325th Glider Infantry Regiment. The 505th Regimental Combat Team was to jump the next night at three air fields closer to Rome due to lack of sufficient transport planes.

Subsequently, a flotilla of one LST (Landing Ship Tank) and three LCIs (Landing Craft Infantry), commanded by Lieutenant Colonel William H. Bertsch of the 319th Glider Field Artillery Battalion, was to land at the mouth of the Tiber River. Bertsch's force included his own artillery battalion, three anti-aircraft batteries, and two anti-tank platoons of the 80th Airborne Anti-Aircraft Battalion, Captain Fred E. Thomas's H Company, and a platoon of A Company, 307th Airborne Engineer Battalion. They would link up with the 504th Regimental Combat Team just like the 325th Regimental Combat Team in the original version of Giant I.

"The most memorable was the briefing for a jump on Rome," recalled Lieutenant Jaubert. "They filled us full of 'smoke' about how good the Italian soldiers were when they had a cause to fight for and of course we remembered the quality of Italian troops in Sicily."[483]

After the battalion commanders had been briefed and they had instructed their company commanders and platoon leaders, the enlisted men learned about Operation Giant II. "We had very little time to be told anything about the mission," recalled Private Albert B. Clark of A Company, "except that we would be jumping on an airfield north west of Rome. After securing the areas of the arrival of more troops and equipment we were to move into Rome on Italian trucks with Italian drivers. We were more concerned about this than we were about securing the field. Once in Rome, we were to set up a defense around the Vatican."[484]

The leading airplane was already in the air when a jeep raced across the runway of Comiso and stopped near the airplane carrying Tucker. An officer jumped out and handed him a message from Ridgway: the mission had been cancelled. Using the plane's radio, this news was quickly spread to the departed planes to return to their base. Jaubert felt relieved about the cancellation: "We were all dressed (parachutes and equipment) to board the aircraft for this drop. Thank God that it was called off. We owe much to General Taylor for his trip to Rome."[485]

At 1830 hours on September 8, Eisenhower announced through a radio broadcast the signing of the armistice with the Italian government. About an hour later, the Italian prime minister, *Marescialle* Pietro Badoglio, confirmed the armistice during a radio speech on Radio Rome. He called upon the Italian troops not to shoot on any American or British forces, whenever and wherever they might show up. *Feldmarschall* Albert Kesselring, commanding all the German forces in Italy, immediately ordered his divisions to execute *Fall Achse*

(Operation Axe). This meant the capture of Italian army units and naval forces and occupation of important military installations. They also tried to capture King Victor Emmanuel II and his cabinet, but they fled from Rome and were brought in safety by the Allies.

As the leading elements of the green U.S. 36th 'Texas' Infantry Division landed on the beaches near Paestum at 0330 hours of September 9, they were greeted by a loudspeaker that announced, "Come on in and give up. We have you covered." This message was not spoken by someone with an Italian accent but by Germans of the 16th Panzer Division of *Generalmajor* Rudolf Sieckenius. His division had originally been destroyed at Stalingrad but was reformed in France in early March 1943 from the 4,000 men who were flown out of the surrounded city in time. They were reinforced by men who were on leave, convalescents, other veterans of destroyed divisions at Stalingrad, and replacements.

In August 1943, the 16th Panzer Division was sent to Salerno, preparing defensive positions. The many hills overlooking the beaches made it a perfect training area, and they divided their strength over Paestum (Panzer Grenadier Regiment 79), Battipaglia, and Montecorvino airfield (Panzer Grenadier Regiment 64) and Salerno (Panzer Aufklärungsabteilung 16). These units fiercely opposed the landings of U.S. VI Corps south of the Sele River toward the town of Agropoli on the south side of the Salerno Bay and British X Corps at north of Salerno Bay through Battipaglia and Salerno. Sieckenius had a large quantity of artillery guns and flak guns at his disposal, as well as his Panzer Regiment 2, consisting of 66 Mark IV tanks and 42 *Sturmgeschütze* (self-propelled 75mm guns).[486]

For Colonel William O. Darby's Ranger Force—including the task force of Lieutenant Colonel William H. Bertsch—who landed near Maiori and the British Commandos of Brigadier Robert Laycock who landed at Vietri, on the north side of Salerno Bay, the opponents were old adversary: elements of the Hermann Goering Division. Second Lieutenant Edward J. Sims, commanding the 1st Platoon of H Company, recalled that "we moved inland and up into the mountains, where we seized some high ground near the Chiunzi Pass, including a vital tunnel. Two battalions of U.S. Rangers, after landing, moved north to positions that commanded the Pagni–Nocera Pass. My platoon occupied positions at the tunnel on the right flank of the company. The company commander borrowed a truck from a local citizen to cover the wide area (about five miles) we had to defend.

"This rugged mountain area was not difficult to defend because the heavy equipment of the Germans was, for the most part, restricted to road use. We had to consider two roads – one from Gragnano through the tunnel, and the other from Sorrento and Amalfi. It was our job to prevent the Germans from using these roads to get through to Salerno."[487]

Second Lieutenant Roy M. Hanna of the attached Machine Gun Platoon recalled that they "traveled up a roadway through vineyards and hills to set up a defensive position along a ridgeline and watched the war progress up the Salerno Valley. The Germans knew we were there and shelled us regularly with artillery. At night a few Germans would come up the slope and fire their machine pistols in the air, I suppose just to harass us. If they got too close we would throw a few hand grenades in their general direction and they would leave us alone."[488]

On September 11, Pfc. Bernard F. Gallagher was sent back as a platoon runner to the H Company CP. He was ambushed but managed to get away and earned a Silver Star: "Gallagher was intercepted by a six-man German patrol who ordered him to surrender. Having been instructed as to the importance of the message, Pfc. Gallagher, courageously, with odds six-to-one against him, fought it out with the enemy, killing two and forcing the remaining four to retreat. He delivered the message in time for his company to withdraw to a defensive position which prevented a possible breakthrough by the enemy."[489]

A second, smaller seaborne landing was carried out on September 9 by the 1st British Airborne Division to take the primary Italian Naval base at Taranto (Operation Slapstick). But although the German resistance was less fanatic in the southern part of Italy, the German Tenth Army commander, *Generaloberst* Heinrich von Vietinghoff, sent the Hermann Goering Panzer Division and the 15th Panzer Grenadier Division south, while the 29th Panzer Grenadier Division was directed north. With these forces, and the already present 16th Panzer

Division, Von Vietinghoff planned to counterattack and drive the Fifth Army back into the Tyrrhenian Sea.

The following days, the battle raged all along the Gulf of Salerno, with the British 46th and 56th Infantry Divisions taking Salerno and Battipaglia and the U.S. 36th Infantry Division occupying the town of Altavilla until a massive German counterattack started on September 12. The dominating Hill 424 near Altavilla was retaken from the 142nd Infantry Regiment and the British 56th Infantry Division lost control over Montecorvino airfield. An American counterattack by the 157th Regimental Combat Team of the U.S. 45th Infantry Division on the Tobacco Factory near the Sele River in the center of the beachhead failed even with fire support of the Battleship *Philadelphia*, which had more targets to fire on after the Battleship *Savannah* had been damaged the day before. The 179th Regimental Combat Team was withdrawn from Persano to help the 157th at the Tobacco Factory on the left flank of the VI Corps Beachhead. This left a gap between the 45th Infantry Division and the 143rd Regimental Combat Team of the 36th Infantry Division near Altavilla.

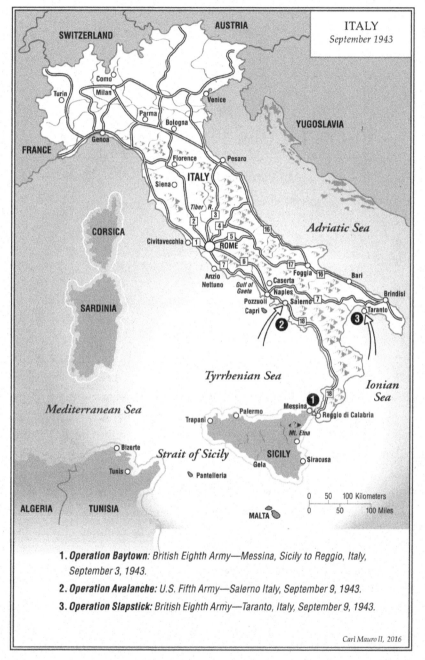

Italy September 1943

CHAPTER 23

EIGHT HOURS TO COUNTDOWN

Salerno Beachhead

SEPTEMBER 13-SEPTEMBER 15, 1943

O n September 13, it became clear to Lieutenant General Mark
W. Clark that reinforcements were desperately needed on his
VI Corps front to stem the German counterattack. Captain Jacob R.
Hamilton, a reconnaissance pilot who had just landed on the make-
shift airfield at Paestum, was sent to Sicily with a message for Major
General Matthew B. Ridgway to send in the 504th that night.

Hamilton landed at Division Headquarters on Licata airfield and
delivered Clark's letter to Ridgway. He immediately consented and
ordered Colonel Reuben H. Tucker to prepare his regiment—less the
detached 3rd Battalion—for a parachute drop at Paestum that night.
Ridgway radioed Fifth Army Headquarters, urging to have all army
and naval anti-aircraft units to withheld fire until the paratroopers had
been dropped. He wanted to prevent at all costs a similar disaster like
Operation Husky.

At Tucker's Regimental Headquarters on Comiso Airfield, Lieutenant Colonel Warren R. Williams, Jr., and Major Daniel W. Danielson were briefed on the mission. Little was known about the actual situation at Salerno other than the fact that they would be dropped well
inside the VI Corps area. The DZ was set near Paestum, but it had the
disadvantage that the terrain was hard and near the sea. Tucker told
Danielson and Williams that Lieutenant Colonel Leslie G. Freeman

and forty-nine pathfinders would jump first to mark the drop zone and set up Eureka beacons. The 52nd Troop Carrier Wing would follow about fifteen minutes later with the remainder of the regiment.

Captain Thomas M. Wight's C Company—less its 1st Platoon—would also jump along with the 504th Parachute Infantry Regiment. He wouldn't make the jump himself as he had injured a leg jumping on Sicily and was advised by his battalion surgeon to travel by ship to Paestum. Lieutenant Colonel Wilbur M. Griffith's 376th Parachute Field Artillery Battalion wouldn't accompany them either as there were simply not enough transport planes available for both the Capua mission of the 505th Regimental Combat Team and the 509th Parachute Infantry Battalion at Avellino, which were both to take place on September 14. Using those planes for the emergency drop at Paestum could slow down the loading process for those two combat jumps. The 509th had the task of capturing the important road and railroad center at Avellino, where any German reinforcements coming from Rome to Salerno would pass through. This would block the major German supply line.

First Lieutenant John S. Lekson, the 1st Battalion S-3 (operations) officer, recalled of the briefing at Comiso Field around 1400 hours, "Bundles were rolled, combat gear was checked, and ammunition was issued. All was in readiness except for the questions: Where? What? Why? Late in the afternoon the battalion commander and his officers were briefed in the bombed-out hangar at Comiso Field. The mission outlined was to parachute onto a secured drop zone about two miles south of Paestum, Italy and report to a representative of VI Corps who would be there with further instructions.

"The troops were briefed with the aid of flashlights and the only available maps, of scale 1/1,500,000. Only in a cursory manner was the situation on Salerno Beachhead known. Company planes were assigned and units began to load bundles. All did not move too smoothly. The last seven planes for B Company did not arrive until 2100 hours. As B Company rapidly loaded into planes, the pilots were being briefed."[490]

First Lieutenant Walter S. Van Poyck, commanding E Company, recalled that "our alert on the 13th was viewed by many as just another dry run. The true mission developed only after we were aboard the aircraft. I remember being handed a map and being told to look for a lighted DZ near Paestum. The understandable reaction from the men in my stick, couched in terms generally unprintable here, was 'Where the Hell is Paestum?' But today, that mission is regarded as history's greatest example of airborne mobility – just eight elapsed hours from alert to commitment against the enemy."[491]

In the Sicilian port of Licata, the 325th Regimental Combat Team, with the 3rd Battalion attached, boarded LCIs in the late afternoon of September 13. Every company—less H Company which had joined the Rangers flotilla at Bizerte—was assigned to a different LCI. They left Licata that evening and set course on a calm Mediterranean Sea for the harbor of Palermo, where they would remain in Fifth Army reserve for Operation Avalanche.

"A series of hurried moves, orders and counter orders finally left us in an olive grove in Sicily having moved up from the Dark Continent," remembered 1st Lieutenant Thomas E. Utterback of Headquarters Company. "We knew we were going into the Italian campaign, but whether by air or water we didn't know. Being loaded on boats one day settled that question for us. Particularly since they were LCIs. I'll go in by air anytime; those beach landings leave you in suspense too long."[492]

Private Earl S. Oldfather of G Company wrote in his diary, "We lined up with our equipment on so Lieutenant [Francis W.] Deignan could look us over. Put it on second time – then off. The third time we went to the airport. Took off in plane – landed somewhere in Sicily – waited. Trucks took us into town – Licata – to the docks. Waited. K-rations issued about 0300 [p.m.] – hadn't eaten since breakfast. Several Army Air Corps men and nurses walked by. Finally loaded on the LCI about 0700 [p.m.]. Looked like I would stay on deck – Lieutenant said he had a place for me down below. They have benches similar to railroad stations. This boat is suppose to accommodate 100 men – they put over 200 – just a little crowded."[493]

Private David K. Finney of Headquarters and Headquarters Company remembered that "the first sergeant called the company together. Captain [Adam A.] Komosa took charge. It was just the usual day, we thought. Then he began speaking: 'The 504th Parachute Infantry

Regiment has been called upon for a very important mission. We will be leaving immediately.' A yell went up from the excited men when the captain turned to leave. We began rechecking our equipment to make sure we had not overlooked anything.

"We were not told more about this mission until we were in the planes: 'The Fifth Army beachhead in Italy is in grave danger of being breached. The 504th is to jump behind friendly lines in the vicinity of the threatened breakthrough. The beach of Salerno will be our DZ (drop zone).' We were honored to have General Mark Clark specifically ask for our regiment to halt the advance of the German Army at Salerno, Italy."[494]

Private Albert B. Clark of A Company was informed that "our mission was to jump in the narrow area between the hospital and the beach, (...) and set up a defense and hold the Germans. If we would not, we were to fight a delaying action, while they [the Fifth Army] evacuated. When we got pushed back to the water, [we had to] start swimming and they would try and pick us up. We didn't think very much about that idea."[495]

At 2045 hours, the pathfinders and Freeman took off from Agrigento airfield and flew across Sicily and the Tyrrhenian Sea to Agropoli on the southern side of the Salerno Bay. Then the pilots turned left and flew in a northern direction towards the DZ at Paestum. At 2314 hours, the pathfinders of the 504th Parachute Infantry Regiment jumped out—the first American pathfinders to jump on a combat operation. They noticed a large burning "T" already on the ground made from burning five-gallon cans of sand and oil.

The 5G transmitter they jumped with smashed on the ground, but within five minutes after the drop, a Eureka beacon had been set up. A second one was held in reserve. The two blue Krypton lights they had with them were not yet turned on. They would be used as soon as all the paratroopers had jumped, to indicate the assembly areas. Lieutenant General Clark and his Fifth Army anxiously awaited the arrival of the remainder of the regiment. They sat out a German bombing raid less than thirty minutes before the arranged drop to avoid the disaster of Operation Husky.

On Sicily, all the sticks were lined up near the C-47s, which would fly them to Salerno as a jeep drove at high speed across the airfield and stopped next to every plane. Colonel Reuben H. Tucker was standing up right next to his driver. "Men, it is open season on Krautheads. You know what to do!" he yelled. Several paratroopers cheered as he drove past their planes. The paratroopers who hadn't boarded their planes yet now climbed aboard. Dusk set in as the first C-47s carrying the main element of the regiment began to taxi to the runway. The supply container under the plane carrying 2nd Lieutenant Reneau G. Breard's 1st Platoon of A Company loosened and fell on the runway: "When we entered the C-47 with all that equipment someone tripped the latch near the door. That's why we were dragging 'chute' and one equipment bundle. The pilot stopped taxiing the plane and two of us jumped out and retrieved the bundle and chute."[496]

Lekson recalled:

> the regimental lift proceeded across the Tyrrhenian Sea without enemy interference. Approximately halfway out the formation ran into a cloud bank. Elements were above, below, and to either side of the battalion S-3's plane. As the lift neared Agropoli several C Company planes flying too close to shore were fired upon by single small caliber weapons with no effect.
>
> Then the red light switched on. Parachutists hustled as they fastened harnesses. Bundles were pushed into the door. Snap fasteners clicked onto the anchor line and down the line came the "readies." Underneath was Agropoli, then the sea, then a shore and a stream.
>
> As the green light switched on, a large flickering "T" appeared below. Out into space went the bundle and, after it, parachutists snapped out one behind the other. The air was crowded with troops and bundles. Below, the 2nd Battalion was already moving on the drop zone toward a bright light. The drop zone was

black specked, dotted with masses of rocks and small trees.[497]

The Regimental Surgeon, Major Ivan J. Roggen, recalled it was "very dark and the jump itself was uneventful except that I, personally, landed on a pile of rocks which wasn't pleasant. Our medical activity primarily involved enduring a rather constant shelling by German 88's and taking care of casualties that resulted and evacuating them to the rear."[498]

Finney remembered it "had been one long day for all of us. Now we wished we could just close our eyes and catch some 'Z's.' I was a smoker but I found the cigarette not really pacifying to me. I continuously kept changing positions in my seat. I rechecked my grenades fastened to my jacket.

"We received the 'stand up and hook up' command and then the check of equipment began. Our waiting time had gotten down to the seconds and then we were moving towards the open door of the plane. Like clock-work we began leaving the plane. The blast of fresh air hit my face and then the snap and jerk of my harness as the parachute opened. We must have jumped at a lower altitude than usual. I was coming down on top of a 105mm howitzer. A quick pull on my left riser steered me away in time to miss it. I could have made a standing landing but preferred falling on my side and get out of my harness in the prone position. One of the guys by the howitzer rushed over and asked if I needed any help. I thanked him, got up and headed inland to form with the rest of the unit."[499]

Second Lieutenant Chester A. Garrison, the 2nd Battalion Adjutant, lay ill with jaundice in a hospital as he learned about the combat jump. Afraid to be left behind and miss all the action, he declared himself fit for duty and made his way to Comiso Airfield:

> The flight was such a last-minute decision that we did not know where we were going or why until after we were airborne. We flew east, inland from the north coast of Sicily and close enough to Mount Etna for me to look down at an angle to see the boiling red

cauldron of its crater. Then I must have fallen asleep, probably because the jaundice tired me.

Just before midnight on September 14, we jumped onto the Salerno Beachhead, where an advance team had set up a guide-in of kerosene fires. This time our 35 planes drew no flak; naval and land forces had been adequately forewarned. Jumping at 800 feet, 22 of the 200 2nd Battalion troopers were injured – more than usual. The rocky ground was probably the cause, as I know that I landed hard.

Quickly we formed up and took to the road. For the third time I saw a ruin that I was not able to investigate. Its Greek temple identified where the colony of Paestum had been. A few times I glanced to my left at its vague outline, but mostly my attention was absorbed by the right where the Germans were said to be.[500]

Several planes failed to arrive and those sticks were unaccounted for. Seven of those eight planes carried B Company, and another contained Lieutenant John Watson's planeload with the battalion's supply section. Since Watson was 2nd Battalion S-4, his duty was temporarily taken over by Major Henry B. Frank, former EGB448 commander and supernumerary to the regimental staff. Lekson accompanied Williams, Danielson of the 2nd Battalion, and Tucker and his principal regimental staff members to a house near the drop zone where they were briefed by Lieutenant Colonel Wiley H. O'Mohundro of VI Corps on the situation in their sector. "He told of the troops that had been cut off at Altavilla," recalled Lekson, "and a gap that existed in the VI Corps line into which the regiment, led by Corps guides, would move. The regiment would 'hold to the last man and the last round.' Troops were to be warned that men of the 36th Division would undoubtedly be drifting through the lines. Then Colonel Tucker made his assignments. The 2nd Battalion would defend the left sector; the 1st Battalion, the right, extending up the slope of Mount Soprano."[501]

Tucker's troopers were attached to the battered 36th 'Texas' Infantry Division of Major General Fred L. Walker, Sr. Earlier that evening, Walker wrote in his diary, "I had divided the Division front into three sectors and placed a brigadier general in command of each sector because the various troopers, except the infantry, are not accustomed to working together, and I want everything possible done to be ready to meet an attack by daylight tomorrow. (...)

"[Brigadier] General [Otto F.] Lange with a taskforce consisting of one company, 636th TD Battalion, one company 751st Tank Battalion, and the 1st and 2nd Battalions, 504th Parachute Infantry (to arrive during the night) is to defend a 4.5 mile sector from the stream junction of Majuri to Tempe."[502]

Division trucks transported the regiment to their frontline sector. "We assembled quickly and easily," recalled Lieutenant Wilfred Jaubert of D Company. "We were trucked and went past the Roman ruins at Paestum and taken to an assembly area several miles from Albanella."[503] For the 1st Battalion, wrote Lekson later, "the positions to be defended was a flat valley floor and the north slopes of Mount Soprano. Ahead some fifteen hundred yards was La Cosa Creek. At 14 September 0200 hours troops unloaded from the trucks and the battalion commander, unable to make a reconnaissance, gave his orders: Company A on the slope of Mount Soprano, swing to east, and tie in with C Company north of the road; Company C from just north of the road, extend across the flat valley to the north, and tie in on Tempone Di San Paolo; dig in before daylight and then continue to develop the position... A battalion command post and an aid station were located behind A Company's position. Wire lines were run to companies. About the command post was located the only planeload from B Company."[504]

In the morning of September 14, the remainder of B Company showed up at the 1st Battalion CP: "Probably due to an insufficient briefing the pilot of the lead plane gave B Company a green light over the mountains some six miles south of the drop zone," recalled Lekson. "Upon landing Captain Charles W. Duncan failed to recognize any landmarks and decided to form a perimeter with his group of four officers and eighty men. When dawn came this group could see the Paestum beaches to their north. At once, they moved off toward the beaches. Near the regimental drop zone they were able to obtain truck transportation and a guide who led them to the battalion defense position. With the coming of B Company, C Company moved to the north and B Company filled in the center of the battalion sector, astride the road, tying in with A Company on the right."[505]

Later that morning Lieutenant General Clark radioed once again to Ridgway, requesting to abort the drop of the 505th Regimental Combat Team at Capua and to replace it with a similar drop as the 504th had carried out near Paestum. They would form Walker's division reserve. Walker wrote that Tucker's paratroopers "looked like excellent soldiers, are in high spirits and fully informed of what they are to do. With these arrangements, my command is quite confident that any German attack anywhere along our front, which will have to cross open ground, will take a severe beating."[506]

During the day, regimental positions were shelled by 88mm flak guns while the German Luftwaffe twice bombed the VI Corps sector. The 3rd Platoon of C Company, 307th Airborne Engineer Battalion helped establish a roadblock near the 1st Battalion CP, while the 2nd Platoon was kept in reserve on guard duty at the Regimental CP. Their platoon leader, 1st Lieutenant John M. Bigler, and the 2nd Squad were missing as their plane didn't make it to the DZ. They arrived during the night and explained that the pilot had flown them back to Sicily on the previous night, as there was a serious technical problem. Seventy-three men in the 504th PIR and five engineers had suffered jump injuries. Twenty-two of these injuries had occurred in the 2nd Battalion.

"The air is constantly full of aircraft," wrote Lieutenant Garrison, "practically all American. (...) Corporal Rowland Briggs of K Company, 143rd Regiment, 36th Infantry Division and two other men are temporarily attached to E Company. At 2200 Lieutenant [Wayne] Hockett and his D Company planeload reported in. His first plane had engine trouble and had to turn back. His second plane dropped them about midnight close to the proper DZ, but they were unable to contact us. Several companies of the 45th Infantry Division arrived by foot and about 1430 went into the line to our left. Reports of German advances and several scattered 88 shells near Battalion CP at 1430.

"[Brigadier] General Lange has set up his CP in our E Company area and is giving directions in our sector. Everything is under control. 15 German tanks have been sighted to our front. Reported that 6 have been knocked out by artillery. First casualty is of E Company – Sergeant [John L.] Satterwhite killed while on patrol three miles forward (1500) and Private [Harold K.] Brinser seriously wounded."[507]

Sergeant John Satterwhite (center) of E Company was killed while on a patrol in Italy. Courtesy: Walt Ranta

Lekson remembered that "lost men of the 36th Division had drifted through the lines with information on the Altavilla attack. Engineers were laying a minefield in front of C Company. With the coming of B Company, C Company moved to the north and B Company filled in the center of the battalion sector, astride the road, tying in with A Company on the right. A wire line had reached battalion from regiment. Except for a German tank attack in a sector north of the battalion position and continual enemy air raids, the day moved uneventfully.

"During the afternoon patrols from C Company moved to the east and across the La Cosa [Creek] without enemy contact. Then the 1st Platoon of B Company [commanded by 1st Lieutenant Milton J. Crochet] was ordered to move out before dark and outpost an unnumbered hill southeast of Albanella. An SCR-511 was sent with this platoon. An order to be prepared to counterattack a German force that was preparing to attack from north of the La Cosa never materialized. After dark Captain Duncan, B Company, took his 2nd Platoon and moved out to join the 1st Platoon south of Albanella since radio contact could not be made."[508]

Lieutenant Jaubert and his 1st Platoon of D Company were sent out just before dusk to make a reconnaissance of the town of Albanella and its surrounding area six miles to the northeast of the Regimental CP. "Our assembly area," recalled Jaubert, "was flat terrain. In the distance was a high flat plateau which I always estimated to be about 6 miles away. We stayed in the assembly area all day and I think it was just before dusk that my platoon was ordered to what I will refer as the Albanella Plateau. We could not see the town from the assembly area."[509]

They walked as quickly as possible through vineyards, orchards, and across mountain streams and climbed up the side of a rugged mountain. "We reached the top by a well used trail as there was no road," recalled Jaubert. They then stood on the large plateau of Albanella and in the darkness reached the outskirts of the town unseen on a few hundred yards distance. Jaubert sent out his three squads to scout the surrounding area. "We spent much of the night searching for Germans, found none, and I then set up a platoon defense on the slope facing Albanella."

Not long after daybreak, a lone Italian farmer passed by and was questioned by Jaubert, who recalled the man "told us that there were two or three Germans hidden in town. They were probably artillery observers. I took a small group and went looking for them but I soon realized that it was an impossible task as there were so many buildings where they could hide."[510]

BIRTH OF A REGIMENT

With one rifle squad, it was beyond their ability to track the three Germans. Jaubert sent a runner for the remainder of his platoon to join him in Albanella. All through that morning and most of the afternoon they were in Albanella and didn't meet a living soul. It felt like they were visiting a ghost town. Then a battalion runner reported to Jaubert, "A messenger arrived telling me to return to the assembly area. During my stay in Albanella we never saw a German and were not shelled. While returning to the assembly area and about half-way there we were heavily shelled by what I thought was from an extreme range as all of the shells landed to our left and we never even 'hit the ground' and kept moving."[511]

In the early evening, Jaubert's exhausted troopers arrived in the D Company area, where he reported to Captain Stanley M. Dolezal as his own men filled their empty water canteens. Jaubert was speechless with anger as Dolezal told him to prepare his platoon at once to march along with the rest of the company back to Albanella! Unknown to Jaubert, the regiment had been ordered to attack: "That's when 'I blew my cool'. We began our attack on Altavilla from the outskirts of Albanella when it was dark."[512]

Throughout the day, small groups and individuals of the retreating 3rd Battalion, 143rd Infantry Regiment filtered through the lines of the 2nd Battalion. "E Company has advanced to the forward slope of its hill," wrote Garrison. "Our artillery in our vicinity set up a heavy pounding at noon. All the attached men are being sent forward to the 141st Regiment which is to our left. F Company was withdrawn from the Sele River where, with tank destroyers, they had been keeping Germans from making a river crossing... Lieutenant [Michael D.] Pobor [of E Company] took out a patrol, was surrounded, escaped, awaiting to hear from the remainder of men (all returned eventually). Blankets have been issued to almost half the men."[513]

"The morning of 15 September dawned clear and hot," recalled Lieutenant Lekson. "Messages from the B Company outpost reported flares during the night and German vehicles observed at some distance, but no enemy contact. Air raids over the beaches and light enemy shelling in the battalion sector were the only visible enemy activity. Rations had been procured by the S-4 but as yet no blankets were available.

"A combat patrol of C Company was sent out in the afternoon toward the valley between Albanella and Altavilla northeast of the battalion sector. Its mission was to make contact with the Germans. The patrol would stay out over night and return the next morning."[514]

That evening, the LCIs carrying the 325th Regimental Combat Team and the attached 3rd Battalion finally left the harbor of Palermo and headed for the Gulf of Salerno. Lieutenant General Clark had decided to transfer them to the Sorrento Peninsula, where Colonel William O. Darby's task force and the British commandos encountered increasing German opposition. The 3rd Battalion of the 504th PIR would land near Paestum as Fifth Army reserve.

Journalist Richard Tregaskis and his colleagues were aboard the LCI carrying Major Emory S. "Hank" Adams, Jr. and Headquarters Company, 3rd Battalion: "The long, low shape of a small ship came sliding directly toward our beam, turned and struck our stern a glancing blow. It was the American LCI which was to guide us to our landing point. The skipper's voice came from the dark, telling us to follow. We swung in a wide circle, blinking toward the other LCIs the information that they should follow along behind us. By this time, however, the LCIs had scattered in an effort to avoid ramming the leader, and they had disappeared into the thickening cold mist."[515]

Oldfather of G Company wrote, "Waded up deep water to the shore. Left shelter half and blanket roll on the beach – scattered out. An enemy plane passed over. Dug slit trench – stayed in it the rest of the night. Got a little sleep. Can hear the roar of the guns."[516]

Utterback, the Headquarters Company Commander, recalled that "we arrived about midnight and had been told to expect a 'hot' beach. The landing craft hit a sand bar offshore, so they dumped us in chin-high water and we waded ashore to hunker among the sand dunes. The situation was totally unreal, very quiet, and we wondered why. Then there was the sound of an approaching vehicle of some kind. Was it an enemy tank?

"Out of the darkness appeared an army 6x6 truck. The driver was looking for some supplies that had been left dumped along the beach.

Upon questioning, the driver told us that the line was five or six miles inland on the hills, and that the 82nd had gone in that direction."[517]

Private Francis X. Keefe of I Company realized shortly after midnight that it was his nineteenth birthday—the first in a combat zone. Little combat was seen, however, as the 3rd Battalion spent the night on the beach not far from Paestum. From the hills above them they could hear the sounds of gunfire, just as they saw gun flashes all along the Gulf of Salerno. The LCIs, meanwhile, returned to Sicily to collect the 376th and 456th Parachute Field Artillery Battalions and the remainder of the 307th Airborne Engineer Battalion.

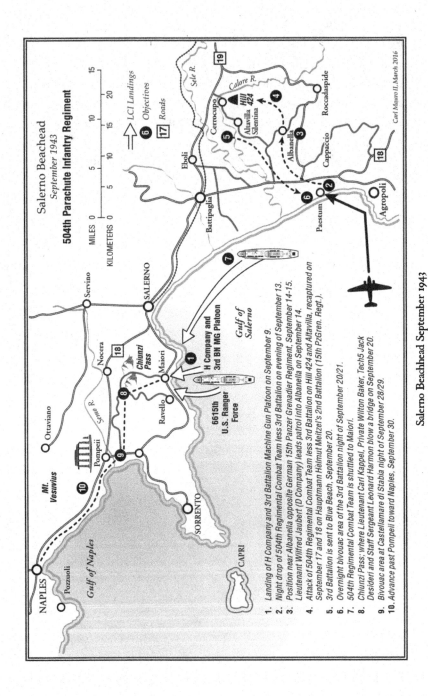

Salerno Beachhead
September 1943
504th Parachute Infantry Regiment

1. Landing of H Company and 3rd Battalion Machine Gun Platoon on September 9.
2. Night drop of 504th Regimental Combat Team less 3rd Battalion on evening of September 13.
3. Position near Albanella opposite German 15th Panzer Grenadier Regiment, September 14-15. Lieutenant Wilfred Jaubert (D Company) leads patrol into Albanella on September 14.
4. Attack of 504th Regimental Combat Team less 3rd Battalion on Hill 424 and Altavilla, recaptured on September 17 and 18 on Hauptmann Helmut Meitzel's 2nd Battalion (15th PzGren. Regt.).
5. 3rd Battalion is sent to Blue Beach, September 20.
6. Overnight bivouac area of the 3rd Battalion night of September 20/21.
7. 504th Regimental Combat Team is shuttled to Maiori.
8. Chiunzi Pass: where Lieutenant Carl Kappel, Private Wilton Baker, Tech5 Jack Desideri and Staff Sergeant Leonard Harmon blow a bridge on September 20.
9. Bivouac area at Castellamare di Stabia night of September 28/29.
10. Advance past Pompeii toward Naples, September 30.

Salerno Beachhead September 1943

CHAPTER 24

REGAINING LOST GROUND

Salerno Beachhead

SEPTEMBER 16-SEPTEMBER 17, 1943

A s dawn broke on September 16, the 504th was still attached to the 36th Infantry Division of Major General Fred Walker, who wrote in his diary, "This morning [Major General Ernest L.] Dawley [of VI Corps] ordered me to retake Altavilla. The 504th Parachute Infantry with one company of the 636th TD Battalion will advance from the south along the high ground during the night to capture Hills 315 and 424."[518]

At 1000 hours on September 16, Colonel Reuben H. Tucker was called to the VI Corps command post and learned from Major General Ernest L. Dawley that in the night of September 13 to 14, the German 15th Panzer Grenadier Regiment had thrown back the 1st and 3rd Battalions of the 142nd Infantry and routed the 3rd Battalion of the 143rd Infantry Regiment in the Altavilla area. It was vital to regain the lost ground at Albanella, Altavilla, and Hill 424. At 1400 hours, Dawley ordered Tucker to move with his regiment to the town of Albanella, south of the Sele River. Having taken Albanella, Tucker's regiment had to advance up northward to the town of Altavilla and its surrounding high ground. Especially the 1,361 meters high Hill 424 west of the Calore River had to be seized. From that hill, the Germans looked down over the entire Salerno Beachhead. The 636th Tank Destroyer Battalion would dispatch a company of tanks to accompany the advance as far as possible. The 132nd Field Artillery Battalion provided forward observers to the 504th Regimental CP as substitute for the absent 376th Parachute Field Artillery Battalion.

An hour later, Tucker briefed Lieutenant Colonel Warren R. Williams, Jr. of the 1st Battalion and Major Daniel W. Danielson of the 2nd Battalion and their battalion staff officers on the mission. The 1st Battalion would capture Hill 424 east of Altavilla, while the 2nd Battalion had to capture Hill 344 and an unnumbered hill east of the town of Albanella. Major Walter F. Winton's 1st Battalion of the 505th would screen the right flank of the regiment.

"From Hill 424 the enemy could see the beaches at Paestum," recalled Lieutenant John S. Lekson. "He could watch movements across La Cosa Creek and the Sele-Calore sector. As long as he held the hill he had excellent observation of the VI Corps sector. On the southwest slope of Hill 424 sat the town of Altavilla, unimportant in itself since the hill commanded it completely. However, as the hub of several roads and numerous trails toward the Calore sector, it served as a focal point toward which German troops could be quickly moved."[519]

At around noon, Lekson received the patrol report from the C Company platoon, which had encountered enemy resistance: "While C Company prepared to move, its combat patrol returned. They had much to report. They had engaged in three fire fights. Considerable enemy artillery and mortar fire had fallen on them. However, the resistance seemed so scattered that it was deemed unimportant. A regimental patrol reported that some forty enemy tanks were located on the reverse slope of a hill about a mile and a half southeast of Altavilla.

"By 1400 the battalion was moving with a file on either side of the dirt road which ran northeast through the defense sector to Albanella. The order of march was A Company, C Company, 3rd Platoon of B Company, and Headquarters Company."[520]

The four miles to Albanella were quickly covered with the 1st Battalion in the lead. Twenty-one-year-old Pfc. Louis C. Marino from Elkhart, Indiana, an assistant machine gunner in the 2nd Platoon of A Company, recalled "it was hot and we were taking salt tablets. We sweat so bad that our uniforms all turned white. We were wearing summer issue uniforms at the time. They could really spot us because of those salt tablets."[521]

Sergeant Otto W. Huebner, the operations sergeant of A Company, remembered:

> the march to the objective was long, hard, and tiresome. The winding trails were narrow and rocky, with overhanging brush in many places, which made it difficult to follow. From the last positions on Mount Soprano to Albanella, the distance was four miles and yet that was only about half the way to the company's objective.
>
> Near Albanella, enemy artillery shells began to drop on the column. It was more harassing than harmful, but it slowed the column down considerably. Gaps began to show between men, and it became very difficult to keep contact. The company commander, Captain Willard E. Harrison, told the point to move faster because the column was behind schedule.
>
> As the 2nd Platoon reached a creek just north of Albanella, two enemy machine guns opened fire on the point, without inflicting a casualty, but caused the front of the column to take cover. It was easy to observe the fire, for the enemy was using tracer ammunition and the fire was about five feet above the ground. The [assistant] 2nd Platoon leader, Lieutenant Horton, put his 60mm mortar into action and knocked out the machine guns in quick order.
>
> After this short action, the column continued to move again, but at a much slower pace. The men were very tired and began to lag. About this time the enemy artillery began to fall with greater intensity and

accuracy. Calls for medics from wounded men in the column could be heard frequently.

The officers and NCOs had to move up and down the column to get the men to their feet and keep them moving. The men had a tendency to lie down when the artillery came close and not watch the individual in front of him, thereby losing contact. (...) About 2200, word came up the column to the company commander that most of C Company and all of Company B had lost contact. Lieutenant Colonel Williams, who was still with Company A, gave the order to Captain Harrison to move anyway to the objective.[522]

Journalists Robert Capa of *Life*, Seymour Korman of the *Chicago Tribune*, Reynolds Packard of the *United Press*, and Richard Tregaskis of the *International News Service* learned at Fifth Army Headquarters about the upcoming assault. They drove in a jeep to the village to be able to write something about the assault. "On the action outskirts of Albanella," Tregaskis wrote later, "we spotted Lieutenant Forrest Richter, adjutant of the 504th Parachute Infantry, who said, 'We jumped behind our lines night before last. (...) The rest of the outfit is coming up now.' And soon, bull-chested Colonel Tucker strode up. He pointed out our objective, Altavilla, high on a ridge to the northeast. It was a collection of light-colored houses etched on the top of a mountain. Puffs of shellfire were spurting from the pattern of the streets and houses. The Germans were in there, and our artillery was attempting to soften up the town.

"Colonel Tucker told us how the attack would be made by his troops. 'We're going to go way around' – he indicated a wide circle to the right – 'and then come up on that ridge overlooking the town.' The calmness of the afternoon was almost startling. While we talked, a line of while ME-109s came over and passed far to the right, curving to dive swiftly into a valley, bombing. 'Nasty, little fellas, aren't they?' said the colonel."[523]

Tucker recalled that his regiment moved out at 1630 hours "from the vicinity of Albanella. At 1800 the advance elements were moving across the floor of the valley northeast of Albanella. An advance command post was established in the valley, just north of Albanella, from which position fire of the 132nd Field Artillery was directed. When the 2nd Battalion came out onto the floor of the valley they were shelled by heavy enemy field artillery. The 1st Battalion proceeded on its mission until it struck an enemy strong point in the vicinity of Hill 315, where it became engaged in battle. The 2nd Battalion proceeded on its mission towards Hill 344."[524]

At 1915 hours, heavy enemy artillery shells came down on the advanced Regimental CP and Tucker decided to move forward with Lieutenant Colonel Leslie G. Freeman, Major Don P. Dunham, Richter, and seven enlisted men, leaving Major Julian A. Cook in charge at his command post. He had hardly left when Korman and Tregaskis entered after wandering through the deserted town of Albanella for some hours. Tregaskis learned that

> the colonel and a couple of battalions had gone ahead, and should be in the valley beyond. Cook was distressed because he had no telephone or radio contact with Colonel Tucker. We asked how we could find him. Cook shrugged his shoulders and pointed down toward the valley. "That's the way," he said.
>
> Darkness had come, and we stumbled down the steep hillside through a rocky orchard. After plumping our weary muscles over the rough ground for half an hour, we had seen no signs of a paratrooper. The darkness was growing quite complete, and we began to wonder if had gone astray. Finally we saw a farmhouse, and decided to seek directions. We asked the farmer, "Dove Americani?" and "Dove Tedeschi?", the customary questions. We gathered that the Americans were only a few hundred yards away and the Germans had passed through here yesterday.

Then we were stumbling down the valley again. We spread out in a single file, listening intently, for the dangers of running into a German patrol, or being shot at by accident, were considerable. Finally we were challenged, but it was an American voice asking for an American countersign. "Red River," said the voice in the dark, and we answered, with a great deal of relief, "Valley." The sentry led us to a little group of men, hunched up at a corner in a dirt road, under the lee of a steep bank. The lieutenant in charge told us that the Germans had been putting interdicting artillery fire into the valley. (...) We decided to go ahead in search of Colonel Tucker, halting when we heard the shells coming. We came out of the valley to a fairly level place, and found the colonel (...) in a drainage ditch.[525]

Tucker's force had meanwhile been reinforced by Captain Thomas M. Wight and part of his C Company, 307th Airborne Engineers Battalion. They were soon joined by Captain Albert E. Milloy and his C Company, less the 3rd Platoon. First Lieutenant James E. Dunn, the 1st Platoon leader, recalled of the march through the hills, "It seemed just that we walked forever! Occasionally we were being stopped by a pillbox or outpost we would have to take care of before proceeding."[526]

Tregaskis continued his story:

Through the trees the colonel pointed out two high hills, or ridges, with a saddle between. "That hill on the left looks right down on Altavilla," he explained. "That's the main objective. Once we get on to it, it's gonna be hard for the Krautheads to stay in Altavilla. That other hill on the right should be in our hands by now."

A clear moon had now risen, and a German artillery observer must have spotted us in the moonlight, for many guns, probably a battalion, began to "zero in" on us. We saw the white flashes from behind the silhouettes of the hills ahead, and in a few seconds, the booming of the guns, the whistling of the shells and the jaw-clenching impact of the explosions, to our left and ahead....

More flashes on the horizon told us that more shells were on the way. Again the booming, and we ducked lower. This time the stick of shells smacked down behind us. We were bracketed. Fragments whizzed through the treetops and we could hear the clipped branches rustling as they hit the ground. Now the other German guns flashed, and we knew these were coming close. The concussion seemed to surround us and crush into our heads, and dirt and heavy limbs of trees came smashing down into our trench in torrents.

"We better get outta here," said the colonel. "They're gettin' the range. Let's go!" We shoved off the heavy boughs that were lying in a tangle on top of us. I was surprised at their weight. We jumped up the bank and sprinted across the field and up a hillside.[527]

The Germans sent in another barrage, and the group jumped into a number of ditches. This time the fragments inflicted a casualty. A large piece of shrapnel hit Wight in his back, and he died in the arms of Freeman and Dunham, who tried in vain to give first aid. Lieutenant Lloyd M. Price, a close friend of the captain, broke down in tears and ran away. He was never seen again by the other airborne engineers. They advanced over a number of hills and along hedgerows until, on a hillside, Freeman suddenly halted and reached over to pick up a black wire. "We'll cut that," he said.

"As we marched down the far side of the ridge, and across the valley," Tregaskis wrote, "we saw the steepest hill of all. Colonel Tucker pointed to it as the first of our two objectives. We walked cautiously as we reached the lower slopes, talking only in the softest whispers, careful to watch for cover. We were in dangerous territory. Artillery fired from *behind* us, German artillery, shooting into our lines.

"The hill rose very steeply, but we slogged along. I went up with the point. As we passed through the regularly spaced trees of an olive grove, half way up the slope, I heard the soft challenge, 'Red River,' and the equally soft response, 'Valley' from one of our men. American paratroopers slipped from the black and silver mosaic of moonlight and shadows. They were an advance patrol."[528]

The news that the patrol had was bad: there was no sign of the remainder of C Company or the rest of the 1st Battalion. Tucker's force had arrived ahead of his forces on the regimental objective instead of following his battalions. Tucker wasted little time and ordered C Company and the engineers to dig in on the hill and set up a small perimeter defense. The waiting was now for other elements of the 504th Parachute Infantry Regiment to appear. Going up the hill, Milloy spotted a light tank on the track and ordered two men to destroy it, which for some reason they failed to do.[529]

Tucker and Milloy captured a German artillery officer and two assistants before they had reached Hill 424, but a German non-commissioned officer said he wanted to return to his foxhole to retrieve a picture of his wife. Accompanied by Tregaskis and a trooper, he walked back, but after he picked up a leather case and showed a picture of his wife and child, he suddenly jumped across the foxhole and dashed away. The guard had been so surprised that he hesitated a moment too long and the German moved out of sight.

Dunham, the Regimental S-3 officer, set up perimeter guards as they bedded down for the night. "Temporary headquarters were set up in the fringe of trees just off the crown of the hill," wrote Tregaskis. "I was wondering whether there were any Germans in the valley just below us, when suddenly we saw tracers flashing in the dark woods and heard the crackle of rifle fire and a few bursts of machine gunning."[530]

Over on the Sorrento Peninsula as darkness was falling on September 16, Corporal Chester H. Aszklar, Pfc. Frank W. Weaver, and Private William O. Gilbert, Jr. of the 2nd Platoon in H Company were captured while in the process of setting up an outpost. "We got ambushed by a German and an Italian," recalled Aszklar. "They had khaki uniforms like we had and one guy put a pistol in my stomach. I pushed it away and said, 'Hey, we've got a job to do! Don't bother us.' Again the gun was in my stomach. When I looked down I saw a Jerry. They held us up and my Sergeant [Alfred R. Wolf] was coming and there was no way of telling that we got captured already. They got him too. (…) After a few days they put us in box cars and moved us to Germany, Stalag VII-A."[531]

Meanwhile, Tucker recalled that "at 0200 the units were in position on Hill 424. We discovered that the enemy had a garrison of approximately a reinforced company in the town of Altavilla, plus one 88mm gun and some small mortars. At approximately 0300, enemy troops began to infiltrate through our lines. Only small arms fire was encountered. These attempts by the enemy were driven back. At 0330 it was found that the ground on Hill 424 was completely surrounded and cut off. Two messengers, sent out at different times, were killed."[532]

The two riflemen from C Company—Privates Frank A. Puhalla and Joseph A. Taylor—who were sent out as messengers were both killed. But while Tucker recalled they were sent out individually, Tregaskis remembered that Dunham was instructed by Tucker to send out a two-man contact patrol to the unnumbered hill from where firing sounded to pass the word that reinforcements were needed. Tregaskis wrote later, "We never heard from them."[533] Puhalla's premonition of being killed in action thus came true.

Meanwhile, the hours ticked by, and they could still hear small arms fire on the unnumbered hill and see lines of white tracers blinking across the sky. Several paratroopers, including Freeman and Richter, were wounded by a German sniper. Dunham tried in vain to locate and kill the sniper but finally returned to the summit and reported he couldn't find him. About that time, the Germans fired amber and green flares, and shortly afterward, they were subjected to a heavy enemy barrage. Tucker recalled that Dunham "volunteered to go out for aid, but was killed in the attempt. Continuous attempts by the enemy, in small forces, throughout the night, to break through our lines were driven back."[534]

Dunham would posthumously be awarded with the Distinguished Service Cross: "When the headquarters of his regiment had been surrounded by enemy forces, Major Dunham volunteered to go out in the face of enemy artillery, machine gun, and rifle fire to obtain reinforcements, after two previous messengers [- Puhalla and Taylor -] had been fatally wounded. In the course of pursuing this mission, Major Dunham was killed. That Major Dunham volunteered to seek reinforcements for his headquarters in the face of almost certain death was an inspiration to the men and officers of his regiment."[535]

Much to their rear the column of the 1st Battalion had suddenly halted. Minutes passed, and Lieutenant Lekson and Captain Charles W. Duncan of B Company moved forward to find out what had happened from 1st Lieutenant Frank W. Gilson, the executive officer of C Company, and the platoon leader of the 3rd Platoon of C Company, 1st Lieutenant George A. Sellner. "Their story was brief," remembered Lekson. "Men had fallen asleep. A man looking up saw that the man who had been in front of him was no longer there. As he called back," he frantically tried to find the column in front of him with no success." Sellner sent out a two-man patrol north on the trail and had reported the break to Lieutenant Gilson at the rear of C Company.

Meanwhile, enemy artillery fire sounded in the vicinity, and German machine gunfire was heard to the east and their rear. The B Company radio operator tried in vain to reach A and C Companies on the SCR-511 radio. In fifteen minutes, the scouts returned and reported no trace of the other column part. Lieutenant Sellner resumed the advance with his platoon until machine pistol fire stopped them near Hill 315. Sellner was ordered to bypass the Germans by swinging off to the right of the trail and moved east. Soon the column climbed the steep slopes of a hill when Headquarters Company reported their 81mm mortar platoon was completely missing. Additional bad news came when Lekson and Duncan looked at a map under a shelterhalf and noticed that Hill 424 was farther to the north.

Williams and Harrison had meanwhile proceeded to Hill 424 after discovering the break in their part of the column. "After proceeding a short distance we came directly into a German occupied position [at Hill 315]," remembered Huebner, "which surprised us as well as the Germans. The small detachment of Germans gave up without a fight. By this time the company knew we were getting deep into enemy territory. As the point came to a small hill, three or four enemy machine guns opened fire. Everybody hit the ground and it looked as if we were going to have a rough fire fight.

"As the men lay on the ground, word came down the column to fix bayonets and get prepared to charge the enemy positions, which were only about fifty yards to the front. The only real concealment one had was the deep darkness of the night. The squad leaders managed to get their squads into a skirmish line."[536]

It was now 2245 hours as A Company found a concrete dugout and captured a small German forward artillery observer team operating a switchboard and telephones. The Germans inside were taken prisoner, and their equipment was destroyed, while Captain Harrison sent his A Company around to the west slope of Hill 315. Suddenly, several machine guns opened fire. Harrison passed word down from the head of the column to avoid the machine gun fire. But the 3rd Platoon in the rear received this message as "Fix bayonets and charge the machine gun." Pfc. Ervin E. Shaffer in the 3rd Platoon recalled that "we didn't have any scouts out because we were moving in with our bayonets. Someone shouted, 'A bayonet charge!' and we all charged forward and I ran in and could make out a bunker in front of me. I dropped down on the ground, facing the bunker. (…) I shot at the muzzle flash and rolled over two times and waited for him to fire. But he didn't fire. So I charged and fell over into a trench."[537]

Unknown to the paratroopers, the cemetery on the northeast slope of Hill 315 lay very close to the Battalion CP of *Hauptmann* (Captain) Helmut Meitzel. This twenty-three-year-old veteran of the invasion of Poland, Stalingrad, Sicily, and Reggio commanded the 2nd Battalion of the 15th Panzer Grenadier Regiment of the 29th Panzergrenadier Division. Meitzel's veteran soldiers had earlier recaptured Altavilla and the surrounding area. *Oberfeldwebel* (Staff Sergeant) Kurt Finke recalled that

> on 16 September the situation became lively. Continuously recon patrols were sent out by all companies and reported unjoyfully that the enemy approached all along our front in stronger force. From our battalion

CP we could see near the shoreline a gathering of 20 to 30 larger and large ships, including at least one battleship. By the afternoon we had to endure the thus far strongest cannonade in this war. The air droned under the intermittent breathtaking loud 380mm shells. Luckily there were no casualties.

In the late afternoon the enemy pressure increased all along the front, which could only be held largely due to the widely spread weak strong points that were several hundred meters apart. The situation sharpened. During the night the enemy managed with several combat patrols to break through the canyon rich and complex terrain. Around 2300 hours [German time – ahead of the American time] the artillery observer, who had set up his battery post on the "Three Houses Hill" [Unnumbered Hill] in the rear of the CP, called and reported that he constantly heard the muffled sound of marching infantry nearby. He asked if they were our troops. At that moment the telephoneline was cut.

The battalion commander shook his head. That was impossible. To obtain certainty an *oberfeldwebel* and two men were sent out to learn more. Almost immediately a call of the 7th Company came in that the enemy had undertaken a flanking maneuver in their sector and part of the enemy were already at the Company CP. The battalion commander wanted to ask something, but then a knack was heard on the line and also this one was out. At that moment firing broke out in the vicinity of the Battalion CP and one man stormed in calling out, "Reinforcements! They are already at the cemetery!" Everyone grasped for their weapons. Only the surgeon remained with the wounded. Few seconds later a tracer bullets from a heavy machine gun kept in reserve rattled through the dark.

When the adjutant wanted to inquire on the situation at the other companies he had to conclude that all lines were out. Also to Regiment no telephone line was intact. Because there had been no artillery fire in the last hour, the lines had to be cut by knives. But the radios still worked and, after the captain had placed all available staff members in a defensive position, he dispatched – standing on the cemetery wall – a radio message to Regiment.

Near midnight a non-commissioned artillery officer stormed in the CP out of breath and reported that the Battery CP on the "Three Houses Hill" had been overrun by a strong enemy combat patrol. He himself had been able to escape after being captured. Shortly after 0100 hours a newly arrived infantry platoon dispatched as reinforcement by another unit was sent to the hill, but they were unable to retake it. The enemy, undoubtfully reinforced, drove them off with strong fire.[538]

On the watches of the Americans, it was shortly before 0200 hours when Captain Harrison had reconnoitered the unnumbered hill with a small group and told his assembled platoon leaders this was the objective. "He ordered the platoon leaders to prepare an all-round defense," recalled Sergeant Huebner, "close to the crest of the hill with the 1st Platoon on the forward slope, 2nd on the left, 3rd on the right, tying in all the way around."[539] Private John B. Isom and others of the 2nd Platoon "tried to dig in but that was impossible because of the rocky soil. There were many rocks up there so we used the rocks to build a safe position."[540]

A Company had seized the unnumbered hill which they erroneously thought was Hill 424 and dug in, awaiting the arrival of the remainder of the 1st Battalion, as Captain Milloy's deployed C Company also lost contact with them just before reaching Hill 315. Corporal Fred J. Baldino of the 2nd Platoon in A Company was placed with Pfc. Joseph Gwiazdowski on an outpost: "We were scared as Altavilla was our first real taste of real combat. The Germans did counterattack that night but they were repulsed."[541]

Meanwhile, Lieutenant Lekson—awaiting the return of a B Company patrol under Sergeant Jerry Murphy—was getting impatient. He halted his part of the 1st Battalion as midnight passed. Finally, at around 0100 hours, Murphy's patrol reappeared. They had contacted Colonel Tucker near a well on Hill 424. Tucker's message was "Bring the battalion down here at once." A platoon of Company C, 307th Airborne Engineer Battalion, and some twenty lost men of B Company, 505th Parachute Infantry Regiment, had meanwhile joined the rear of column.

Murphy guided the entire group to Hill 424 and at 0200 hours halted the column at the well. Lieutenants Lekson and William S. Jones walked a few yards ahead along the trail and ran into Lieutenant Colonel Williams, who had just left A Company. Williams led the column up the hill and assigned their dispositions. A patrol was sent out to find the missing 81mm mortar platoon. It became clear to Williams that they were probably on the unnumbered hill and that Tucker was on Hill 424 with C Company. They decided to await first light so they could orient themselves better.[542]

The 2nd Battalion followed the 1st Battalion in its tracks, recalled Lieutenant Chester A. Garrison: "That evening I travelled in the dark with the mortar platoon that carried into combat its tube, base-plate, and supply of shells. Since they were all heavy and awkward, particularly the iron base-plate, the men kept changing them around for relief. I joined in and soon dreaded my turn with the base-plate. Marching cross-country through rough fields and up a path on a steep hill, men passed out from the exertion until before dawn we finally took a break. Exhausted from the climb in addition to my lingering jaundice, I flopped down asleep in a field."[543]

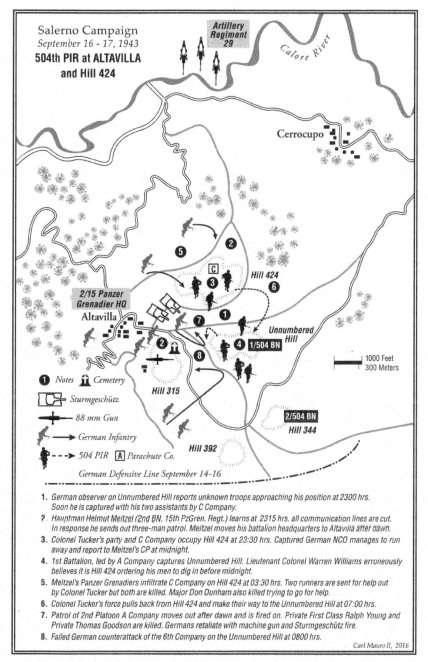

Salerno Campaign
September 16 - 17, 1943
**504th PIR at ALTAVILLA
and Hill 424**

Artillery Regiment 29

Calore River

Cerrocupo

2/15 Panzer Grenadier HQ

Altavilla

Hill 424

Unnumbered Hill

1/504 BN

Hill 315

2/504 BN
Hill 344

Hill 392

1000 Feet
300 Meters

① Notes   🪦 Cemetery

🗡️ Sturmgeschütz

✝ 88 mm Gun

🔫 → German Infantry

🪂 - - → 504 PIR   Ⓐ Parachute Co.

German Defensive Line September 14-16

1. German observer on Unnumbered Hill reports unknown troops approaching his position at 2300 hrs. Soon he is captured with his two assistants by C Company.
2. Hauptman Helmut Meitzel (2nd BN, 15th PzGren. Regt.) learns at 2315 hrs. all communication lines are cut. In response he sends out three-man patrol. Meitzel moves his battalion headquarters to Altavilla after dawn.
3. Colonel Tucker's party and C Company occupy Hill 424 at 23:30 hrs. Captured German NCO manages to run away and report to Meitzel's CP at midnight.
4. 1st Battalion, led by A Company captures Unnumbered Hill. Lieutenant Colonel Warren Williams erroneously believes it is Hill 424 ordering his men to dig in before midnight.
5. Meitzel's Panzer Grenadiers infiltrate C Company on Hill 424 at 03:30 hrs. Two runners are sent for help out by Colonel Tucker but both are killed. Major Don Dunham also killed trying to go for help.
6. Colonel Tucker's force pulls back from Hill 424 and make their way to the Unnumbered Hill at 07:00 hrs.
7. Patrol of 2nd Platoon A Company moves out after dawn and is fired on. Private First Class Ralph Young and Private Thomas Goodson are killed. Germans retaliate with machine gun and Sturmgeschütz fire.
8. Failed German counterattack of the 6th Company on the Unnumbered Hill at 0800 hrs.

Carl Mauro II, 2016

504th PIR at Altavilla and Hill 424 16-17 September 1943

CHAPTER 25

ON THE WRONG HILL

Salerno Beachhead

SEPTEMBER 17, 1943

W hen it became light in the morning of September 17, soldiers were seen on Hill 424 to the northeast. Captain Willard E. Harrison of A Company ordered 2nd Lieutenant Mearle D. Duvall to take a strong patrol to investigate Hill 424. Privates Louis C. Marino and Thomas J. Goodson were in a slit trench when "Sergeant [Robert] Lowe came over. He wanted to send out a patrol and Goodson was one of the guys that he picked to go out."[544] Sergeant Otto W. Huebner saw them cautiously move down the northwestern slope: "As the lead scout, Pfc. Ralph R. Young went down the crest about two hundred yards, he spotted troops to his front. Thinking they were friendly troops he did not take cover and was fired upon and killed. The platoon leader, Lieutenant Duvall went out to help him and was hit in the legs with shrapnel."[545] Duvall had to be evacuated quickly before another shell or bullet would kill him.

PFC Ralph Young of A Company was killed near Hill 424
by German fire. Courtesy: Doug Mokan

Right at that moment, Harrison appeared over the hillcrest and
decided to go out in the open to bring Duvall to safety. He ordered
the 2nd Platoon men, who wanted to aid their comrades, back into
their foxholes. While they covered him, he ran out and briefly checked
Young before picking up the wounded Duvall. All were impressed by
this valor.[546]

Marino was horrified as he saw his close friend Goodson "stood
behind a little tree, put his bayonet on his rifle and started waving that
darn thing back and forth like he was hunting wild Indians or something. It kind of amused me but I knew that he shouldn't be doing that,
because the Germans spotted him right away and as soon as he moved
away from behind that tree he got cut down by one of their burp guns.
That is when Captain Harrison (...) crawled up to him, took his rifle
and then crawled back and left the body there. Goodson had been in
the same squad. In fact he was right ahead of me when we were making a single march going into the battle the day before."[547]

Private Edward B. Hill, Jr. of Headquarters Company kept firing and received a Silver Star when he "voluntarily covered the flank
of his patrol of five men when it encountered an enemy position of

an estimated hundred men. Private Hill, in a position of little cover, remained in position under heavy automatic fire and protected the patrol in its withdrawal."[548]

At around 0800 hours, Lieutenant John S. Lekson observed the German 6th Company "moving from the edge of Altavilla into the valley toward us. As Lieutenant Colonel Williams and I watched this force of some seventy-five to one hundred Germans moving, another smaller enemy force appeared from the south edge of Altavilla and swung around Hill 315. As the Germans approached within three hundred yards of B Company, our men opened fire. The Germans broke into small groups that moved forward from bush to bush and terrace to terrace."[549]

While the Germans sought cover, accurate mortar fire of the 60mm mortar squad of the 3rd Platoon of B Company rained down on them. Sergeant Edmund Q. Moorehead directed the mortar fire from the crest while his mortar crew was some fifteen feet behind him. His platoon leader, 1st Lieutenant William A. Meerman, called out targets to Moorehead from a position further down the forward slope. Almost unable to pinpoint the German gun positions in the disappearing morning mist, Moorehead decided to expose himself. For this act, he would be decorated with the Silver Star: "Sergeant Moorehead, in charge of a mortar squad, removed his jump coat and exposed himself on top of a hill to draw enemy fire and pick out their gun positions. His courageous action and his excellent direction of the close up fire of his squad aided materially in the repulse of all enemy counter attacks."[550]

Moorehead recalled decades later that "on the hill we had orders not to fire, to give us time to dig our foxholes. We were heard by the Germans and two of their machine guns 100 yards apart began spraying our hill with effective fire for fifteen minutes, halting most troopers from digging and wounding others trying to dig in. I called out orders, degrees and distances to my mortar men. My first shell scored a hit on the close target. It took two more to silence the distant machine gun fire. All digging then commenced in silence."[551]

Pfc. Norman H. Plaisted from Dover, New Hampshire, of Moorehead's squad, was cited for gallantry in action on September 17:

"Plaisted was an observer for mortar crews. Plaisted, while out on operational action, spotted enemy movement. He opened fire, causing the enemy to disperse and stay put, until other men could get up the line to fire at them. He was under 88mm fire while performing this act. Private First Class Plaisted drew the enemy's attention to himself, thereby giving our riflemen a chance to build up an effective first line."[552]

Pfc. William L. Clay earned also a citation for gallantry in the same action as Plaisted: "Clay was manning a Browning Automatic Rifle during an enemy 88mm and mortar barrage concentration on his position. He remained in his position where he took up the fire on the enemy again. Later in the same day he manned an observation post on an exposed flank under fire to observe and warn the company of enemy movements."[553]

Another commended for bravery was Pfc. Edwin E. Decker who "regardless of personal safety, and under an intense artillery barrage, aided in removing critically wounded men from fox holes to positions of temporary safety. This action took place in daylight on the forward slope of [the] unnumbered hill within 700 yards of blistering tank fire."[554]

Lekson recalled that "as the German attack slowed down and then dropped back, Lieutenant Colonel Williams ordered the mortar to stop firing. It had expended much of its ammunition and resupply was not certain. Enemy artillery concentrations of thirty or forty rounds each and mortar fire hit the slopes of the hill. Then a mist began to gather in the valley obscuring Altavilla and parts of Hill 424. The battalion waited. Though the mist did not last more than a half hour, it seemed much longer. The troops on the forward slope were tense and word was being passed back and forth to watch for enemy infiltrations."[555]

When the mist thinned, three German *Sturmgeschütze* appeared on the road that ran along Hill 424 at the northeastern edge of Altavilla. They soon began to fire into foxhole after foxhole. First on the A Company sector, then along the 2nd and 3rd Platoons of B Company. The Mortar Squad Leader of the 2nd Platoon in A Company, Sergeant Fred L. Lanning, wrote to the sister of 1st Lieutenant Ned E. Wall that "we had captured a hill during the night and that morning had moved over to close a gap in the lines. Infantry troops (ours) had been driven off several times so there were foxholes and slit trenches in the area. As I was looking over a place to set up the mortar, the Germans opened up fire. I hit a ditch but just to the side of me and uphill was where Ned and 1st Sergeant Edwin Rouse were located. About 15 to 20 feet from me. They hid into slit trenches there and were doing just right. A shell came in that was time released. In other words it exploded above the ground sending shrapnel downward. That shell killed both Lieutenant Wall and Sergeant Rouse. A little to the left and I would have been gone and my people may have been contacting your Ned. I noted such in the margin of a prayer book that I carried."[556]

Letter by Lieutenant Colonel Warren Williams, Jr. to the parents of Lieutenant Ned Wall to explain the impact of his loss in the 1st Battalion. Courtesy: Gary Wall

A direct hit fell on a 2nd Platoon, B Company bazooka position. Dug in among a cluster of trees on the right flank, Staff Sergeant Henry P. Paquet was killed by a *Sturmgeschütz* shell burst and Private Emanuel J. Weinberger had both legs blown off. The incident shocked the platoon, as Paquet had been in the original cadre.

Second Lieutenant Stanley J. Whitman, the 1st Platoon leader of A Company, and his platoon medic, Technician 5th Grade Amilcar J. Pollet, jumped up and ran forward to render first aid. They were joined by Weinberger's platoon leader, 1st Lieutenant William W. Magrath, and Private Guy L. Stokes, the first aid man of the 2nd Platoon, B Company. As they were busy placing tourniquets on Weinberger's cut-off legs to stop the bleeding, shrapnel from an exploding tank shell wounded Whitman in the face. They then dragged Weinberger to the first aid post of Captain Charles E. Pack, Jr. For this action, Magrath, Pollet, and Whitman were cited for meritorious service while the medic was awarded the Silver Star: "Stokes, under heavy 88mm gun and mortar fire in the direct range of the enemy on the forward slope of a hill, repeatedly went forward to render first aid and bring back wounded men and officers to the battalion aid station behind the ridge of the hill. Previous to this attack, Private Stokes having jumped by parachute on 14 September, worked through the area to find injured jumpers, render first aid, and evacuate them to safety."[557]

Second Lieutenant Stanley Whitman of A Company was wounded in the face by shrapnel while trying to aid a paratrooper from B Company on Hill 424. Courtesy: Charles and Ned Whitman

"As the tanks fired," wrote Lekson, "a German attack was launched from the northwest along the draw against the 1st Platoon of A Company. In a short fire fight the German force was driven back with some loss. (...) While the tanks had been active, the artillery observer had gained radio contact. Soon, VI Corps artillery was firing on Altavilla and on the tanks. As the German tanks and infantry withdrew, enemy artillery began to pound the hill. I, with a command post detail, moved to the aid station to collect ammunition from the wounded. Some of the troopers had reached a critical low in small arms [ammunition]. In the aid station were some twenty wounded."[558]

Oberfeldwebel Kurt Finke provides the recollection of that morning from the German side:

> Dawn on 17 September brought upon all the ground a heavy, milky fog. That should be favorable for us. Due to the situation the Battalion Commander decided to regroup the battalion, pull the 7th Company sharp to the 5th Company and move the 6th Company, facing no enemy, for disposal to Altavilla. Upon these orders were issued to the company commanders through the telephonelines, which meanwhile had been repaired by the tireless operators, the Battalion CP was relocated to the castle [in the center of Altavilla].
>
> Under cover of the fog the regrouping was carried out unseen for the enemy. As the sun broke through and the fog disappeared, we could observe how the enemy held the Cemetery Hill [315] and thus our former Battalion CP. Our artillery and two *Sturmgeschütze* prepared them a warm welcome. Before 1000 hours it was reported the Americans [of the small A Company patrol] probed forward (...) Their objective was clear. The enemy wanted to cut Altavilla off and thus prepare the same fate which we had done with them a few days earlier.

Now struck the hour for the 6th Company. Halfway up the hill came the clash with the numerical stronger enemy forces. Yet again the German grenadiers proved superior, even in the most difficult hours. The enemy was forced back and the company dug in for defense. Thus they created the battle conditions that enabled to hold the city as long as possible in light of the overall situation. Enemy pressure increased before noon in front of the 6th Company and for nearly three hours the artillery pounded the city and the positions. Also the 5th and 7th Companies could hardly resist the opponent. Due to the attack of the 6th Company the original objective of the enemy was prevented: he strove now with strong forces to the nearby target – the city itself.[559]

Finke wrongly interpreted Tucker's target, which were Hills 315 and 424 and not Altavilla. During the night, he and Captain Albert E. Milloy had tried in vain to contact other elements by radio. A patrol led by Lieutenant Fordyce Gorham moved at daybreak down the southwest slope of Hill 424 toward Altavilla to oust a machine gun out of the church tower.[560] On a rocky steep trail along the hill, they encountered a *Sturmgeschütz* and a light tank, the same that Milloy saw abandoned hours earlier. Gorham took his group back, requested a bazooka, and they were once again descending when a stronger German combat patrol moved up and drove them back.

Staff Sergeant James O. Eldridge recalled that "a German machine gun kept giving us plenty of trouble [from the north], and we had trouble locating it. A patrol of five men was picked out of our section and [Private Warren W.] 'Zoomie' [Zumwalt] was among the five. The plan was to locate the machine gun nest, then split up and creep and crawl up at five different angles, and, when every man was loose enough, to toss a couple of hand grenades each, then charge in.

"Well, everything went all right and every man was in position, but then the Germans turned loosed another burst. 'Zoomie' thought they had spotted some of the patrols, so instead of waiting on the grenades, he jumped into the machine gun nest alone, and tried to take it single-handed. But, another machine gun, located where it could cover this first one, opened up on him and nearly cut him in two. The machine gun was taken care of, but we lost 'Zoomie.' He was one of the swellest fellows I ever knew."[561]

Master Sergeant Henry S. Furst was awarded the Silver Star for driving off German attacks during the night: "When his unit was surrounded and enemy troops were filtering through the lines, was instrumental in effectively organizing the positions of his unit and checking further hostile advance. Master Sergeant Furst directed activities without regard for personal safety under heavy machine gun, rifle and artillery fire. His action was an inspiration to his men to successfully repulse all attacks."[562]

Meanwhile, war correspondent Richard Tregaskis had just finished his foxhole on top of the hill when Sergeant Ray Justice of C Company crawled over. "We're all getting out of here," he said. Tregaskis wrote:

> I scrambled out of my shelter and joined the thin column of men which had begun to move. It was not clear just what the strategy might be, but we were retiring, at least temporarily. I saw the chesty little Colonel Tucker striding along the path. "We're moving over to another ridge," he said. "The 1st Battalion should be there." Freeman and Richter hobbled along with the column. It was the first time I had seen them since they were winged last night. Both were well plastered with dried blood, and, under their ripped shirts, bandages showed. Their faces were drawn, but quite cheerful.
>
> Richter told me, "We were coming across the saddle last night when two Krauts jumped up. They got the first shots." Richter's arm seemed quite stiff; a bullet had pierced the rear part of the shoulder. Colonel Freeman carried his arm in a sling, and his face was gray.[563]

Shortly after the German morning attack had been repulsed on the unnumbered hill, Colonel Reuben H. Tucker's group joined forces with the remainder of the 1st Battalion. Lekson recalled that "he demanded, 'Where in the hell have you been?' In a brief conference it was decided that A Company would move out at once to seize Hill 424. C Company would reorganize and then follow A Company. B Company would take over the defense of the Unnumbered Hill until the 2nd Battalion could be brought up."[564]

The number of wounded was rising, and there was still no contact re-established with regimental headquarters at Albanella. Reinforcements—and most of all, food and water—were badly needed. Lieutenant Colonel Leslie G. Freeman, the wounded executive officer, led some ten light-wounded enlisted men, Captain Forrest Richter, and Lieutenants Duvall and Whitman off the hill to Albanella. "Korman and I decided to go back with the walking wounded to write our stories of the night's battle," recalled Tregaskis. "Stretchers with their loads of wounded humanity lay on the sloping hillside, near a ditch. Some figures of men, bandaged, sat forlornly on the ground. Medical corpsmen moved about, helping to administer morphine and apply bandages.

"The walking wounded were rounded up – a sad group, ragged and blood-stained and bandaged. One, with a smashed nose, complained that his girl would never look at him again. We assured him that he would be fixed up. Some of the group did not seem to be bona-fide walking wounded, for they had risen from stretchers and could barely hobble. But they insisted they could move under their own power. Trying that long walk through a gauntlet of Germans would be preferable to lying there on the hillside, in the open, with only the ditch for shelter, while the enemy began another artillery concentration."[565]

They awaited until the artillery barrage had stopped, and it was silent again. "Let's go!" ordered Freeman as he and Richter led the column of walking wounded off the south side of the unnumbered hill. "The two officers held their .45s in their good hands," recalled Tregaskis, "and somewhere along the little column two other men had automatics. This was the armed strength of our expedition – and we might have to run a gauntlet of German infantrymen, armed with *Schmeissers* and rifles, on the way to the rear. If we ran into a German patrol they could make short work on us. (...)

"As we began to move, the shells screeched again, but we stayed on our feet, hurrying as much as the sad column of limping men could hurry.... (...) We could hear the muffled banging of shelling back in the direction of the ridge which we had left. (...) We moved cautiously through the wooded paths, watching the trees and the bushes while our nerves waited for a quick signal to jump."[566]

They encountered a lone German soldier who had a leg wound. He begged them to help him as he been laying there all night long. Freeman told him it was impossible as many were wounded themselves. They would send some medics at the earliest possibility. Not to be deterred, the German dragged himself up and slowly hobbled after the column. "An hour later," wrote Tregaskis, "we saw an American soldier and were challenged. We were getting close to our lines; and shortly afterward reached a field dressing station under the grape arbor of a farmhouse. We were only a couple of miles from Albanella. We could see it, high up on top of a hill, across a valley. There was phone communication with the rear from this station. There were stretchers and morphine for the men who had hobbled so courageously through the long distance, and fresh bandages for who had been bleeding heavily."[567]

Seymour Korman and Tregaskis said their goodbyes and hitchhiked back to Fifth Army Headquarters where they started to write their articles. Tregaskis's eyewitness account of the battle near Altavilla and the death of Major Don P. Dunham appeared in U.S. newspapers in December 1943.[568]

At the Regimental Aid Station, the wounded were treated by Major Ivan J. Roggen and his medics, ably assisted by the Regimental Dentist, Captain Robert M. Halloran. "As a medic with a brassard, I was grateful to be within range and not be shot at," recalled Halloran. "Almost all Germans respected the Geneva Convention. We, as medics, were briefed so we could support combat units, patrols, etc. We 'leapfrogged' our aid stations as the troops advanced, so were constantly on the move, searching adequate buildings for aid stations treating wounded and sick, and evacuating to field hospitals. We often saw 'shell shock' and sometimes treated it with Sodium Amitol, or got them to sleep. Medical care in front lines was chiefly 'first aid.' Stop bleeding, splinting, preventing infection, etc. and evacuating to evacuation hospitals in the least time possible.

"When we were in reserve I worked a long day trying to take care of the dental needs of 2000 men. Needless to say, the dental care was inadequate, but we all tried hard. Dental field equipment was very absolete and incomplete. I had dentists back home send me that I needed to perform just basic dentistry, and later improvised extensively. Our medical care was adequate, but supplies and equipment forced our M.D.'s to render less care than they wanted to."[569]

Private Robert Larsen, ammunition bearer in Sergeant Fred Lanning's
A Company mortar squad, posing for Albert Clark to take a photo.
Hill 424, September 1943. Courtesy: Albert Clark

Sergeant Fred Lanning, mortar squad leader of the 2nd Platoon in A Company,
photographed by Albert Clark on Hill 424. Courtesy: Albert Clark

CHAPTER 26

RECAPTURE OF HILL 424

Salerno Beachhead

SEPTEMBER 17, 1943

L ieutenant Colonel Leslie G. Freeman's request at the regimental command post in Albanella for desperately needed reinforcements and ammunition was taken seriously by Major Robert B. Acheson. The Regimental S-4 officer arranged five jeeps loaded with ammunition and set off toward the unnumbered hill along with 1st Lieutenant George F. Taliaferro, the 1st Battalion S-4 officer, and some men from Service Company. They didn't get very far, as recounted in his Distinguished Service Cross Citation: "At the La Cosa Creek, the trucks were unable to proceed because of heavy enemy rifle, mortar, and artillery fire. With complete disregard to his own safety, Major Acheson then voluntarily proceeded alone across the valley to the encircled battalion.

"While crossing the valley, Major Acheson came upon a group of riflemen who were pinned down by enemy fire. He reorganized and directed their force so effectively that they cleared the opposition from the slope [of Hill 315]. Although he was wounded in the chest and sustained severe shell fragment wounds in the right arm, which later required amputation, Major Acheson completed his assigned mission before accepting medical attention."[570]

Major General Fred L. Walker, Sr. wrote in his diary, "The 504th Parachute Infantry occupied Hill 315 early this morning but soon thereafter Colonel Tucker reported the enemy was heavily shelling his position. Later he reported that the enemy was bringing up reinforcements for counterattack and that he was having heavy losses."[571]

At around 1030 hours, A Company moved down the gully with the 1st Platoon, now led by 2nd Lieutenant Reneau G. Breard, and up Hill 424. A machine gun suddenly opened fire, recalled Sergeant Otto W. Huebner: "The 3rd Platoon, which was in the rear of the column, moved around the west side of the hill in a flanking movement, attacked the position and eliminated it quickly. The 3rd and 1st Platoons abreast moved up to the top of the hill at once, with the 2nd Platoon following. As the platoons reached the top of the hill, Captain Harrison ordered the 1st Platoon to move to the right, 3rd to the front, and 2nd to the left."[572]

Pfc. Ervin Shaffer of the 3rd Platoon vividly remembered that as "the whole company went over the hill we found foxholes where they had already been doing some fighting two days before. (...) I found a hole and jumped into it and the Germans then were coming up from the side of the hill. We bore the brunt of three German counterattacks. Almost everyone in our squad actually were decorated or given a citation for bravery. None of the men in the squad were killed, but there had been men killed all around us from artillery fire."[573]

Huebner continued:

> Just as the platoons were moving to the crest in their sector, a strong force of Germans started moving over the crest on the opposite side. Company A immediately set up a hasty defense. One advantage the company had was the fact that we were on the hill while the main German force was still climbing. (...)
>
> Finally, the 2nd Platoon drove the Germans back over the crest and closed in fast, taking up positions along the crest. The 2nd Platoon then swung part of its fire to the right in front of the 3rd Platoon, causing the Germans to withdraw in that sector. Every step the Germans would take backward, the company would

take forward, using every available means of cover. Finally, the company with all three platoons abreast held the entire crest of the hill. The fire soon ceased; the attack was repelled, but the company suffered eight casualties, though the enemy suffered many times more.

Immediately, the company commander ordered a hasty defense set up in a moon shape design with the 2nd Platoon on the west overlooking Altavilla, the 3rd Platoon to the north, and the 1st Platoon to the east, all tying in. Company headquarters to the rear and center of the company, and a couple of small security positions to the rear facing the unnumbered hill.[574]

Hill 424 had a perfect view of the beachhead and whoever held it could see everything that went on. The slope had been badly contested, as Huebner noticed:

The sight on the hill was an unpleasant one. This was the same place that the 1st Battalion of the 142nd Infantry, 36th Division four days previously was finally forced to withdraw after great losses were inflicted on both sides. The hill was infested with scattered dead Germans and American soldiers, supplies, and ammunition. There were machine guns still in their original emplacements, rifles, packs clothing, ammunition belts, machine gun [ammunition] boxes, and stacks of 60mm mortar shells scattered all over the hill.

The ammunition was gathered up and distributed through the company as soon as possible. The platoons began digging positions in their sectors. Foxholes dug by the 142nd Infantry were improved and used in many cases. Slit trenches were also used in many instances instead of foxholes, because the hard ground made digging difficult.

The officers and NCOs directed the exact spots of positions. We tried to arrange them to cover the most likely enemy approaches, have each position give mutual support to the one on the right and left, with observation, fire, and depth in that order of priority. To add firepower, the machine guns that were left on the hill by the 142nd, were put in the platoon positions.[575]

At around 1100 hours, the Germans launched a counterattack to retake Hill 424, supported by *Sturmgeschütze III* armed with 75mm gun. They systematically started to shell the top of the hill, forcing A Company to remain in their foxholes. Huebner recalled that

the men were quite hungry about this time, for they had not had any rations since the day before. A few were lucky enough to find a little bread and jam in the dead Germans' packs. Water was also scarce. There was a well down the draw to [the] northwest, about two hundred yards, but every time anyone would go for water, they would either get in a fire fight or be shelled.

The company radio operator had finally gotten through to battalion on the unnumbered hill. Lieutenant Colonel Williams, the battalion commander, told Captain Harrison, the company commander, that Company C would be on their way to help. It was impossible at this time to evacuate the wounded, but the company medical personnel were doing a fine job of taking care of them. Their greatest assistant was the little morphine syringe.

The shelling increased with mortar and heavy artillery falling and everyone stayed low in his hole. At noon the shelling became almost unbearable. It was so bad that the sides of the foxholes began caving in. The air was thick with smoke and dust from the bursting shells, and then – all quiet. The quiet period continued for only a minute, as heavy enemy machine guns began blasting away from the front of the 1st and 3rd Platoons areas, supporting a German assault force approaching the positions.

The men ducked their heads in the foxholes to escape the machine gun fire, approximately two feet off the ground in most places, and yelled to the men to get their hands up and start firing – which they did. The platoons laid down a heavy base of fire with every possible weapon being fired. The 60mm mortars were deployed singly with each platoon. The 1st and 3rd Platoon mortars began laying down fire within a hundred yards of the front line positions traversing back and forth. The company radio operator finally managed to communicate with battalion again on the unnumbered hill."[576]

Privates First Class Robert L. Jones and Bernard E. Carter of the 1st Platoon took off their bag packs so the digging would be easier. Carter always carried his Bible with him, loved to sing his favorite song, "Cool Waters," and talked about his guitar. Their platoon sergeant, Staff Sergeant George A. Siegmann, was digging nearby. Carter had just taken off his back pack, when a mortar shell landed and shrapnel exploded through his back. Siegmann and Jones, who quickly turned their friend over, watched him die. Carter had followed Siegmann wherever he went, and had been a foxhole buddy of Jones on several occasions. Now they had to dig a grave and both paratroopers carried this horrible moment forever in their memory.[577]

Lekson, on the unnumbered hill, recalled that "Harrison radioed a request for artillery to Lieutenant Colonel Williams."[578] He had spotted two *Sturmgeschütze* at the cemetery north of Hill 315. While a forward observer relayed the fire mission to the 32nd Field Artillery Battalion, Lieutenant Colonel Warren R. Williams, Jr. asked Captain Willard Harrison to adjust over a different radio channel.

As the assaulting panzer grenadiers of *Hauptmann* Helmut Meitzel's 7th Company stormed up the northern and eastern slopes of Hill 424, they shouted war cries. Meitzel had copied this tactic from his encounters with Russians in Stalingrad. But unlike what the Germans had experienced a few days earlier with the Texans, the paratroopers opened up with their rifles, Browning Automatic Rifles (BAR), and .30-caliber light machine guns. "When the company opened up its final protective fire," Huebner wrote, "it momentarily stopped the assault. After a few minutes of hesitation, the Germans began rushing the positions in groups, while another group would support by fire, but for some reason their fire was inaccurate."[579]

One soldier of Swiss origin, Pfc. Peter R. Schneider in the 1st Platoon, called out orders in German. He yelled *"Kommen Sie hier!"* and as the Germans advanced, Schneider and his fellow soldiers from A Company picked off eighteen of them like sitting ducks. He was decorated with the Silver Star for his ingenuity. Schneider himself remembered that "I heard the German officers giving their commands and their men were talking as they came up. I knew just where they were heading. So I was able to tell our fellows just where to fire. We crouched low and picked them off. Some of the German privates started to fall back and their officers cursed them, calling them yellow, and urged them on. Several German soldiers protested, crying, 'Those Americans shoot too straight.'

"I thought this was a good time for me to speak up and I did in German, of course. I started shouting commands to the Heinies to move right or left and back and forward. Each of my commands brought them in direct line of one of our boys' fire and those Germans were shot down like sitting ducks. The other Germans were completely disorganized and had enough."[580]

Pfc. Daniel W. Shaffer was decorated with the Silver Star when he "deliberately exposed himself to enemy small arms fire to locate and point out enemy dispositions to his squad leader. He killed two enemy soldiers, which action enabled his squad leader to properly dispose his squad and repulse attacks on his squad front."[581]

The Germans kept coming up the hill by leaps and bounds and at several places close combat actions were fought. Huebner wrote,

> Soon, the hand grenades flew like snowballs from both sides, but for every shot or grenade from the Germans on the 1st and 3rd Platoons, they got two back. The officers and NCOs were up in the front foxholes firing with the men. Heavy artillery began falling on the hill, only this time it was falling in the middle of the enemy position, which was deeply appreciated by the company, because shortly after, the attack seemed to become disorganized and easier to control by fire.
>
> Before long the Germans began to withdraw down the crest. Once the 1st Platoon leader had to yell at a couple of men to get back in their foxholes, for they began to pursue the enemy. The company had killed approximately 50 Germans, but had suffered almost half that number in casualties. (...)
>
> Shortly after this small fire fight, the enemy started shelling the hill again. Much to our delight, Company C had just come up the hill to help. The battalion commander and his CP group were with them, including the battalion medical officer. The medical officer was needed greatly and performed miracles, including two amputations, with his meager stock of medical supplies. The battalion aid station was set up in a gully near the battalion CP. Evacuation of the wounded was still impossible, and to add to the evacuation problem a heavy concentration began falling

on the hill, including air bursts, which caused many
additional casualties.[582]

Williams feared that A Company might be completely cut off and
called up the remainder of his force—including twenty stray paratroopers of C Company, 505th Parachute Infantry—to Hill 424. "Company
C was placed in position along the north side of side Hill 424," recalled
Lekson, "tying in with A Company on its left. The east flank of C Company was covered by the engineers and the 505th men."[583]

At around 1500 hours, the German 5th Company struck against
A Company from the west slope of Hill 424 and against C Company
from the northwest. This attack, preceded by a heavy artillery and
mortar fire, lasted almost an hour. Due to covering fire from machine
guns, Lekson erroneously estimated the attacking strength at two German companies. During this attack, Pfc. Willard N. Young of A Company earned a Silver Star when he "crawled forward of the front lines
and tossed a grenade into a machine gun position. This action helped
to break up an attack on his squad front."[584]

Lieutenant James E. Dunn of C Company, "by his own courageous
conduct and his direction of the fire of his platoon from an exposed
position, successfully repelled two determined enemy attacks, thus
making it possible for friendly troops to retain possession of Hill
424."[585] He also received a Silver Star for gallantry in action.

Huebner recalled:

> The Germans began advancing by fire and move-
> ment, taking advantage of the cover afforded by the
> good approaches. They were hitting all three pla-
> toons of Company A with the main force coming up
> the western slope. Due to the shape of the hill mass,
> it was impossible to lay down a good final protective
> line. The field of fire was very limited, in places only
> 50 yards. One outpost was cut off and later eliminated,
> while the other fought its way back, giving the com-
> pany very little notice of the attack. With the large vol-
> ume of fire the enemy was laying down, it sounded as

if the entire German Army was attacking. Mortar targets were picked and fired upon as close as 50 yards in front of the troops. Its fire was very effective and most valuable in disorganizing assaults....

The company commander kept calling back to battalion for artillery fire. The battalion commander said the only thing he could get was from the naval boats off the beaches, and it was very dangerous to fire so close to friendly troops. The company commander said he had to take the chance and the battalion commander agreed.

The fire fight continued on, and in its second hour casualties began mounting on both sides. The word was passed along for the men to get deep down in their holes as the Navy began firing. The shell bursts, landing on the northwest slope, seemed to rock the entire hill. The foxholes cracked like glass and the topsoil around sprinkled into the foxholes with every burst. On could hear terror-stricken screams coming from the Germans along the slope of the hill, which made one's backbone quiver. A few Germans still tried to come forward, but the bombardment disorganized them completely, and before long the enemy withdrew. The hill was still ours, although Company A suffered twenty more casualties during that attack. The Germans suffered many, many more."[586]

Private Gordon Gould of the 1st Platoon noticed Sergeant William C. Hauser was hit by 88mm fire: "Although seriously wounded, the sergeant crawled to where he could better direct the action of his men. The never to be forgotten noise of a German 88 – the explosion – we carried him back and put him in a slit-trench. A good many soldiers would have welcomed the protection offered by an slit-trench at that moment. But not Sergeant Hauser. Believed to be dying, he again crawled forth to help check the attack of the enemy. The enemy's attack was finally driven back... Sergeant Hauser was among the wounded to leave Salerno aboard a hospital ship, homeward bound. (...) His right arm had to be amputated."587

Oberfeldwebel Kurt Finke wrote about A Company seizing Hill 424 from the German perspective: "As the danger in front of the 6th Company increased and the enemy threatened to outflank it on the left, the Captain decided to pull the 5th and 7th Companies out of their positions and commit them on the left flank of the 6th Company. With the remaining available troops he wanted to defend the city under all conditions (...)

"Shortly before 1400 hours the new positions were occupied. Continuously pounded the ship artillery. At 1430 hours the order reached the Battalion through a regimental orderly officer that we were to leave the Altavilla area. Not one second earlier as ordered the last battalion member left the city. Only the other day we learned, after being informed on the overall situation, in what kind of 'trap' we had been and which meaning it was that the city was held so long. We had recaptured it against numerically stronger enemy forces and had held it against even stronger units, until ordered to pull back."588

Meanwhile, the 2nd Battalion had relieved B Company on the unnumbered hill at 1300 hours. Lieutenant Chester A. Garrison wrote:

> F Company and most of the 81mm mortar platoon became detached from us in the dark and are somewhere to our rear. About 0830 a P-38 flew over dropping two bombs in D Company area, killing (...) Pfc. John C. Di Rinzo, Private James E. Lechner, Pfc. John C. Le Count, Private John J. Monti and Private James H. King, Jr.
>
> By 1130 the artillery fire directed at this hill ceased. At 1145 Captain Pack of 1st Battalion came through with several men. Said he had heard that the 1st Battalion was to evacuate their [unnumbered] hill as best as the individuals were able. This is in conflict with orders

we have received (signed 0955) from regiment, which we have not understood, to the effect that we are to move onto the 1st Battalion hill.

Headquarters Company has for duty 13 officers and 107 enlisted men, 3 officers and 16 enlisted men attached. Lieutenant [William L.] Wilson with his F Company platoon reported in about 1130 but has had no contact with his company – though he saw Lieutenant Tom Collins of his company at the regimental aid station (...) We moved out with E Company in the lead, F Company, Battalion CP, Headquarters Company and D Company. Another climb. It took at least three hours to get everybody there. [B and HQ Companies of] the 1st Battalion had not moved out by the time we reached our hill. Two dead paratroopers and one German were in the immediate area and the dead of other units everywhere. The artillery became particularly stiff about 1700, one barrage was constant for two minutes. Other casualties, but not yet officially reported. Colonel Tucker has set up in our Battalion CP area (many of regimental staff are casualties). Our phone is through.[589]

The situation on Hill 424 started to look graver while the walking wounded had left the unnumbered hill. Williams, realizing casualties were mounting, ordered Captain Charles W. Duncan by radio to reinforce them with his B Company. Colonel Reuben H. Tucker remembered that "the 1st Battalion suffered many casualties from enemy field artillery timed fire. Four separate and distinct attacks by the enemy from the north, east and west of our position, were driven back, with heavy casualties resulting for the enemy. It is estimated that the enemy forces amounted to one regiment, supported by 88mm guns, heavy howitzers and mortars. At least three enemy tanks [*Sturmgeschütze*] brought fire down on position. Our casualties were comparatively light. Evacuation of the wounded and supplying the troops was a major problem, since any movement of the supply train by ambulances was done under enemy observed field artillery fire."[590]

Private Howard Albert, one of the medics, received a Silver Star for administering first aid and evacuating wounded paratroopers "to safety while under extremely heavy and accurate artillery fire without regard for his own personal safety. His courageous conduct was instrumental in saving the lives of many wounded comrades."[591]

Walker wrote in his diary that day, "General Ridgway came to see me and asked for the 180th Infantry Regiment to reinforce Tucker's command. Army Headquarters refused this but VI Corps directed Tucker to hold out until night, then to return to the vicinity of Albanella. Later, Tucker's troopers found the going easier and occupied both Hills 315 and 424. He was told to remain there overnight."[592]

At around 1730 hours, a messenger from U.S. VI Corps headquarters reached Tucker on the unnumbered hill. The message contained an order to withdraw to Albanella as Major General Ernest Dawley feared that the 504th would be soon surrounded. Tucker decided to ignore this order after the hard fighting his regiment had endured, since naval artillery played its part from that Friday afternoon: "We were able to set up our mortars and give the Germans some of that as well as rifle fire. We established communications with the main force and our big guns came into action. Their accuracy was deadly and the Germans did not like to take more than they give. American bombers and fighter bombers came over delivering more wallops and our naval guns helped the cause along.

"Our position on the hill was still pretty precarious tho and I was ordered to evacuate under cover of darkness Friday night. I sent a message back that we hadn't come back to retreat and talked the high command out of enforcing the order."[593]

The VI Corps' order to retreat from Hill 424, Garrison recalled, "was much to our disgust as we have the hill and are not suffering undue casualties. We have water, but no rations have come through to us. Contact by phone was finally established with rear higher echelons and we are to remain in this area unless otherwise notified. The 81mm mortar platoon and F Company intact have caught up with us and are in place. One platoon of F Company under Lieutenant Wilson remained on the hill we left.

"Sergeant [Dale E.] Decker of this platoon was killed during afternoon by an airburst. One incident of the early evening was the use of a heavy (U.S. Navy) barrage directed at Altavilla directly below us and too close for comfort. Private [Vince A.] Madona of E Company was seriously wounded. Two slight wounds in F Company. In Headquarters, one man killed – Private Harry [A.] Wensil."[594]

That evening, a sound-powered phone line was laid down from VI Corps to the Regimental CP. Dawley once again expressed his fear that the 504th would soon be cut off and ordered Tucker to withdraw. Tucker's legendary response was "Retreat, Hell! Send me my other battalion!" referring to Major William R. Beall's 3rd Battalion—less H Company—that had landed by sea and was held in Corps reserve near Paestum. Beall had just assumed command after Major Emory S. Adams, Jr. had contracted malaria.

"During the morning we dried out and [in the evening] moved to a village on a hilltop half way to the front," recalled 1st Lieutenant Thomas E. Utterback of the 3rd Battalion on September 17. His Headquarters Company had made a wet landing on the beach the night before. "I was now a company commander and thus was taken forward on recon with the Major [Beall]. From the top of the hill at Albanella we gazed into the valley between there and Altavilla, and it was plenty hot. Eighty-eight shells were coming in all over the place, and mortars were crunching in too. No wonder I didn't smile when I heard that we were crossing that valley that night."[595]

Early that evening, the 3rd Battalion was returned to regimental control, and Tucker ordered them to take over Hill 344 from Lieutenant William L. Wilson's F Company Platoon. Private Earl S. Oldfather of Captain George J. Watts's G Company was "told we were going about 4 miles to Albanella. Left our musette bags here. Boy, what a hike! (...) Just on the other side of the town we stopped. Went to a house to get water and grapes. An old man and woman were handing it out. Told to dig in – minute later we moved on. Its amazing how much the human body can stand. Marched along high cliffs – one step to the side and you would have been a goner. Hiked all night."[596]

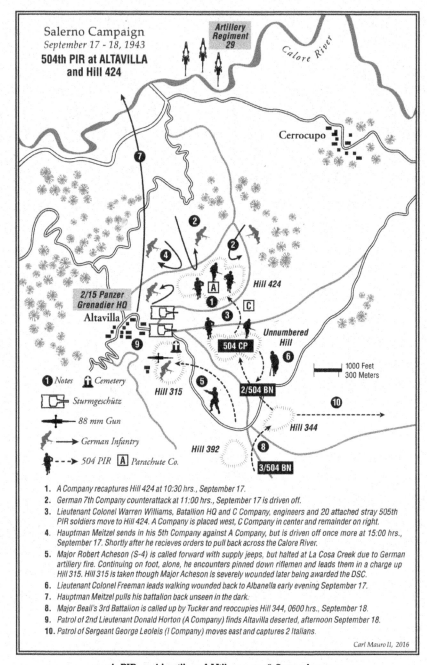

Salerno Campaign
September 17 - 18, 1943
**504th PIR at ALTAVILLA
and Hill 424**

Artillery
Regiment
29

Calore River

Cerrocupo

⑦

②

②

④

Hill 424

Ⓐ

2/15 Panzer
Grenadier HQ
Altavilla

①

③

Ⓒ

Unnumbered
Hill

504 CP

⑥

⑨

⑤

Hill 315

2/504 BN

⑩

1000 Feet
300 Meters

① *Notes* ⛪ *Cemetery*

Sturmgeschütz

88 mm Gun

German Infantry

504 PIR Ⓐ *Parachute Co.*

Hill 344

Hill 392

⑧

3/504 BN

1. *A Company recaptures Hill 424 at 10:30 hrs., September 17.*
2. *German 7th Company counterattack at 11:00 hrs., September 17 is driven off.*
3. *Lieutenant Colonel Warren Williams, Battalion HQ and C Company, engineers and 20 attached stray 505th PIR soldiers move to Hill 424. A Company is placed west, C Company in center and remainder on right.*
4. *Hauptman Meitzel sends in his 5th Company against A Company, but is driven off once more at 15:00 hrs., September 17. Shortly after he recieves orders to pull back across the Calore River.*
5. *Major Robert Acheson (S-4) is called forward with supply jeeps, but halted at La Cosa Creek due to German artillery fire. Continuing on foot, alone, he encounters pinned down riflemen and leads them in a charge up Hill 315. Hill 315 is taken though Major Acheson is severely wounded later being awarded the DSC.*
6. *Lieutenant Colonel Freeman leads walking wounded back to Albanella early evening September 17.*
7. *Hauptman Meitzel pulls his battalion back unseen in the dark.*
8. *Major Beall's 3rd Battalion is called up by Tucker and reoccupies Hill 344, 0600 hrs., September 18.*
9. *Patrol of 2nd Lieutenant Donald Horton (A Company) finds Altavilla deserted, afternoon September 18.*
10. *Patrol of Sergeant George Leoleis (I Company) moves east and captures 2 Italians.*

Carl Mauro II, 2016

504th PIR at Altavilla and Hill 424 17-18 September 1943

CHAPTER 27

STRIKE AND HOLD

Salerno Beachhead

SEPTEMBER 18-SEPTEMBER 30, 1943

P rivate Earl S. Oldfather recorded it was well after midnight as G Company "arrived atop a mountain. Other soldiers were there. We dug in. The Germans were shelling the other hill where the 2nd Battalion is. I was on ration detail this afternoon. Had 6 mules – loaded them up with K-rations and water cans – took same to the 2nd Battalion. Captain [Andrew W.] Row was in charge. Two mules fell – what a time. Saw 3 dead soldiers – 2 troopers, 1 infantry. Made two trips – then back to our area. Got K-rations. Our platoon moved over the hill – dug in."[597]

First Lieutenant Thomas E. Utterback of Headquarters Company recalled of Albanella, "In this position we were to dig in and prepare to hold for the rest of the division which was in trouble and might have to retreat. Colonel Tucker, commanding officer of the 504th, was told to retreat during the night. He replied, 'To hell with retreating, just send up my other battalion.' So we went up during the night, and by noon the next day the situation had stabilized. Tucker's reaction became a battle cry for the 504th. In case of doubt, charge and get it over with. Just at first light we made contact with the troops on the mountain on the other side. There we were introduced in a grand way to what 88s can be like."[598]

By 0600 hours on September 18, Major William R. Beall and his 3rd Battalion were on Hill 344 south of the unnumbered hill. "Going up the hill we took an awful lot of artillery fire. The ground was soft enough to dig holes," remembered Private Francis X. Keefe of I Company.[599]

"A few artillery rounds came in early last night but no action thereafter," wrote Lieutenant Chester A. Garrison on September 18. "There was little action during the day. Artillery fire came in fairly solid about 1340. Three men and one officer (Lieutenant [John E.] Scheaffer of D Company) were casualties. E Company had three men hit ([Privates Arvil H.] Webster, [Leonard W.] Smith and [Lawrence O.] Frenning) and one man killed – Pfc. Thomas T. Gillilan. Captain [Ralph N.] Bogle was here in the morning but has not yet cleared our area of the dead.

"Our patrols have not contacted the enemy. The 1st Battalion has patrols in Altavilla. D Company believed they had spotted a group of camouflaged tanks or halftracks. Artillery refused the mission. Patrols disclosed they were only vineyards. K-rations finally reached us by 1800, 1/3 ration which worked throughout the night. Lieutenant [Ernest L.] Walker is now acting S-4 as Major [Henry B.] Frank has gone to regiment. The rest of the regimental headquarters has moved into our area. Patrols to our front 4 miles reported no enemy."[600]

Colonel Reuben H. Tucker had transferred Major Frank, a supernumerary officer like Major Julian A. Cook, from the 2nd Battalion to regimental headquarters as the new S-3. Tucker wrote about September 18: "No supplies were received until the late afternoon of the 18th. It was necessary to use carrying parties and mules requisitioned from the natives to supply the troops. Well water was available, but the wells were under constant enemy artillery fire."[601]

Sergeant Robert J. Lowe of A Company volunteered with another man to obtain water from a well for the 2nd Platoon at the bottom of the wooded hill in "no man's land" for the 2nd Platoon. Lowe recalled:

> We rounded up 17 canteens and started down crawling all the way in hopes the enemy wouldn't see us. Finally, we reached the well and had just filled two

canteens when a machine gun opened up on us. It was so hot we had to drop the canteens and return to our lines. We were lucky to get back at all.

Then we really got mad. Some of the guys were beginning to suffer from thirst. There was water – and our own canteens – so near and yet so far. We made two more attempts. Every time we would get to the well that one machine gun would cut loose and drive us back. There was only one thing to do. The next time I took several men and worked down through the woods to the gunner's flank while the others started for the well from the front to distract him.

It worked like a charm. He was ready to blaze away again on our men when I cracked him from the side. I killed him with the first shot and the assistant gunner ran off. We all ran out, filled the canteens and made it back to our lines.[602]

At dawn on September 18, a patrol of the 1st Platoon of A Company, consisting of 2nd Lieutenant Reneau G. Breard and Privates Amos R. Cundiff, Willard H. Edstrom, Irving T. Fairbrother, and Barney Walters moved down the side of the ridge into Altavilla. War correspondent Reiman Morin wrote an article about their experiences:

It was dark and they neither saw nor heard any human beings in the streets. Then behind the door of a house they heard voices. They rapped on the door softly, and after a moment a shivering peasant opened it. They asked the man some questions. Before each answer he hesitated. No information.

After the peasant closed the door again the men heard someone speaking German inside the house. They broke in the door and captured eight German soldiers.

The terrified Italian cried out that the Germans had stood behind him touching his neck with a pistol and told him what to say to the Americans.

While they were approaching one of the Germans suddenly yelled. Some of the others yelled too. They were trying to draw fire and they did draw fire. The street was suddenly alive with bullets and the sounds of Germans moving, but the patrol slipped away and made its way back up the slope.[603]

A second A Company combat patrol led by 2nd Lieutenant Donald F. Horton in the afternoon did not encounter any Germans at all. That same day, two fatal casualties were sustained in B Company: Pfc. Myer Hesselberg and Private Vernon A. Weeks.

A sleeping paratrooper from A Company on Hill 424,
photographed by Albert Clark. Courtesy: Albert Clark

The morning of September 19, all appeared to be quiet. "We were elated when we heard silence," recalled Private David K. Finney of Headquarters and Headquarters Company. "Being so quiet didn't feel natural to the ears but we quickly adjusted."[604] Garrison recalled that "suddenly it ceased. The quiet was eerie. I waited without moving. Little noises of pebbles falling suggested that troopers were moving to peek out of their foxholes to discover that shell holes pitted the area between the foxholes but neither killed nor wounded anybody. A shell can be effectively only with a foxhole hit."[605]

The day passed by real quiet. Garrison recorded in the battalion journal, "No action all day long. Regimental medics have moved in with 2nd Battalion medics. Supplies are beginning to stream in. Cigarettes, toilet articles, D-rations and C-rations along with K-rations came in during the afternoon. Captain Bogle has a detail clearing our area of the dead. All of the American dead have been removed. Details from the 143rd Regiment (36th Infantry Division) were looking for their men.

"During noon, General Ridgway visited the area to see Colonel Tucker. He expressed his approval of our maneuvers and accomplishments. Several other high ranking officers from different outfits and newspaper men also were in the area. Major Danielson called a CO's meeting in the evening after attending a battalion CO's meeting. We are to pull out of this area to return to our first Italian bivouac area."[606]

Seymour Korman of the *Chicago Tribune* entered the town on September 19 and wrote that "Altavilla was as heavily pounded as any city I have seen in Tunisia, Pantelleria, and Sicily. It had been a No Man's land for the contesting forces, each trying to prevent the other from controlling it. Shells, bombs, and mortars had torn up the streets, toppled buildings, and ripped out the utilities. There wasn't a yard of level ground.

"The first reports had been that most of the civilian residents had evacuated. This was found to be untrue. These civilians were pinned down by the cross-fire and were unable to get out of the city, and some of them had been killed. The Allied Military Government (AMG) already was on the job to help resurrect the city."[607]

Oldfather of G Company wrote in his diary, "Corporal [Paul D.] Wilson came after us – said we were moving out. Back to our holes after equipment. Order was changed – back to the outpost. Company I came thru while I was on guard. The officer in charge didn't like the way I challenged."[608]

Beall dispatched a six-man strong combat patrol from I Company led by Sergeant George "Greek" Leoleis to the Calore River, a mere three miles east of Hill 344, to find out what the Germans were up to. "We went out late afternoon and walked across a number of hills and through a valley down to the river," recalled Keefe. "We followed some German wires up a hill. It must have been a German observation post. Along the river bank we saw two Italian soldiers bathing in the river. We asked if they had seen any 'Tedeschi.' They said they had seen some a couple of days earlier. We broke it down in the conversation that they tried to get back to their homes in Sicily since the war for them was over.

"A little higher up a hill was a completely deserted town on the river. We saw a German staff car on the other side going north. Sergeant Leoleis said we could wade across, but I stayed on the western side as we had orders not to cross the river. He and the others went while I stayed with the Italians. They returned after a while from across the river and reported they hadn't seen any Germans. We took the two Italians back to battalion headquarters as it was getting dark."[609]

On September 20, the regiment was finally relieved from its positions by elements of the 36th Infantry Division. The 3rd Battalion—once again led by Major Emory S. Adams, Jr., who had recovered sufficiently from his malaria—moved to Blue Beach near Paestum in the evening and slept in holes on the beach. "Got ready to move again," wrote Oldfather, "marched to the side of the hill – waited. This afternoon we started walking – trucks are supposed to pick us up. One did come along. Woods and I got on – sure crowded. More beautiful scenery. Kind of rough riding. Back thru Albanella. Truck left us off at the area we left the 17th – that was wrong. Started walking down the road – Colonel of the 325th stopped – said we were loading on LCI's with them – trucks be along after us. (…) Finally got to the beach."[610]

Altavilla proved to be a test case for 504th Regimental Combat Team. Despite being cut off from other VI Corps units, with little or no radio communication, being surrounded and shelled by the Germans, they held on. In the six days fighting near Albanella and Altavilla, the regiment lost twenty-two men, and 150 paratroopers were wounded. It was an indication that the struggle ahead to the heart of the Third Reich would be long and hard.

The 504th RCT—including C Company of the 307th Airborne Engineer Battalion—received great credit from Lieutenant General Mark Clark for rescuing his beachhead. But despite that praise, many paratroopers regretted the cancellation of Giant II. They believed it was a missed opportunity to liberate Rome. Tucker, however, remained proud on the outstanding performance of his unit, even though he knew that "the heights could not have been held without the superior support of the 36th Division Field Artillery."[611] His exclamation, "Retreat, hell! Send me my other battalion!" was epitomized in the motto that the 504th Regimental Combat Team adopted: Strike and Hold.

Hauptmann Helmut Meitzel received a Knights Cross—the highest German medal—for his leadership at Altavilla, whereas his opponent was awarded the Distinguished Service Cross: "Colonel Tucker observed that the enemy was digging in on Hill 424, Army objective of the 1st Battalion of his regiment, the advance of which had been delayed by terrain, organized a small group of twenty-three men, and with utter disregard for his own safety, Colonel Tucker led this small group through heavy enemy artillery fire, attacked and drove the enemy from Hill 424. In this action five of the men became casualties, but Colonel Tucker and the remaining eighteen men held Hill 424 against enemy counterattacks and against enemy forces that were retreating in front of the 1st Battalion, until the 1st Battalion was able to occupy and hold the hill. By his heroic actions, Colonel Tucker enabled the 1st Battalion to attain its important Army objective."[612]

Captured soldiers of Hauptmann Helmut Meitzel's 2nd Battalion of the 15th
Panzer Grenadier Regiment at Altavilla. Courtesy: Mandle family

Colonel Reuben Tucker stands next to Lieutenant General Mark Clark at Castelvetrano
Airfield, December 8, 1943. Fourth from the left 1st Lt. William Kellogg of C
Company, 307th AEB. All were awarded the DSC by President Franklin D.
Roosevelt - in Tucker's case for his leadership at Altavilla. Courtesy: U.S. Army

Major General Fred L. Walker, the 36th Infantry Division commander, told Tucker and his paratroopers they had performed "a grand job over unbelieveably difficult terrain and against insuperiable odds." The journalist, Korman, returned to the devastated town of Altavilla and asked Tucker for his comments on the battle since he had left. "With added forces I went up the hill again," related Tucker to Korman. "The *Boche* [Germans] started giving us the business in a big way, using 88s, tank destroyer shells, mortars, machine guns, and machine pistol and rifle fire. We got into our foxholes, but whenever we had a chance we came out and threw some stuff back at them. That afternoon – Friday – we were able to set up our mortars and give the Germans some of that as well as rifle fire. (...)

"Our position on the hill was still pretty precarious tho and I was ordered to evacuate under cover of darkness Friday night. I sent a message back that we hadn't come back [to Hill 424] to retreat and talked the high command out of enforcing the order. We took lots of shelling Friday night and some more Saturday morning, but by Saturday afternoon the Germans couldn't take much more of the beating we were delivering. Their fire slackened and stopped and Saturday night some of our patrols entered Altavilla."[613]

Meanwhile, a number of changes took place on a higher level. Major General Ernest P. Dawley, the VI Corps commander, was relieved and replaced by Major General John P. Lucas. His staff was shifted to lead the operations in the northern sector of the Fifth Army beachhead, while the II Corps staff came over from Sicily to the southern sector. Major General Geoffrey Keyes, the corps commander, ordered the 504th Parachute Infantry Regiment to send patrols in the area while the unit rested and refitted. The Regimental CP was in the town of Roccadaspide.

"Battalion commanders meeting at 1000," wrote Garrison on September 21. "Major Danielson returned with the information that the battalion was to be prepared to move by 1400. We are the extreme right flank of the II Corps, to patrol the area to the south of Castelcivita."[614]

Before the 3rd Battalion troopers—who had camped overnight on the beach—boarded an LST to travel to the Sorrento Peninsula, they had to wait for several hours in the morning and afternoon. Keefe remembered that he and others of I Company "liberated" ration boxes of the partially sunken ship.

"On the LST transferring us from the Salerno beachhead to Minori," wrote Corporal Francis W. McLane of I Company, "I had a foolish altercation with Lieutenant Willis J. Ferrill. It was around noon and I went to a drinking fountain located on the right side of the ship at the foot of a stairway. Lieutenant Ferrill, at the request of the ship's captain, was directing people away from the area. This was to keep the passages clear. I, of course, went to the duplicate fountain, on the other side. I was filling my canteen when the lieutenant appeared. He was pretty ticked off and told me he wouldn't forget this and when were not so involved, he would me instruct me as to what it meant to ignore an officer's orders.

"Time went by and after a period of combat action, we landed in a rest area. Sergeant [Lloyd V.] Engebretzen had gone to collect the PX rations. When he returned he handed me a carton of Lucky Strikes, saying that Lieutenant Ferrill told him to give them to me. At that time I smoked Camels. Ferrill smoked Luckies. That was the end of the water fountain incident and another notch up in my respect for Lieutenant Ferrill. We sailed up the coast and landed at a town named Minori, walked a short distance to its twin town Maiori."[615]

Near Chiunzi Pass on the Sorrento Peninsula, H Company was incorporated again by the 3rd Battalion. "We had constant patrols because the Germans were said to be infiltrating dressed as civilians," recalled McLane. "My patrol (…) went up to an ancient castle right on the pass. Everything beyond that was exposed to direct artillery fire."[616]

That same day, Lieutenant Colonel Wilbur M. Griffith's 376th Parachute Field Artillery Battalion was finally unloaded on the beach near Paestum. They had been awaiting shipment by both glider and sea for weeks and every time the plans had changed. Tucker was glad to see them as they made his 504th Regimental Combat Team nearly complete. From now on they would provide artillery support in all the campaigns that lay ahead.

The 3rd Battalion moved up to the front line on September 22, and Private Darrell G. Harris of the Demolition Squad recalled that "as we moved up a road toward Chiunzi Pass (which came to be known as '88 Pass'), we were under almost constant German artillery fire. There were shouts for 'medics' up and down the line after every shell burst. Sometime during this campaign was the first time I remember seeing paratrooper bodies being hauled by the trailer load behind a jeep."[617]

On September 24, Harris was "dug in near a hilltop. I had just opened a pack of K-rations when I heard 'incoming mail,' and I dove for my foxhole, leaning my rifle against a tree. When the shelling was over, I found that my rifle was cut completely in two by a piece of shrapnel. Only the sling held the two halves together. It was here that we lost our battalion commander who was suffocated when a near miss caved in his foxhole."[618]

The deep foxhole of Major Beall, the 3rd Battalion executive officer, took a direct hit. Major Adams was one of those who started to dig him out with his hands and tried to massage Beall's heart but to no avail. The last song that had been played when William Beall danced with his wife Jean just before leaving the States, "Sentimental Journey," had come true. The death of Beall was not only devastating news for his wife Jean and their children but also for everyone in the 504th Parachute Infantry Regiment who knew him. When Adams informed Major General Matthew B. Ridgway and stated he would write Beall's widow, Ridgway looked at him sternly and said sharply, "*I'll* write his wife."[619]

The Germans nearly broke through the 3rd Battalion's defensive position that afternoon, but some H Company troopers saved the day. Private John J. Foley, Jr. was placed with another soldier on an outpost overlooking a bridge that was demolished by 1st Lieutenant Carl W. Kappel, Staff Sergeant Leonard Harmon, Jr., and Privates Wilton A. Baker and Jack O. Desideri in the face of nearing German troops. The bridge span crossed a 120-foot deep chasm and was the only road connection from the German-held plain south of Naples and the American taskforce in the mountains north of Maiori. Within two minutes, the bridge was wired for demolition and blown. Baker was decorated with the Silver Star for his part in the destruction of the bridge: "Under observed enemy rifle and machine gun fire Private Baker placed explosives on a bridge, demolishing it and rendering it useless to the enemy, contributing to the successful withdrawal of the Company to which he was attached."[620]

"We saw the bridge being blown up and figured it was done by our troops," recalled Foley. "After the bridge was blown our platoon withdrew through a mountain tunnel, but we were not told of this maneuver. I could then see some German engineers who tried to fix the bridge, but they couldn't without a lot of equipment – which they didn't have. It took me and the other trooper about four or five days until we spotted a jeep coming out of a tunnel and managed to rejoin H Company."[621]

In the morning of September 25, after a few days of rest and resupply, Tucker finally received word to board LCIs on Red Beach near Paestum with his regiment to join his 3rd Battalion on the Sorrento Peninsula. Garrison wrote about the preparations for this move:

> Company commanders are meeting in preparation for a problem given by Division. The 1st Battalion will go through it tomorrow night, the 2nd Battalion the next night. At 2130 sudden call from regiment for all battalion staff to report to regiment immediately. The 504 (1st Battalion, 2nd Battalion, and Regimental Headquarters) to move out tomorrow to join the 3rd Battalion (...) Company commanders meeting at 2300.

> September 26 – Up at 0500, left bivouac by 0700, entrucked to beach by 0815 at Paestum. Boarded LCIs (6 per battalion) by wading from beach to gangplank (chest deep). Moderately rough trip. Major Danielson went with Colonel Tucker by jeep. Landed at Maiori, two English light cruisers firing into hills. (...) Entrucked on 14 vehicles and drove up the valley into the hills. Steep climb. Established battalion headquarters along road, E Company in reserve, F and D Companies up into ridge. In bivouac by 1530. Dug in in vineyards, most of E Company went into ridge position about 2130. Occasional mortar or artillery fire on

our positions, also some rifle fire in area. Light rain. Relieved the 2nd Battalion, 325th Glider Infantry.[622]

Finney of Headquarters and Headquarters Company had a different hike up than the 3rd Battalion just days earlier: "We walked most of the day and were happy not having to hide and sweat out incoming shells and pot shots from snipers. About two hours before dark, we took up positions at Chiunzi Pass."[623]

On September 28, the 504th Regimental Combat Team moved out in the early afternoon into the coastal plain south of Naples under command of British X Corps. Oldfather saw from his position how an armored column was struck by artillery fire: "The Germans are shelling the road – the convoy was stopped – trucks all along the way. Don't know what the damage is. I'm writing this at a height of 24,000 feet – so I'm told. Oh yes, we could hear bells ringing in the valley when the Allies went in. Sure wish I could take a picture of this valley and the volcano in the background. We moved down into the valley this afternoon – didn't take the road – a trail. Sure a long ways down. Got caught in a hail storm."[624]

Troopers of the 2nd Platoon of A Company in Castallamare drying their clothes, September 1943. Courtesy: Albert Clark

On October 1, Tucker's troopers entered Naples, and the final objective of Operation Avalanche was achieved. "We decided to stay in one of the hangars at the airfield," remembered Keefe of I Company, "but soon engineers told us to move out as it had not yet been checked for booby-traps. We then slept in house doorways of some apartment buildings between the airport and the cemetery. Some squads were kept at the airport however. Muri and I were twice sent out patrolling the street that first night."[625]

Utterback, the Headquarters Company Commander of the 3rd Battalion, recalled that "we were in Naples for some time helping root out German troops and Fascist sympathizers and establishing order in general. The harbor became jammed with our shipping. Airports around Mt. Vesuvius became busy Allied air bases. A typhus epidemic broke out among the native Italians, so we were all given shots."[626]

The regiment would stay over three weeks in Naples to rest and recuperate before their next step in the liberation of Italy. Captain Robert E. Kile of Battle Creek, Florida joined them as a replacement officer in December 1943: "I never forget the mountains around Venafro and the bearded dirty Willies and Joes holed up there. I arrived there in the middle of the night and we managed to get out ahead of the lines and expected 'to get it' from our own troops at any time." Kile was sent to G Company: "Most of them I didn't have enough contact with to get to know personally but they were a gutsy bunch and I wouldn't give anything for the experience with G Company."[627]

Kile lasted a little more than a month until his landing ship was bombed as it approached the beach at Anzio. "I was never quite sure what the ship was that took me back to Naples," he wrote afterward, "but I do remember two men talking and their Limey language gave me the impression it was a British ship. (...) Apparently the only fatal casualties were from the gun crew next to where I was standing. (...) Sergeant [Mike] Vincent and the G Company clerk came to the Naples General Hospital a couple of times to see me. I was the first Anzio casualty back, and they naturally wanted to know what had happened to G Company."[628]

If the reader wants to continue the regimental history, I advise to read *Spearhead of the Fifth Army*, covering late September 1943 to early April 1944. Subsequently, *The Battle of the Bridges* will enable you to pick up the story from April 1944 to November 1944. Book 4 in this regimental history series, *Blocking Kampfgruppe Peiper*, covers November 1944 throughout the Battle of the Bulge to the Huertgen Forest. *End of an Odyssey* finalizes the epic saga of Tucker's troopers from February 1945 across the Rhine and Elbe Rivers into Berlin, closing with the New York Victory Parade. By then, Colonel Reuben H. Tucker could look back with enormous pride; showing the regiment he had activated and trained since the spring of 1942 had completed an inspiring saga. May the reader tell and keep alive the WWII legacy of the 504th Parachute Infantry Regiment. Strike and Hold!

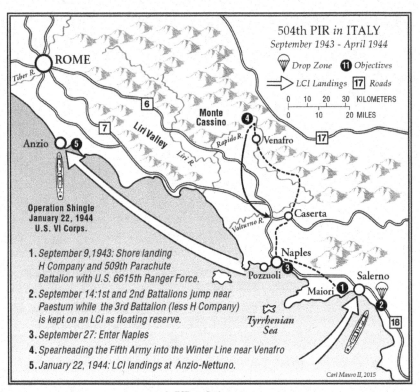

504th PIR in ITALY
September 1943 - April 1944

🪂 Drop Zone   ⬤11 *Objectives*
⇒ *LCI Landings*   17 *Roads*

0   10   20   30 KILOMETERS
0   10   20 MILES

ROME

Tiber R.

Monte Cassino

Liri Valley

Rapido R.

Liri R.

Venafro

17

6

7

Anzio ⬤5

**Operation Shingle
January 22, 1944
U.S. VI Corps.**

Volturno R.

Caserta

4

1. *September 9, 1943: Shore landing H Company and 509th Parachute Battalion with U.S. 6615th Ranger Force.*
2. *September 14: 1st and 2nd Battalions jump near Paestum while the 3rd Battalion (less H Company) is kept on an LCI as floating reserve.*
3. *September 27: Enter Naples*
4. *Spearheading the Fifth Army into the Winter Line near Venafro*
5. *January 22, 1944: LCI landings at Anzio-Nettuno.*

Naples

Pozzuoli 3

Maiori 1

Salerno 🪂

2

18

Tyrrhenian Sea

Carl Mauro II, 2015

504th PIR in Italy 1943-1944

CHAPTER 28

PRISONERS OF WAR

Oflag 64 and Stalag II-B

JULY 1943-MAY 1945

T he first paratroopers who were captured fell into enemy hands during the first night of Operation Husky on July 10, 1943. Of all the men who were captured, these men may have been the most unfortunate ones—knowing they would never participate in any of the battles that lay ahead and, moreover, spend many months, if not years, behind the barbed wire. Among the first ones to be captured were several 3rd Battalion officers. Lieutenant Herman Littman of H Company was first "sent up to [Oflag III] Luckenwalde and put in solitary by the Krauts in order to extract information about my unit. When I wouldn't answer his questions day by day the interrogator blew his stack."[629] Littman was eventually transported to Oflag 64.

Lieutenant Louis W. Otterbein had also been captured on Sicily and was interrogated in Oflag III Luckenwalde: "A Nazi captain used every method on me from cajolery to mental torture. Daily my life was threatened."[630] For long weeks, he was kept in solitary confinement and contracted a severe case of jaundice due to the lack of proper food. Finally, the Germans learned they couldn't extract any information from Otterbein that they had been expecting to obtain and sent him to Oflag 64, a former school complex in Szubin, Poland. It was improvised in 1939 into an army camp for a Polish cavalry unit by placing wooden barracks on the school grounds. The Germans converted the cavalry base into a prisoner of war camp and renamed the village Alt-burgund. They initially used the camp for British, French, and Soviet POWs, but in June 1943, the *offizierslager* was renamed Oflag 64 and the original "inhabitants" were moved to another camp. Now it would be used to house American officers only. Twenty Russian POWs performed menial tasks for the German guards, while ten British orderlies and eighteen enlisted Americans would assist the American officers.

The next officer who arrived in December 1943 was Lieutenant Colonel Charles W. Kouns, who had already on Sicily made plans to escape along with British Lieutenant Eric Davies of the 2nd Battalion South Staffordshire Regiment. Davies's glider crash-landed during Operation Husky in the vicinity of Catania, and he was captured. He was separated from his men, and during the first night, he was placed in a cell with Kouns. Davies recalled, "He had some U.S. gold seal dollars with him and we all but had the sergeant of the guard bribed, but he was afraid of the private soldiers, and nothing came of it. During the day I had been interrogated in style, was taken into a room with the window closed so as to be in twilight. The interrogating officer sat behind a desk and tried all the usual approaches. The two sentries fixed bayonets and loaded their rifles with elaborate flourishes, and because my identity discs had been taken off me on capture he threatened to have me shot as a spy. Later he tried to bribe me and then the effect of flattery and finally that he would have me shot. I told him to go to hell and get on with it, that I had given my name rank and number and that was all he was going to get. There was a big map on the wall, and I was able to get out of him that we were in Piazza Armerina."[631]

From Piazza Armerina, Kouns, Davies, Pilot Officer Ian Samuels, and Lieutenant R.G. Williams of the 2nd South Staffords were transported in trucks to Messina. Davies remembered that

> twice on route we were machine gunned by [P-38] Lightnings. When this happened the Italian guards dived for the ditch covering the trucks with their rifles and threatening to shoot the first man to get off the truck. Luckily we were not hit. Along the route we saw

groups of burnt-out vehicles which had been shot up by Allied aircraft.

At Messina the Germans were ferrying men and vehicles across the Straits, so we were taken south of the town and lodged in a jail. There we were joined by other prisoners. For 24 hours we had had no food or water.

During the trip to Messina Colonel Kouns and I planned an escape from the vehicles by cutting the canvas and jumping when the trucks slowed down. The hole was discovered and sewn up. We cut it again, and again it was sewn up. The rear truck was brought up to within 30 yards with Tommygunners sitting on the front wings covering us. Two men sat on the front wings of our truck facing backwards with the same task. (...)

The next day we were taken across the Straits in assault craft after nearly being lynched by the civilian population in Messina. The trip only took 20 minutes and gave us no time to put Colonel Kouns' plan - to rush the Italian guards and German crew and take over the boat - into operation. After the crossing we were taken by rail to P.W. camp at Capua, where the officers were put in a separate compound. It was then the 16th July, and we remained there until about mid-August. We occupied our time planning escapes and assembling escape kits.[632]

Kouns continued his story from here: "On August 27th I was sent to Chiete, where I remained until October 2nd. On October 3rd, while enroute to Germany, I jumped from the train and remained at large for nine days, when I was recaptured at Riva. Italian civilians were nice to me during the nine days at liberty.

"I was transferred to Moosburg, Germany, where I was kept in solitary confinement for twenty days. While enroute to [Oflag III] Luckenwalde, I cut my way out of a freight car and escaped near Munich. I bribed civilians for food, but could get no aid otherwise."[633]

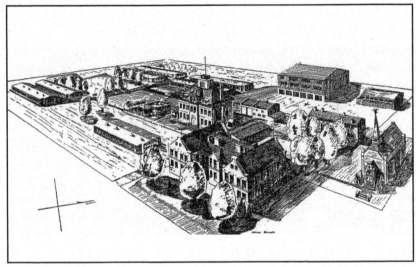

OFLAG 64 was the camp where most of the captured officers of the 504th Parachute Infantry Regiment were held prisoner. Courtesy: James Bickers

Although it was certainly on almost every officer's mind, finding means to escape was not the only activity at Oflag 64. There were educational courses in French, German, Italian, Spanish, Art, and Music. The Red Cross supplied not only Red Cross food parcels but also clothing and Y.M.C.A. items for setting up education and recreational facilities. Musical instruments, textbooks and novels, notebooks, basketballs, footballs, tennis rackets, and hockey sticks—it all made life more bearable in the camp. Otterbein was the stage manager of each theater production in Oflag 64. Although the resources were meager, he always managed to provide with his team a good stage for every performance that was given. Littman organized a weight lifting squad, and Bill Fabian, who had never worked with oils before, painted a number of portraits.

Compared to the hardships that the captured enlisted paratroopers were subjected to, the officers had for the most part an easier time.

Non-commissioned officers and enlisted men ended up far more widely spread over Germany and Poland. The Germans had created four types of camps as the war broke out: the *oflags* for officers, the *stalags*—a contraction of two words, *stamm* and *lager* (main camp)—the *stalag luft* camps for the thousands of shot-down Allied air crews, and finally, Oflag III and Stalag III at Luckenwalde near Berlin as specialized interrogation centers.

Sergeant Edward Haider of I Company was transported to Stalag II-B Hammerstein in East Prussia: "We had heard that this was the worst stalag in all of Germany because of the mean staff of guards. Upon our arrival we were unloaded from the train at the camp and immediately counted. They counted us three times before they were satisfied we were all there. (...) We were all whistled out of the barracks eight to ten times a day and made to stand in lines, behind one another, just to be counted."[634]

Private William R. "Buffalo Bill" Grisez, the Regimental Demolition Platoon, also stayed in Stalag II-B and worked on three different farms. From French forced laborers he obtained a white towel and, using a red and a blue pencil, worked for several nights by candlelight to create an American flag. Grisez carefully stored it under his clothes in case the Germans would search his bunk or barracks. He planned to use it when the liberation came to identify himself as an American.[635]

On August 28, one paratrooper, Pfc. Franklin P. Reed, was killed by German guards along with a soldier of the 168th Infantry Regiment, Pfc. Dean W. Halbert. Reed and Halbert were assigned to a *Kommando* (work party) at Gambin in the district of Stolp. While working in the fields, they asked their guard permission to relieve themselves in the edge of the forest. The German consented, and they walked to the forest and disappeared between the trees.

After several minutes, the guard became suspicious, raised the alarm, and ran into the woods to find them. Sometime later, he returned with Halbert and Reed and informed his superior of the incident. Two Kommando guards were then instructed to take the two Americans back to the *Kommando* barracks in Stolp. Several shots were heard after they had disappeared out of sight. The work detachment overheard the guards reporting to their superior that Halbert and Reed had been shot while trying to escape. Prisoners were then ordered to collect the bodies and bring them back to the barracks. These shootings were no exception in Stalag II-B and more would take place in 1943 and 1944.[636]

Private Elmer Kaberlein of H Company kept a diary while being a prisoner at Stalag II-B. Here are some interesting extracts of his story:

August 15, 1943 - Left Hammerstein for Arbeitskommando at Alt-Ristow, near Schlaive. Rode most all day on truck in rain. Arrived at farm late at night. Ate boiled potatoes and drank milk (situation looked good, then).

August 16, 1943 - Got up early in the morning—first job on a farm—stacked wheat in field—10 hours per day. Kinds of work I've done since being on this farm: stack wheat, throw wheat on wagon and pack, stack wheat on pile in field. Put wheat in barn, thrash, rake hay, weed turnips, pull turnips, pull carrots, cover turnips, pick potatoes, cover potatoes, grade potatoes, uncover potatoes, shovel potatoes in several hills, repair road, cut and saw wood, clean stables, work on dung pile, cut straw, haul lime, carry sacks.

December 25, 1943 - CHRISTMAS DAY. (Saturday) No work. Received a #9 box and a special Christmas box. My thoughts were of my wife and my folks all day long.

January 15, 1944 - Received my first letter! It was from Marian (wife), it made me feel so much better.

February 29, 1944 - Met [Corporal] George [C.] Wilson, a Para-trooper from my Company; he was captured February 9th at Anzio, Italy. He told me news of the Company and the outcome of the Sicilian affair.

March 12, 1944 - Went to church at Stalag Chapel.

March 1944 - Given a lagerdienst (freedom from work) good until operation.

March 31, 1944 - Last day of March and the end of a very bad snowy month. It was cold and miserable most every day. I was thankful for not having to work on kommando. During this month I did much reading, thinking of home and sleeping.

April 2, 1944 - Palm Sunday - and I didn't even know it until late in the afternoon. I then layed on my bunk and thought of the Palm Sundays of years gone by. This day my thoughts are especially of my wife and my mother.

April 7, 1944 - Good Friday - the Jerries gave the American Stalag an American Flag and there was a dedication of same in the morning. It was quite a thrill to see Old Glory again and the meaning it has behind it (Freedom). An American Captain gave a little talk about it and the Acting Chaplain led us in prayer on this Good Friday. The dedication was ended by everyone singing "God Bless America."

April 8, 1944 - Regular Saturday inspection in morning. Enrolled in American night school, taking three courses, namely: algebra, commercial law and German.

April 9, 1944 - Easter Sunday and a very beautiful day, sun shining and the air just a little cool (one of the few good weather days I've seen in Germany). Went to church at the Stalag Chapel; while there I visualized being in my own church, and sitting on each side of me were Marian and my mother, and listening to Rev. Frey's sermon. This is my third Easter away from home; here's hoping it'll be the last.

April 20, 1944 - Received letter from mother dated December 9th.

April 30, 1944 - End of another month. The weather for past few weeks was rainy and cold. Spent most of time reading, sleeping and thinking of home.

May 6, 1944 - Saw German film at theater in Hammerstein.

May 13, 1944 - Left Hammerstein, returned to Alt-Ristow kommando.

May 15, 1944 - Began work on farm - planting spuds. Very tired at end of day.

June 6, 1944 - Very good news today - Invasion of France (won't last long now!)

July 9, 1944 - Planted turnips—One year ago jumped at Sicily.

July 11, 1944 - Prisoner one year—(It can't last forever!)

August 17, 1944 - Received 12 letters today - got 8 pictures from Marian.

September 9, 1944 - Third birthday away from home! (28 years old)

September 18, 1944 - Received birthday card from Marian. Saw "our boys" going over today (about 500 [B-17 Flying] Forts), beautiful sight!

September 18-23, 1944 - Picked up spuds all week long - legs and back very stiff - 10 hours per day.

September 30, 1944 - End of another month; won't this war ever end? Picked spuds all week - two days got soaked, worked in rain.

October 20, 1944 - The worst guard we ever had left for the front. Good riddance.

November 9, 1944 - Five men returned to Hammerstein - Dewey Williams [of the 16th Infantry Regiment], [Corporal Oma L.] Fleming [of D Company, captured at Anzio], [Pfc. Charles G.] Haratsis [of H Company, captured on Sicily], [Pfc. Ronald P.] Ellis [of HQ/1 Company, captured east of Nijmegen], Rullo. Received six letters—2 Marian, 1 Dad, 3 Mother.

November 12, 1944 - First snowfall of season.

November 30, 1944 - THANKSGIVING DAY, my second in Germany. Worked eight hours digging reservoir. Bought chicken. Four of us fellows cooked up big meal—fried chicken, potatoes with gravy and coffee. Best meal I've had all year. My thoughts tonight are again of home—wishing I were there.

December 21, 1944 - First day of winter - received 26 letters in the past two days.

December 24, 1944 - Christmas Eve. No work. Sang Christmas carols and old tunes. Went to bed [at] 12 o'clock.

December 25, 1944 - CHRISTMAS DAY. Slept till noon. Ate turkey and spaghetti, cake. Got all dressed up in new clothes. Heard Glenn Miller orchestra broadcast from Paris—#1 on Hit Parade—I'll Walk Alone. Very homesick today—thoughts were on Marian and my family all day. Next year Christmas I must be home.

February 8-17, 1945 - Much confusion on farm. Russians pushing like hell. Volksturm meetings, not too much work. No more mail from home or packages. On our last two Red Cross boxes—Valentine's Day and thinking much of my wife today.

February 20, 1945 - Left Alt-Ristow Kommando. (Destination unknown.) Began walking for Stettin with packs on back.

February 21-28, 1945 - Walked each day averaging 25 kilometers per day.

March 1-31, 1945 - Same as last month. Half starved to death.

April 13, 1945 (FRIDAY THE THIRTEENTH) Friday the 13th!!! THE HAPPIEST DAY OF MY LIFE!!!! P.O.W DAYS OVER!!!!! Liberated by U.S. Army - 102nd Recon.

April 14-15-16, 1945 - Took over German village (Peckfitz) - ate their food - lived like a king, ate chicken, fresh meats, eggs, white bread.

April 17, 1945 - Left Peckfitz by 6 x 6 trucks. rode approx. 130 kilos. Passed thru Hannover, the town in almost total ruins.

April 18-20, 1945 - Arrived at Hildesheim (28 kilometers from Hannover). Here took a shower, deloused and sweated out leaving by plane.

April 20, 1945 - Left Hildesheim by plane C-47 arrived at LeHavre, France, a trip of 500 miles. Rode G.I. trailer 45 miles back to R.A.M.P. Camp Lucky Strike. Here shower, deloused and a good meal, steak and all its trimmings. Eaten out of a brand new G.I. mess kit. I'm in the Army again, sweating out all kinds of lines, but I'm sure as hell not complaining!

April 20-30, 1945 - Remained at Camp Lucky Strike. Was issued new clothing, processed, given tetanus shot in arm and prepared to go aboard ship for U.S.A.[637]

Some paratroopers were not directly sent to POW camps in Germany and were able to escape from Camp 59 in Italy when on September 8 the Italian government switched sides. "We were taken by Italian guards from one camp to another until we were up almost to the border," recalled Sergeant Peter J. Ranti of G Company. "We heard about the Italian armistice and the rumors started flying. Thousands of Germans were floating through the Brenner Pass, they said, and we would be shipped pronto up into Germany. Two days after the armistice, we 'blew' and the guards (mostly Italian) didn't seem to give a damn. Some of them fired shots in the air but no one was really stopped from leaving that particular camp. I've never valued my knowledge of Italian, even though it was a Calabrian dialect with an American inflection, more than when I started the trip through Italy."[638]

Ranti first sold his uniform and later his army shoes for money to buy food. In one town, he stole a bicycle and made his way south. At a farmhouse, he earned 800 lires after working there three weeks. Another place he was captured by Italian soldiers, "but after they discovered I was an Italian-American they let me push on. But just as I was nearing the British lines down on the Adriatic, a Nazi sentinel grabbed me, and boy, things looked black. There I was in enemy territory, wearing civilian clothes. They tried to arrest me as a spy but my 'dog tag' showed them that I was an American soldier. They threw me into an Italian controlled camp and there I met up with a British officer who was trying every which way to escape."

It took several days before they convinced the Italian camp commander that the officer's father was a general in the Eighth Army and their release would mean for him a good treatment if the British troops would get there. He directed them to a small motor launch which they used to motor to a British-held coastal town. On December 4, recalled Ranti, "they investigated me there and turned me over to American authorities in Bari."[639]

Staff Sergeant Robert K. Binnix of the Machine Gun Platoon also made his escape. He recalled that their final Camp 59 was in northern Italy and in their rooms were only slat boards for springs, straw mattresses, and one blanket. Later, at the end of August, some overcoats were provided. By September 14, Binnix and several others had completed a hole in the prison wall and successfully crawled to freedom. Binnix's group traveled mostly at night to the south, avoiding civilians and soldiers and sleeping in the day. Their long trek down the Adriatic coast went well until they approached the city of Foggia. German patrols were numerous in the countryside, and thus, the group split up. Binnix and Sergeant Theodore Macauley of I Company slipped through German outposts near a river and the next day, wearing long beards and ill-fitted Italian clothes, ran into a Canadian patrol. Their ordeal was over, and both became instructors at the Parachute School in Fort Benning.

Sergeant Walter V. Ott of Service Company escaped from an Italian prison hospital in Fermo along with a British corporal helped by two Italian orderlies. They took them to a large landowner, Andrew Nochi, who lived some one-half mile from Fermo and had earlier spent several years in Argentina. They remained there for four and a half months until March 1944, when Ott and several British airmen and one South African purchased a small boat with loaned money from Nochi. The motorless boat was launched on March 17 at Porto San Giorgio and sailed to a British-held port. From there, Ott was first sent to Bari and then back to the United States. Pfc. Sterling E. Oberholtzer, the fourth man to escape in Italy, reached the British lines on the Sangro River near Casoli on December 9, 1943.

POSTSCRIPT

Lieutenant Colonel Charles W. Kouns was last photographed by Robert Capa as a free man just hours before he jumped on Sicily, where he was captured. It wasn't until October 23, 1943 that his wife Marion received a telegram from the War Department with the official report that Kouns was a prisoner of war. He arrived in Oflag 64 in December 1943, and another couple of photos of him were made while being a "Kriegy" behind barbed wire. Kouns stayed there until January 21, 1945 when he was put on a forced march out of the camp. Escaping soon after, a long journey brought him through Rembertow, Odessa, and the Mediterranean Sea back home.

After the war, Kouns sent review comments to the Office of the Chief of Military History (OCMH) in Washington when they worked on the official history of the campaigns on Sicily and Italy, titled *Sicily and the Surrender of Italy*. He also supplied info to General Matthew B. Ridgway's biographer Clay Blair. Kouns retired in the 1960s with the rank of colonel and died on March 9, 2004 at age ninety in Alexandria City, Virginia.

Lieutenant Colonel William P. Yarborough felt betrayed in early 1945 when he learned in Washington of the disbandment of his 509th Parachute Battalion. He attended the Command and General Staff College and returned to Europe to command the 473rd Infantry Regimental Combat Team in Italy for the last months of the war and earned a Silver Star. Yarborough was named Provost Marshall of 15th Army Group and later of the U.S. Forces in Vienna before serving from 1947 to 1949 at the Armed Forces Information School at Carlisle Barracks.

In 1950, Yarborough attended the British Staff College at Camberley before being assigned to the NATO Plans Section and entering the Army War College as a student in 1952. He stayed three years in Carlisle, both as a student and teacher. In 1956, he became Deputy Chief to the U.S. Military Advisory and Assistance Group to Cambodia. The following year, Yarborough commanded the 1st Battle Group of the 7th Infantry Regiment before leading a counterintelligence unit in Stuttgart.

In January 1961, President John F. Kennedy appointed Brigadier General Yarborough as commander of the U.S. Army Special Warfare School in Fort Benning, where he arranged authorization of the Green Beret as official headgear of the Special Forces. Other postings to the UN Command Military Armistice Commission in Korea, the Pentagon, and finally, Chief of Staff and Deputy Commander in Chief of the U.S. Army Pacific followed. Lieutenant General Yarborough retired in 1971 and contributed to numerous books about the history of the American Airborne Forces. He passed away on December 6, 2005 at ninety-three and was buried next to his wife in Arlington Cemetery at Section 4, grave 3099-D.

Lieutenant Colonel Leslie G. Freeman was awarded a Silver Star in May 1945 for "gallantry in action on 13 and 14 November 1943, in the vicinity of Colli, Italy. As commanding officer of a parachute battalion, Colonel Freeman undertook the mission of capturing a strategically important hill. He led two depleted companies across a river and through an area saturated with anti-personnel mines. Skillfully maneuvering his troops for an attack on the crest of the hill, under intense mortar and small arms fire, Colonel Freeman brilliantly directed his men in dislodging a numerically superior enemy force to capture the objective. With this position taken, the enemy was forced to withdraw from an adjacent hill position. The prodigious courage displayed by Colonel Freeman in the face of heavy odds won the admiration and esteem of his men, and his performance is exemplary of the finest traditions of the Armed Forces of the United States."[640]

He returned to the United States in April 1944 and was assigned to the Parachute School in Fort Benning as S-3 Officer until he was made acting Commandant of the school under Colonel George Van Horn

Moseley, Jr. in November 1944. This meant a promotion to full colonel. He reverted to S-3 in June 1945 when Colonel James W. Coutts of the 513th Parachute Infantry Regiment returned from Europe.

On September 13, 1945, Freeman was succeeded as S-3 officer by Lieutenant Colonel Warren R. Williams, Jr., who had enough points to come home. Freeman was tapped to take command of the 2nd Parachute Training Regiment. He passed away in April 1977 at sixty-eight in Sun City, Arizona and was buried in Taylor Cemetery in Taylor, New York.

After being severely wounded and left for dead in a Sicilian roadside ditch, 2nd Lieutenant Rudyard M. Swagler was shipped home in August 1943. Once more or less recovered, he refused a disability discharge and was posted in late October as an instructor to the 2nd Parachute Training Regiment in Fort Benning, Georgia. By December 1943, he served as munitions officer in the 513th Parachute Infantry Regiment and later as supply officer of the 2nd Paratrooper Training Regiment.

Lieutenant Rudyard Swagler receiving a Purple Heart with two Oak Leaf Clusters from Major General Fred Walker, Commandant of the Parachute School, in October 1944. Courtesy: Leslie Swagler Fligg

One day in the spring of 1944, he encountered 1st Lieutenant Warren E. Tobias, Jr. whom he had last seen before being wounded. For both paratroopers, it was an unusual but treasured reacquaintance. Although being a supply officer suited Swagler well, he started to experience seizures, dizzy spells, and serious headaches that forced him to relinquish his position on February 4, 1945. His commanding officer, Colonel George Van Horn Moseley, Jr. wrote in a commendation letter that day, "I wish to take this opportunity to commend you on your past service as Supply Officer of the Processing of Overseas Replacements. Due to your organizing ability and complete thoroughness in your duties a high degree of efficiency has been attained which has permitted the 2nd Parachute Training Regiment to succeed in making Parachute Replacement shipments accurately supplied in accordance with Army Ground Forces directives.

"Your recent hospitalization, which occurred during the processing of the largest shipment ever made by this unit, was exceedingly regrettable; however, due to the excellence of the section which you organized with much disregard for your personal health, the shipment was well coordinated and highly successful. But for your ability, effort and organizing qualities, that particular shipment may very well have failed. It is my sincere wish that your services be recognized and commended."[641]

It took another nineteen months before the War Department was convinced that Swagler was eligible for a 100 percent medical discharge.[642] He received an honorable discharge as a captain on September 6, 1946. Swagler continued to experience seizures that gradually subdued in the 1950s, although it cost him his driver's license when he was fifty. He worked as a counselor for homeless veterans before successfully selling stocks and mutual funds and eventually leading a regional office. His daughter Leslie recalled that her father kept having trouble with severe headaches until later in his life. Captain Rudyard Malcolm Swagler passed away on October 27, 2000, fifty-seven years after his life nearly ended on Sicily. He is buried in the Conejo Mountain Funeral Home & Cemetery in Camarillo, California.

LIST OF OFFICER TRANSFERS
JUNE 1942–APRIL 1943

Rank	First name	Initial	Last name	To	Month
MAJ	John	B	Shinberger	First Spec. Serv. Force	June 1942
MAJ	Ward	S	Ryan	Parachute School	July 1942
LTC	Richard	NMI	Chase	Troop Carrier Command	July 1942
MAJ	Herbert	F	Batcheller	505th PIR	July 1942
CAPT	Mark	J	Alexander	505th PIR	July 1942
CAPT	James	E	McGinity	505th PIR	July 1942
CAPT	Julius	H	Scruggs	505th PIR	July 1942
CAPT	Walter	F	Winton	505th PIR	July 1942
2LT	Ivey	K	Connell	505th PIR	July 1942
1LT	Patrick	J	Gibbons, Jr.	505th PIR	July 1942
1LT	John	H	Sanders	505th PIR	July 1942
MAJ	Charles	H	Chase	506th PIR	July 1942
CAPT	Ernest	H	La Flamme	506th PIR	July 1942
CAPT	Robert	L	Wolverton	506th PIR	July 1942
1LT	Carl	A	Buechner	506th PIR	July 1942
1LT	Herman	E	Dickerson	506th PIR	July 1942
1LT	Henry	P	Stoffregen, Jr.	506th PIR	July 1942
CAPT	Arthur	A	Maloney	507th PIR	July 1942
1LT	Frank	R	Duke	507th PIR	July 1942
1LT	Henry	J	Muller, Jr.	507th PIR[1]	July 1942
1LT	Benjamin	F	Pearson, Jr.	507th PIR	July 1942

[1] Later a cadre member for the 511th PIR and eventually the G-2 Officer of the 11th Airborne Division.

1LT	Gordon	K	Smith	507th PIR	July 1942
CAPT	John	M	Cook	507th PIR	August 1942
CAPT	Robert	E	Eby	101st Airborne Division	August 1942
1LT	John	L	Alhart	Air Corps	October 1942
CAPT	Ralph	R	Bates	D/503rd PIR	October 1942
2LT	Donald	E	Abbott	D/503rd PIR	October 1942
2LT	Thomas	P	McNerney	D/503rd PIR	October 1942
1LT	James	C	Meade	D/503rd PIR	October 1942
1LT	John	R	Richmond	D/503rd PIR	October 1942
1LT	John	P	Rucker	D/503rd PIR	October 1942
1LT	Joseph	A	Turinsky	D/503rd PIR	October 1942
2LT	Arthur	C	Vandivort	D/503rd PIR	October 1942
CAPT	Philip	S	Gage, Jr.	501st PIR	November 1942
2LT	Billy	P	Kelso	501st PIR	November 1942
COL	Theodore	L	Dunn	Transportation Service	December 1942
MAJ	David	A	DeArmond	32nd Infantry Division	December 1942
CAPT	Frederick	J	Swift	513th PIR	December 1942
1LT	Earl	S	Wycoff	511th PIR	January 1943
CAPT	Melvin	NMI	Zais	513th PIR[2]	January 1943
CAPT	Roger	K	Kalina		February 1943
1LT	William	H	Hooker, Jr.		February 1943
1LT	Ira	A	McDonald		February 1943
1LT	John	E	Minter, Jr.	Parachute School	February 1943
2LT	John	B	Roesler		February 1943
MAJ	Gerald	R	Cox	?	March 1943
MAJ	George	W	Rice	?	March 1943
CAPT	Robert	O	Erickson	ROTC unit	March 1943
CAPT	David	NMI	Rosen	513th PIR	March 1943
1LT	Richard	A	Daly	515th PIR	March 1943
2LT	Charles	D	Edwards		March 1943
2LT	William	L	Geddes	501st PIR	March 1943
2LT	Edmund	E	Grubb	513th PIR	March 1943
2LT	Harold	A	Hoggard	502nd PIR	March 1943
CAPT	William	L	Lindsey	515th PIR	March 1943
1LT	Roger	N	Meadows		March 1943

---

[2] Later a cadre member and XO of the 517th PIR.

2LT	Francis	R	Ringa, Jr.	506th PIR	March 1943
1LT	Arthur	L	Robichaux	515th PIR	March 1943
CAPT	Abdallah	K	Zakby	513th PIR[3]	March 1943
1LT	Charles	R	Barrett	Airborne Comd & 542nd PIR	March 1943

---

[3] Cadre member of the 515th PIR in June 1943. Rejoined the 504th PIR later as a replacement officer.

ORDER OF BATTLE IN THE UNITED STATES

May 1, 1942

Lieutenant Colonel Theodore L. Dunn	-	Regimental Commander
Lieutenant Colonel Richard Chase	-	Regimental Executive
Major Reuben H. Tucker III	-	No duty assigned
1st Lieutenant Julian A. Cook	-	Regimental S-1
Captain Leslie G. Freeman	-	Regimental S-2
Captain Ward S. Ryan	-	Regimental S-3
Captain Warren R. Williams, Jr.	-	Regimental S-4
Captain Robert E. Eby	-	Regimental Surgeon
1st Lieutenant Henry J. Muller, Jr.	-	Personnel Officer
1st Lieutenant Joseph P. Fagan	-	HQ&HQ Company
Captain Charles W. Kouns	-	Service Company
Captain Robert L. Wolverton	-	1st Battalion Commander
Vacated	-	1st Battalion Executive
Major John B. Shinberger	-	2nd Battalion Commander
Captain Robert O. Erickson	-	2nd Battalion Executive
Captain Charles H. Chase	-	3rd Battalion Commander
Captain William Colville, Jr.	-	3rd Battalion Executive
1st Lieutenant Daniel W. Danielson	-	Adjutant and Company Commander

September 1942

Colonel Theodore L. Dunn	-	Regimental Commander
Major Reuben H. Tucker III	-	Regimental Executive

1st Lt. Harry J. Cummings	-	S-1 (Personnel)
Captain William Colville, Jr.	-	S-2 (Intelligence)
Captain Charles W. Kouns	-	S-3 (Operations)
Captain Gerald R. Cox	-	S-4 (Supply)
Major Warren R. Williams, Jr.	-	1st Battalion Commander
Captain George W. Rice	-	1st Battalion Executive
Major David A. DeArmond	-	2nd Battalion Commander
Major Daniel W. Danielson	-	2nd Battalion Executive
Major Leslie G. Freeman	-	3rd Battalion Commander
Captain Julian A. Cook	-	3rd Battalion Executive

December 1942

Lieutenant Colonel Reuben H. Tucker III	-	Regimental Commander
Major Leslie G. Freeman	-	Regimental Executive
Captain Melvin Zais	-	S-1 (Personnel)
Captain William Colville, Jr.	-	S-2 (Intelligence)
Major Emory S. Adams, Jr.	-	S-3 (Operations)
Major Julian A. Cook	-	S-4 (Supply)
Major Warren R. Williams, Jr.	-	1st Battalion Commander
Captain Abdallah K. Zakby	-	1st Battalion Executive
Major Daniel W. Danielson	-	2nd Battalion Commander
Captain Melvin S. Blitch, Jr.	-	2nd Battalion Executive
Major Charles W. Kouns	-	3rd Battalion Commander
Major George W. Rice	-	3rd Battalion Executive

March 1943

Lieutenant Colonel Reuben H. Tucker III	-	Regimental Commander
Lieutenant Colonel Leslie G. Freeman	-	Regimental executive officer
Captain Robert R. Johnson	-	S-1 (Personnel)
Captain William Colville, Jr.	-	S-2 (Intelligence)
Major Emory S. Adams, Jr.	-	S-3 (Operations)
Major Julian A. Cook	-	S-4 (Supply)
Lieutenant Colonel Warren R. Williams, Jr.	-	1st Battalion Commander
Captain Edward N. Wellems	-	1st Battalion Executive
Lieutenant Colonel William P. Yarborough	-	2nd Battalion Commander
Major Daniel W. Danielson	-	2nd Battalion Executive
Major Charles W. Kouns	-	3rd Battalion Commander
Major William R. Beall	-	3rd Battalion Executive

When Major Beall was sent to North Africa with the advance party, Captain Herbert C. Kaufman (S-3) became acting 3rd Battalion Executive.

ORDER OF BATTLE FOR OPERATION HUSKY - JULY 9/10, 1943

Regimental Staff

Colonel Reuben H. Tucker III	-	Regimental Commander
Lieutenant Colonel Leslie G. Freeman	-	Regimental executive officer
Captain Robert R. Johnson	-	S-1 (Adjutant)
Captain William Colville, Jr.	-	S-2 (Intelligence)
Captain Melvin S. Blitch, Jr.	-	S-3 (Operations)
Major Julian A. Cook	-	S-4 (Supply)
Major Ivan J. Roggen	-	Regimental Surgeon
Captain Francis G. Sheehan	-	Assistant Regimental Surgeon
Captain Kenneth I. Sheek	-	Surgeon
1st Lieutenant Francis R. Cannizzaro	-	Assistant Surgeon
1st Lieutenant Robert M. Halloran	-	Regimental Dental Officer
1st Lieutenant Delbert A. Kuehl	-	Protestant Chaplain
Captain Edwin J. Kozak	-	Catholic Chaplain
Captain William A.B. Addison	-	Munitions Officer
1st Lieutenant Shirley H. Dix	-	Special Services Officer

HQ&HQ Company

Captain Adam A. Komosa	-	Company Commander
1st Lieutenant Jack P. Simpson	-	Executive Officer
2nd Lieutenant Virgil F. Carmichael	-	Regimental Communications Platoon
2nd Lieutenant James B. Beld	-	Assistant Platoon Leader
1st Lieutenant Erwin B. Bigger	-	Regimental Demolition Platoon

1st Lieutenant Carl W. Kappel	-	Assistant Platoon Leader
2nd Lieutenant Floyd E. Fry	-	Assistant Platoon Leader
1st Lieutenant Willard J. Hill	-	Grave Registration Officer
WO Wilbur H. Hall	-	Band Leader

Service Company

Captain Otis A. Danneman	-	Company Commander
Captain Harry J. Cummings	-	Personnel Officer
WO George E. Bishop	-	Administrative Clerk Class I
1st Lieutenant Eugene R. Cohen	-	Motor Transport Officer
2nd Lieutenant Dick Owen	-	Motor Maintenance Officer
Captain Wylie Cooper	-	Parachute Maintenance Officer
WO John A. Ward	-	Assistant Parachute Maintenance Officer
2nd Lieutenant Clifford E. Hall	-	
WO Benjamin L. Leslie	-	Technical Signal Communication Center
WO Leighton E. Lott	-	

1st Battalion Staff

Lieutenant Colonel Warren R. Williams, Jr.	-	Battalion Commander
Captain Edward N. Wellems	-	Executive Officer
1st Lieutenant Thomas J. Foley, Jr.*	-	S-1 (Personnel)/S-2 (Intelligence)
1st Lieutenant John S. Lekson	-	S-3 (Operations)
1st Lieutenant Kenneth T. Munden	-	S-4 (Supply)
1st Lieutenant Harold C. Allen	-	Communications Platoon
2nd Lieutenant William S. Jones	-	Assisting Platoon Leader
1st Lieutenant Gus M. Gerard	-	Mess Officer
2nd Lieutenant Harold M. Gutterman	-	Recon Platoon Leader
Captain Charles E. Pack, Jr.	-	Battalion Surgeon
1st Lieutenant Joseph S. Holbrook	-	Assistant Battalion Surgeon

Captain Willard E. Harrison	-	**A Company**
1st Lieutenant George A. Noury	-	Executive Officer
1st Lieutenant Ned E. Wall	-	1st Platoon Leader
2nd Lieutenant Stanley J. Whitman	-	Assistant Platoon Leader
2nd Lieutenant Robert D. Condon	-	2nd Platoon Leader
2nd Lieutenant Mearle D. Duvall	-	Assistant Platoon Leader
1st Lieutenant John M. Randles	-	3rd Platoon Leader
2nd Lieutenant Alexander Neilson	-	Assistant Platoon Leader

1st Lieutenant Charles W. Duncan	-	**B Company**
1st Lieutenant Thomas C. Helgeson	-	Executive Officer
1st Lieutenant Milton J. Crochet	-	1st Platoon Leader
2nd Lieutenant Joseph G. Wheeler	-	Assistant Platoon Leader
1st Lieutenant George F. Taliaferro	-	2nd Platoon Leader
2nd Lieutenant Henry B. Justice	-	Assistant Platoon Leader
1st Lieutenant William W. Magrath	-	3rd Platoon Leader
2nd Lieutenant William A. Meerman	-	Assistant Platoon Leader

1st Lieutenant Albert E. Milloy	-	**C Company**
1st Lieutenant Edson R. Mattice	-	Executive Officer
1st Lieutenant Francis W. Payne	-	1st Platoon Leader
2nd Lieutenant James E. Dunn	-	Assistant Platoon Leader
1st Lieutenant James H. Goethe	-	2nd Platoon Leader
2nd Lieutenant Lyle Nightingale	-	Assistant Platoon Leader
1st Lieutenant George A. Sellner	-	3rd Platoon Leader
2nd Lieutenant Horace V. Carlock	-	Assistant Platoon Leader

Captain Jack M. Bartley	-	**HQ Company**
1st Lieutenant Frank W. Gilson	-	Executive Officer
1st Lieutenant G.P. Crockett	-	Mortar Platoon
2nd Lieutenant Calvin J. Billman	-	Assistant Platoon Leader
1st Lieutenant Richard F. Mills	-	Machine Gun Platoon
2nd Lieutenant Michael N. Sweeney	-	Assistant Platoon Leader

*) This was 1st Lieutenant Stuart E. Power, who accidently shot himself in the heel of his foot on July 9 and was eventually transferred out of the unit. Power later served with the OSS in Burma. Either Lieutenant Foley or Lieutenant Jones replaced him before the combat jump.

2nd Battalion Staff

Lieutenant Colonel William P. Yarborough	-	Battalion Commander
Major Daniel W. Danielson	-	Executive Officer
1st Lieutenant Mack C. Shelley	-	S-1 (Personnel)
1st Lieutenant Lewis P. Fern	-	S-2 (Intelligence)/S-3 (Operations)
1st Lieutenant John L. Watson	-	S-4 (Supply)
1st Lieutenant Hubert H. Washburn	-	Battalion Surgeon
1st Lieutenant William P. Jordan	-	Assistant Battalion Surgeon

2nd Lieutenant Ross I. Donnelly	-	Mess Officer
Captain Stanley M. Dolezal	-	**D Company**
1st Lieutenant Joseph H. Boes	-	Executive Officer
1st Lieutenant G. Wilfred Jaubert	-	1st Platoon Leader
2nd Lieutenant Earl F. Morrison	-	Assistant Platoon Leader
1st Lieutenant Woodrow W. Ridler	-	2nd Platoon Leader
2nd Lieutenant Arthur W. Lesage, Jr.	-	Assistant Platoon Leader
1st Lieutenant Beverly T. Richardson	-	3rd Platoon Leader
2nd Lieutenant Robert K. Vermilyea	-	Assistant Platoon Leader
1st Lieutenant Herbert H. Norman	-	Additional officer
Captain Arthur W. Ferguson	-	**E Company**
1st Lieutenant Walter S. Van Poyck	-	Executive Officer
2nd Lieutenant Reynard E. Anderson	-	1st Platoon Leader
2nd Lieutenant Louis A. Bowman	-	Assistant Platoon Leader
2nd Lieutenant William L. McIntosh	-	2nd Platoon Leader
2nd Lieutenant Chester A. Garrison	-	Assistant Platoon Leader
1st Lieutenant Richard E. Thompson	-	3rd Platoon Leader
2nd Lieutenant Gilbert R. Stocum	-	Assistant Platoon Leader
2nd Lieutenant John E. Scheaffer	-	Additional officer
Captain Melvin W. Nitz	-	**F Company**
1st Lieutenant Zigmund C. Lutcavage	-	Executive Officer
2nd Lieutenant Edward J. Sims	-	1st Platoon Leader
2nd Lieutenant William L. Wilson	-	Assistant Platoon Leader
1st Lieutenant Calvin P. Messner	-	2nd Platoon Leader
2nd Lieutenant Louis A. Hauptfleisch	-	Assistant Platoon Leader
1st Lieutenant Charles A. Drew	-	3rd Platoon Leader
2nd Lieutenant Thomas D. Collins	-	Assistant Platoon Leader
2nd Lieutenant Fred M. Harris, Jr.	-	Additional officer
1st Lieutenant Malcolm A. Nicolson	-	**HQ Company**
1st Lieutenant Robert J. Cellar	-	Executive Officer
1st Lieutenant John J. O'Malley	-	Communications Platoon
2nd Lieutenant Hugh A. Henderson	-	Assistant Platoon Leader
1st Lieutenant Carl L. Patrick	-	Mortar Platoon
2nd Lieutenant Earnest H. Brown	-	Assistant Platoon Leader
2nd Lieutenant Edmund H. Kline	-	Machine Gun Platoon
2nd Lieutenant John S. Thompson	-	Assistant Platoon Leader

2nd Lieutenant Martin E. Middleton - Additional officer

3rd Battalion Staff

Lieutenant Colonel Charles W. Kouns - Battalion Commander
Major William R. Beall - Executive Officer
1st Lieutenant Forrest E. Richter - S-1 (Personnel)
1st Lieutenant T. Moffatt Burriss - S-2 (Intelligence)
Captain Herbert C. Kaufman - S-3 (Operations)
1st Lieutenant Rudyard M. Swagler - S-4 (Supply)
Captain William W. Kitchin - Battalion Surgeon
1st Lieutenant Hyman D. Shapiro - Assistant Battalion Surgeon
1st Lieutenant Thomas E. Utterback - Mess Officer
2nd Lieutenant Floyd E. Fry - 3rd Squad Regimental Demolition Platoon

1st Lieutenant Marshall C. McOmber - **G Company**
1st Lieutenant George W. Cline II - Executive Officer
2nd Lieutenant Harry G. Stewart - 1st Platoon Leader
2nd Lieutenant James G. Breathwit - Assistant Platoon Leader
2nd Lieutenant Louis W. Otterbein, Jr. - 2nd Platoon Leader
2nd Lieutenant Charles R. Witt - Assistant Platoon Leader
2nd Lieutenant Clyde F. Baley - 3rd Platoon Leader
2nd Lieutenant Harry E. Evans - Assistant Platoon Leader

Captain Lawrence P. Jordan - **H Company**
1st Lieutenant Frank J. Kent - Executive Officer
1st Lieutenant William H. Davidson - 1st Platoon Leader
2nd Lieutenant Herman Littman - Assistant Platoon Leader
1st Lieutenant Richard D. Aldridge - 2nd Platoon Leader
2nd Lieutenant Warren E. Tobias, Jr. - Assistant Platoon Leader
1st Lieutenant George J. Watts - 3rd Platoon Leader
2nd Lieutenant James C. Ott - Assistant Platoon Leader

1st Lieutenant George M. Warfield - **I Company**
1st Lieutenant Fred E. Thomas - Executive Officer
2nd Lieutenant Willis J. Ferrill - 1st Platoon Leader
2nd Lieutenant Harold A. Hurst - Assistant Platoon Leader
2nd Lieutenant Henry B. Keep - 2nd Platoon Leader
2nd Lieutenant Bill E. Fabian - Assistant Platoon Leader
1st Lieutenant Donald L. Holmes - 3rd Platoon Leader

2nd Lieutenant Richard H. Briggs	-	Assistant Platoon Leader
1st Lieutenant John S. Messina	-	**HQ Company**
1st Lieutenant Elbert F. Smith	-	Executive Officer
1st Lieutenant Calvin A. Campbell	-	Communications Platoon
2nd Lieutenant Frank J. Lavis	-	Assistant Platoon Leader
1st Lieutenant Peter J. Eaton	-	Mortar Platoon
2nd Lieutenant Franklin L. Thomas	-	Assistant Platoon Leader
2nd Lieutenant Francis W. Deignan	-	Machine Gun Platoon
2nd Lieutenant Roy M. Hanna	-	Assistant Platoon Leader
1st Lieutenant Edward C. Digan	-	Anti-Tank Platoon
2nd Lieutenant Herbert Rosenthal	-	Assistant Platoon Leader

ORDER OF BATTLE ON
SICILY – JULY 22, 1943

Regimental Staff

Colonel Reuben H. Tucker III	-	Regimental Commander
1st Lieutenant Harry G. Stewart	-	S-1 (Personnel)
Captain William Colville, Jr.	-	S-2 (Intelligence)
Major Melvin S. Blitch, Jr.	-	S-3 (Operations)
Captain Andrew W. Row, Jr.	-	S-4 (Supply)
Major Ivan J. Roggen	-	Regimental Surgeon
Captain Delbert A. Kuehl	-	Protestant Chaplain
Captain Edwin J. Kozak	-	Catholic Chaplain

1st Battalion Staff

Lt.Col. Warren R. Williams, Jr.	-	Battalion commander
Captain Edward N. Wellems	-	Executive battalion commander
2nd Lieutenant William S. Jones	-	S-1 (Personnel) / S-2 (Intelligence)
1st Lieutenant John S. Lekson	-	S-3 (Operations)
1st Lieutenant George A. Taliaferro	-	S-4 (Supply)
Captain Charles Pack, Jr.	-	Battalion Surgeon
Captain Willard E. Harrison	-	A Company
Captain Charles W. Duncan	-	B Company
1st Lieutenant Albert E. Milloy	-	C Company
Captain William A.B. Addison	-	HQ Company

2nd Battalion Staff

Lieutenant Colonel William P. Yarborough	-	Battalion commander
Major Daniel W. Danielson	-	Executive battalion commander
2nd Lieutenant Chester A. Garrison	-	S-1 (Personnel)
1st Lieutenant Lewis P. Fern	-	S-2 (Intelligence)
1st Lieutenant Malcolm A. Nicolson	-	S-3 (Operations)
1st Lieutenant John Watson	-	S-4 (Supply)
1st Lieutenant William P. Jordan	-	Battalion Surgeon
Captain Stanley M. Dolezal	-	D Company
Captain Arthur W. Ferguson	-	E Company
1st Lieutenant Beverly T. Richardson	-	F Company
Captain Robert R. Johnson	-	HQ Company

3rd Battalion Staff

Major Emory S. Adams, Jr.	-	Battalion commander
Major William R. Beall	-	Executive battalion commander
1st Lieutenant James C. Ott	-	S-1 (Personnel)
1st Lieutenant T. Moffatt Burriss	-	S-2 (Intelligence)
1st Lieutenant George A. Noury	-	S-3 (Operations)
2nd Lieutenant Herbert Rosenthal	-	S-4 (Supply)
Captain William W. Kitchin	-	Battalion Surgeon
1st Lieutenant Richard D. Aldridge	-	G Company
1st Lieutenant Warren E. Tobias, Jr.	-	H Company
1st Lieutenant Fred E. Thomas	-	I Company
1st Lieutenant Peter J. Eaton	-	HQ Company

ORDER OF BATTLE FOR OPERATION AVALANCHE – SEPTEMBER 9, 1943

Regimental Staff

Colonel Reuben H. Tucker III	-	Regimental Commander
Lieutenant Colonel Leslie G. Freeman	-	Regimental executive officer
Captain Forrest E. Richter	-	S-1 (Personnel)
Captain William Colville, Jr.	-	S-2 (Intelligence)
Major Don B. Dunham	-	S-3 (Operations)
Major Robert B. Acheson	-	S-4 (Supply)
Major Ivan J. Roggen	-	Regimental Surgeon

1st Battalion Staff

Lieutenant Colonel Warren R. Williams, Jr.	-	Battalion commander
Major Abdallah K. Zakby	-	Executive battalion commander
1st Lieutenant Gus Gerard	-	S-1 (Personnel)
1st Lieutenant William S. Jones	-	S-2 (Intelligence)
1st Lieutenant John S. Lekson	-	S-3 (Operations)
1st Lieutenant George A. Taliaferro	-	S-4 (Supply)
Captain Charles Pack, Jr.	-	Battalion Surgeon
Captain Willard E. Harrison	-	A Company
Captain Charles W. Duncan	-	B Company
1st Lieutenant Albert E. Milloy	-	C Company
1st Lieutenant George A. Noury	-	HQ Company

2nd Battalion Staff

Major Daniel W. Danielson	-	Battalion commander
Major Melvin S. Blitch, Jr.	-	Executive battalion commander
2nd Lieutenant Chester A. Garrison	-	S-1 (Personnel)
1st Lieutenant Lewis P. Fern	-	S-2 (Intelligence)
1st Lieutenant Malcolm A. Nicolson	-	S-3 (Operations)
1st Lieutenant John L. Watson	-	S-4 (Supply)
1st Lieutenant William P. Jordan	-	Battalion Surgeon
Captain Stanley M. Dolezal	-	D Company
Captain Arthur W. Ferguson	-	E Company
1st Lieutenant Beverly T. Richardson	-	F Company
Captain Robert R. Johnson	-	HQ Company

3rd Battalion Staff

Major Emory S. Adams, Jr.	-	Battalion commander
Major William R. Beall	-	Executive battalion commander
1st Lieutenant Franklin L. Thomas	-	S-1 (Personnel)
1st Lieutenant T. Moffatt Burriss	-	S-2 (Intelligence)
1st Lieutenant George A. Noury	-	S-3 (Operations)
2nd Lieutenant Herbert Rosenthal	-	S-4 (Supply)
Captain William W. Kitchin	-	Battalion Surgeon
Captain George J. Watts	-	G Company
Captain Fred E. Thomas	-	H Company
Captain George M. Warfield	-	I Company
1st Lieutenant Thomas E. Utterback	-	HQ Company

List of Distinguished
Service Cross Recipients

Those listed with an (*) were posthumously awarded

Rank	First name	Initial	Last name	Company	Place of action
Major	Robert	B	Acheson	Regt S-4	Altavilla
Captain	Harry	J	Cummings*	Personnel Off	Sicily
Major	Don	B	Dunham*	Regt S-3	Altavilla
Private	Shelby	R	Hord	H	Sicily
Colonel	Reuben	H	Tucker	Regt CO	Altavilla

However, without downplaying the heroic feats of these men, one must remember that undoubtfully countless other acts of bravery went unnoticed or were uncredited. Perhaps this is best summed up in a letter of 1st Lieutenant Robert C. Blankenship of I Company to Corporal Francis W. McLane on July 28, 1944: "The guy with all the ribbons isn't always the guy that has seen the most action."

LIST OF CONTRIBUTING VETERANS

B etween 2001 and 2018, I interviewed and/or corresponded with the following veterans. Ranks given are the highest-held in the regiment. Most of them have sadly passed away. Without their contributions, this regimental history could never have been written.

Regimental Headquarters: Capt. Delbert Kuehl (Protestant Chaplain), Capt. Henry Muller, Jr. (Personnel Officer), Maj. Ivan Roggen (Regimental Surgeon), Pfc. Warren Tidwell (A Co. and Capt. Fordyce Gorham's jeep driver).

HQ & HQ Company: 1st Lt. Erwin Bigger (Demolition Platoon), Pfc. David Finney (Communications Platoon), Pfc. William Grisez (Demolition Platoon), Pfc. Darrell Harris (Demolition Platoon), 1st Lt. Herman Hupperich (Demolition Platoon), Cpl. Thomas Zouzas (S-2 section).

1st Battalion: Pfc. James Addis (A Co.), Cpl. Fred Baldino (A Co.), 1st Lt. Reneau Breard (A and B Co.), Sgt. Albert Clark (A Co.), Sgt. George Cutting (HQ/1 Co.), Sgt. Virgil Danielson (A Co.), 1st Lt. James Dunn (A and C Co.), Pfc. John Getway (A Co. and 509th PIB), S/Sgt. John Isom (A Co.), Sgt. Robert Jones (A Co.), S/Sgt. John Kaslikowski (HQ/1 Co.), 2Lt. Billy Kelso (C Co.), Pfc. Roger Lambert (A Co.), Sgt. Ben Lesselroth (B Co.), Tec4. Robert Lowery (C Co.), 1Lt. William Magrath (A and B Co.); Pfc. Louis Marino (A Co.), Capt. Albert Milloy (C Co.), T/Sgt. Mitchell Rech (A Co.), 1Lt. George Sellner (C Co.), Sgt. Ervin Shaffer (A Co.), Sgt. Dennis Speth (A Co.), Sgt. Elmer Swartz (C Co.), Sgt. Robert

Waldon (B Co.), Pfc. Anthony Zdancewicz, Capt. Charles Zirkle, Jr. (1st Battalion Surgeon).

2nd Battalion: 2nd Lt. Angelo Boccino (E Co.), 1st Lt. Lewis Fern (S-2), 1st Lt. Leonard Greenblatt (E and D Co.), Pfc. Leo Hart (F Co.), Cpl. Paul Kunde (E Co.), 2nd Lt. Arthur LeSage, Jr. (D Co.), 1st Lt. Zigmund Lutcavage (F Co.), S/Sgt. Ernest Parks (D Co.), 1st Lt. Lauren Ramsey (HQ/2 Co.), Pfc. James Sapp (HQ/2 Co.), Sgt. Willis Sisson (E Co.), Sgt. Roy Tidd (E Co.), Sgt. Bennie Weeks (HQ/2 Co.), 1st Lt. William Watson (HQ/2 and F Co.).

3rd Battalion: Pvt. Alfred Burgreen (I Co.), Capt. Moffatt Burriss (HQ/3 Co.), 1st Lt. Francis Deignan (HQ/3 and G Co.), Sgt. John Foley, Jr. (H Co.), Pfc. James Gann (G Company), Sgt. Edward Haider (I Co.), 1st Lt. Roy Hanna (HQ/3 Co.), Pvt. Francis Keefe (I Co.), Pvt. James Legacie, Jr. (H Co.), Sgt. George Leoleis (I Co.), Pfc. William Leonard (I Co.), 1st Lt. Herman Littman (H Co.), T/5 Herbert Lucas (HQ/3 Co.), Cpl. Francis McLane (I Co.), Pfc. Paul Mentzer (HQ/3 Co.), T/Sgt. Louis Orvin, Jr. (I Co.), 2nd Lt. James Ott (H and G Co.), Pfc. Bonnie Roberts (HQ/3 Co.), Pfc. John Schultz (H Co.), 1st Lt. Edward Sims (F and H Co.), Cpl. Walter Souza (H Co.), Sgt. Don Zimmerman (H Co.).

Veterans, other American units: Capt. Paul Donnelly (376th Parachute Field Artillery Battalion), Lt.Col. Jack Downhill (62nd Troop Carrier Squadron), Pfc. Raymond Fary (80th Airborne Anti-Aircraft Battalion), S/Sgt. Mike Ingrisano (44th Troop Carrier Squadron), Major Benjamin Kendig, Jr. (44th Troop Carrier Squadron), M/Sgt. Leonard Lebenson (82nd Airborne Division HQ), 1st Lt. Harold Roy (376th Parachute Field Artillery Battalion), 1st Lt. Charles Strooband (376th Parachute Field Artillery Battalion).

Published Works

Anzuoni, Robert P. *I'm the 82nd Airborne Division!* Atglen, PA: Schiffer Publishing, 2005.

Blair, Clay. *Ridgway's Paratroopers: The American Airborne in World War II*. Annapolis, MD: Naval Institute Press, 1985; 2002.

Bos, Jan. *Circle and the Fields of Little America. The History of the 376th Parachute Field Artillery Battalion, 82nd Airborne*. Privately published DVD book, 2007.

Breuer, William B. *Geronimo!* New York, NY: St. Martin's Press, 1989; 1992.

———. *They Jumped At Midnight*. New York, NY: Jove Books, 1990.

Burriss, T. Moffatt. *Strike and Hold. A Memoir of the 82nd Airborne in World War II*. Washington, D.C.: Brassey's, 2001.

Carter, Ross S. *Those Devils in Baggy Pants*. Kingsport, TN: Kingsport Press, 1979.

Clark, Mark W. *Calculated Risk*. New York, NY: Enigma Books, 2007.

Dawson, W. Forrest. *Saga of the All American*. Atlanta, GA: Albert Love Enterprises, 1946; 1978.

Devlin, Gerard M. *Paratrooper!* New York, NY: St. Martin's Press, 1979.

Ellis, Jr., John T. *The Airborne Command and Center*. (The Army Ground Forces, Study No. 25.) Historical Section – Army Ground Forces; Washington 1946.

Follain, John. *Mussolini's Island. The Battle for Sicily 1943 by the people who were there*. London: Hodder and Stoughton, 2005.

Garrison, Chester A. *An Ivy-League Paratrooper*. Corvallis, OR: The Franklin Press, 2002.

Gavin, James M. *On to Berlin: Battles of an Airborne Commander 1943–1946*. New York, NY: Viking Press, 1978.

Golla, Karl-Heinz. *Zwischen Reggio und Cassino. Das Kriegsgeschehen in Italien im zweiten Halbjahr 1943*. Bonn, Germany: Bernard & Graefe Verlag, 2004.

Götte, Franz and Herbert Peiler. *Die 29. Falke Division 1936-1945. Eine Dokumentation in Bildern*. Friedberg, Germany: Podzum-Pallas Verlag, 1984.

Haggard, Allen W. *Stray Bullets Have No Eyes*. Chattanooga, Tennessee: self-published, 1999.

Harris, Darrell G. *Casablanca to VE Day. A Paratrooper's Memoirs*. Pittsburgh, PA: Dorrance Publishing, 1995.

Kurowski, Franz. *Fallschirmpanzerkorps Hermann Goering*. Würzburg, Germany: Flechsig Verlag, 2010.

Langdon, Allen L. *"Ready." The History of the 505th Parachute Infantry Regiment, 82nd Airborne Division, World War II*. Indianapolis, IN: Western Newspaper Publishing Co., Inc. 2016 (1986).

Leoleis, George. *Medals*. New York, NY: Carlton, 1990.

Liberation Museum Groesbeek. *Roll of Honour 82nd Airborne Division World War Two*. Nijmegen, the Netherlands: Nijmegen University Press, 1997.

LoFaro, Guy. *The Sword of St. Michael: The 82nd Airborne Division in World War II*. Cambridge, MA: Da Capo Press, 2011.

Lunteren, Frank van. *The Battle of the Bridges. The 504th Parachute Infantry Regiment in Operation Market Garden*. Havertown, PA: Casemate Publishing, 2014.

———. *Blocking Kampfgruppe Peiper. The 504th Parachute Infantry Regiment in Operation Market Garden*. Havertown, PA: Casemate Publishing, 2015.

———. *Spearhead of the Fifth Army. The 504th Parachute Infantry Regiment at Venafro and Anzio*. Havertown, PA: Casemate Publishing, 2016.

Mandle, William D. and David H. & Whittier. *Combat Record of the 504th Parachute Infantry Regiment*. Paris, France, 1946; Nashville, TN: The Battery Press, 1976.

Mrozek, Steven J., ed. *Propblast. Chronicle of the 504th Parachute Infantry Regiment*. Fort Bragg, NC: 82nd Airborne Division Historical Society, 1986.

Nigl, Alfred J. and Charles A Nigl. *Silent Wings, Savage Death*. Santa Ana, CA: Nigl & Nigl, 2007.

Nordyke, Phil. *All American All the Way. The Combat History of the 82nd Airborne Division in World War II*. St. Paul, MN: Zenith Press, 2005.

———. *More than Courage. The Combat History of 504th Parachute Infantry Regiment in World War II*. Minneapolis, MN: Zenith Press, 2008.

Pierce, Wayne. *Let's Go! The Story of the Men Who Served in the 325th Glider Infantry Regiment*. Chapel Hill, NC: Professional Press, 1997.

Rapport, Leonard and Arthur Northwood, Jr. *Rendezvous With Destiny. A History of the 101st Airborne Division* (Greenville, Texas: 101st Airborne Division Association, 1965.

Ruggero, Ed. *Combat Jump. The Young Men Who Led the Assault into Fortress Europe, July 1943*. New York, NY: Perennial, 2004.

Schmidt, Julius (Ed.), *29. Falke Division. Das Buch der Falke Division*. Bad Nauheim, Germany: Podzun Verlag, 1960.

Schmitz, Günther. *Die 16. Panzer-Division. Bewaffnung – Einsätze – Männer 1938-1945*. Eggolsheim, Germany: Dörfler Verlag, 2004.

Turnbull, Peter. *"I Maintain the Right": The 307th Airborne Engineer Battalion in WWII*. Bloomington, IN: AuthorHouse, 2005.

Unpublished AND PRIVATELY PUBLISHED Sources

Memoirs and Histories

Finney, David K. "My Time with the 504th." Privately printed memoir. San Diego, 2006.

Lunteren, Frank W. van , "Brothers in Arms: A Company, 504th Parachute Infantry Regiment, 82nd Airborne Division, from North

Africa to Berlin." Privately printed company history. Arnhem: the Netherlands, 2007.

Parks, Ernest W. "The War Years (WWII)." Unpublished memoir, 2008.

Smith, Elbert F. "Just a Little Bit of History or, How it came to Be." Unpublished memoir, 2005.

ABOUT THE AUTHOR

B orn in Arnhem, the Netherlands, Frank van Lunteren is the Chair of the History Department CSG Het Streek Lyceum. He has authored three highly acclaimed volumes on the 504th PIR, and is an honorary member of the 504th Parachute Infantry Regiment.

ENDNOTES

1   Clay Blair, *Ridgway's Paratroopers* (Annapolis, MD: Naval Institute Press, 2002), 52.

2   Lt. Col. John T. Ellis, Jr., *The Airborne Command and Center*. The Army Ground Forces, Study No. 25. (Historical Section – Army Ground Forces; Washington 1946), 3.

3   Ellis, Jr., *The Airborne Command and Center*, 4.

4   Ellis, Jr., *The Airborne Command and Center*, 4.

5   Ibidem, 7-8.

6   Richard Chase and Janet Campbell Green, "Shooting Chuters" (January 1942). Courtesy of Pamela Chase Hain.

7   Ibidem, 9.

8   Letter Adjutant General Eustace M. Peixotto to the commanding general of I Army Corps, as quoted from Lt. Col. John T. Ellis, Jr., *The Airborne Command and Center*, 121-122.

9   Ibidem.

10 Captain David E. Thomas, "Selection of the Parachutist," *Military Surgeon*, Vol. 91 (1942), 81-82.

11 Ellis, Jr., *The Airborne Command and Center*, 96.

12 504th Parachute Infantry Regimental newspaper *Propblast*, October 1942, 10.

13 Reuben H. Tucker, *Propblast*, September 1, 1942.

14 Cornelius Ryan, interview with Colonel Julian Cook, February 25, 1968. Cornelius Ryan Collection of WWII Papers, box 102, folder 17. Ohio University, Athens, Ohio. Major James E. McGinity was killed in action on June 6, 1944 while serving in the 505th Parachute Infantry Regiment.

15 Reuben H. Tucker, *Propblast*, September 1, 1942.

16 Henry J. Muller, telephone interview with the author, January 22, 2017.

17 Charles W. Kouns, letter to Clay Blair, April 9, 1983. A copy was kindly sent to the author by his granddaughter Kim Kouns.

18 Muller, telephone interview with the author.

19 Muller, telephone interview with the author.

20 In Company B, for instance, these four cadre members were 1st Sergeant Charles W. Holland and Staff Sergeants Jack Bishop, James C. Hesson and Henry P. Paquet. Only the last three would go overseas with the regiment. Paquet was killed in Italy and Bishop and Hesson eventually both received a battlefield commission. Bishop would even serve in three different companies: A, B and F.

21 Major John S. Lekson, *The Operations of the 1st Battalion, 504th Parachute Infantry (82nd Airborne Division) in the Capture of Altavilla, Italy, 13-19 September 1943, (Naples-Foggia Campaign)* (Infantry School 1947-1948), 7.

22 "Lt. E.J. Kozak Received Early Education In City," *The Baltimore Sun*, July 12, 1943 and his obituary in *The Baltimore Sun*, April 9, 1944.

23 "A Silver Star Chaplain."

24 Ibidem.

25 "A Silver Star Chaplain."

26 "Ward S. Ryan 1938," accessed September 5, 2015, https://apps.westpointaog. org/Memorials/Article/11321.

27 Frederic Kelly, telephone call with Roy M. Hanna, March 5, 1968. Cornelius Ryan Collection of WWII Papers, box 102, folder 27. Ohio University, Athens, Ohio.

28 Roy M. Hanna, email to the author, May 2005.

29 Charles W. Kouns, letter to Clay Blair, April 9, 1983. A copy was kindly sent to the author by his granddaughter Kim Kouns.

30 Clay Blair, *Ridgway's Paratroopers* (Annapolis, MD: Naval Institute Press, 2002), 34-35.

31 Ridgway as quoted from Clay Blair, *Ridgway's Paratroopers* (Annapolis, MD: Naval Institute Press, 2002), 35.

32 Ernest W. Parks, *The War Years (WWII)*, 1. A copy of this unpublished memoir was kindly sent to the author.

33 Parks, *The War Years*, 2.

34 Edward P. Haider, *Blood In Our Boots* (St. Paul, MN: Trafford Publishing, 2002), 1.

35 Ibidem, 5-6.

36 Ibid, 9.

37 Alfred Burgreen, letter to the author, April 16, 2018.

38 Herbert C. Lucas, response to author's questionnaire.

39 Arthur W. Ferguson, *Jump Happy* (privately printed booklet, New York, Christmas 1942), 5-7.

40 Herman C. Hupperich, response to author's questionnaire. During the remainder of the war, Hupperich served as a pilot and flight instructor in the United States. He retired with the rank of colonel in 1965.

41 Darrell G. Harris, *Casablanca to VE Day. A Paratrooper's Memoirs* (Pittsburgh, PA: Dorrance Publishing, 1995), 2. A copy of this book was kindly provided to the author by Darrell Harris.

42 Charles W. Kouns, letter to Clay Blair, April 9, 1983. A copy was kindly sent to the author by his granddaughter Kim Kouns.

[43] George Leoleis, telephone interview with the author, May 10, 2008.

[44] "Philip S. Gage, Jr.'s interview for the Veterans History Project at Atlanta History Center," accessed January 14, 2018, https://www.youtube.com/watch?v=up1I10Z-G38.

[45] Colonel William T. Calhoun, *Bless 'Em All* (2001). Edited by Paul F. Whitman. Retrieved on March 15, 2008. http://corregidor.org/Bless%20'em%20All/features/503_509.html.

[46] Calhoun, *Bless 'Em All*.

[47] William R. Beall, *Propblast*, October 1942, 11.

[48] Lewis P. Fern, telephone interview with the author, November 11, 2007.

[49] Thomas Zouzas, response to author's questionnaire.

[50] Robert D. Condon, training diary. Courtesy of his son Robert B. Condon.

[51] James E. Dunn, response to author's questionnaire.

[52] Dunn, questionnaire.

[53] Baldino, email to the author, January 2005.

[54] Albert B. Clark, interview with the author, September 20, 2004.

[55] Fred J. Baldino, "Odyssey of the Pfc. 'General'!" *The Airborne Quarterly*, August 2001.

[56] Bob Gillette, "Origins of the Static Line," *Static Line*, Volume XLVIII, Number 9. October 2003.

[57] Gordon Gould, letter to Harriet Wentworth, October 22, 1942. Courtesy of their daughter Linda Brown.

[58] Gordon Gould, "Strictly G.I." (March 5, 1948) – college paper assignment. This original document was kindly sent to the author by his daughter Linda Brown.

[59] Gould, letter to Harriet Wentworth, November 16, 1942.

[60] Gould, letter to Harriet Wentworth, November 22, 1942.

[61] *Propblast*, December 1942.

[62] "Would Like To Live Here After The War, Paratroopers Who Visited Town State," *Charleroi Mail*, 5 December 1942. A copy of this article was kindly provided by Kathleen Buttke.

[63] Charles W. Kouns, letter to Clay Blair, April 9, 1983. A copy was kindly sent to the author by his granddaughter Kim Kouns.

[64] Matthew B. Ridgway as quoted from Clay Blair, *Ridgway's Paratroopers* (Annapolis, MD: Naval Institute Press, 2002), 42.

[65] Christopher Tucker, email to the author, October 15, 2012.

[66] Cornelius Ryan, interview with Colonel Julian Cook, February 25, 1968. Cornelius Ryan Collection of WWII Papers, box 102, folder 17. Ohio University, Athens, Ohio.

[67] Warren R. Williams, Jr. as quoted from Clay Blair, *Ridgway's Paratroopers* (Annapolis, MD: Naval Institute Press, 2002), 36.

[68] Blair, *Ridgway's Paratroopers*, 42.

[69] Reuben H. Tucker, *Propblast*, February 1943, 2.

[70] Doyle ironically died on Reuben Tucker's twenty-fourth birthday, and in the very year, he would graduate from West Point...

[71] Charles W. Kouns, letter to Clay Blair, April 9, 1983. A copy was kindly sent to the author by his granddaughter Kim Kouns.

[72] Ibidem, 28.

[73] "Conversations between Lieutenant General William P. Yarborough and Colonel John R. Meese and Lieutenant Colonel Houston P. Houser III," U.S. Army Military History Research Collection. Senior Debriefings Program, 28.

[74] Darlene Milloy (Captain Milloy's wife), telephone interview with the author, May 26, 2008.

[75] Robert W. Lowery, telephone interview with the author, May 26, 2008.

[76] Darlene Milloy, telephone interview.

[77] Fred L. Lanning, notes added to A Company photo (January 1943). A copy was kindly provided by his widow Vera.

[78] Gordon Gould, letter to Harriet Wentworth, January 4, 1943. Courtesy of their daughter Linda Brown.

[79] Gould, letter to Harriet Wentworth, February 5, 1943.

[80] *Propblast*, December 1942.

[81] "Headquarters and Headquarters Company goes to Washington," *Propblast*, February 1943, 4.

[82] *Propblast*, February 1943.

[83] Charles W. Kouns, letter to Clay Blair, April 9, 1983. A copy was kindly sent to the author by his granddaughter Kim Kouns.

[84] Clay Blair, *Ridgway's Paratroopers* (Annapolis, MD: Naval Institute Press, 2002), 57.

[85] *Propblast*, February 1943.

[86] Ibidem.

[87] Gould, letter to Harriet Wentworth, February 15, 1943.

[88] *Propblast*, 6.

[89] Information supplied by Marcia Ray Decker, whose father Edwin was a friend of Stanley Daniszewski.

[90] Ross S. Carter, *Those Devils in Baggy Pants* (Kingsport, TN: 1978), 12.

[91] Ibidem, 12.

[92] Nicholas J. Bonilla, letter to his wife, March 12, 1943. Courtesy of the Birmingham Public Library.

[93] Ivan J. Roggen, response to author's questionnaire.

[94] Roggen, questionnaire.

[95] Ivan J. Roggen, response to author's questionnaire.

[96] Roggen, questionnaire.

[97] Robert M. Halloran, questionnaire sent to the United States Army Military History Institute.

[98] Ken Thieme, grandson of Robert O. Erickson, e-mail to the author, January 21, 2017.

[99] David Rosenkrantz, letter to his sister, March 17, 1943. Courtesy of his nephew Dr. Phil Rosenkrantz.

[100] Elbert F. Smith, *Just a Little Bit of History or, How it came to Be* (2005), 8. Unpublished manuscript. A copy was kindly provided to the author by his son Travis.

[101] Leonard Rapport and Arthur Northwood, Jr., *Rendezvous With Destiny. A History of the 101st Airborne Division* (Greenville, Texas: 1965), 35.

[102] Ethel Betry as quoted from Emilie Hornak, "Bride said goodbye and never saw husband again," *The Porterville Recorder*, November 11, 2003.

[103] Edward P. Haider, *Blood In Our Boots* (St. Paul, MN: 2002), 16-17.

[104] Charles W. Kouns, letter to Clay Blair, April 9, 1983. A copy was kindly sent to the author by his granddaughter Kim Kouns.

[105] Kouns, letter to Clay Blair, April 9, 1983. A copy was kindly sent to the author by his granddaughter Kim Kouns.

[106] Peter Puhalla, nephew of Frank A. Puhalla, telephone interview with the author, January 19, 2017.

[107] Julie Johnson-Jones, granddaughter of Captain Beall, email to the author, May 10, 2008. Her grandmother told her this story just weeks before she passed away in 2008.

[108] "Army Officer Says AWOL Soldiers Are Impeding War Effort," *The Cumberland News*, April 10, 1943.

[109] David Rosenkrantz, letter to his parents, April 15, 1943. Courtesy of his nephew Philip Rosenkrantz.

[110] Kouns, letter to Clay Blair, April 9, 1983.

[111] Elbert F. Smith, *Just a Little Bit of History or, How it came to Be* (2005), 8-9. Unpublished manuscript.

[112] Robert M. Halloran, questionnaire sent to the United States Army Military History Institute.

[113] Albert B. Clark, written account (August 2005), 3.

[114] Gordon Gould, letter to Harriet Wentworth, April 24, 1943. Courtesy of their daughter Linda Brown.

[115] Kouns, letter to Blair, April 9, 1983.

[116] Clark, written account, 3.

[117] Haider, *Blood In Our Boots*, 20-21.

[118] Darrell G. Harris, *Casablanca to VE Day. A Paratrooper's Memoirs* (Pittsburgh, PA: Dorrance Publishing, 1995), 2.

[119] Lewis P. Fern, telephone interview with the author, February 1, 2009.

[120] Lucas, questionnaire.

[121] Clark, written account, 4.

[122] Ivan J. Roggen, response to author's questionnaire.

[123] Halloran, questionnaire.

[124] Kouns, letter to Blair, April 9, 1983.

[125] Edgar D. Stephens, letter to his wife, July 30, 1943. A digital copy was kindly provided to the author by his son Edgar.

[126] Elbert F. Smith, *Just a Little Bit of History or, How it came to Be* (2005), 9. Unpublished manuscript. A copy was kindly provided to the author by his son Travis.

[127] Kouns, letter to Blair, April 9, 1983.

[128] Lucas, questionnaire.

[129] Halloran, questionnaire.

[130] Smith, *Just a Little Bit of History or, How it came to Be*, 9.

[131] Kouns, letter to Blair, April 9, 1983.

[132] Charles W. Kouns, letter to Clay Blair, April 9, 1983. A copy was kindly sent to the author by his granddaughter Kim Kouns.

[133] James C. Ott, response to author's questionnaire.

[134] Thomas E. Utterback, written account (1944). Courtesy of his granddaughter Laurie Utterback.

[135] David K. Finney, *My Time With The 504th*. Self-published memoir, (Santee, CA: 2006) n.p. Only four copies of this memoir were distributed – the author was fortunate and honored to receive one of them.

[136] Finney, *My Time With The 504th*.

[137] Ibidem.

[138] Ibid.

[139] Finney, *My Time With The 504th*.

[140] John B. Isom, telephone interview with the author, March 12, 2005.

[141] Isom, telephone interview.

[142] Ibidem.

[143] Ibid.

[144] Francis W. McLane, *World War II Journal*, 1. Unpublished manuscript. A copy was kindly provided to the author by Francis X. Keefe.

[145] McLane, *World War II Journal*, 1.

[146] Ibid, 2.

[147] Ibid.

[148] McLane, *World War II Journal*, 2.

[149] Ibid, 3.

[150] Fred W. Thomas, letter to his parents, May 20, 1943. A copy was kindly provided to the author by his son David.

[151] Donald Zimmerman, telephone interview with the author, August 7, 2010.

[152] Adam A. Komosa, "Airborne Operation, 504th Parachute Infantry Combat Team (82nd Airborne Division). Sicily, 9 July – 19 August 1943," 5-6. Courtesy of the Donovan Library in Fort Benning, Georgia.

[153] Charles W. Kouns, letter to Clay Blair, April 9, 1983. A copy was kindly sent to the author by his granddaughter Kim Kouns.

[154] Ivan J. Roggen, response to author's questionnaire.

[155] Thomas J. Leccese, diary entry June 3, 1943. A transcription of this diary was kindly provided to the author by his nephew Pasquale Freni.

[156] Leccese, diary entry, June 5, 1943.

[157] Ott, questionnaire.

[158] Herbert C. Lucas, response to author's questionnaire.

[159] Kouns, letter to Clay Blair, April 9, 1983.

[160] James C. Powers is buried at Carthage, plot A, row 20, grave 4.

[161] Leccese, diary entry, June 12, 1943.

[162] Ernest W. Parks, *The War Years (WWII)*, 3. Unpublished manuscript.

[163] Leccese, diary entry, June 16, 1943.

[164] T. Moffatt Burriss, *Strike and hold. A Memoir of the 82nd Airborne in World War II* (Washington D.C.: 2000), 30.

[165] Edgar D. Stephens, letter to his wife, July 30, 1943. A digital copy was kindly provided to the author by his son Edgar.

[166] Thomas E. Utterback, written account (1944). Courtesy of his granddaughter Laurie Utterback.

[167] Lucas, questionnaire.

[168] McLane, *World War II Journal*, 4.

[169] Albert B. Clark, written account (August 2005), 5-6.

[170] Clark, written account, 6.

[171] Don Whitehead, "It's Okay And Away With Paratroops; Ridgedly Trained Before Invasion of Sicily Of The Sky Soldiers," *The Bee* (Danville, Virginia), July 15, 1943.

[172] Burriss, *Strike and hold*, 30-31.

[173] Komosa, "Airborne Operation, 504th Parachute Infantry Combat Team," 6.

[174] Earnest H. Brown, written account. Courtesy of Terry Brown, who kindly sent a copy of his late father's notes on his wartime service to the author.

[175] Leccese, diary entry, June 30, 1943.

[176] Charles W. Kouns, letter to Clay Blair, April 9, 1983. A copy was kindly sent to the author by his granddaughter Kim Kouns.

[177] Peter Turnbull, *"I Maintain The Right": The 307th Airborne Engineer Battalion in WWII* (Bloomington, IN: AuthorHouse, 2005), 10. Captain Gurfein was later assigned to the Fifth Army Airborne Training Center in Oujda.

[178] Michel De Trez, *The way we were. Doc McIlvoy and his parachuting medics* (Wezembeek-Oppem, Belgium; 2004), 16.

[179] Clay Blair, *Ridgway's Paratroopers* (Annapolis, MD: Naval Institute Press, 2002), 77.

[180] Lieutenant Colonel William P. Yarborough and 1st Lieutenant Lewis P. Fern, "Intelligence Information Bulletin No. 1," (July 8, 1943).

[181] Blair, *Ridgway's Paratroopers*, 86.

[182] Thomas E. Utterback, written account (1944). Courtesy of his granddaughter Laurie Utterback.

[183] T. Moffatt Burriss, *Strike and hold. A Memoir of the 82nd Airborne in World War II* (Washington D.C.; 2000), 34.

184 Charles W. Kouns, letter to Clay Blair, April 9, 1983. A copy was kindly sent to the author by his granddaughter Kim Kouns.

185 Roy M. Hanna, email to the author, May 2005.

186 Edward P. Haider, *Blood In Our Boots* (St. Paul, MN: 2002), 35.

187 Darrell G. Harris, *Casablanca to VE Day. A Paratrooper's Memoirs* (Pittsburgh, PA: Dorrance Publishing, 1995), 4-5.

188 "News Of Redlands Men In Service Of Company," *The San Bernardino County Sun*, July 8, 1943. Lieutenant Power later broke his ankle in August 1943 and was shipped back home. He then joined the OSS and was assigned to Detachment 101 in Burma where he served as a field security officer.

189 James H. Goethe, letter to his nephews Joe and John (1990). Courtesy of his daughter Priscilla Elledge.

190 "News From Men In The Service," *The Escabana Daily Press*, August 29, 1943.

191 Harris, *Casablanca to VE Day*, 5.

192 Charles W. Kouns, letter to Clay Blair, April 9, 1983. A copy was kindly sent to the author by his granddaughter Kim Kouns.

193 Elbert F. Smith, *Just a Little Bit of History or, How it came to Be* (2005). Unpublished manuscript, 10.

194 Smith, *Just a Little Bit of History or, How it came to Be.*

195 Robert Capa, "Geronimo," *Illustrated*, January 15, 1944.

196 Robert DeVore, "Paratroops Behind Nazi Lines," *Collier's Magazine*, September 18, 1943. A copy of this article was kindly sent to the author by Robert B. Condon, son of the late 1st Lieutenant Robert D. Condon of A Company.

197 Wallace Wood, "Kilroy Was Stuck Here," accessed December 11, 2009, http://www.kilroywashere.org/001-Pages/01-0KilroySightings-3.html. Robert Capa became famous for his D-Day photos of Omaha Beach.

198 Charles W. Kouns as quoted from "Paratroopers just before jump," *The Daily Iowan*, July 14, 1943.

199 Charles W. Kouns, letter to Clay Blair, April 17, 1983. A copy was kindly sent to the author by his granddaughter Kim Kouns.

200 Thomas E. Utterback, written account (1944). Courtesy of his granddaughter Laurie Utterback.

201 Haider, *Blood In Our Boots*, 38.

202 Francis W. Deignan, written account (2001), 1.

203 Roy M. Hanna as quoted from Julie Brennen, "Just doing the job for which he volunteered," *The Express* (Lockhaven, Pennsylvania), November 30, 2009.

204 Haider, *Blood In Our Boots*, 37.

205 T. Moffatt Burriss, *Strike and hold*, 35.

206 Lewis S. Frederick, Jr. as quoted from http://ww2flyers53rdtc.com/13_53rd%20 19430709%20HUSKY%20reports%20from%204%20parachutists.pdf, Accessed June 14, 2020.

207 Lieutenant Colonel Charles W. Kouns as quoted from "How the Invasion Began," *Time Magazine*, July 19, 1943.

208 Robert Capa as quoted from "How the Invasion Began," *Time Magazine*, July 19, 1943.

209 Charles W. Kouns, report sent to Major General James M. Gavin on his experiences, April 1946. A copy was kindly provided to the author by his granddaughter Kim Kouns.

210 Kouns, report sent to Major General Gavin, April 1946.

211 Pfc. Sterling E. Oberholtzer as quoted from MIS-X report 124, January 7, 1944. Reel A1315 of the Maxwell Air Force Base Archives. A copy was upon request kindly provided to the author.

212 Kouns, report sent to Major General Gavin, April 1946.

213 Staff Sergeant Robert K. Binnix as quoted from MIS-X report 81, December 16, 1943. Reel A1315 of the Maxwell Air Force Base Archives. A copy was upon request kindly provided to the author.

214 Francis W. Deignan, telephone interview with author, April 5, 2008.

215 "Chutists Tell Experience In Escaping From Nazis," *The Bayonet* (Fort Benning), March 9, 1944.

216 Pfc. Sterling E. Oberholtzer as quoted from MIS-X report 124, January 7, 1944. Reel A1315 of the Maxwell Air Force Base Archives. A copy was upon request kindly provided to the author.

217 Kouns, report sent to Major General Gavin, April 1946.

218 Kouns, report sent to Gavin.

219 Deignan, written account (2001), 1-3.

220 Deignan, written account (2001), 1-3.

221 Roy M. Hanna as quoted from Julie Brennen, "Just doing the job for which he volunteered," *The Express* (Lockhaven, Pennsylvania), November 30, 2009.

222 Roy M. Hanna, written account.

223 Hanna as quoted from Julie Brennen, "Just doing the job for which he volunteered."

224 Hanna, written account.

225 Ibidem.

226 Hanna, written account.

227 "Thrilled on Seeing Picture of Husband With Paratroops," *The Irvington Gazette*, July 15, 1943.

228 Utterback, written account (1944).

229 Roy M. Hanna, email to the author, May 12, 2008.

230 The 1LT John Messina Trophy was awarded to an Edward Little High School in June 1944 for the most outstanding basketball player in honor of his talented officer. His own basketball legacy also led to his posthumous induction in 1978 to the University of Rhode Island Sports Hall of Fame.

231 Thomas E. Utterback, written account (1944). Courtesy of his granddaughter Laurie Utterback.

232 T. Moffatt Burriss, *Strike and hold*, 36-37.

233 Burriss, *Strike and hold*, 37.

[234] T. Moffatt Burriss, *Strike and hold. A Memoir of the 82nd Airborne in World War II* (Washington D.C.: 2000), 39.

[235] Burriss, *Strike and hold*, 40.

[236] Russel F. Looney as quoted from John A. Moroso III, "Race Across Dunes, Advance of 13 Miles, Told by Eyewitnesses," *The Binghampton Press*, July 16, 1943.

[237] John C. Turner, *Sicily History as I remember it*, 1. A copy of this document was kindly sent to the author by Kathleen Buttke, niece of Private Walter Muszynski of I Company.

[238] John C. Turner, *Sicily History as I remember it*, 1.

[239] Turner, *Sicily History as I remember it*, 1.

[240] Major William E. Beall, "Airborne Assault Operations – 9-14 July, 1943," (August 21, 1943), 4.

[241] Turner, *Sicily History as I remember it*, 1.

[242] Ibidem.

[243] Flint Whitlock, *The Rock of Anzio. From Sicily to Dachau: A History of the U.S. 45th Infantry Division* (Boulder, CO: 1998), 44-45.

[244] Darrell G. Harris, *Casablanca to VE Day*, 4.

[245] Darrell G. Harris as quoted from from the IDPF of Pfc. Roy N. Heaton, who is still MIA.

[246] Forrest E. Humphrey as quoted from the IDPF of Pfc. Roy N. Heaton, who is still MIA.

[247] Harris, *Casablanca to VE Day*, 5-6.

[248] Harris, *Casablanca to VE Day*, 5-6.

[249] Floyd E. Fry as quoted from Floyd Carl, "Makes Way Back To Lines After Being Caught Behind Forces Of Enemy On Sicilian Front," *Northwest Arkansas Times* (Fayetteville, Arkansas), June 3, 1944.

[250] William R. Grisez, telephone interview with the author, January 31, 2010.

[251] "Night Death Fight In Sicily Recalled," *The New York Times*, September 20, 1945.

[252] "Paratrooper Among First Men to Land in Sicily," *Reading Eagle* (Pennsylvania), September 1, 1943.

[253] Major William E. Beall, "Airborne Assault Operations – 9-14 July, 1943," (August 21, 1943), 4.

[254] Peter J. Ranti as quoted from the *Berkshire County Eagle* (Pittsfield, Massachusetts), January 26, 1944.

[255] Obituary for Wallace Telford, *Faith and Victory*, newsletter of the Church of God Servant in Guthrie, Oklahoma, April 1996.

[256] Karl Goldschmidt as quoted from Franz Kurowski, *Fallschirmpanzerkorps Herman Göring.* (Würzburg, Germany: Flechsig, 2010), 115. Translation from German language by the author.

[257] IDPF of Pfc. Roy N. Heaton, statement of March 15, 1944 by Colonel Thomas Drake through the American Legation in Switzerland.

[258] Milton F. O'Quinn, V-mail letter to his wife Betty, September 23, 1943. A copy was kindly provided to the author by his niece Ferne O'Quinn.

[259] George J. Watts, letter to Francis McOmber, October 10, 1943. A copy was kindly provided to the author by Mike Bigalke.

[260] Watts, letter to Francis McOmber.

[261] "Parachute Lt. Kent one of the first Americans to land in Sicily," *The Bayonet*, February 10, 1944.

[262] Herman Littman, interview with his granddaughter Tiffany Skidmore, 2012. Courtesy of Tiffany Skidmore.

[263] Elmer C. Kaberlein, "WWII Diary." A digital copy was kindly sent to the author by Eric and Margaret Beringer.

[264] Jack Wallace, diary entry, July 12, 1943, accessed May 1, 2018, http://www.ottawacitizen.com/news/Jack+Wallace+wartime+diary+Invading+Sicily+1943/8683896/story.html.

[265] "200 Italians Dined Their Captors," *Los Angeles Daily News*, July 16, 1943.

[266] Statement of 1LT William H. Davidson, accessed June 14, 2020, http://ww2flyers53rdtc.com/13_53rd%2019430709%20HUSKY%20reports%20from%204%20parachutists.pdf.

[267] James H. Legacie, Jr., telephone interview with the author, February 13, 2011.

[268] "Sicily Invasion Described by Paratrooper," *The Courier-News* (Bridgewater, New Jersey). April 12, 1944.

[269] "Wounded Servicemen Urge All To Support War Loan Campaign," *The Ambler Gazette* (Ambler, Pennsylvania), December 7, 1944.

[270] Chester H. Aszklar, interviewed by Philip Elbaum, March 7, 2003. Library of Congress, Veterans History Project, accessed October 18, 2016, http://memory.loc.gov/diglib/vhp/story/loc.natlib.afc2001001.39248/mv0001001.stream?start=0.

[271] Herbert C. Lucas, response to author's questionnaire.

[272] George J. Watts, letter to Francis McOmber on October 10, 1943. A copy was kindly provided to the author by Mike Bigalke.

[273] James C. Ott, response to author's questionnaire.

[274] Silver Star Citation for Private Elmer E. Lindsey. Headquarters 82nd Airborne Division, General Orders #29, 20 August 1943.

[275] H. Donald Zimmerman, telephone interview with the author, August 7, 2010.

[276] Zimmerman, telephone interview.

[277] Warren E. Tobias, Jr. as quoted from the IDPF of Private Roy N. Heaton, who is still MIA.

[278] Rudyard M. Swagler as quoted from "Proceedings of Army Retiring Board For Officers," April 17, 1945. A copy of these records was kindly shared with the author by his daughter Leslie Fligg.

[279] Franz Kurowski, *Fallschirmpanzerkorps Hermann Goering* (Flechsig Verlag, Würzburg 2010), 111.

[280] Kurowski, *Fallschirmpanzerkorps Hermann Goering*, 109.

[281] Captain George M. Warfield, letter to Mrs. Wallace Ritch, April 14, 1944. I am indebted to his granddaughter Lisa Ware for a digital copy of the letter.

[282] Francis X. Keefe, telephone interview with the author, December 11, 2009. Captain Warfield told Keefe about his experiences of the jump after the war.

[283] Statement of 1LT Donald L. Holmes, accessed June 14, 2020, http://ww2flyers53rdtc.com/13_53rd%2019430709%20HUSKY%20reports%20from%204%20parachutists.pdf.

[284] Statement of 1LT Donald L. Holmes, accessed June 14, 2020, http://ww2flyers53rdtc.com/13_53rd%2019430709%20HUSKY%20reports%20from%204%20parachutists.pdf.

[285] Chester J. Botwinski, telephone interview with the author, April 16, 2008.

[286] Betsy Luce, "No Choir Sang in Sicily," *New York Post*, July 24, 1944.

[287] Theodore F. Macauley as quoted from *The Brooklyn Daily Eagle*, September 27, 1943.

[288] Sergeant Walter V. Ott as quoted from MIS-X report 305, April 22, 1944. Reel A1314 of the Maxwell Air Force Base Archives. A copy was upon request kindly provided to the author.

[289] Haider, *Blood In Our Boots*, 39-40.

[290] Haider, *Blood In Our Boots*, 40-42.

[291] Ibidem, 44.

[292] Haider, *Blood In Our Boots*, 46.

[293] This may have been Private Donald P. Thomas of H Company, who was not captured.

[294] Haider, *Blood In Our Boots*, 49.

[295] "Parents Lean Captain Johnson Killed in Sicilian Operation," *The Great Falls Tribune*, July 8, 1944.

[296] Ibidem, 51-52.

[297] Albert C. Haggard as quoted from Allen W. Haggard, *Stray Bullets Have No Eyes* (Privately printed 1999), 66-67.

[298] Haggard as quoted from Allen W. Haggard, *Stray Bullets Have No Eyes*, 67-68.

[299] Alfred Burgreen, letter to the author, April 16, 2018.

[300] Shelby R. Hord as quoted from "TPS Welcomes 1st EM Almumnus To Get DSC," *The Bayonet*, July 27, 1944.

[301] Distinguished Service Cross Citation for Private Shelby R. Hord. Headquarters U.S. Seventh Army, General Orders #24. September 11, 1943.

[302] Hord as quoted from "TPS Welcomes 1st EM Almumnus To Get DSC."

[303] Silver Star Citation for Private Thomas E. Lane. Headquarters 82nd Airborne Division, General Order #29, August 20, 1943.

[304] Willis J. Ferrill as quoted from John Thompson, "Tribune Writer Finds Chutists A Fighting Band," *Chicago Tribune*, July 27, 1943.

[305] Silver Star Citation (posthumously) for 2nd Lieutenant Edward C. Digan. Headquarters 82nd Airborne Division, General Order #27, May 31, 1944.

[306] Clay Blair, *Ridgway's Paratroopers* (Annapolis, MD: Naval Institute Press, 2002), 91-92.

[307] Blair, *Ridgway's Paratroopers*, 100.

[308] Robert D. Condon, *The big day had come*, n.d. This version was changed slightly by the author on some points from the present to the past present. A copy of this account was kindly provided by Robert B. Condon.

[309] William P. Yarborough, interview with Colonel John R. Meese and Lieutenant Colonel Houston P. Houser III, 28 March 1975 (U.S. Army Military History Research Collection), 29.

[310] Lewis P. Fern, telephone interview with author, February 1, 2009.

[311] Ross S. Carter, *Those Devils in Baggy Pants* (Kingsport, TN: 1978), 18.

[312] William P. Yarborough, interview by John R. Meese and H. P. Houser III, 30. The William P. Yarborough Papers, Box "oral interview," Folder "Section One (Duplicate)," USAMHI.

[313] Fern, telephone interview with author, February 1, 2009.

[314] Lauren W. Ramsey, telephone interview with author, April 8, 2008.

[315] Delbert A. Kuehl as quoted from Patrick K. O'Donnell, *Beyond Valor* (New York, NY; 2002), 52.

[316] Condon, *The big day had come.*

[317] Carter, *Those Devils in Baggy Pants,* 18.

[318] It is certain Captains Cummings and Danneman were on board of this plane, but as both of them were not officially listed as passengers, their cause of death was unknown for a long time. Cummings was killed by machine gun fire as he tried to leave the aircraft. Captain Danneman drowned. Both bodies were found in the water near Scoglitti, Sicily.

[319] This was a standard procedure during the airborne operations in the European Theater during World War Two. Lieutenant Colonel (Ret.) Jack E. Downhill (62nd Troop Carrier Squadron), telephone interview with the author, February 18, 2009.

[320] Pete Jones, "David E. Mondt, Lt. Col. Retired, WWII C-47 Pilot," accessed February 18, 2009, http://www.francissteelevfwpost817.org/DavidMondt.html.

[321] Condon, *The big day had come.*

[322] Albert B. Clark, written account, 7.

[323] Condon, *The big day had come.*

[324] Willard E. Harrison as quoted from Thomas B. Ketterson, *82nd Airborne Division in Sicily and Italy, Part II – Sicily,* 7.

[325] Condon, *The big day had come.*

[326] John Savage as quoted from "Paratrooper Literally Runs Nazi To Death," *The Bayonet,* August 17, 1944.

[327] Silver Star for 2nd Lieutenant Calvin J. Billman. Headquarters 82nd Airborne Division, General Order #29, August 20, 1943.

[328] Silver Star for Corporal Harry A. Gordon. Headquarters 82nd Airborne Division, General Order #33, September 15, 1943.

329 Henry P. Paquet as quoted from "Sicily Hates Duce, Lansingite Writes," *Lansing State Journal*, September 26, 1943.

330 Henry P. Paquet as quoted from "Escaped Germans," *The Escabana Daily Press*, August 29, 1943.

331 Ronald Crockett, nephew of T.J. Crockett, telephone interview with the author, April 30, 2018.

332 Lawrence W. Stimpson, accessed October 2010, http://www.kued.org/productions/worldwar2/untoldStories/LawrenceStimpson.pdf.

333 Edwin E. Decker, letter to his parents, August 7, 1943. Courtesy of Marcia Decker Ray.

334 James O. Eldridge as quoted from a letter to his sisters in the local Gastonia (North Carolina) newspaper of September 1943. Scans were kindly provided to the author by his son Jimmy Eldridge.

335 Robert W. Lowery, *Jumping Into War* (written account, 2001). A copy of this account was kindly sent to the author by Mike St. George, while Robert's son Walter gave permission to use it.

336 "Just Jumped Out – and Let Bullets Zip," *Chicago Tribune*, August 17, 1943.

337 James E. Dunn, response to author's questionnaire.

338 James H. Goethe, letter to his nephews Joe and John (1990). Courtesy of his daughter Priscilla Elledge.

339 Carter, *Those Devils in Baggy Pants*, 23-24.

340 Ibidem, 26.

341 William P. Walsh, statement during the Nashville Convention of the 82nd Airborne Division Association in the early 1980s. Courtesy of his son John Walsh.

342 Keith K. Scott as quoted from Thomas B. Ketterson, *82nd Airborne Division in Sicily and Italy, Part II – Sicily*, 9-10.

343 Scott as quoted from Thomas B. Ketterson, *82nd Airborne Division in Sicily and Italy, Part II – Sicily*, 10.

344 Silver Star Citation for Staff Sergeant Cecil W. Anderson, Headquarters 82nd Airborne Division, General Order #29, August 20, 1943.

345 "Paratrooper wounded by own shrapnel," *Long Island Daily Press* (Jamaica, NY), November 2, 1943.

346 David K. Finney, email to the author, 2004.

347 William B. Breuer, *Drop Zone Sicily* (Novato, CA: 1983), 153.

348 Komosa, 13-14. Komosa copied most of this account from the first regimental history by William D. Mandle and David H. Whittier.

349 Robert M. Halloran, questionnaire sent to the United States Army Military History Institute.

350 Breuer, *Drop Zone Sicily*, 146-147.

351 Ivan J. Roggen, response to author's questionnaire.

352 Fielding J. Armstrong as quoted from William B. Breuer, *Geronimo!* (New York, NY: 1992), 93.

353 Bos, *Circle and the Fields of Little America*, 66 and Ivan J. Roggen, telephone interview with author, February 19, 2009.

354 Breuer, *Dropzone Sicily, 148 and Ivan J. Roggen, telephone interview with author, February 19, 2009.*

355 Roggen, response to author's questionnaire.

356 Silver Star Citation (posthumously) for Pfc. James R. Brooks. Headquarters 82nd Airborne Division, General Orders #98, June 28, 1945.

357 Distinguished Service Cross Citation for Captain Harry J. Cummings. Headquarters Seventh Army, General Order #16, August 18, 1943.

358 Breuer, *Dropzone Sicily, 148-149.*

359 Lieutenant Colonel (Ret.) Jack E. Downhill (62nd Troop Carrier Squadron), telephone interview with the author, February 18, 2009.

360 Fielding J. Armstrong as quoted from William B. Breuer, *Geronimo! (New York, NY: 1992),* 94.

361 Julian A. Cook, interview with Cornelius Ryan, February 25, 1968. Courtesy of the Cornelius Ryan Collection, Alden Library, Ohio University.

362 Albert N. Garland and Howard McGaw, *Sicily and the Surrender of Italy* (Washington D.C.: 1965), 179.

363 Cook, interview.

364 The last interment of James Denkins and James Edwards, as well as all the other KIAs of C Company, 307th Airborne Engineer Battalion and the 376th Parachute Field Artillery Battalion can be found in the appendices.

365 Delor M. Perow as quoted from "Lt. Perow Tells About Allied Attacks On Own Paratroopers At Sicily," *The Escabana Daily Press,* May 2, 1944.

366 Peter Turnbull, *"I Maintain The Right": The 307th Airborne Engineer Battalion in WWII* (Bloomington, IN: AuthorHouse, 2005), 19.

367 Edward J. Sims, written account. Courtesy of Edward J. Sims.

368 Delbert A. Kuehl as quoted from Patrick K. O'Donnell, *Beyond Valor* (New York, NY: 2002), 52.

369 O'Donnell, *Beyond Valor,* 53.

370 Ibidem, 54.

371 Kuehl as quoted from Patrick K. O'Donnell, *Beyond Valor,* 54.

372 Charles A. Drew as quoted from Thomas B. Ketterson, *82nd Airborne Division in Sicily and Italy, Part II – Sicily,* 8.

373 Letter Richard H. Gentzel to his best friend Ernie B. McChesney, February 1944. Courtesy of Karen Dugan.

374 Zigmund C. Lutcavage, telephone interview with the author, April 2008.

375 Ivan J. Roggen, telephone interview with author, February 19, 2009. Major Roggen spoke with 1st Lieutenant Shelley about the crash a few weeks after it had happened.

376 William B. Breuer, *Drop Zone Sicily,* 150-151.

377 Ivan J. Roggen, response to author's questionnaire.

378 John J. O'Malley as quoted in William B. Breuer, *Geronimo!* (*New York, NY;* *1992*), 92.

379 William P. Yarborough, interview by John R. Meese and H. P. Houser III, 31. The William P. Yarborough Papers, Box "oral interview," Folder "Section One (Duplicate)," USAMHI.

380 Lewis P. Fern as quoted from the *Unit Journal of the 2nd Battalion, 504th Parachute Infantry, 82nd Airborne Division,* entry July 11, 1943.

381 Walter S. Van Poyck, Sr., "Mission Possible With Reminiscences," *Paraglide* (Spring 1972), 9.

382 Chester A. Garrison, *An Ivy-League Paratrooper* (Corvallis, OR: 2002), 83-85.

383 Paul A. Kunde, telephone interview with the author, August 1, 2012.

384 Ernest W. Parks, *The War Years* (unpublished memoir), 4-5.

385 G. Wilfred Jaubert, letter to William B. Breuer, September 14, 1982. A scan was kindly provided by his son Jack Jaubert.

386 Jaubert, letter to William B. Breuer.

387 Stanley M. Dolezal as quoted from Charles U. Daly, 'Glory! Glory! What A Helluva Way To Die', *Cavalier,* August 1961, 82.

388 Daly, 'Glory! Glory! What A Helluva Way To Die', *Cavalier,* 82.

389 William L. Watson, interview with Karen Dugan, December 29, 2008.

390 John S. Thompson as quoted from Phil Nordyke, *All American All The Way. The Combat History of the 82nd Airborne Division in World War II* (St. Paul, MN: 2005), 83.

391 Thompson as quoted from Phil Nordyke, *All American All The Way,* 83-87.

392 "Chute officer Experiences Hair-Raising Adventure," *The Bayonet,* February 10, 1946.

393 Earnest H. Brown, written account. Courtesy of Terry Brown, who kindly sent a copy of his late father's notes on his wartime service to the author.

394 Ketterson, *82nd Airborne Division in Sicily and Italy,* 13.

395 Hord as quoted from "TPS Welcomes 1st EM Almumnus To Get DSC."

396 Alfred Burgreen, letter to the author, April 16, 2018.

397 Major William E. Beall, "Airborne Assault Operations – 9-14 July, 1943," (August 21, 1943), 3.

398 Herbert C. Lucas, response to author's questionnaire.

399 Federico Peyrani (unit historian 504th schwere Panzer-Abteilung), email to the author, January 31, 2011.

400 Earl Wills as quoted from Harold Boyle, "U.S. Paratroops and Nazis Make War-Time Bargain," *St. Petersburg Times,* August 15, 1943.

401 Wills as quoted from Boyle, "U.S. Paratroops and Nazis Make War-Time Bargain."

402 Peyrani, email to the author, January 31, 2011.

403 George J. Watts, letter to Francis McOmber on October 10, 1943. A copy was kindly provided to the author by Mike Bigalke.

404 Thomas Utterback, written account (1944). Courtesy of his granddaughter Laurie Utterback.

[405] Thomas E. Utterback, letter to his family, July 21, 1943. Courtesy of his granddaughter Laurie Utterback.

[406] Yarborough, interview with Colonel John R. Meese and Lieutenant Colonel Houston P. Houser III on March 28, 1975 (U.S. Army Military History Research Collection), 33.

[407] Yarborough, interview.

[408] Lewis P. Fern, *Unit Journal of the 2nd Battalion, 504th Parachute Infantry, 82nd Airborne Division,* entry for 13 July 1943.

[409] John S. Thompson as quoted from Phil Nordyke, *All American All The Way. The Combat History of the 82nd Airborne Division in World War II* (St. Paul, MN; 2005), 90.

[410] John Thompson, "Tells How 410 Paratroopers Died Off Sicily," *Chicago Tribune,* March 19, 1944. The article was delayed since July 22.

[411] Fern as quoted from the *Unit Journal of the 2nd Battalion, 504th Parachute Infantry, 82nd Airborne Division,* entry for July 14, 1943.

[412] Fern as quoted from the *Unit Journal of the 2nd Battalion,* July 15, 1943.

[413] Ketterson, *82nd Airborne Division in Sicily and Italy,* 19.

[414] Edward J. Sims, written account.

[415] "Ike Visits Sicily," *New York Times,* July 13, 1943.

[416] Ridgway, "Reported Loss of Transport Planes and Personnel due to Friendly Fire," 3 and 5.

[417] Edward J. Sims, written account.

[418] Ivan J. Roggen, response to author's questionnaire.

[419] 52nd Troop Carrier Wing, "A-2 Section, Consolidated Report – Husky Mission No.2," August 5, 1943.

[420] "410 American Airborne Troops Lost When Planes Shot Down," *The News* (Frederick, Maryland), March 17, 1944.

[421] Drew Pearson, "The Washington Merry-Go-Round," *Nevada State Journal,* March 25, 1945.

[422] Fern as quoted from the *Unit Journal of the 2nd Battalion, 504th Parachute Infantry, 82nd Airborne Division,* entry for 19 July 1943.

[423] Walter S. Van Poyck, Sr., "Mission Possible With Reminiscences," *Paraglide* (Spring 1972), 9.

[424] Edward J. Sims, written account.

[425] Albert B. Clark, written account, 8.

[426] Clark, written account, 8.

[427] Ivan J. Roggen, response to author's questionnaire.

[428] Sims, written account.

[429] Fern, *Unit Journal of the 2nd Battalion, 504th Parachute Infantry, 82nd Airborne Division.*

[430] Richard H. Gentzel, letter to his best friend Ernie B. McChesney. Courtesy of Karen Dugan.

[431] Yarborough, interview with Colonel John R. Meese and Lieutenant Colonel Houston P. Houser III, March 28, 1975 (U.S. Army Military History Research Collection), 34.

[432] Fern, *Unit Journal of the 2nd Battalion, 504th Parachute Infantry, 82nd Airborne Division.*

[433] Gentzel, letter.

[434] Fern, *Unit Journal of the 2nd Battalion, 504th Parachute Infantry, 82nd Airborne Division.*

[435] Yarborough, interview, 34.

[436] Fern, *Unit Journal of the 2nd Battalion, 504th Parachute Infantry, 82nd Airborne Division.*

[437] Headquarters 62nd Armored Field Artillery Battalion, "Account of action: D to D + 8," July 28, 1943, accessed December 20, 2009, http://www.alpinegarden.com/CombatJournalandBattalionCommandersNarratives.htm.

[438] Richard H. Gentzel, letter to his best friend Ernie B. McChesney. Courtesy of Karen Dugan.

[439] Silver Star Citation for Staff Sergeant James C. Turner. Headquarters 82nd Airborne Division, General Order #117, September 4, 1945.

[440] Silver Star Citation for Staff Sergeant Abraham Bloomfield. Headquarters 82nd Airborne Division, General Order #119, September 13, 1945.

[441] Silver Star Citation for Technician 5th Grade Levern H. Miller. Headquarters 82nd Airborne Division, General Order #33, September 15, 1943.

[442] Fern, *Unit Journal of the 2nd Battalion, 504th Parachute Infantry, 82nd Airborne Division.*

[443] John Thompson, "Tribune Writer Finds Chutists A Fighting Band," *Chicago Tribune* July 27, 1943. The article was delayed since July 22.

[444] Yarborough, interview, 34-35.

[445] Komosa, "Airborne Operation, 504th Parachute Infantry Combat Team," 25.

[446] Yarborough, interview, 35-37

[447] Van Poyck, "Mission Possible With Reminiscences," 9.

[448] Yarborough, interview, 38.

[449] Paul C. Mentzer, letter to his parents, July 25, 1943. A copy was kindly shared with the author.

[450] "News From Men In The Service," *The Escabana Daily Press*, August 29, 1943.

[451] Fred W. Thomas, letter to his parents, August 10, 1943. A copy was kindly sent to the author by his son Dave.

[452] Fern, *Unit Journal of the 2nd Battalion, 504th Parachute Infantry, 82nd Airborne Division.*

[453] Fred J. Baldino, email to the author, May 19, 2005.

[454] Edward J. Sims, written account.

[455] Ibidem.

[456] Chester A. Garrison, *An Ivy-League Paratrooper* (Corvallis, OR: 2002), 87.

[457] Sims, written account.

[458] Ned E. Wall as quoted from *The Sun* (Topeka, Kansas), August 28, 1943.

[459] Earl S. Oldfather, "My Time in the Army," diary entries May 10 – August 22, 1943. I am indebted to Bob Davis for providing copies of this unique source.

[460] Oldfather, "My Time in the Army," diary entries, August 24-25, 1943.

[461] John J. Foley, Jr., telephone interview with the author, February 25, 2012.

[462] Thomas J. Zouzas, "Tales from a Baggy Pants Devil. Corporal Thomas Zouzas, 504th Parachute Infantry." Courtesy of Thomas J. Zouzas.

[463] Zouzas, "Tales from a Baggy Pants Devil."

[464] Francis X. Keefe, telephone interview with the author, January 18, 2009.

[465] Keefe, interview with author.

[466] Keefe, telephone interview with the author, December 22, 2015.

[467] McLane, *World War II Journal*, 4-5.

[468] Reneau G. Breard, letter to author, February 18, 2005.

[469] Edward W. Kennedy, letter to his sister Rose, June 17, 1943. A retyped version was kindly sent to the author by his nephew Edward J. Kennedy.

[470] Robert M. Halloran, questionnaire sent to the United States Army Military History Institute.

[471] James O. Eldridge, letter to his friend Dameron Williams, October 28, 1943. This letter was printed in the local Gastonia (North Carolina) newspaper and kindly provided to the author by Jimmy Eldridge.

[472] Regis J. Pahler, questionnaire sent to the United States Military History Institute.

[473] Thomas, letter to his parents, August 25, 1943. A scanned copy was kindly sent to the author by his son David.

[474] Richard Tregaskis, *Invasion Diary* (New York, NY: 1944), 97.

[475] G. Wilfred Jaubert, letter to William B. Breuer, September 29, 1982. A scan was kindly provided by his son Jack Jaubert.

[476] Earl S. Oldfather, "My Time in the Army," diary entry, September 1, 1943.

[477] Thomas E. Utterback, written account sent to his wife, 1944. A retyped copy was kindly sent to the author by his granddaughter Laurie Utterback.

[478] Tregaskis, *Invasion Diary*, 99.

[479] G. Wilfred Jaubert, letter to William B. Breuer, September 29, 1982. A scan was kindly provided by his son Jack Jaubert.

[480] Ibidem , *Invasion Diary*, 99-100.

[481] Ibid, 100.

[482] Clay Blair, *Ridgway's Paratroopers* (Annapolis, MD: Naval Institute Press, 2002), 319.

[483] Jaubert, letter to William B. Breuer, September 29, 1982.

[484] Albert B. Clark, written account (August 2005).

[485] Jaubert, letter to Breuer, September 29, 1982.

[486] Günter Schmitz, *Die 16. Panzer-Division. Bewaffnung – Einsätze – Männer 1938-1945*. (Eggolsheim, Germany: Dörfler Verlag 2004), 123.

[487] Edward J. Sims, written account.

[488] Roy M. Hanna as quoted from Julie Brennen, "Just doing the job for which he volunteered," *The Express* (Lockhaven, Pennsylvania), November 30, 2009.

[489] Silver Star Citation for Pfc. Bernard F. Gallagher. Headquarters 82nd Airborne Division, General Orders #75, May 22, 1945.

[490] Major John S. Lekson, *The Operations of the 1st Battalion, 504th Parachute Infantry (82nd Airborne Division) in the Capture of Altavilla, Italy, 13 September-19 September 1943* (Fort Benning 1947-1948), 6. Courtesy of the Donovan Research Library, Fort Benning, Georgia.

All further quotations of Lieutenant Lekson are taken from this account. I have slightly edited his account. When he wrote the "1st Platoon," I changed this into the "2nd Platoon" and vice versa, as I discovered that he wrote about the 2nd Platoon when he mentioned the 1st and the other way round. Lieutenant Duvall, for instance, served in the 2nd Platoon and not in the 1st, as Lekson remembered it. Duvall did serve in the 1st Platoon in the States but succeeded Lekson when the latter became the S-3 officer.

[491] Walter S. Van Poyck, Sr., "Mission Possible With Reminiscences," *Paraglide* (Spring 1972), 9-10.

[492] Thomas E. Utterback, written account sent to his wife, 1944. A retyped copy was kindly sent to the author by his granddaughter Laurie Utterback.

[493] Oldfather, "My Time in the Army," diary entry September 13, 1943.

[494] David K. Finney, *My Time With The 504th*. Self-published memoir (Santee, CA: 2006) n.p.

[495] Clark, written account.

[496] Reneau G. Breard, letter to author, June 2005.

[497] Lekson, *The Operations of the 1st Battalion, 504th Parachute Infantry (82nd Airborne Division) in the Capture of Altavilla, Italy*, 7-8.

[498] Ivan J. Roggen, response to author's questionnaire.

[499] Finney, *My Time With The 504th*. n.p.

[500] Chester A. Garrison, *An Ivy-League Paratrooper* (Corvallis, OR: 2002), 93.

[501] Lekson, *The Operations of the 1st Battalion, 504th Parachute Infantry*, 8.

[502] Fred L. Walker, *From Texas to Rome with Fred L. Walker.* (Eldorado Hill, CA: Savas Publishing, 2014), 262-263.

[503] G. Wilfred Jaubert, letter to William B. Breuer, September 29, 1982. A scan was kindly provided by his son Jack Jaubert.

[504] Lekson, *The Operations of the 1st Battalion, 504th Parachute Infantry*, 8-9.

[505] Ibid, 9.

[506] Walker, *From Texas to Rome with Fred L. Walker*, 264.

[507] Chester A. Garrison as quoted from the *Unit Journal of the 2nd Battalion, 504th Parachute Infantry, 82nd Airborne Division*. Abbreviations have been edited in full words. John L. Satterwhite is buried in Texas.

[508] John S. Lekson, *The Operations of the 1st Battalion, 504th Parachute Infantry (82nd Airborne Division) in the Capture of Altavilla, Italy, 13 September-19 September 1943* (Fort Benning 1947-1948), 9-10.

509 G. Wilfred Jaubert, letter to William B. Breuer, October 13, 1982. A scan was kindly provided by his son Jack Jaubert.

510 Jaubert, letter to Breuer, October 13, 1982.

511 Jaubert, letter to Breuer, October 13, 1982.

512 G. Wilfred Jaubert, letter to William B. Breuer, October 13, 1982. A scan was kindly provided by his son Jack Jaubert.

513 Garrison, *Unit Journal of the 2nd Battalion, 504th Parachute Infantry, 82nd Airborne Division*, entry for September 15, 1943.

514 Lekson, *The Operations of the 1st Battalion*, 10.

515 Richard Tregaskis, *Invasion Diary* (New York, NY; 1944), 111.

516 Oldfather, "My Time in the Army," diary entry September 15, 1943.

517 Thomas E. Utterback, written account sent to his wife, 1944. A retyped copy was kindly sent to the author by his granddaughter Laurie Utterback.

518 Walker, *From Texas to Rome with Fred L. Walker*, 268.

519 Lekson, *The Operations of the 1st Battalion*, 14.

520 Ibidem, 11.

521 Louis C. Marino, telephone interview with author, November 2005.

522 First Lieutenant Otto W. Huebner, *The Operations of Company A, 504th Parachute Infantry (82nd Airborne Division) in the Defense of Hill 424 near Altavilla, Italy, 17 September-19 September 1943, (Naples-Foggia Campaign), (Personal Experience of the Company Operations Sergeant and Acting First Sergeant)*, (Infantry School, 1948-1949) 10-12. Courtesy of the Donovan Research Library at Fort Benning, Georgia.

   All further quotations of Otto Huebner are taken from this account. I have changed one thing in his account. When he wrote the "1st Platoon," I changed this into the "2nd Platoon" and vice versa, as I discovered that he wrote about the 2nd Platoon when he mentioned the 1st and the other way round. Lieutenant Duvall, for instance, served in the 2nd Platoon and not in the 1st, as Huebner remembered it.

523 Tregaskis, *Invasion Diary*, 114.

524 Reuben H. Tucker, Report of the 504th Parachute Combat Team, Operation Avalanche. (October 1943). A copy of this document was kindly provided to the author by Mike Bigalke.

525 Tregaskis, *Invasion Diary*, 114-115.

526 James E. Dunn, response to author's questionnaire.

527 Tregaskis, *Invasion Diary*, 115-117.

528 Ibidem, 117-118.

529 Lekson, *The Operations of the 1st Battalion*, 22.

530 Richard Tregaskis, *Invasion Diary* (New York, NY: 1944), 120.

531 Chester H. Aszklar, interviewed by Philip Elbaum, March 7, 2003. Library of Congress, Veterans History Project, accessed October 18, 2016, http://memory.loc.gov/diglib/vhp/story/loc.natlib.afc2001001.39248/mv0001001.stream?start=0.

532 Colonel Reuben H. Tucker, *Report of the 504th Parachute Combat Team, Operation Avalanche* (October 1943), 1. A copy of this document was kindly sent to the author by Mike Bigalke.

533 Tregaskis, *Invasion Diary*, 120.

534 Tucker, *Report of the 504th Parachute Combat Team, Operation Avalanche* (October 1943), 1.

535 Distinguished Service Cross Citation for Major Don P. Dunham. Headquarters Fifth Army, General Orders #84 (November 11, 1943).

536 Huebner, *The Operations of Company A, 504th Parachute Infantry (82nd Airborne Division) in the Defense of Hill 424 near Altavilla, Italy, 17 September-19 September 1943*, 12.

537 Ervin E. Shaffer, telephone interview with the author, March 19, 2005.

538 Kurt Finke as quoted from Julius Schmidt (compiler), *29. Falke Division. Das Buch der Falke Division* (Bad Nauheim, 1960), 317-318. Translated by the author.

539 Huebner, *The Operations of Company A*, 12-13.

540 John B. Isom, telephone interview with the author, February 21, 2005.

541 Baldino, email to the author, October 12, 2004.

542 Lekson, *The Operations of the 1st Battalion*, 23-24.

543 Chester A. Garrison, *An Ivy-League Paratrooper*, 93.

544 Marino, telephone interview with the author, November 2005.

545 Huebner, *The Operations of Company A*, 13-14. Ralph R. Young is buried at the National Cemetery in Gettysburg, Pennsylvania at plot 2, grave 544.

546 Fred J. Baldino, email to author, February 2005.

547 Marino, telephone interview with the author.

548 Silver Star Citation for Private Edward B. Hill, Jr. Headquarters 82nd Airborne Division, General Orders #36, October 15, 1943.

549 Lekson, *The Operations of the 1st Battalion*, 27-28.

550 Silver Star Citation for Sergeant Edmund Q. Moorehead. Headquarters 82nd Airborne Division, General Orders #36, October 15, 1943.

551 Edmund Q. Moorehead, "My 50th VE Special," (1995), 1. A copy was kindly provided to the author by Marcia Ray Decker.

552 Headquarters 82nd Airborne Division, letter of commendation to Pfc. Norman H. Plaisted, October 13, 1943. A copy was kindly sent to the author by his son Norman.

553 "Clay Glowingly Praised," newspaper clipping of 1944 provided by Cooper Beverley-Meise.

554 A copy of this citation was kindly shared with the author by Edwin Decker's daughter Marcia Ray Decker.

555 John S. Lekson, *The Operations of the 1st Battalion*, 28.

556 Fred K. Lanning, letter to Hazel Wall, October 9, 1995. A copy was kindly sent to the author by Gary Wall.

557 Silver Star Citation for Private Guy L. Stokes. General Orders #36, Headquarters 82nd Airborne Division, 1943.

[558] Lekson, *The Operations of the 1st Battalion*, 29.

[559] Kurt Finke as quoted from Julius Schmidt (compiler), *29. Falke Division. Das Buch der Falke Division* (Bad Nauheim, 1960), 318-319. Translated by the author.

[560] "Officer Husband of Local Girl is Hero," *The Pilot* (Southern Pines, NC), October 8, 1943.

[561] James O. Eldridge, letter to his friend Dameron Williams, October 28, 1943. This letter was printed in the local Gastonia (North Carolina) newspaper and kindly provided to the author by Jimmy Eldridge.

[562] Silver Star Citation for Master Sergeant Henry S. Furst. Headquarters 82nd Airborne Division, General Orders #36, October 15, 1943.

[563] Tregaskis, *Invasion Diary*, 125.

[564] Lekson, *The Operations of the 1st Battalion*, 29-30.

[565] Tregaskis, *Invasion Diary*, 126-127.

[566] Ibidem, 128-129.

[567] Ibid, 130.

[568] Richard Tregaskis, "Tregaskis tells of major's heroic death," *The Lowell Sun*, December 9, 1943.

[569] Robert M. Halloran, questionnaire sent to the United States Army Military History Institute.

[570] Distinguished Service Cross Citation for Major Robert B. Acheson. Headquarters Fifth Army, General Order #84, 1943.

[571] Walker, *From Texas to Rome with Fred L. Walker*, 268.

[572] Otto W. Huebner, *The Operations of Company A*, 15.

[573] Ervin E. Shaffer, telephone interview with the author, March 19, 2005.

[574] Huebner, *The Operations of Company A*, 15-17.

[575] Ibidem, 17-18.

[576] Ibid, 18-20.

[577] Robert L. Jones, telephone interview with Linda Field, daughter of the late George A. Siegmann, May 10, 2010. A transcript was kindly sent by Linda to the author.

[578] Lekson, *The Operations of the 1st Battalion*, 30.

[579] Huebner, *The Operations of Company A*, 20.

[580] Peter R. Scheider as quoted from Seymour Korman, "General Hails Yanks' Victory Atop Hill 424," *Chicago Tribune*, September 23, 1943. A copy was kindly provided to the author by Bill McKinley.

[581] Silver Star Citation for Pfc. Daniel W. Shaffer. Headquarters 82nd Airborne Division, General Orders #36, October 15, 1943.

[582] Huebner, *The Operations of Company A*, 20-22.

[583] Lekson, *The Operations of the 1st Battalion*, 31.

[584] Silver Star Citation for Pfc. Willard N. Young. Headquarters 82nd Airborne Division, General Orders #36, October 15, 1943.

[585] Silver Star Citation for 1st Lieutenant James E. Dunn. Headquarters 82nd Airborne Division, General Orders #36, October 15, 1943.

[586] Huebner, *The Operations of Company A*, 22-24.

[587] Gordon Gould, "Strictly G.I." (March 5, 1948) – college paper assignment. This original document was kindly sent to the author by his daughter Linda Brown.

[588] Finke as quoted from Julius Schmidt (compiler), *29. Falke Division. Das Buch der Falke Division* (Bad Nauheim, 1960), 318-319.

[589] Chester A. Garrison, *Unit Journal of the 2nd Battalion, 504th Parachute Infantry, 82nd Airborne Division.*

[590] Tucker, *Report of the 504th Parachute Combat Team, Operation Avalanche* (October 1943), 2.

[591] Silver Star Citation for Private Howard Albert. General Orders #36, Headquarters 82nd Airborne Division, October 6, 1943.

[592] Walker, *From Texas to Rome with Fred L. Walker*, 268.

[593] Colonel Tucker as quoted from Seymour Korman, "General Hails Yanks' Victory Atop Hill 424," *Chicago Tribune*, September 23, 1943. A copy was kindly provided to the author by Bill McKinley.

[594] Garrison, *Unit Journal of the 2nd Battalion, 504th Parachute Infantry, 82nd Airborne Division.*

[595] Thomas E. Utterback, written account sent to his wife, 1944. A retyped copy was kindly sent to the author by his granddaughter Laurie Utterback.

[596] Oldfather, "My Time in the Army," diary entry, September 17, 1943.

[597] Oldfather, "My Time in the Army," diary entry, September 18, 1943.

[598] Utterback, written account.

[599] Francis X. Keefe, telephone interview with the author, July 26, 2010.

[600] Chester A. Garrison, *Unit Journal of the 2nd Battalion, 504th Parachute Infantry, 82nd Airborne Division.*

[601] Tucker, *Report of the 504th Parachute Combat Team, Operation Avalanche* (October 1943), 2.

[602] "Rochesterian Volunteers," *Democrate and Chronicle* (Rochester, NY), November 27, 1943.

[603] Reiman Morin, "Patrols Assists in Taking Altavilla," accessed January 24, 2006, www.strikehold504th.com/forums.

[604] David K. Finney, *My Time With The 504th.* Self-published memoir, (Santee, CA: 2006) n.p.

[605] Chester A. Garrison, *An Ivy-League Paratrooper* (Corvallis, OR: 2002), 94.

[606] Chester A. Garrison, *Unit Journal of the 2nd Battalion, 504th Parachute Infantry, 82nd Airborne Division.*

[607] Seymour Korman, "General Hails Yanks' Victory Atop Hill 424," *Chicago Tribune*, September 23, 1943. A copy was kindly provided to the author by Bill McKinley.

[608] Oldfather, "My Time in the Army," diary entry, September 19, 1943.

[609] Keefe, telephone interview with the author, August 2, 2010.

[610] Oldfather, "My Time in the Army," diary entry, September 20, 1943.

[611] Tucker, *Report of the 504th Parachute Combat Team, Operation Avalanche* (October 1943), 2.

612 Distinguished Service Cross Citation for Major Robert B. Acheson. Headquarters XVIII Airborne Corps, General Order #8, (November 14, 1944).

613 Colonel Reuben Tucker as quoted from Seymour Korman, "General Hails Yanks' Victory Atop Hill 424," *Chicago Tribune*, September 23, 1943. A copy was kindly provided to the author by Bill McKinley.

614 Chester A. Garrison, *Unit Journal of the 2nd Battalion, 504th Parachute Infantry, 82nd Airborne Division*.

615 Francis W. McLane, *World War II Journal*, 5-6.

616 McLane, *World War II Journal*, 6.

617 Darrell G. Harris, *Casablanca to VE Day. A Paratrooper's Memoirs* (Pittsburgh, PA: Dorrance Publishing, 1995), 7.

618 Harris, *Casablanca to VE Day*, 7.

619 Matthew B. Ridgway as quoted from Clay Blair, *Ridgway's Paratroopers* (Annapolis, MD: Naval Institute Press, 2002), 163.

620 Silver Star Citation of Pvt Wilton A. Baker. Headquarters 82nd Airborne Division, General Orders #37, October 31, 1943.

621 John J. Foley, Jr., telephone interview with the author, February 25, 2012. Baker would receive a Silver Star.

622 Chester A. Garrison, *Unit Journal of the 2nd Battalion, 504th Parachute Infantry, 82nd Airborne Division*.

623 David K. Finney, *My Time With The 504th*. Self-published memoir, (Santee, CA: 2006) n.p.

624 Oldfather, "My Time in the Army," diary entry, September 28, 1943.

625 Francis X. Keefe, telephone interview with the author, December 22, 2015.

626 Thomas E. Utterback, written account sent to his wife, 1944. A retyped copy was kindly sent to the author by his granddaughter Laurie Utterback.

627 Robert E. Kile, letter to Earl S. Oldfather, December 2, 1993. The original letter was kindly donated to the author by Dennis Kennedy.

628 Kile, letter to Oldfather.

629 Herman Littman, email to Elodie Caldwell, August 22, 2008. A copy of this email was kindly provided to the author.

630 Louis W. Otterbein, Jr. as quoted from "Don't Worry. Families Told Liberated Bloomfield Officer Says Boys Can Take Care of Themselves," Local New Jersey newspaper, May 1945. Courtesy of John Otterbein.

631 Statement of No.207782 Lieut. E.J. Davies 2nd Bn The South Staffordshire Regiment - Escaped Prisoner of War. October 27, 1943.

632 Statement Lieutenant Davies.

633 Colonel Charles W. Kouns as quoted from Colonel Doyle R. Yardley and Charles A. Turnbo (edited), *Home was Never Like This. The Yardley's Diaries* (Evergreen, CO: 2002), 115.

634 Edward P. Haider, *Blood In Our Boots* (St. Paul, MN: 2002), 67.

635 William R. Grisez, telephone interview with the author, January 31, 2010.

[636] Military Intelligence Service, *Stalag II-B : The Final Report* (November 1, 1945), accessed on February 3, 2010, <http://darbysrangers.tripod.com/id64.htm>.

[637] Elmer C. Kaberlein, "WWII Diary." A digital copy was kindly sent to the author by Eric and Margaret Beringer.

[638] Peter J. Ranti as quoted from the *Berkshire County Eagle* (Pittsfield, Massachusetts), January 26, 1944.

[639] Peter J. Ranti as quoted from the *Berkshire County Eagle* (Pittsfield, Massachusetts), January 26, 1944.

[640] "Gets Silver Star," *The Bayonet*, May 17, 1945.

[641] Colonel George Van Horn Moseley, Jr., letter to 1st Lieutenant Rudyard M. Swagler. A copy was kindly sent to the author by his daughter Leslie Fligg.

[642] "Proceedings of Army Retiring Board for Officers," Lawson General Hospital, April 17, 1946. A copy was provided by Leslie Fligg.

INDEX

1st Battalion, 504th Parachute Infantry
Regiment, *10*
  break in column of, 344
  in campaign to retake Altavilla,
    348
  failure of Army Ground Forces
    test, 33
  first combat injuries in, 276–277
  leadership changes in, 71
  move to Castellammare del Golfo,
    290
  patrols in Altavilla, 378
  plan to seize Hill 424, 359
  See also individual units
1st British Airborne Division, 317
1st Canadian Infantry Division, 167
1st Parachute Brigade, British, 190
2nd Armored Division, 274, 285
2nd Battalion, 504th Parachute
  Infantry Regiment, *10*
  advance up western coast of Sicily,
    275–276, 277–279
  bivouac area near Biscari, 266–
    269
  bivouac area near Santa
    Margherita, 285
  campaign to retake Altavilla, 348
  Castellammare del Golfo, capture
    of, 288
  failure of Army Ground Forces
    test, 33

  garrisoning duty of, 293
  Lauren Ramsey on ill-
    preparedness of, 210
  move to Salemi, 290
  See also individual units
3rd Battalion, 504th Parachute
  Infantry Regiment, *10*
  advance up western coast of Sicily,
    285
  arrival in Naples, 390
  casualties and captured during
    Sicily Campaign, 295
  Charles Kouns on Sicily mission,
    131–142
  command changes, 265
  departure for Palermo, 322
  as Fifth Army reserve, 332–333
  Francis Deignan on Sicily mission,
    142–147
  on Hill 344, 378
  landing in Sicily, 127–130
  leadership changes, 71
  in Licata, Sicily, 311
  move to Blue Beach, 382
  move up the Sorrento Peninsula,
    386–389
  Operation Husky planning, 118–
    119
  orders to take over Hill 344, 375
  passing of Army Ground Forces
    test, 33

post-landing assembly in Gela, 265

prisoners of war and casualties from, 295

replacements assigned to, 301

Roy Hanna on Sicily mission, 147–150

Salerno Beachhead departure wait, 385–386

as "X" Battalion, 114

See also individual units

4th Livorno Division, 116

5th Company, German Army, 356–357, 370, 372

6th Company, German Army, 352, 356–357, 372

7th Company, German Army, 356–357, 372

8th Infantry Division, 2

9th Infantry Division, 2–3

15th Panzer Grenadier Division, 116–117

16th Panzer Division, 316, 317–318

20th Combat Engineer Regiment, 288, 289

29th Panzer Grenadier Division, 317, 345

36th Infantry Division, 316, 318, 335, 381, 382

39th Regimental Combat Team, 2nd Armored Division, 274

45th Infantry Division, 173, 207, 270, 318, 329

52nd Troop Carrier Wing, U.S. Navy, 214, 271–272, 308, 321

56th Infantry Division, 318

81mm Mortar Platoon, 220, 344, 348, 372, 374–375

82nd Airborne Division

conversion to airborne division, 21–22

division review of, 78

move to Fort Bragg, 34, 35

parade, 99, *100*

troop strength, 86

See also individual units

83rd Chemical Mortar Battalion, 280, 285

'88 Pass. *See* Chiunzi Pass

101st Airborne Division, 22, 69

142nd Infantry, 365–366

179th Regimental Combat Team, 318

180th Infantry Regiment, 163–164, 242, 374

206th Coastal Defense Division, Italian, 179

307th Airborne Engineer Battalion, 17, 115, 210, 275, 278, 328. *See also* C Company, 307th Airborne Engineer Battalion

307th Airborne Medical Battalion, 115

325th Glider Infantry Regiment, 115, 308, 311–312, 314

325th Regimental Combat Team, 322, 332

376th Parachute Field Artillery Battalion, 210, 269, 321, 386

376th Parachute Infantry Battalion, 17–18

501st Parachute Battalion, 2, 6, 36, 86

502nd Parachute Battalion, 2, 6

502nd Parachute Infantry Regiment, 15, 51, 69

503rd Parachute Infantry Regiment, 6, 33, 35–37

504th Parachute Battalion activation, 3, 6, 33

504th Parachute Infantry Regiment activation of, 5

assault demonstration, 69
Casablanca arrival, *82, 83*
casualties and captured during
Sicily Campaign, 295
first death of members of, 23
friendly fire casualties, 269
May 1, 1942 cadre photos, *9, 10*
odyssey of, *105*
original cadre, 11–19
plan to move up western coast of
Sicily, 274–275
Salerno Beachhead campaign
success of, 383
Salerno Beachhead jump injuries,
328
Sicily Campaign landings, *151*
See also individual units
504th Parachute Infantry Regimental
Band, 55
504th Regimental Combat Team,
17–18
504th Schwere Panzer-Abteilung, 139,
163
505th Parachute Infantry Regiment
advance up western coast of Sicily,
285
at Biazzo Ridge, 169
campaign to retake Altavilla, 348
Capua mission plans, 311, 321,
328
casualties and captured during
Sicily Campaign, 295
choice of, for Operation Husky,
114–115
I Company troops with, 191
Matthew Ridgway's search for,
206–207
in Niscemi, 146
Operation Husky planning, 119

plan to move up western coast of
Sicily, 274–275
regimental jump, 71
replacements, 113
Roy Hanna on, 149–150
stray paratroopers from, on Hill
424, 370
506th Parachute Infantry Regiment,
20, 29, 301
513th Parachute Infantry Regiment,
86, 303
636th Tank Destroyer Battalion,
335–336

A

A Company, 1st Battalion, *41, 389*
accidental injuries in
Castellammare del Golfo, 291
campaign to retake Altavilla, 345–
348
Fred Lanning's notes on photo of,
53–54
German attack on, 353–354, 356
in leading aircraft for Sicily drop,
214–220
patrol in Altavlla, 379–380
plan to seize Hill 424, 359
post-landing assembly in Gela,
260
reconstitution of, 37–46
release of, to the 503rd PIR, 36
Reneau Breard's assignment to,
304–305
retaking of Hill 424, 364–372
accidental injuries, 103, 122, 291–292.
See also noncombat deaths
Acheson, Robert B., 363
Adams, Emory S., Jr.
as 3rd Battalion commander, 265

death of William Beall and, 387
illness of, 375
on *Monrovia*, 115, 206, 207
move to Blue Beach, 382
as Regimental S-3, 56
Salerno Beachhead landing, 332
Addison, William A., 16
advance units, in North Africa, 79,
106–107
Airborne Command, formation of
the, 5
Albanella, Italy
casualties, 382–383
D Company reconnaissance of,
330–331
march of the wounded to, 359–
360
march to, 336–338
orders to withdraw to, 374
supplies sent from, 363
Thomas Utterback on, 375, 377
war correspondents in, 339
See also Hill 424; unnumbered hill
Albert, Howard, 374
Alcamo, Sicily, 288, 289
Aldridge, Richard D., 185, 186, 265
Alexander, Mark J., 20–21
Algeria. *See* Oujda, Algeria
Allied Military Government (AMG),
381
Allied negotiations with Italy, 311
Altavilla, Italy, 349, 376
36th Infantry Division and, 318,
329
casualties, 382–383
German account of, 356–357
patrols in, 378, 379–380
Reuben Tucker's plan of attack on,
338–339
Seymour Korman on, 381, 385

Wiley O'Mohundro's briefing on,
326
Wilfred Jaubert on attack of, 331
See also Hill 315; Hill 424;
unnumbered hill
Amaral, George R., 161
Anderson, Cecil W., 227
Anderson, Reynard, 33, 34
Andreas, Jack, 230
animal mascots, 119–120
Anzio, Italy, 390
Armstrong, Fielding J., 212, 232, 235
Army Ground Forces inspection,
32–33
Aszklar, Chester H., 182, 342–343
AWOL soldiers, 75

B

B Company, 1st Battalion
2nd Battalion's relief of, on
unnumbered hill, 372–373
briefing on Salerno Beachhead,
321
defense of unnumbered hill, 359
fatal casualties in, 380
German attack on, 355
jump exercise, 56
mortar fire from, 352
orders to reinforce A Company on
Hill 424, 373
prisoners of war from, 295
reinforcements for A Company, 37
Salerno Beachhead jump, 327–
328
Sicily drop, 220–221
B Company, 307th Airborne Engineer
Battalion, 115
Bachenheimer, Theodore H., 43–44,
69–70

Badoglio, Pietro, 311, 313–314, 315
Baker, Wilton A., 387–388
Baldino, Fred J., 41–42, 43–44, 54, 277, 291, 348
Baley, Clyde F., 170, *171*, 172
band, regimental, 55
Barbour, Bill, 184
Barnes, Robert E., 245
Bartley, Jack M., 29, 59
Bartow, Richard A., 245
Bassett, James A., 1, 2
Bates, Ralph, 36–37
Battalion medical detachments, 61–62
Battipaglia, Italy, 318
The Bayonet, 140–141
beach landings, 184, 314, 322, 332, 382, 386
Beall, Jean, 74–75
Beall, William R., *10, 37, 41*
    cadre photo and, 6
    command of 3rd Battalion, 375
    death of, 387
    departure on *HMT Andes,* 76
    Fred Lanning's notes on photo of, 54
    G Company command and, 265
    on Hill 344, 378
    I Company patrol orders, 382
    learning of Charles Kouns's capture, 261
    post-landing assembly in Gela, 260
    pre-deployment date with wife, 74–75
    reconstitution of A Company, 37–40
    Regimental Advance Party and, 71
    Sicily Campaign and, 152, 166–168
Beanie (jackass), 119–120

Bedell, Edwin A., 76
Bertolette, Richard, 61
Bertsch, William H., 314–315, 316
Biddle, Charles J., 70
Biello, Dominic, 57
Bigger, Erwin B., 31–32, 210
Bigler, John M., 237, 328
Billingslea, Charles, 266, 277, 309
Billman, Calvin J., 220
Binnix, Robert K., 130, 139, 140, 195, 402
Biscari, Sicily, 248, 266–269
Biscari Airfield, 163, 173, 189, 221
Bishop, Jack B., 37
Black, Lee, 179
Blevins, Howard K., 194
Blitch, Melvin S., Jr., 52, 56, 266, 292
Bloomfield, Abraham, 283
Bodnar, William T., 171
Boggs, Alvin H., 226
Bogle, Ralph N., 378, 381
Bonilla, Nicholas, 60
Botwinski, Chester J., 191
Boyd, Frank D., 210
Bradley, Omar N., 99, 116
Brady, Kenneth E., 181
Brancato, Jacob S., 121
Breard, Reneau G., 304–305, 324, 364, 379
Breathwit, James G., 173
bridge demolition by H Company, 387–388
Briggs, Richard H., 187, 191
Briggs, Rowland, 328
Brinser, Harold K., 329
British 46th and 56th Infantry Divisions, 318
British Eighth Army, 116, 274, 307–308
British X Corps, 307, 316, 318, 389

Brooks, James R., 234

Brown, Earnest H., 113, 256–259

Bruggeman, William, 61

Burgreen, Alfred, 28, 200–201, 261

Burriss, Moffatt, 106, 112, 118, 126, 158–161

Butler, Raymond J., 212

Byrd, James E., 212, 231–232

C

C-47 tank reinforcement recommendation, 273

C Company, 1st Battalion
break in column, *121*, 344
death of Floyd Quinn of, 103
death of Jack Bartley of, 59
death of Merle Williams of, 23
death of messengers from, 343
photo of, 53
plan to seize Hill 424, 359
reinforcements for Hill 424, 370
replacements for, 305–306
Salerno Beachhead campaign, 336
Sicily drop, 221–227, 237

C Company, 307th Airborne Engineer Battalion
death of commander of, 341
fatalities in, 269
on Hill 424, 342, 348
Mark Clark's crediting of, 383
mine removal by, 278, 289
as part of 504th Regimental Combat Team, 17
roadblock established by, 328
Sicily drop, 210–211

Camp Edwards, Massachusetts, 77–78, 81

Camp Leautey, 81, 94–95, 98, 297–298

Camp Lyautey. *See* Camp Leautey

Campbell, Calvin, 29, 166

Campbell, Ernest H., 237

Cannizzaro, Francis "Frank" R., 63, 230

Capa, Robert, 123–124, 127, 128, 338, 405

Capua, Italy
planned mission for, 308, 310, 311–312, 328
prison camp at, 142, 177–179, 395

Cargill, Thomas C. "Doc," 252

Carney, Herbert C., 156

Carter, Bernard, E., 367

Carter, Ross S., 59, 209, 211, 225

Casa Iacono, 262–264

Casablanca, Morocco, *82, 83*
advance detail's arrival at, 79
David Finney on, 94–95
departure for Oujda, Algeria, 83
replacements' arrival at, 97–98, 296–297, 301
SS George Washington's arrival at, 80–81
Thomas Utterback on, 89

Castellammare del Golfo, Sicily, 287–288, 289, 290, 291

Castellano, Giuseppe, 311, 312

Castle Nocera, 181, 183, 184, 201–202, 204

chaplains, 18–19, 79, 300, 399

Chapman, William E., 33, 230

Chase, Charles H., 6, *10, 12,* 20, 290

Chase, Richard, 3, 6, *12,* 20

Chenery, William L., 123

Chicago Tribune
Jack Thompson of the, 124, 268, 284

Seymour Korman of the, 310, 338, 381

Chiunzi Pass, 316, 386–387, 389

civilians
  Salerno Beachhead campaign and, 278, 381, 395
  Sicily campaign and, 133, 139, 146, 183

Clark, Albert B., 43
  on arrival in Casablanca, 78, 80
  on Camp Edwards, 77
  on first combat injuries, 276–277
  on flight to Sicily, 216
  on Operation Giant II, 315
  reconstitution of A Company, 42–43
  on Salermo Beachhead mission, 323
  on train travel, 78, 108–111

Clark, Mark W., 99, 100, 384
  awarding of Edward Kennedy's Soldier's Medal, 305
  Capua mission and, 311–312, 328
  command of William Yarborough and, 292
  Earl Oldfather on, 298
  Italy invasion plans, 307, 308
  in Morocco, 99, 100
  order for reinforcements at Salerno Beachhead, 320
  request for 504th as reinforcement, 323
  Salerno Beachhead mission, 332
  on success of Salerno Beachhead campaign, 383
  trip to London as airborne observer, 52

Clay, William L., 353

Clements, Rell, Jr., 53

Clevenger, Charles A., 245

Cline, George W., 173

Coen, Edward, 284

Cohen, Eugene R., 232, 233

Collier's Magazine, 123

Collins, Arthur E., 230

Collins, Tom, 373

Colville, William, Jr., 6, 10

Comiso Field, 309, 315, 320–321, 325

command changes
  3rd Battalion, 265
  after Altavilla battle, 385
  after Sicily Campaign, 292–293
  James Gavin and, 115
  pre-deployment, 47–48, 64, 65, 71

communications devices, 309–310, 321, 323

Communications Platoon, 166, 182

Comstock, Ira K., Jr., 230

Condon, Robert D., 41, 291
  on awaiting zero hour, 211
  on flight to Sicily, 214–217, 218–219
  on night before combat drop, 207–208
  reconstitution of A Company and, 39, 40
  wounding of, 277, 291

Conklin, James C., 230

Conley, Henry F., 161

Connolly, William, 57

Conover, Clayton F., 230

Conrath, Paul, 116–117, 189

Cook, Julian A., 15, 213
  as 3rd Battalion executive officer, 21
  communications loss and, 339
  Henry Muller on, 13
  on joining the paratroopers, 7
  officer assignments and, 11–12
  as Regimental S-4, 64

on Reuben Tucker, 47–48
on Sicily drop, 235–236, 237
Cope, Leonard J., 245
Corey, Albert W., 37
Coutts, James "Lou" W., 11, 13–14, 407
Cox, Gerald R., 64
Crane, Newton L., 246
Crawford, Kenneth R., 174
Crawford, Willard, 181
Crochet, Milton J., 56, 330
Crockett, T.J., 221
Crouch, Joel L., 309, 310
Cummings, Harry J., 33, 34, 212, 232, 233–235
Cundiff, Amos R., 379
Cupples, Joseph, 57

D

D Company, 2nd Battalion, 57, 58
bombing of, 372
command changes in, 47
death of James Powers of, 103
death of Roy Gray of, 46
patrols in Altavilla, 381
prisoners of war from, 295
Propblast article on, 56–57
reconnaissance of Albanella, 330
Salemi area mission, 290–291
Salerno Beachhead drop, 328
Sicily jump, 251–254
Tumminello Pass battle, 281
Danielson, Daniel W.
as 2nd Battalion commander, 47
as assistant to David DeArmond, 21
briefing of, by Wiley O'Mohundro, 326

briefing on Salerno Beachhead mission, 320–321
call for commanding officers' meeting, 381
move to Sorrento Peninsula, 388
orders to leave Salerno Beachhead, 385
orders to retake Altavilla, 336
William Yarborough and, 52, 292
Daniszewski, Stanley J., Jr., 59
Danneman, Otis A., 212, 232, 233
Darby, William O., 274, 316–317, 332
Davidson, William H., 180–181
Davies, Eric, 394
Davis, Marquis E., 173, 178
Davis, Ola, 29
Dawley, Ernest, 335, 374, 375, 385
D'Crenzo, Sam, 33, 305
De Vore, Russell W., 245
Dean, Robert P., 193
DeArmond, David, 20, 21, 47
deaths. *See* killed in action; noncombat deaths
Decker, Dale E., 375
Decker, Edwin E., 221, 353
Deignan, Francis W.
33rd Infantry Regiment and, 51
Earl Oldfather on, 322
as jumpmaster, 130
on preparations for first combat mission, 125
Robert Binnix and, 140
Sicily mission and, 142–147
Delloto, Angelo M., 193
Demeritt, William J., Jr., 35, 47
Demolition Platoon. *See* Regimental Demolition Platoon
Denkins, James W., 237
dental care, 361
Denton, Daniel V., 230

Desideri, Jack O., 387
Di Rinzo, John C., 372
Dickerson, Albert, 303
Dickerson, Robert L., 314
Digan, Edward C., 183, 204–205
Distinguished Service Cross
    Acheson, Robert B., 363
    Cummings, Harry J., 234–235
    Dunham, Don P., 343–344
    Hord, Shelby R., 202, 203
    recipient list, 425
    Tucker, Reuben, 383
Division Advance Detachment, 76–77
Dix, Shirley, 33, 34
Dixon, Russell K., 230
Dolezal, Stanley M., 47, 252, 254, 331
Dooley, Harold L., 33
Doyle, Thomas A., 50
Drew, Charles A. "Hoss," 242–243,
    245, 281–282
drop zones, Operation Husky, 117–
    118
Dudley, William R., 33
Dugan, Galen W., 230
Duncan, Charles W.
    assignment to C Company, 15
    break in column and, 344
    orders to reinforce A Company on
    Hill 424, 373
    Salerno Beachhead jump, 327–
    328, 330
    Sicily drop, 220
Dunham, Don P., 339, 341, 342,
    343–344, 360
Dunlop, Lawrence, 181
Dunn, James E., 39, 40, 41, 224, 340,
    370
Dunn, Mike, 273
Dunn, Theodore L., 12
    background of, 5–6

Fred Lanning's notes on photo of,
    53
Henry Muller on, 13
loss of officers to new parachute
    regiments and, 20–21
parachute jump of Matthew
    Ridgway and, 24
reconstitution of A Company and,
    37, 38
regimental colors presentation, 11
replacement of, 47, 48
status of regiment of, 32, 34
Durendo, Joseph R., 173
Durham, John C., 246
Duvall, Mearle D., 39–40, 41, 350,
    351, 359
dysentery, 83–84, 155

E

E Company, 2nd Battalion
    briefing on Salerno Beachhead,
    321–322
    casualties in, 375, 378
    at Ribera, Sicily, 275–276
    Salemi area mission, 290–291
    at Salerno Beachhead, 328–329
    Sicily drop, 248–250
    Tumminello Pass battle, 281
E Company, 20th Combat Engineer
    Regiment, 289
Eaton, Peter J., 161–164, 264–265
Eby, Robert E., 17, 22
Eden, Anthony, 69
Edstrom, Willard H., 379
Edwards, James R., 237
EGB447, 79, 86, 97–98, 296, 303
EGB448, 80, 97, 296–303
Eide, John W., 230

Eighth Army, British. *See* British
  Eighth Army
Eisenbruch, Harold C., 173
Eisenhower, Dwight D., *100*
  82nd Airborne parade and, 99,
    100
  on armistice with Italy, 315
  friendly fire investigation and, 270,
    272
  James Coutts as advisor to, 14
  Maxwell Taylor's message to, from
    Rome, 314
  Operation Giant II and, 312
  practice jump for, 103, 181
Eldridge, James O., 221–223, *223*,
  305–306, 357–358
Ellis, Ronald P., 400
Ellis, Vernon P., 237, 278
Engebretson, Lloyd, 199–200, *200*,
  386
equipment delivery procedure
  training, 66–69
equipment seizure from Italians, 284
Erickson, Robert O., 6, *10*, *12*, 20, 64,
  64
escapes and escape attempts,
  American POW, 397–398,
  401–403
Eureka beacons, 309–310, 321, 323
Evans, Harry E., 170
Evans, Lucian A., 193

F

F Company, 2nd Battalion
  advance up western coast of Sicily,
    276, 277–279
  Salemi area mission, 290–291
  Sicily drop, 239–246
  Tumminello Pass battle, 279–284

Fabian, Bill E., 70, 193, 396
Fairbrother, Irving T., 379
Farello Airfield, 207, 237, 260
Fasano, Alex R., 33
fatalities. *See* killed in action;
  noncombat deaths
Fattore, Louis F., 284
Ferguson, Arthur W., 30–31, 250
Ferguson, Frederick J., 136, 137–138,
  138
Fern, Lewis P.
  as 2nd Battalion S-2 Officer, 52
  advance up western coast of Sicily,
    278–279
  background of, 26
  command changes and, 292
  on entering Ribera, 275
  on flight of officers, 210
  on Italian POWs, 289
  on Salemi area mission, 290–291
  on salvaged Italian equipment,
    284
  on Sicily drop, 248
  on trip on *SS George Washington*,
    79
  on troop strength, 266–267, 268–
    269
  on Tumminello Pass battle, 280,
    281
Ferrari, Henry E., 199
Ferrill, Willis J., 183, 201, 202, 204,
  265, 386
Fetters, Wayne M., 74
Fifth Army
  3rd Battalion as reserve for, 332–
    333
  Italy invasion plans, 307–308
  mission to reinforce, 322–323
Fillion, Adrian, 245
Findley, Holley A., 33

Finke, Kurt, 345–347, 356–357, 372
Finney, David K., 92–95, 228–229,
   322–323, 325, 380
first jump
   of Alfred Burgreen, 28
   of Arthur Ferguson, 30–31
   of Francis McLane, 97
   of Fred Baldino, 42
   of Herbert Lucas, 28–29
   of Ivan Roggen, 60
   of John Isom, 96
Flaville, Charles K, 243–244
Fleming, Oma L., 400
Foise, Jack, 273
Foley, John J., Jr., 301, 387–388
Follmer, Willard R., 206
food. See rations
Fort Benning, Georgia, 10
   activation of the 504th, 3–5, 6–7
   David Finney's training at, 93–94
   departures of original officers,
      20–21, 31–32
   Dickerson, Albert, 303
   Francis McLane on training at, 97
   John Isom on training at, 96
   original cadre at, 11–19
   Test Platoon, 1–2
   training at, 7–9, 23–33
Fort Bragg, North Carolina, 57, 58
   82nd's move to, 34, 35
   A Company, reconstitution of,
      37–46
   deaths during training at, 59–60
   Elbert Smith on training at, 66–69
   leadership changes, 47–48, 64, 71
   medics' training at, 61, 62–63
   preparations for departure from,
      76
   training at, 55–56
Fort Hamilton, New York, 74

Fowler, John "Jack" M., 123
Frank, Henry B., 303, 326, 378
Frazier, James R., 173
Frederick, Lewis S., Jr., 127–128
Freeman, Leslie G., 15
   bag of gold seal dollars and, 233
   campaign to retake Altavilla and,
      339, 341, 343
   command of 3rd Battalion, 21
   post-war life of, 406–407
   as regimental executive officer,
      51–52
   request for reinforcements and
      supplies from, 363
   Richard Tregaskis on, 358
   Salerno Beachhead mission and,
      320–321, 323
   Sicily jump of, 232
   walk back to Albanella, 359, 360
   wounding of, 235
Frenning, Lawrence O., 378
friendly fire
   on C Company, 221, 224, 225
   casualty totals, 269–270
   on D Company, 251–252, 253
   on E Company, 248–249
   Earnest Brown on, 257
   on F Company, 241, 242, 245
   Headquarters and Headquarters
      Company jump and, 235–238
   investigation into, 270–271
   John S. Thompson on, 255
   media reports of, 273
   on William Yarborough's plane,
      247
Fry, Floyd E., 165
furlough to Washington, D.C., 54–55
Furst, Henry S., 358

G

G Company, 3rd Battalion
  boat transport, 322
  command changes, 265
  march to Albanella, 375
  practice loading and unloading
    boats, 311
  Robert Kile on, 390
  at Salerno Beachhead, 332, 377
  Sicily Campaign and, 150, 168–
    175
Gage, Philip S., Jr., 35
Gallagher, Bernard F., 317
Gann, James L., 172–173
Gardiner, William T., 313–314
Garrison, Chester A.
  on 2nd Battalion's relief of B
    Company, 372–373
  on casualties of September 18th,
    378
  on order to evacuate Hill 424,
    374–375
  on orders to leave Salerno
    Beachhead, 385
  on patrols in Altavilla, 378
  on preparations for move to
    Sorrento Peninsula, 388
  on quiet of September 19th, 380–
    381
  on Salerno Beachhead drop, 325–
    326, 328–329
  on Salerno Beachhead mission,
    331
  on Sicily drop, 249–250
  on transfer, 292–293
  on traveling with heavy
    equipment, 348
garrison duty, in Sicily, 288–294
Gavin, James M., 101

advance up western coast of Sicily,
    285
  Capua landing plans and, 308
  command structure changes, 115
  fly over of Sicily, 117–118
  Matthew Ridgway's search for,
    206
  Operation Husky and, 114
  transfer of Lewis Fern to OCS, 26
Gaygan, James F., 276
Gela, Sicily
  army cemetery at, 174
  drop plans, 119, 125, 126
  E Company drop, 249
  friendly fire over, 250, 255
  German bombing of convoy at,
    225
  Monrovia's arrival at, 206
  post-landing assembly in, 260–
    265, 268–269
Gela-Niscemi road mission, 134–136,
    164
General Order Number 2, 5
Gentzel, Richard H., 243–245, 279,
    280, 282–283
Gerard, Gus M., 292
German airborne operations, 1
German Army
  5th Company, 356–357, 370, 372
  6th Company, 352, 356–357, 372
  7th Company, 356–357, 372
  counterattack at Hill 424, 366–
    370
  defensive forces on Sicily, 116–
    117
  intelligence, 109, 113
  Operation Axe, 315–316
  POWs, 181, 255–256, 342, 344,
    345, 384

Salerno mission to halt advance of, 323

Sicily mission casualties, 136, 137

See also Hermann Goering Panzer Division

German bombers, 224–225

German propaganda radio, 109, 113

Gibson, John M., 212, 231, 235

Gilbert, William O., Jr., 342

Gillilan, Thomas T., 378

Gilson, Frank W., 344

Goethe, James H., 38, *41*, 121, *121*, 224–225

Goldschmidt, Karl, 171–172, 262–264

Goodson, Thomas J., 350, 351

Gordon, Harry A., 220

Gorham, Fordyce, 38–39, *41*, 54, 121, 357

Gorniak, Frank X., 227

Gough, Harry W., 159–161

Gould, Gordon, 44–46, 54, 56, 77–78, 371–372

Grainger, Fred, 62

Gray, Roy W., 46

Green, Hubert D., 127

Green, Paul, 310

Gregory, Howard L., 33, 37

Griffin, Henry, 250

Griffith, Wilbur M., 17, 210, 386

Grisez, William R. "Buffalo Bill," 165, 397

Gruenther, Alfred, 99

Grün, Eugen, 262–263

Guba, John G., 245

Gulf of Salerno, 307–308, 317–318

Gurfein, Joseph I., 115

Gurley, Abraham, 184

Gutterman, Harold M., 210

Guzzoni, Alfredo, 116, 117

Gwiazdowski, Joseph, 348

H

H Company, 3rd Battalion

bridge demolition by, 387–388

in campaign to retake Altavilla, 342–343

command changes, 265

David Rosenkrantz's letter on training of, 64–66

Edward Kennedy's assignment to, 305

Elbert Smith on equipment delivery training, 66–69

fatal casualties in, 98, 295

post-landing assembly in Gela, 260–261

reincorporation by 3rd Battalion, 386

replacements assigned to, 301

Sicily Campaign and, 176–188

training jump in North Africa, 111–112

Haggard, Albert C., 199–200

Hahn, Werner, 262–263

Haider, Edward P.

background of, 26–28

on boarding the *SS George Washington*, 78–79

on company mascots, 119–120

on engagement with Germans in Sicily, 196–198

on Henry Keep's generosity, 70–71

on last-minute knowledge of mission, 125–126

on night of first combat mission, 124–125

as prisoner of war, 165, 397

on Sicily drop, 195–196

Haire, James P., Jr., 193

Halbert, Dean W., 397–398

Hall, Ralph C., 221

Hall, Wilbur, 55

Halloran, Robert M.
    on arrival at Casablanca, 80
    on Cape Cod staging area, 77
    on food, 83
    as Regimental Dental Surgeon,
      63–64
    on replacements, 305
    on Sicily drop, 231
    treatment of wounded near
      Altavilla, 360–361

Hamilton, Jacob R., 320

Hanna, Roy M., 22–23, 119, 125,
    147–150, 317

Haratsis, Charles G., 400

Hardridge, Alex I., 246

Harmon, Leonard, Jr., 387

Harris, Darrell G., 32, 79, 120–121,
    122, 164–165, 386–387

Harrison, George M., 184

Harrison, Willard E., *100*
    campaign to retake Altavilla, 344,
      347
    in flight to Sicily, 214, 217–218
    at Hill 315, 344
    march to Albanella and, 337, 338
    order for patrol of Hill 424, 350
    picking up of wounded Mearle
      Duvall, 351
    request for artillery by, 368
    retaking of Hill 424, 364, 366

Hart, Joseph H., 230

Hartgraves, William D., 192

Haugen, Orin D., 14

Hauptfleisch, Louis, 29

Hauser, William C., 44–45, 371–372

Hawkins, Clarence G., 230

Headquarters and Headquarters
    Company
    command changes in, 265
    furlough to Washington, D.C. of,
      54–55
    missing in action form from, 161
    Moffatt Burriss on Sicily
      Campaign and, 158–161
    move up Sorrento Peninsula, 389
    Operation Husky, 228–237
    organization of, 16
    Thomas Utterback on Sicily
      Campaign and, 152–158

Headquarters Company, 1st Battalion,
    220

Headquarters Company, 2nd
    Battalion, 254–256

Heaton, Roy N., 173

Henderson, Hugh A., 245

Hennessey, James H., 193

Henry, Homer, 37

Hermann Goering Panzer Division
    1st Battalion engagement with,
      163
    American intelligence on, 116–
      117
    American POWs taken by, 165,
      171, 194
    Castle Nocera battle and, 204
    counterattack orders of July 10th,
      189
    Edward Haider on, 196
    field hospital of, 177
    Fifth Army and, 317–318
    G Company 2nd Platoon drop
      and, 169
    H Company and, 316–317
    James Ott's attack on, 183–184

Hesselberg, Myer, 380

Hill, Edward B., Jr., 351–352

Hill, George B., 192–193

Hill 315, 339, 344–345, *349*, 363–364, 368

Hill 344, 336, 375, 378

Hill 424, *349, 376, 380*
    campaign to take, 336, 340, 341–344
    A Company patrol of, 350
    German counterattack on, 318
    plan to seize, 335–336, 359
    retaking of, 364–375
    Reuben Tucker's message from, 348
    Reuben Tucker's success at, 383
    Richard Tregaskis on leaving, 358
    VI Corps orders of September 16th, 335

Hines, Wesley C., 46, 251–252

Hinton, Woodrow, 46

Hirsch, Joseph, 277

HMT Andes, 76, 79

Hockett, Wayne, 328

Holbrook, Joseph S., 63

Holmes, Donald L., 190–191

Honea, Woodrow, 20

Honey (dog), 53

Hope, Bob, 300, 307

Hord, Shelby R., 201–203, 261

Hornby, William E., 16, 54–55

Horton, Donald F., 337, 380

Howell, George P., Jr., 51

Huckins, Walter R., 181–182

Huebner, Otto
    on advance to Hill 424, 344–345
    campaign to retake Altavilla and, 347
    on march to Albanella, 337–338
    order for patrol of Hill 424, 350

reconstitution of A Company and, 37, 46
    on retaking of Hill 424, 364–366, 368, 369, 370–371

Humphrey, Forrest E., 164, 165

Hupperich, Herman C., 31

I

I Company, 3rd Battalion
    arrival in Naples, 390
    arrival in New York, 78–79
    command changes, 265
    fatal casualties in, 98
    Francis Keefe's assignment to, 304
    mascots of, 119–120
    observation patrol from, 381–382
    post-landing assembly in Gela, 261
    Salerno Beachhead departure wait, 386
    in Sicily Campaign, 189–205

illness and disease, 83–84, 94, 155

Illustrated magazine, 123

infiltration obstacle course training, 303–304

intelligence
    Allied, 116–117
    German, 109, 113

Isom, John B., 95–96, 347

Italian Army
    4th Livorno Division, 116
    POWs, 275, 282, 284, 288–289
    on Sicily, 116

Italy, *319, 392*
    Allied negotiations with, 311
    armistice agreement, 312, 315–316
    plans for invasion of, 307–310
    See also Salerno Beachhead; Sicily

J

Jahay, Sidney A., 184
Jaubert, Wilfred, *254*
  on Capua mission briefing, 310
  on Operation Giant II, 315
  on Salerno Beachhead mission,
    327, 330–331
  on Sicily jump, 252–253
  on travel to Trapani, Sicily, 312
Jeffery, James J., 193
Jepson, Jesse M., 74
Jerry (dog), 127
Johnson, Harry L., 171
Johnson, Lawrence P., 64, 98, 197
Johnson, Robert R., 236, 292
Jones, Doris, 252
Jones, George M., 36
Jones, Robert L., 37, 367
Jones, William S., 309, 348
Jordan, Lawrence, 261
Jordan, William P., 63
jump towers, 1–2, 96
jump training
  accidents, 122
  B Company exercise, 56
  David Finney on, 93–94
  David Rosenkrantz's letter on,
    64–66
  Elbert Smith on, 66–69
  Michael Losyk's death during,
    59–60
  regimental practice jumps, 71,
    102–103
  of replacements, 308–309
  stages of, 7–9
  of Test Platoon, 1–2
  See also first jump
jump wings, 3, 9
Justice, Ray, 358

K

Kaberlein, Elmer C., 173, 178–179,
    398–401
Kacala, Joseph S., 193
Kairouan, Tunisia, *213, 214*
  advance units in, 106–107
  briefing on Capua mission in, 310
  camel shooting incident in, 120–
    121
  Francis Keefe's assignment in, 304
  Francis McLane on, 108
  Thomas Utterback's return to,
    265–266
  Thomas Zouzas on, 302
  training in, 111–113, 308
  See also North Africa
Kalina, Roger K., 35
Kanapkis, Edward, 161
Kappel, Carl W., 122, 387
Kaufman, Herbert C., 71–72, 152,
    153, 158, 174
Keefe, Francis X., 302–304, 333, 378,
    382, 386, 390
Keep, Henry, 28, 29, 70–71, 192
Keerans, Charles L., Jr., 124, 212, 232,
    235
Kelley, Richard D., 130, 134
Kellogg, William, *384*
Kemble, Mickey, 33
Kendall, Herbert H., 191
Kennedy, Edward W., 305
Kennedy, John F., 406
Kent, Frank J., 176–177, 261
Kerns, Ralph, 230
Kesselring, Albert, 117, 189, 315–316
Ketterer, John J., 46
Kettren, Augustine, 192
Keyes, Geoffrey, 274–275, 385
Kichman, Paul G., 184

Kile, Robert E., 390
Kilgore, Harley M., 273
killed in action
    in advance up western coast of
        Sicily, 278
    Beall, William, 387
    Byrd, James, 231–232
    in campaign to retake Altavilla,
        343–344
    Carter, Bernard, 367
    Danneman, Otis, 233
    Decker, Dale, 375
    Digan, Edward, 205
    Dunham, Don, 360
    of F Company, 241, 242
    of G Company, 171, 173
    Gillilan, Thomas, 378
    Goodson, Thomas, 351
    Hesselberg, Myer, 380
    of I Company, 192–193
    Paquet, Henry, 355
    Rouse, Edwin, 354
    at Salerno Beachhead, 329
    in Tumminello Pass battle, 284
    on unnumbered hill, 372
    Wall, Ned, 353–354
    Weeks, Vernon, 380
    Wensil, Harry, 375
    Wight, Thomas, 341
    Young, Ralph, 350
    Zumwalt, Warren, 357–358
    See also noncombat deaths
King, James H., Jr., 98, 113, 372
Kisko, Joseph, 61
Kitchin, William W., 63, 84, 166–168
Knights Cross, 383
Kobak, Henry J., 245
Komosa, Adam A., 99, 112–113, 228,
    230–231, 285, 322–323
Kopstein, Joseph, 245

Korman, Seymour
    assignment to the 504th, 310
    mission to take Altavilla and, 338,
        339, 359, 360, 381, 385
Kouns, Charles W., 15
    on Army Ground Forces
        inspection, 32–33
    on being attached to the 505th,
        114
    on being taken prisoner, 141–142
    on bivouac inspection, 81
    departure from New York and, 78
    Elbert Smith's assignment and,
        122–123
    final briefing before Operation
        Husky takeoff, 124
    fly over of Sicily, 117–118
    on improvement in camp
        conditions at Oujda, 84–85
    James Ott's contact with in Sicily,
        183–184
    on landing in Sicily, 127–130
    on Lesley McNair's training visit,
        55
    Operation Husky planning, 118–
        119
    on original cadre, 12–13
    post-war life of, 405
    as prisoner of war, 394, 395–396
    on regimental jump, 71
    on replacement groups, 86
    on Reuben Tucker, 52, 77, 101
    on ship-to-shore move at
        Casablanca, 80–81
    on Sicily mission, 131–138, 139–
        140
    on Thomas Utterback's serving of
        wine to troops, 91–92
    on training exercise accidents, 103

view on leadership of the 504th,
46–47
on weapons training and battle
indoctrination, 23
William Beall as replacement for,
261
Kouns, Marion, 150–151
Kozak, Edwin J., 18, 79
Krause, Edward C. "Cannonball,"
117–118
Kuehl, Delbert A., 18–19, 29, 79, 211,
241–242
Kunde, Paul A., 250

L

Labinsky, Myron F., 152, 154, 155,
156
Labre, John R. "Jack," 122, 289–290
Landing Craft Infantry training, 311.
See also beach landings
Landing Ship Tanks (LSTs). *See* beach
landings
Lane, Thomas E., 203–204
Langdon, Allen L., 98, 113
Lange, Otto F., 327, 329
Langford, Frances, 307
Lanning, Fred L., 53–54, 353–354,
362
Larsen, Robert, 362
Lavis, Frank J., 301
Laycock, Robert, 316
LCIs. *See* beach landings; Landing
Craft Infantry training
Le Count, John C., 372
Leccese, Thomas J., 102, 103, 104, 113
Lechner, James E., 372
Lee, Nelvis M., 241
Lee, William C., 1–2, 5, 52–53
Legacie, James H., Jr., 181

Lekson, John S., *41*
on break in column, 344
briefing by Wiley O'Mohundro,
326
C Company patrol report, 336
campaign to retake Altavilla, 348
Fred Lanning's notes on, 54
on German attack on A Company,
356
on German attack on Hill 424,
352, 353
on organization of 1st Battalion,
16
on reconstitution of A Company,
38
on reinforcements for Hill 424,
370
on Reuben Tucker, 359
on Salerno Beachhead drop, 324–
325
on Salerno Beachhead mission,
321, 327–328, 329–330, 331–
332
transfer to battalion staff, 207
on Willard Harrison's request for
artillery, 368
Leoleis, George, 33, 382
LeSage, Arthur W., 252
Lewis, Harry L., *101*, 308
Licata, Sicily, 311, 322
Lindsey, Elmer E., 184–185
Littman, Herman, 177–178, 179, 393,
396
Livesay, James L., 46
Lockhart, Joseph L., 284
Long, Richard F., 166
Looney, Russell F., 161
Los Angeles Daily News, 180
Losyk, Michael, 59–60
Lowe, Robert J., 350, 378–379

Lowery, Robert W., 224
Loyal Edmonton Regiment, 179–180
LSTs. *See* beach landings
Lucas, Herbert C.
    background of, 28–29
    on camp at Oujda, 83
    on Charles Kouns's capture, 261
    on regimental practice jumps, 103
    on Sicily jump, 182
    on travel to Tunisia, 108
    on trip across the Atlantic, 79
Lucas, John P., 385
Lutcavage, Zigmund C., 245, 291–292

M

Macauley, Theodore F., 193–195, 402
MacDonald, James M., 245
Machine Gun Platoon, C Company,
    225–226
Machine Gun Platoon, HQ Company,
    125, 130 –147, 255–256,
    267–269
Madona, Vince A., 375
Magrath, William W., 38, 53, 309, 355
Malone, Raleigh E., 74
Maloney, Arthur A., 21
Mandle, William D., 303
Manley, Roland K., 152, 153, 158
Mann, Aubrey, 171
Marino, Louis C., 336–337, 350, 351
marriages, pre-deployment, 69–70
Marshall, George C., 56, 69
Martin, Sande H., 113
mascots, company, 53, 119–120, 127
Massey, Charles T., 191
McAllister, Helen, 50
McCarthy, Thomas J., 37, 54
McDermott, Russell J., 191
McEachern, Joseph J., 173

McEwen, David C., 173
McGinity, James E., 7, 20–21
McGrath, William W. *See* Magrath,
    William W.
McKeever, William, 302–303
McLane, Francis W.
    background of, 96–97
    on departing New York, 98
    on Francis Keefe, 304
    on leaving Sarerno beachhead,
        386
    transfer to I Company, 113
    on travel to Tunisia, 108
McNair, Lesley J., 4–5, 55
McNally, Arthur, 245
McNamara, James M., 230
McOmber, Marshall C., 75, 173, 174–
    175, 182, 265
McPhail, William W., 230
medical equipment, 118
medics
    assignments and training of, 61–
        64
    Fort Bragg training, 55
    in original cadre, 17
    replacements for, 305
    Silver Star award, 374
    treatment of wounded near
        Altavilla, 360–361
Meerman, William A., 352
Meintzer, Wade M., 115
Meitzel, Helmut, 345, 368, 383
Mentzer, Paul C., 289
Messina, John S., 152, 158, 265
Meyerson, David, 280–281
MIAs. *See* missing in action
Migues, Eddie, 61
Miles, Albert E. "Woody," 173
Miley, William W., 2

military bases, activation and training,
73
Miller, Glenn, 75
Miller, Levern H., 283
Millett, George, 14
Milloy, Albert E., 53, 224, 340, 342,
348, 357
Mills, Richard F., 225–226, 227
missing in action
of 3rd Battalion, 295
of 376th Parachute Field Artillery
Battalion, 237
after Sicily jump, 161, 173
Crawford, Kenneth R., 174
in friendly fire incident, 270
of I Company, 190–191, 192
Lindsey, Elmer E., 184–185
Ray, Robert E., 164, 165
Ritch, Wallace, 190
Sheridan, Hugh A., 177
Mitchell, Willis W., 127
Mohammed ben Yusef, 99
Mondt, David E., 212
Monrovia (transport vessel), 115, 206,
207
Montecorvino airfield, 318
Montgomery, Bernard L., 116, 307,
308, 312
Monti, John J., 372
Moorehead, Edmund Q., 352
Moreland, Tommy D., 256
Morin, Reiman, 379–380
Morrow, Delmer G., 245
Mortar Platoon, 1st Battalion, 352–
353
Mortar Platoon, 2nd Battalion, 220,
256, 257–259, 280
Mortar Platoon, 3rd Battalion, 161–
164, 264–265
Morton, Howard W., 98

Moseley, George Van Horn, Jr., 406–
407, 408
Moseley, Norman, 197
Muller, Henry J., Jr., 11–12, 13–14, *15*
Mulloy, Patrick J., 237
Murfield, Ethel, 70
Muri, Leo P., 304, 390
Murphy, Jerry, 348
Mussolini, Benito, 290, 311
Muston, Raymond L., 98
Myrtle Beach Problem, 71

N

Neptune, Robert H., 210
Neumeyer, Lawrence W. "Bucky," 185
The New York Times, 166, 270
Nicoll, Ken, *209*
Nicolson, Malcolm A., 292
Niscemi, Sicily, 132, 141, 142, 146,
194–195. *See also* Gela-Niscemi
road mission
Nitz, Melvin W., 239, 277, 279
Noguès, Charles, *99*
noncombat deaths
Gray, Roy W., 46
in North Africa, 98, 103, 113
training accidents, 59–60
Vernier, Gilbert A., 32
Williams, Merle R., 23
North Africa
arrival of *SS George Washington* in,
80–81
EGB448 in, 296–306
pathfinder tests, 310
regimental practice jumps in,
102–103
See also Casablanca, Morocco;
Kairouan, Tunisia; Oujda,
Algeria

O

Oates, James, 46

Oberholtzer, Sterling E., 130, 134, 135, 139, 403

Officer Candidate School, recommendations for, 29

officers
A Company, *41*
departures of original cadre, 20–21
in original cadre, *9*, 11–15, *12, 15*
prisoner of war experience of, 396–397
See also command changes

Oflag 64, 173, 178, 393–396, *396*

Oldfather, Earl S.
on I Company patrol, 381–382
on loading onto LCIs, 322
on march to Albanella, 375
move to Blue Beach, 382
on move up Sorrento Peninsula, 389
on ration detail, 377
on Salerno Beachhead landing, 332
on time in North Africa, 296–301
on training for Operation Giant I, 311

O'Malley, John J., 246

O'Mohundro, Wiley H., 326

Operation Avalanche, 307, 314, 316, *319*. *See also* Salerno Beachhead

Operation Axe, 316

Operation Baytown, 307, *319*

Operation Giant I, 308, 310–312

Operation Giant II, 312–315

Operation Husky. *See* Sicily

Operation Mincemeat, 116

Operation Shingle, 392

Operation Slapstick, 317–318, *319*

O'Quinn, Milton F., 174

Orgaz Yoldi, Luis, 99, *99*

original cadre, *9, 10,* 11–19, *12, 15,* 20–21

Orvin, Louis E., Jr., 191

Ott, James C.
background of, 86–87
capture of Charles Kouns and, 261
command changes and, 265
mission in Sicily, 135, 137, 141, 183–184, 186
on night jumps in Africa, 103

Ott, Walter V., 193–195, 403

Otterbein, Louis W., Jr., 169, *169*, 393–394, 396

Oujda, Algeria
arrival of advance detail, 79
camp conditions at, 83–84
noncombat deaths in, 98
parades in, *99*, 99–100, *100*
Thomas Utterback on, 87–90
See also North Africa

Ourganian, George, 191–192

P

Pack, Charles E., Jr., 63, 355, 372–373

Packard, Reynolds, 338

Paestum drop zone, 320–322, 332

Pagni-Nocera Pass, 317

Pahler, Regis J., 306, 309

Palermo, Italian surrender at, 285

Papa, Paul D., 131, 139

Pappalardo, Joseph S., 191

Paquet, Henry P., *12,* 220–221, 355

Parachute Maintenance Detachment, 16, 210

parades, Oujda, *99*, 99–100, *100*

paratrooper training. *See* training

paratroopers, physical requirements for, 4–5
Parker, Willard E., 74
Parks, Ernest W., 24–26, 103–104, 251–252
pathfinders, 308–310
Patrick, Carl L., 256
Patton, George S., 99, 102, 116, 207, 274
Paulk, Dan I., 284
Payne, Francis W., 224
Pearson, Benjamin F., 21
Perow, Delor M., 237
Personal Affairs checklist, 71–72
Phillips, George B., 278
physical requirements for paratroopers, 4–5
Pilla, Carlo J., 74, 152, 154, 155, 156
Plaisted, Norman H., 352–353
Pobor, Michael D., 331
policing duties in Sicily, 288–294
Pollet, Amilcar J., 355
Ponte Olivo Airfield, 119, 176
Power, Stuart E., 121
Powers, James C., 103
Price, Lloyd M., 237, 341
prisoners of war, American
from B Company, 221
campaign to retake Altavilla, 342–343
Charles Kouns as, 142
escapes by, 401–403
G Company, 168–169, 170–171
Grisez, William, 165
Haider, Edward, 165
I Company, 193, 194
Kent, Frank J., 176–177
in Oflag 64, 393–396
Schaefer, William H., 163–164
in Stalag II-B, 397–401

prisoners of war, German, 181, 255–256, 342, 344, 345, 384
Propblast (regimental newspaper), 46, 54, 56–57
Provisional Parachute Group, 2–5, 6, 51, 52
Puhalla, Frank A., 74, 343, 344
Purple Heart
Gorniak, Frank X., 227
Hines, Wesley C., 252
Pyle, Ernie, 123

Q

Queale, Charles E., 127
Quinn, Floyd V., 103, 113

R

Ramsey, Lauren W., 52, 210, 280
Rangers, 274, 316–317
Ranti, Peter J., 168, 401–402
rations, 83, 84–85, 91–92, 209, 294, 366
Ray, Robert E., 164, 165
Reed, Franklin P., 397–398
regimental band, 55
Regimental Demolition Platoon, 16, 31–32, 164–165, 210, 281
regimental newspaper. See Propblast
regimental practice jumps, 65–66, 71, 102–103
Regimental Reconnaissance Platoon, 121, 210, 230, 232
Reilly, John E., 127
replacements
after Sicily Campaign, 296–306
Charles Kouns on, 86
for G Company, 390
pre-combat assignments, 113

training of, 308–309
See also EGB447
Reserve Officer Training Course
  (ROTC), 39, 40
Ribera, Sicily, 275–277
Rice, George W., 21, 71
Richter, Forrest, 159–161, 338, 339,
  343, 358, 359
Ricketts, Floyd I., 230
Ridgway, Matthew B., 99, *100*
  cancellation of equipment delivery
    training exercise, 68
  Capua mission and, 308, 311–312,
    315, 328
  Charles Keerans, assignment of,
    124
  choice of the 505th for Operation
    Husky, 114–115
  command changes by, 265
  comments at Division Review, 78
  conversion of the 82nd to an
    airborne division, 21
  Emory Adams and, 56
  friendly fire and, 237–238, 270–
    271
  knowledge of German units on
    Sicily, 117
  Operation Giant II plans, 313
  parachute jump of, 24
  pathfinders plan and, 308–310
  plan to move up western coast of
    Sicily, 274
  reinforcements at Salerno
    Beachhead and, 320
  reinforcements for Reuben
    Tucker, 374
  release of A Company to the
    503rd PIR, 35–36
  Reuben Tucker's promotion and,
    101, *101, 102*

search for paratroopers on Sicily,
  206–207
Theodore Dunn's replacement
  and, 47
Tumminello Pass battle, orders
  after, 284
visit to Altavilla area, 381
William Beall's death and, 387
William Yarborough's
  reassignment by, 292
rifle companies, organization of, 16,
  35–36
Ritch, Wallace, *15*, 190
Roberts, Bonnie, 29
Roberts, Edman, 173
Rodt, Eberhard, 116–117
Roepke, Paul M., 245
Roggen, Ivan J.
  assignment of, 60–61
  on common casualties, 277
  crash landing in Sicily, 232, 233–
    234
  on friendly fire, 271
  on George Patton's speech, 102
  on identifying bodies of plane
    crash, 246
  on medical detachments, 61–62
  on medics' training, 62–63
  on Salerno Beachhead drop, 325
  on *SS George Washington* trip, 80
  treatment of wounded near
    Altavilla, 360
Rome, Italy, 311, 312–316
Roosevelt, Eleanor, 55
Roosevelt, Theodore, Jr., 253
Rosen, David, 47, 64
Rosenkrantz, David, 29, 64–66, 76,
  179, 180
Rosenthal, Herbert, 159, 167–168,
  265

Rossi, Carlo, 142
Rouse, Edwin, 354
Roush, Raymond, 212, 231, 232, 235
Row, Andrew W., 377
Rozman, Albin V., 232, 235
Rozzell, Richard W., 184
Ryan, Ward S., 20, 21
Ryder, William T., 1, 2

S

Salaparuta, Sicily, 293
Salemi, Sicily, 290–292, 293
Salerno Beachhead, 334, 349, 376
    36th Infantry Division and, 318, 329
    campaign to take Hill 424, 336, 340, 341–344
    casualties, 382–383
    A Company patrols, 379–380
    D Company reconnaissance, 330–331
    defense of, 316–318
    drop, 324–329
    German account of, 356–357
    LCIs landing, 332–333
    march of the wounded, 359–360
    march to Albanella, 336–338
    move up Sorrento Peninsula, 385–389
    Operation Avalanche, 316, 318
    orders to retake Altavilla, 335
    orders to withdraw to Albanella, 374
    patrols, 350, 378, 379–380
    preparation for, 320–324
    retaking of Hill 424, 364–375
    Reuben Tucker's plan of attack on, 338–339
    Seymour Korman on, 381, 385
    Thomas Utterback on, 375, 377
    VI Corps orders of September 16th, 335–336
    war correspondents in, 339
    Wiley O'Mohundro's briefing on, 326
    Wilfred Jaubert on attack of, 331
Salter, Winford H., 148
Sambuca, Sicily, 285
Samuels, Ian, 394
Sanford, Teddy, 314
Santa Margherita, Sicily, 279, 284, 285, 293
Satterwhite, John L., 329, 329
Savage, John, 219–220
Sayre, Edwin, 146, 169
Schaeffer, William H. "King Kong," 163–164
Scheaffer, John E., 378
Schmalz, Wilhelm, 189
Schneider, Peter R., 368
Schrack, William H., 245
Schwark, Clarence W., 245
Schwere Panzer-Abteilung 504, 139, 163, 171, 262
Scicli, Sicily, 179–180
Scoglitti, Sicily, 167, 232
Scott, Keith K., 225–227
Secondine, Alfred, 284
"Selection of the Parachutist" (Thomas), 4–5
Sellner, George A., 344
Sergeant York (movie), 21
Service Company, 13, 16, 83
Shaffer, Daniel W., 369
Shaffer, Ervin E., 345, 364
Shapiro, Hyman D., 63, 84
Sheehan, Francis G., 17, 35, 63
Sheek, Kenneth I., 17, 63
Sheffield, Wilbert D., 245

Shelley, Mack C., 245, 246, 292

Shinberger, John, 6, *10, 12,* 13, 20

Sicily, *151, 286*

  2nd Battalion drop, 254–256

  3rd Battalion drop, 127–130

  advance up western coast, 274–279

  American casualties and captured, 295

  C Company drop, 221–227

  Castellammare del Golfo capture, 287–288

  Charles Kouns account of mission in, 131–138, 139–140

  choice of the 505th for, 114–115

  command changes after campaign in, 292–293

  Communications Platoon in, 166

  D Company drop, 251–254

  Demolition Platoon in, 164–165

  E Company drop, 248–250

  F Company drop, 239–246

  fly over across preselected drop zones, 117–118

  Francis Deignan on, 142–147

  G Company in, 168–175

  garrison duty in, 288–294

  H Company in, 176–188

  Headquarters and Headquarters Company jump, 228–237

  I Company in, 189–205

  Lewis Fern's notes on troop strength, 266–267, 268–269

  missing in action in, 161

  Moffatt Burriss on, 158–161

  Mortar Platoon in, 161–164

  Operation Giant II plan, 313

  pathfinder teams in, 309

  planning stage of campaign for, 118–119

  post-landing assembly in Gela, 260–264

  preparation for Salerno Beachhead attack, 320–324

  Roy Hanna on, 147–150

  Thomas Utterback on, 152–158

  Tumminello Pass battle, 275–285

Sieckenius, Rudolf, 316

Siegmann, George A., 37, 367

Silver Star

  Albert, Howard, 374

  Anderson, Cecil W., 227

  Baker, Wilton, 387

  Billman, Calvin J., 220

  Bloomfield, Abraham, 283

  Brooks, James R., 234

  Digan, Edward C., 205

  Dunn, James E., 370

  Freeman, Leslie, 406

  Furst, Henry S., 358

  Gallagher, Bernard F., 317

  Gordon, Harry A., 220

  Gorniak, Frank X., 227

  H Company, 184–185

  Hill, Edward B., Jr., 351–352

  Lane, Thomas E., 203–204

  Miller, Levern H., 283

  Moorehead, Edmund Q., 352

  Schneider, Peter, 368

  Shaffer, Daniel, 369

  Stokes, Guy L., 355

  Turner, James C., 283

  Whitman, Stanley, 355

  Yarborough, William, 405

  Young, Willard N., 370

Simonds, Guy, 167

Simpson, Jack P., 54–55, 278

Sims, Edward J.

  on accidental injuries, 292

advance up western coast of Sicily, 277–278

on defending Salerno Bay, 316–317

on fate of planes' flight into Sicily, 269

on friendly fire investigation, 271

on garrisoning duty, 293

on march up western coast of Sicily, 276

on Sicily jump, 239–241

Smith, Carl O., 230

Smith, Chester A., 301

Smith, Elbert F.
  command changes, 265
  as commander of the motorized detachment, 122–123
  improvement of camp conditions at Oujda, 84–85
  on orders to move to New York City, 77
  Thomas Utterback's replacement of, 87
  on training in Casablanca, 81
  on weapons and equipment delivery, 66–67

Smith, Gordon K., 21

Smith, Leonard W., 378

Smith, Stanley G., 74

Smith, Walter Bedell, 312

Sneddon, Edward W., 181

Snodgrass, James L., 193–195

Soldier's Medal, 305

Sorrento Peninsula, move up the, 385–389

Spaatz, "Tohey," 99

SS *George Washington*, 78, 79–81, 86, 94, 97–98, 296

Stalag II-B, 165, 171, 179, 221, 397–401

Stampone, Nicholas N., 184

Starbuck, Lacy R., 46

Starling, Andrew E., 108–111

Stars and Stripes newspaper, 273

Stephens, Edgar D., 81, 106

Stevenson, Clinton G., 245

Stewart, Harry G., 173–174

Stimson, Henry, 273

Stokes, Guy L., 355

Strouse, Elwood, 178

Swagler, Rudyard M., 187–188, *188, 407*, 407–408

Swift, Frederick J., Jr., 17, 35

Swing, Joseph M., 270

T

Tague, Robert A., 181

Taliaferro, George F., 363

Taylor, Joseph A., 343, 344

Taylor, Maxwell D., 79, *213*, 312, 313–314, 315

Telford, Wallace G., 168–169

Test Platoon, 1–2

Thomas, David E., 4–5

Thomas, Fred E., 198–199, 315

Thomas, Fred W., 98, 262–264, 265, 290, 307

Thompson, John S., 124, 255–256, 267–268, 284

Timson, William, 111–112

Tobacco Factory, 318

Tobias, Warren E., Jr., 187, 265, 408

Tolson, John J., III, 36

Topczewski, Albin S., 152, 158

training
  chaplains' participation in, 18–19
  deaths during, 59–60, 103
  Edward Haider on, 27

of EGB448 in North Africa, 296–300
at Fort Benning, 7–9
Francis McLane on, 97
Gordon Gould on, 45–46
Herbert Lucas on, 28–29
John Isom on, 96
of medics, 61, 62–63
for Operation Giant I, 311
phases of, 3
of replacements, 303–304, 308–309
Roy Hanna on, 22–23
in Tunisia, 111–113
weapons qualification and battle indoctrination, 23
See also jump training
Trapani, capture of, 288
Tree Rivers Regiment, 179
Tregaskis, Richard
assignment to the 504th, 310
on campaign to retake Altavilla, 338, 339–343
on Capua mission cancellation, 312, 313, 314
on leaving Hill 424, 358
on Salerno Beachhead landing, 332
on walk back to Albanella, 359–360
troop strength, notes on, 266–267, 268–269
Tucker, Lyman, 50, 51
Tucker, Margaret, 51
Tucker, Reuben H., *10, 12, 213, 384*
on the activation of the 504th, 6
address to men before Salerno Beachhead drop, 324
on Altavilla, battle for, 385
arrival in Naples, 390

on arrival of the 376th Parachute Field Artillery Battalion, 386
assignments for Salerno Beachhead mission, 327
background of, 49–51
on bivouac inspection, 81
briefing by Wiley O'Mohundro, 326
briefing on Salerno Beachhead mission, 320–321
campaign to retake Altavilla, 338–339, 341, 343, 348
Capua landing plans, 308
Charles Kouns on, 77, 103
on choice of the 505th for Operation Husky, 114–115
command changes under, 51–53, 56, 292
command of the 504th, 47
Distinguished Service Cross award to, 383
effort to stop friendly fire, 237–238
equipment delivery procedure training and, 68
final pre-deployment personnel changes, 64
Henry Muller on, 13
on Hill 424 casualties, 373–374
Italian POWs and, 289
July 11th drop orders, 207
Lesley McNair's training visit and, 55
orders for policing duties in Sicily, 288
orders to retake Altavilla, 336
orders to retreat from Hill 424, 374–375, 377
post-landing assembly in Gela, 268–269

post-landing assembly in Vittoria, 260

preparations for move to Sorrento Peninsula, 388

promotion of, 101, *101*, 102

ration supply and, 85

as regimental executive officer, 21

Richard Chase and, 3

Richard Tregaskis on, 310

Robert Neptune as artillery liaison officer for, 210

Rome attack plans, 312–313, 314

Sicily drop, 235, 236–237

on training of the original cadre, 11

transfer of Fordyce Gorham to S-2 section, 121

transfer of Henry Frank as S-3, 378

on unnumbered hill, 373

welcome of replacements, 300

Tucker, William, 51

Tucker's Tumbler, 305

Tumminello Pass battle, 279–285

Tunisia. *See* Kairouan, Tunisia; North Africa

Turner, James C., 283

Turner, John C., 161–163

Turner, John W., 230

U

Ueckert, Fred, 74

University of Maryland, 39–40

unnumbered hill

B Company and, 330, 359, 372–373

communications on, 366, 367, 368

message to Reuben Tucker on, 374

patrol sent to, 343

seizure of, 346–348, 353

U.S. 45th Division, 241, 242, 257–258, 267

U.S. military bases, 73

U.S. Navy, friendly fire from. *See* friendly fire

Utterback, Thomas E., *157*

arrival in Naples, 390

command changes, 265

on going into the Italian campaign, 322

letter home from, 265–266

on Operation Giant I plan, 311

on Operation Husky, 118, 124

on Salerno Beachhead, 332–333, 375, 377

on setting up base in Tunisia, 106–107

in Sicily Campaign, 152–158

on trip and assignment to Oujda, 87–90

V

Van Poyck, Walter S., 248–249, 275–276, 288–289, 321–322

Vangilder, Dean W., 173

Vernier, Gilbert A., 32

VI Corps

artillery fire on Altavilla, 356

briefing by Wiley O'Mohundro on situation of, 326

command changes in, 385

German attacks on, 316, 328

Operation Avalanche and, 307

order for evacuation of Hill 424, 374, 375

reinforcements for, 320–321, 326
Reuben Tucker's call to command
    post of, 335
Victor Emmanuel II, 311, 316
Vincent, Mike, 390
Vittoria, Sicily, 172, 174, 260, 267–268
Volturno River, 308, 310
volunteers, paratrooper, 2–3, 4, 26
Von Vietinghoff, Heinrich, 317–318

W

Wagner, Richard R., 232, 235
Walker, Ernest L., 378
Walker, Fred, 407
    on Hill 315 shelling, 363–364
    on orders to retake Altavilla, 335
    on performance of the 504th, 385
    on request for reinforcements
        from the 180th, 374
    on working with the 504th, 327,
        328
Wall, Ned, 294, 295, 353–354
Wallace, Elbridge H., 46
Wallace, Jack, 179–180
Walsh, William, 225
Walters, Barney, 379
war correspondents, 272–273, 310,
    338
War Department, 2, 21, 273, 408
Warfield, George M., 28, 120, 190
Warren, James R., 230
Washburn, Hubert H., 63, 245, 246
Washington, D.C. furlough, 54–55
water, mission to get, 378–379
Watson, John, 326
Watson, William, 191, 254–255
Watts, George J., 174–175, 182–183,
    204, 260–261, 265
weapons delivery procedure, 66–69

weapons training, 23
weather, 98, 106–107, 112, 336–337
Weaver, Frank W., 342
Webster, Arvil H., 378
Weeks, Vernon A., 380
Weinberger, Emanuel, 355
Wellems, Edward N., 64, 71
Welsh, Harry F., 29
Wensil, Harry A., 375
Wheeler, William, 29, 182
White, Arlos A., 173
Whitehead, Don, 111–112
Whitman, Stanley J., 294, 304–305,
    355, 355, 359
Wienecke, Robert H., 84
Wight, Ted M., 210, 237, 278
Wight, Thomas M., 17, 321, 340, 341
Wilczynski, Henry J., 284
Williams, Dewey, 400
Williams, Merle R., 23
Williams, Paul L., 273
Williams, R.G., 394
Williams, Warren R., Jr., 12
    advance to Hill 424, 344
    arrangements for rifle protection
        for mortar crews, 220
    on B Company jump exercise, 56
    briefing by Wiley O'Mohundro,
        326
    briefing on Salerno Beachhead
        mission, 320–321
    campaign to retake Altavilla, 348
    command changes and, 51, 64
    command of 1st Battalion, 21
    German attack on Hill 424 and,
        352, 353
    German intelligence on, 109, 113
    jump instruction for Matthew
        Ridgway, 24

letter to parents of Ned Wall from, 354
orders to B Company to reinforce Hill 424, 373
orders to retake Altavilla, 336
orders to Willard Harrison, 338
radio communications and, 366, 368
as Regiment S-3 officer, 7
regimental reorganization, 268–269
reinforcements for Hill 424, 370
on replacement of Theodore Dunn, 48
Sicily jump of, 210
Wills, Earl, 263–264
Wilson, George C., 398
Wilson, Harry, 1
Wilson, Paul D., 381
Wilson, William L., 54–55, 373, 375
Winton, Walter F., 336
Witt, Charles R., 169
Wolf, Alfred R., 343
Wolverton, Robert, 6, *10, 15,* 20
Woodworth, William P., 184
Wright, Arthur M., 226

X

"X" Battalion. *See* 3rd Battalion
X Corps, 307, 316, 318, 389
X Force, 274–275

Y

Yarborough, William P.
advance up western coast of Sicily, 275
assignment to 2nd Battalion, 52–53

on being left out of Sicily operation planning, 209
Castellammare del Golfo, capture of, 287–288
on lack of preparation for Sicily drop, 210
as mayor of Alcamo, 289
parachute qualification badge design of, 3
post-war life, 405–406
reassignment of, 292
regimental bivouac area near Biscari, 266, 268
on Sicily drop, 246–248
Tumminello Pass battle, 279–280, 284, 285
Yelverton, John A., 83
Yocum, Alvin L., 150
York, Alvin C., 21
Young, Ralph, 350, *351*
Young, Willard N., 370

Z

Zais, Melvin, 52, 56
Zakby, Abdallah K., 64
Zimmerman, Donald, 98, 185–187
Zouzas, Thomas J., 301–302
Zumwalt, Warren W., 305–306, 357–358